Hands-On Turbo C®++

Stephen R. Davis

Addison-Wesley Publishing Company, Inc.

Reading, Massachusetts Menlo Park, California New York
Don Mills, Ontario Wokingham, England Amsterdam Bonn
Sydney Singapore Tokyo Madrid San Juan

Many of the designations used by manufacturers and sellers to distinguish their products are claimed as trademarks. Where those designations appear in this book and Addison-Wesley was aware of a trademark claim, the designations have been printed in initial capital letters.

Library of Congress Cataloging-in-Publication Data

Davis, Stephen R., 1956-
    Hands on Turbo C++ / by Stephen R. Davis.
        p. cm.
    Includes index.
    ISBN 0-201-57052-1
    1. C++ (Computer program language) 2. Turbo C++ (Computer program) I. Title.
QA76.73.C153D38   1990
005.26'2--dc20   90-48410
                                                                     CIP

Copyright © 1991 by Stephen R. Davis

All rights reserved. No part of this publication may be reproduced, stored in a retrieval system, or transmitted, in any form or by any means, electronic, mechanical, photocopying, recording, or otherwise, without the prior written permission of the publisher. Printed in the United States of America. Published simultaneously in Canada.

Set in 11 point Times by Benchmark Productions
Cover design by Mike Fender
ABCDEFGHIJ-MW-943210
First Printing, December, 1990

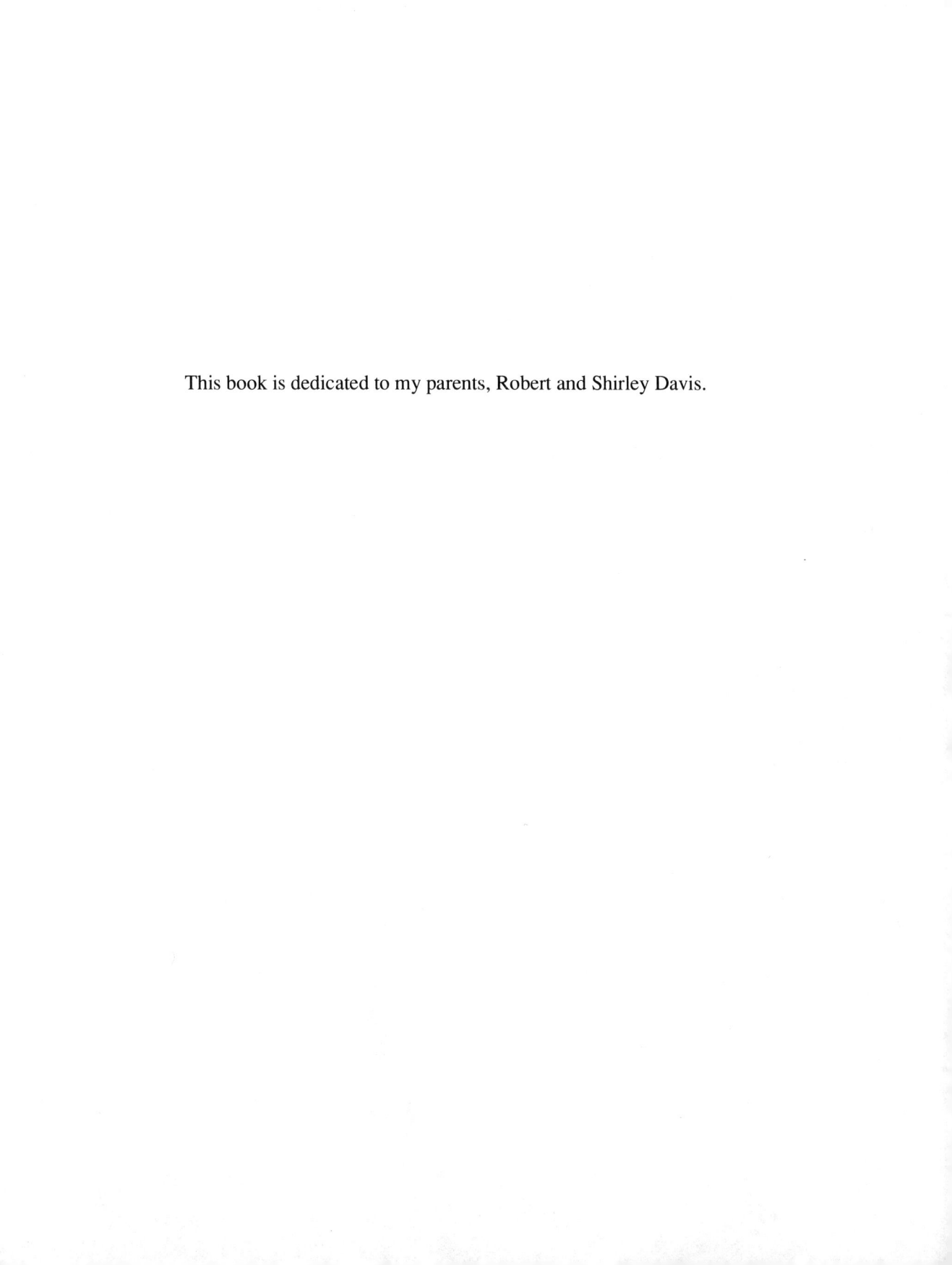

This book is dedicated to my parents, Robert and Shirley Davis.

Table of Contents

Introduction — xiii

Chapter 1 *Introduction to Turbo C++*
  Object-oriented Programming — 3
    Defining Our Terms — 3
    Evolving Concepts — 5
    Why Bother? — 8
  From C to C++ — 11
    C++ and ANSI C — 11
      Function Prototyping — 11
      `void` — 14
      `volatile` and `const` — 15
      Register Variables — 17
      #pragmas — 18
      Quiet Changes — 20
  From Turbo C to Turbo C++ — 21
    Interactive Development Environment — 21
    VROOMM — 23
    Support for Assembly Language — 23
  Conclusion — 24

Chapter 2 *Using C++*
  Classless Primitives — 27
    Strong Typing — 27
    Reference Operator — 28
    Declarations Within Blocks — 31
    Inline Functions — 33
    `new` and `delete` — 34
    Expanded Role for `const` — 35

Scope Resolution Operator	35
// Comments	36
Anonymous Unions	37
Overloading Functions	38
Classes	41
Classes in C	41
Fixing `struct` with class	45
Class `Address`	48
Constructors and Destructors	50
Format	51
Creating and Destroying Objects	52
Overloading Operators	56
Inheritance	62
Initializing Derived Classes	64
Complete `BusinessAddress` Class	65
Multiple Inheritance	66
When to Use a Derived Class	67
Virtual Functions—Polymorphism	67
Stream I/O	70
Conclusion	75

Chapter 3 *The Classless Primitives*

Strong Typing	79
Declaring Simple Objects	79
Typed Expressions	85
Addressing in the 80x86 Processor Family	87
Declaring Pointers in C++	93
Pointers and Defaults	98
Tentative Declarations	99
Void Pointers	100
Huge Objects	100
Reference Operator	101
Reference Types	104
Functions with Referential Arguments	105
Referential Functions	107
Passing Constants as Referential Arguments	108
Declaring Variables Within Blocks	109
Inline Functions	112

Efficiency Considerations	112
Problems with Inline Functions	115
When Inline is Outline	116
The `new` and `delete` Keywords	118
Conclusion	120

Chapter 4 *Overloading Functions*

Differentiating Functions	123
Typesafe Linking	128
Linking C++ with C Modules	132
Conclusion	134

Chapter 5 *Classes*

Organization of Classes	137
What is `this`?	142
Arrays of Class Objects	144
Pointers to Class Members	147
Static Class Members	150
Enumeration Members	153
Friends of Classes	155
Unions	157
Conclusion	159

Chapter 6 *Constructors and Destructors*

Constructors	163
The Default Constructors	164
Other Constructors	166
Class Constants	168
The Copy-Initializer Constructors	169
Initializing an Object with Another Object of the Same Class	170
Passing an Object by Value	171
Returning an Object by Value	173
A Look Under the Hood	177
Constructing Member Objects	180
Constructors and `new`	182
Calling `new` from a Constructor	182
Calling a Constructor from `new`	186
Destructors	187

Invoking Destructors	187
Destructing Member Objects	189
Virtual Destructors	190
Initializing Other Types of Objects	191
Executing Before or After `main()`	192
Global constructors	192
`atexit()`	192
Start-up and Exit Pragmas	193
Order of Execution	195
Conclusion	196

Chapter 7 *Overloading Operators*

Friend Operators Versus Member Operators	204
Coercion Operators	209
Virtual Arrays	212
Virtual File Array	213
Virtual EMS Array	216
Overloading `new` and `delete`	229
Simple `operator new()`	230
Compound `operator new()`	233
Variable Sized Structures	237
Conclusion	239

Chapter 8 *Class Inheritance*

Simple Inheritance	243
Access to Inherited Members	244
Constructors for Derived Classes	248
Derived Versus Containing Classes	249
Subclasses	251
Linked List Examples	254
Polymorphism	260
The `isA()` Method	263
Another Linked List Example	264
Abstract Classes	269
Multiple Inheritance	270
Using Multiple Inheritance	270
Implementing Multiple Inheritance	273
Ambiguous Objects	273
Ambiguous Classes	275

Base Class Addresses	276
Doubly Linked Lists	279
Containing Class Solution	280
Multiple Inheritance Solution	282
Virtual Inheritance	284
Conclusion	287

Chapter 9 *Stream Input/Output*

Conventional C I/O	291
Older C++ Streams	291
C++ 2.0 Streams	292
Inserters	295
Inserter Types	297
Format Control	299
Buffering	305
Custom Inserters	306
Custom Manipulators with Restricted Argument Types	308
Custom Manipulators with General Argument Types	315
Extractors	320
Custom Extractors	323
Input/Output to Files	330
User Files	331
Seeking Within a Stream	334
Tying Streams	335
Pointers to Streams	335
Handling Errors in Streams	336
Other Stream Methods	339
Mixing I/O with `stdio`	340
Incore I/O	340
Conclusion	342

Chapter 10 *Turbo C++ Advanced Features*

Virtual Run-time Object-oriented Memory Manager	345
Conventional Overlay Systems	345
VROOMM System	348
Using VROOMM	351
Inline Assembly Language	355
Pseudo-Registers and `geninterrupt()`	358
Keyword `asm`	366

`__emit__`	371
Assembly Level Debugging	373
Interrupt Functions	375
Special Forms of Flow Control	377
Signals	377
Control-break Handler	384
Conclusion	386

Chapter 11 Task Class Application

Theory	
`setjmp/longjmp`	390
Rescheduler	395
Task Class	396
Comparison of Features	398
Implementing Class Task	400
Task Creation	403
Task Rescheduling	408
Task Termination	411
Starting and Stopping the Scheduler	415
Task Return Value	416
Intertask Message Passing	420
Time	426
Task Output	434
Sample Application	437
Example 1: Orbiting Planets	438
Example 2: Worms	447
Areas for Improvement	456
Comparisons with AT&T Task Class	457
Conclusion	458

Theory   389

Appendix A *Program Listing of Task Class*	**459**
Appendix B *Source Code for Example 1—Orbit*	**481**
Appendix C *Source Code for Example 2—Worms*	**491**
Bibliography	**501**
Index	**505**

Hands-On Turbo C++

Introduction

Hands-On Turbo C++ is an introduction to the world of C++, especially Turbo C++ for the C programmer. This book will familiarize the reader with C++ and the other enhancements contained in Turbo C++ from Borland International.

While change is inevitable, changes in programming languages are only warranted when some benefit accrues. Unlike other C++ books, *Hands-On Turbo C++* does not assume that the reader has already decided to drop C in favor of this new language. A healthy level of skepticism, mixed with a certain amount of patience, is both understandable and desirable when approaching a new language.

Approaching C++ from a basis in C is similar to mastering complex numbers after working with real numbers. All of the operations that work with real numbers work in the complex number plane (but often for a slightly different reason). Complex numbers expand the meaning of many of the operations. Initially, the mathematician may see little reason to go through the mental change of gears necessary to become comfortable with complex numbers. Having adopted the expanded number plane, however, few mathematicians limit themselves to real numbers again.

Hands-On Turbo C++ builds upon the reader's knowledge of C. The book is divided into three sections. Chapters 1 and 2 are an overview of the object oriented programming methodology in general and C++ in particular. This section aims to make the reader comfortable with the new structures of the C++ language. It also explains some of the whys behind C++ along with the whats.

Chapters 3-10 reexamine each of the C++ constructs in more detail. In this section we will analyze the specifics, including exceptions to the rules. *Hands-On Turbo C++* explains how some constructs are implemented as well. We will take an occasional look "under the hood" at the assembly language generated to see what makes Turbo C++ run.

Finally, Chapter 11 and the three appendices feature a sample application: a multitasking application written completely in C++. The `Task` class from this example can be used for multitasking capabilities, including message passing and process control, under DOS.

Who Needs This Book?

Hands-On Turbo C++ is written for C programmers who are interested in learning Turbo C++. Most readers will have been exposed to the C language, at least in its original Kernighan and Ritchie form, by the time they approach C++. This book assumes the reader knows enough C to be able to write a small program. *Hands-On Turbo C++* does not assume any knowledge of the object-oriented paradigm or the languages that support it.

Why Should I Learn C++?

Despite the popularity that C enjoys in the programming community, something is wrong. As user demands escalate, the difficulty, and hence the cost, in developing application software is rising exponentially.

Ten years ago structured programming was heralded as the salvation of the programming industry. It was believed that structured techniques would bring software costs under control and that schedules would have meaning again. While production costs are much less than they would have been with prior programming techniques, structured programming has not lived up to its promise.

Larger programs generally involve larger numbers of programmers. Increasing the number of programmers leads to an exponential rise in the number of communication paths. Since a change in one module can affect any number of other modules, the process involves coordination among many programmers. Soon programmers are spending more time checking and correcting communications problems between modules and themselves than they are producing new code.

Introduction

Using techniques such as data abstraction and encapsulation, the object-oriented methodology reduces the number of interactions between modules and, hence, between programmers. These techniques force a greater level of communication earlier in a project when fewer programmers are involved and the cost of a change is much less.

Reusing existing code is the most effective way to reduce development costs. Procedural programming techniques designed in the lab to increase reusability fail in practice. The object-oriented methodology attempts to enhance reusability by encapsulating every detail of a user-defined data type in one place.

Many early object-oriented languages were interpretive, rendering them useless for application programs. C++, by comparison, was designed to generate highly efficient real time machine code. C++ brings the power of object-oriented languages out of the lab and into the real world.

What is Turbo C++?

Turbo C++ is a hybrid compiler, supporting both ANSI C and AT&T C++ Version 2.0. Turbo C++ represents another step in a long line of Borland compilers, many of them breakthroughs in their day.

Turbo Pascal was the first compiler to offer the "all-in-one" Turbo environment. Its lightning compiles and immediate error messages ushered in a new era in compiler convenience. That Turbo Pascal never generated the smallest or the fastest executables in the world didn't seem to matter, compared to its high level of user convenience.

The long-awaited Turbo C 1.0 brought "Turbo" to the C world in the early summer of 1987. While Turbo C was a much larger package than Turbo Pascal, the compiles were just as fast and the environment was even more convenient. Microsoft responded with Quick C and the battle of the C languages was joined.

Turbo C 2.0, introduced in the fall of 1988, took ease of use one step further by adding debugging capability to its onscreen interface. Turbo C++ continues that tradition by adding an improved, mouse-supporting windowed interface and support for the object-oriented language, C++.

C++ was developed by AT&T as a preprocessor in the early 1980s. To compile a C++ program, the programmer executed the `cfront` translator which took the C++ program and output a C program. The programmer then compiled the C program into an executable. Turbo C++ is a true compiler. As with its Turbo predecessors, entering the compile command from the interactive environment generates an executable program directly and almost instantaneously. Gone are the two-step compilations, the confusing error messages, and the need to purchase a separate compiler.

Conventions

Before we begin, it should be noted that throughout *Hands-On Turbo C++,* I have adopted the naming convention suggested by Borland. All object names appear completely in lower case with the following exceptions:

- structure, class and union names begin with capital letter (e.g., `struct Base`)
- #defines appear in all capitals (e.g., `#define MAXARGS`)
- in multiple-word variable names, all words after the first are capitalized (e.g., `struct Base baseObject`)
- pointer type variable names end in Ptr (e.g., `baseObjectPtr`).

In addition, when C++ keywords, the names of variables, and other C++ source code-related constructs appear within the text, they are printed in the same font as code examples to distinguish them from the rest of the text.

Chapter 1

Introduction to Turbo C++

Introduction to Turbo C++

Turbo C++ is the newest member of a long line of compilers from Borland beginning with Turbo Pascal 1.0 and extending through Turbo C 2.0. The similarity of Turbo C++ to its predecessors is unmistakable.

However, Turbo C++ is much more than a maintenance release of Turbo C. Turbo C++ includes support for Version 2.0 of C++, the object-oriented version of the king of real-time programming languages, C.

The next two chapters examine Turbo C++. Chapter 1 discusses the concepts behind object-oriented programming, then studies the similarities between C and C++, and concludes with a comparison of Turbo C and Turbo C++. Chapter 2 introduces the features unique to C++. Chapter 3 begins a more detailed examination of the features of C++.

When examining any new language, the programmer should be skeptical. Why was this language written? What advantages does it have over the languages the programmer already knows and uses? The next two chapters will examine C++ and, specifically, Turbo C++ from this viewpoint. What is C++ and what advantages does it have over C?

Object-oriented Programming

C++, inextricably linked with the concept of **object-oriented programming** (sometimes shortened to **OOP**), is the result of adding object-oriented features to the C language. (C++ is not the only possible result. The language Objective C is another attempt at the same thing. Although the principles are similar, the implementation is not.) Before we can understand C++, we must understand something of object-oriented programming.

Defining Our Terms

Many definitions boil down to "object-oriented programming is good," as if any recent worthwhile development in programming theory must be object-oriented and vice versa.

Object-oriented programming is often confused with the language Smalltalk. Smalltalk is the original, purely object-oriented language and, as such, often comes up in discussions of the topic. Smalltalk was one of the first languages to endorse the Xerox PARC/Macintosh "Point and

Shoot" user interface, which leads some people to confuse the Graphic User Interface with object-oriented programming. The implication is that object-oriented programs must somehow have a graphics interface. These two aspects of Smalltalk are not related.

Pinson and Wiener define object-oriented programming languages as follows: "Computer languages are object-oriented if they support the four specific object properties called abstraction, encapsulation, inheritance, and polymorphism." (Pinson and Wiener, *An Introduction to Object-Oriented Programming and Smalltalk*, 1988.) Although this definition is probably a good one, it requires a bit of explanation.

Object-oriented programming is a programming **paradigm**. A programming paradigm can be described as a method or style of programming but at its core lies an important point. People develop certain approaches to solving problems. Without being reevaluated, these solutions may become ingrained.

A programming paradigm is a mind set that a person uses to solve programming problems. Programmers set about coding sometimes massive projects with strong mind sets as to the best approach. However, a programmer's opinions represent just one way of solving the problem. Programmers occasionally need to analyze their own paradigms to determine if they are still optimal in light of the knowledge they have accumulated through years of experience. C++ challenges the reader to examine the object-oriented programming paradigm.

A language is said to be an **object-oriented language** if it supports the object-oriented paradigm. Of course, support is a relative term. It has been argued that assembly language supports structured programming because structured code can be written in assembly language. However, assembly language is not generally thought of as a structured programming language. Bjarne Stroustrup, the father of C++, puts it as follows: "A language is said to support a style of programming if it provides facilities that make it convenient to use that style." (Stroustrup, "What is Object-Oriented Programming?", 1987.)

It is virtually impossible for a general purpose language to enforce any particular programming style. Who has not heard the boast, "I can write Fortran code in any language."? For example, it is possible to write unstructured programs in Pascal, even though Pascal is widely held to be the standard-bearer of structured programming languages. In fact, Pascal includes a `goto` statement even though use of that construct was widely purported to be the antithesis of structured programming.

C++ is an object-oriented language because it supports the object-oriented paradigm. As a superset of C, C++ also supports earlier paradigms. C++ is a hybrid. Hybrids of other languages exist as well, including Objective Pascal from Apple and Turbo Pascal 5.5 from Borland for Pascal, Neon for Forth, Flavors, ExperCommonLisp and CommonObjects for Lisp, and even ObjectiveLogo for Logo. In fact, object-oriented versions of most programming languages exist or are in the works. (See Peter Wenger's article, "Learning the Language," March 1989 for a discussion of the taxonomy of these and other languages.)

Evolving Concepts

The earliest programming paradigm could be best described as **chaos**. In this model all thought is directed solely to the solution of the problem with little or no thought given to how the solution is to be achieved. Languages that typify the chaos paradigm include the earlier forms of BASIC (which lack even a subroutine construct). Under chaos the user is not distracted by thoughts of organization or expendability. All attention is focused on the particular problem. When chaos works at all, it works only for very simple programs (less than a few hundred lines). In programs of any size, the number of paths through the code that invariably arise make debugging and testing a nightmare (the classic "spaghetti code" problem).

The first improvement on chaos was **procedural programming**, typified by such languages as Fortran and Cobol. In this paradigm, the programmer attempts to divide the problem into constituent functions. In theory the programmer can treat each function as a single statement. The complexity of each function is abstracted away. A wall is erected between the source code and the data. All thought is directed toward abstraction of the code, with none directed toward the data.

A later variation on this theme is **structured programming** wherein the abstraction of code extends beyond just the function. Rather than allow chaos to reign within the functions, as does procedural programming, structured programming adopts rules that allow the programmer to view each control structure (e.g., `for`, `while`, and `if` blocks) as a small subfunction that can be further abstracted. Users can view a `for` loop, for example, as an independent entity because they know that all paths enter and exit the same way with no paths springing into the middle of the loop to execute a few instructions and then jump out again later. To support structured programming, a language must provide a complete set of control structures, such as those found in Pascal.

The structured programming paradigm no longer ignores the data aspect of programming. Rules exist for passing data between functions. Functions are obliged to access only the data that they accept as input arguments. Communication through global variables is discouraged.

These restrictions responded to weaknesses in the procedural model. It was difficult to treat a function as an abstracted entity if it could access and change global variables. Since documenting these secondary effects is difficult, communications paths were adopted that are easier to describe. However, adherence to these rules is voluntary and, therefore, not common.

Most structured programming languages encourage programmers to define new data types that more accurately describe the real object. In C, simple data types may be defined via `enum` or `typedef` statements. Composite data types invariably require the declaration of a structure of some sort. The structure definitions serve to keep similar data together in a single entity that more closely resembles the real world object after which it is modelled.

The paradigm used by most programmers today is something between procedural and structured programming.

In **modular programming**, an extension of the structured programming style, functions are further divided into separately compilable source files known as **modules**. Each module has a set of data and functions that only it can access. A separate set of data and functions is accessible to all modules. All similar functions are grouped into one module. Not all of the functions defined need be known outside of the module. Limiting the number of globally defined functions reduces the number of communication paths between modules, thus reducing the overall system complexity.

This paradigm also makes possible **data hiding** or **encapsulation**, where data being used by the individual functions is hidden from other modules. The programmer can declare a new data structure and define a set of functions to manipulate it. Modules outside the defining module can view the structure as a new data type using only the functions provided publicly to access it. Data known outside the modules are said to be **public** whereas other data, which the modules might use to implement the new data type and which are not visible outside the module, are said to be **private**. In C, elements declared static or automatic are private whereas others are public.

This is a pretty strong paradigm. Having examined the problem, the programmer first defines all of the new data types that will be needed to implement a solution. A separate defining module is built for each. Within each defining module the programmer might build functions to create, delete, display, and otherwise operate on the individual type. Once these new types exist, the remaining program becomes smaller and easier to read. The programmer can implement an algorithm with less worry about manipulating the data structures. Details of the structure type are hidden in the defining module. Modifications to the data structures can often be made by changing the defining module without involving the core modules. The best C programs use this programming paradigm.

Unfortunately, adherence to this paradigm in C is voluntary. If an illegal value ends up in a structure member, the programmer cannot be sure whether one of the access functions incorrectly stored it there or whether some miscreant module is accessing the structure members directly. Languages that support data encapsulation enforce the use of access functions.

The syntax of any newly created type does not resemble that of the types built into the language, however. Languages that support **data abstraction** allow the programmer to define the intrinsic operators for the newly defined types. Having defined a new type Complex, for example, the programmer can then define the simple math operators (+, -, *, and /) for Complex. That is, the programmer can define what it might mean to enter:

```
Complex A, B, C;

C = A + B;
```

Notice that I did not say **redefine**. The math operators continue to exist for the intrinsic types.

Data abstraction allows the programmer to further ignore the details when implementing an algorithm. Besides C++, Ada is the most commonly used real-time language that supports data abstraction.

Defining a new data type, including all of the operators that it might employ, can be an involved process, especially if one always has to start from the beginning. In addition, defining data types in terms of the basic intrinsic types obscures relationships that might exist between user-defined types. It is easier and more descriptive to derive new data types from existing user-defined types.

For example, a college student is a special case of the more general student. The two types share many properties. It is instructive to define a new type `CollegeStudent` in terms of `Student` to highlight the relationship between the two. This is known as **inheritance**.

Having created such a definition, it must be possible to move back and forth between the two types. A `CollegeStudent` must be able to access the functions defined for a `Student`. Thus, a function that expects to receive a pointer to `Student` might rightfully receive a pointer to `CollegeStudent` since a college student is a student. The ability to sort out inherited types is known as **polymorphism**.

This brings us back to our definition of object-oriented languages. An object-oriented language supports encapsulation, abstraction, inheritance, and polymorphism. C++ supports these properties as well as the same structured programming supported by its parent C language. We will return to these four properties at length in the remainder of the book.

Why Bother?

Many texts on C++ and object-oriented programming fail to address the question, Why bother? It is not entirely true that C programmers can move immediately and painlessly to C++. While existing C code can be compiled to generate the same results under C++, if C programmers intend to write the same programs with C++ that they would have written with C, there is no reason to make the switch. C++ is a different language. Although most constructs are the same, there is a learning curve with C++ that must be addressed.

Cost is the primary reason for all of the changes in paradigm through which the programming world has gone. While the chaos method worked when memory constraints kept the largest program to a few hundred lines, it began to fail when program sizes grew into the kilobytes. Similarly, the structured programming methodology that works in the classroom falls apart in the lab when programs reach many megabytes in size and involve dozens of people.

C++ and object-oriented programming reduce the cost of developing quality programs. AT&T reports that on large systems "its use, compared to conventional approaches, greatly reduced software integration time." (Coplien et al., "C++: Evolving Toward a More Powerful Language," 1988.) In addition, "it reduces the need for communication among implementers late in the project and throughout the maintenance phase" by increasing communication earlier in the project when the costs are much lower.

The level of software reuse has an even larger effect on the cost of a program. Projects can achieve a significant reduction in development cost and time if they can reuse existing code. The proper use of data abstraction to isolate data type-related functions can significantly increase the amount of reused code between projects because all user-defined data types that the projects have in common can be reapplied without additional effort.

However, no matter how cheaply developed, a program is not useful if its performance does not meet requirements. In moving from chaos to procedural programming, some programmers objected to the loss of efficiency. Calling a function to perform an operation adds overhead over simply inserting the code to perform the operation inline. With the addition of structured programming, concern over efficiency increased as overhead increased. Pushing arguments onto a stack required CPU cycles when the same data could be referenced globally without the overhead.

For small functions the overhead could be easily calculated. Recoding functions using different programming paradigms and comparing the number of resulting CPU instructions was a common exercise. In the real world, however, these analyses are flawed. In all but the most extreme cases, even large amounts of overhead (more than 100 percent) make little or no difference except in a very few, time-critical routines. This is a result of the "10 percent of the code consumes 90 percent of the time" rule of thumb.

In addition, such analyses assume that two programmers attacking the same nontrivial problem with two different programming paradigms would arrive at essentially the same solution. My experience has been quite different. Programmers tend to construct solutions that are not optimal. How far from optimal is not only a function of experience level and personal style, but also a result of the programming paradigm. A programmer who uses a more advanced approach will almost always reach a more optimal solution to a nontrivial problem than one who uses a less advanced approach. The higher level of abstraction prevents the programmer from not seeing the forest for the trees, which completely negates the speed advantage inherent in the simpler paradigm.

C++ was designed with efficiency as a prime consideration. The AT&T study noted that "code that used only the C subset of C++ produced the same code as an ordinary C compiler would have." The same study also reported that "after programmers cultivated an understanding of the object paradigm of how to use C++ features to complement each other, no code efficiency was lost while they took advantage of the language's power to increase productivity."

In Table 1–1, tests conducted comparing Turbo C 2.0 with Turbo C++ on the famous sieve of Eratosthenes benchmark show that the two compilers generate files of essentially the same size that execute in the same length of time. The only noticeable difference was in the compilation process itself, which Turbo C 2.0 completed faster.

Table 1–1   Sieve of Eratosthenes timing comparison

	Turbo C 2.0	*Turbo C++*
Size of .OBJ file [bytes]	1,085	1,125
Size of .EXE file [bytes]	19,072	18,323
Time to execute [sec]	58	57
Time to compile [sec]	3	7

My experience on other programs seems to bear out these numbers. While Turbo C++ is somewhat slower in compilation, the resulting programs were neither slower nor larger than their C equivalents would have been.

From C to C++

C++ is a superset of C. All of the constructs of C are present in C++. Programs that compile under C should compile under C++. Programs that follow the Kernighan and Ritchie standard may generate errors when subjected to C++ and will certainly generate warnings. Programs that generated no warnings under Turbo C 2.0 (provided, of course, that all warnings were enabled) should not generate any errors when compiled under Turbo C++.

To ensure that this is the case, Turbo C++ can differentiate between a C and a C++ program by examining the extension. If the source file name ends with a .C it is assumed to be a C program; if it ends with a .CPP, it is assumed to be a C++ program, unless the **C++ always** option is enabled in the Options/Compiler menu.

C++ and ANSI C

C++ and ANSI C share more than a common heritage. Many of the extensions in ANSI C, such as its function declaration format and the use of strong typing, come from C++. In addition, C++ has been expanded to include later ANSI features to retain maximum compatibility. C++ shares the following features with ANSI C with few, if any, minor differences.

Function Prototyping   In the older Kernighan and Ritchie C, it was generally sufficient to declare a variable by its size and a function by its return type. Failure to declare a function resulted in its being assigned the default type of `int`. This was predicated on the assumption that a returned integer fits in a register of the CPU and that throwing away a value left in a register causes the processor no problems.

Both C++ and ANSI C enforce a much higher level of type checking. Programmers can no longer mix storage types that are not assignment compatible (one can still mix character, integer, and floating point values in the same expression since C knows how to promote from one to the other). The following assignment is not acceptable even though a pointer to an integer may have the same format in memory and be the same size as a pointer to a character on a PC.

```
int*   a;
char*  b;

a = b;              /*not acceptable without a cast*/
a = (int*)b;        /*acceptable with the cast*/
```

The addition of the cast (int*) changes the type of b from char* to int* to match the type of a. In C a cast always appears as a type within parentheses immediately in front of the value to be cast.

The purpose of strong typing is not to make the programmer's work more difficult. Some early languages, most notably PL/1, took the approach that the compiler should attempt to make sense out of almost anything the programmer entered in order to save the programmer effort. If the programmer used a variable without declaring it, the language would declare it automatically, inferring its type from the way the variable was used or spelled.

The problem with this approach was that when the compiler attempted to make sense out of questionable constructs, it was often wrong. A variable that was never declared might have been a misspelled version of a properly declared variable. Pointing out the misspelling with an error message directs the programmer to the error. By creating a new variable, the compiler introduced a bug that the programmer had to correct.

Strong typing attempts to catch errors as early in the programming process as possible. By adopting a stricter set of rules, the compiler can better catch programming mistakes.

Stronger type checking extends to functions as well as variables. ANSI C allows not only the return type of functions to be declared, but also the type of each argument. When the function is referenced, the type of each argument is compared to the function's argument list. Describing a particular function as an **integer function** is not sufficient. It is now **a function taking an integer and a character and returning an integer**, for example.

This leads to two problems: (1) the difficulty of defining a function before referencing it in a module (ask any Pascal programmer) and (2) knowing the type of functions defined in other modules and only included at link time. To solve this problem, C allows the programmer to declare the type of a function without defining it. This is known as a **prototype declaration**. Although always available, but often ignored in K&R C, the prototype declaration has been raised to a fine art in ANSI C and C++. Both languages have adopted a new format for function declarations to accommodate prototype declarations. In the new format, the names and types of all arguments appear on the same line, for example:

```
unsigned func(unsigned a, int b);
```

rather than:

```
unsigned func(a, b)
    unsigned a;
    int      b;
```

The function definition then appears as:

```
unsigned func(unsigned a, int b) {
           .
           .
           .
}
```

When the programmer does not want to say anything about the number and type of arguments to a function, ellipses may be used. The following two prototypes declare a function `f1()` which takes a single integer followed by any number of arguments and a function `f2()` which accepts any number of any type arguments.

```
void f1(int a, ...);
void f2(...);
```

Current style is to build a prototype declaration for all functions defined within a module. These are often placed in a .H or a C++ .HPP include file for inclusion by modules that call any of the functions. Calling a function that has no prototype generates a warning in Turbo C++ and can lead to some strange errors.

`void` C++ shares with ANSI C the keyword `void`. Originally, functions declared without a return type were assumed to return an integer, i.e., the declaration `fn()` was the same as the declaration `int fn()`. The reason for this was that functions which return integers do so by leaving the value in one of the registers (AX on 80x86 machines). If the calling function chose to ignore that value, no harm came of it. It was not necessary to differentiate the two cases to the compiler. Unfortunately, this made it impossible to determine when a function was being called properly. Did the function really not return a value but the programmer thought it did? Had the programmer called the wrong function?

Early in the evolution of C the term `void` was introduced to indicate a function that returns no value. Such a function was declared `void fn()`. (The default return type for functions is still `int`.) Now the compiler could tell when the function was being called incorrectly.

Since then the role of `void` has expanded. It can now be used to declare a function that takes no arguments. In ANSI C the prototype declaration `int fn()` is equivalent to `int fn(...)`, i.e., a function that returns an integer and accepts any number of any type arguments. ANSI C uses a declaration of `int fn(void)` to indicate a function that takes no arguments. In C++ a declaration of `int fn()` is equivalent to `int fn(void)`, but the latter form is allowed to enhance compatibility.

In addition, a variable may be declared to be a `pointer to void`. A pointer to void cannot be incremented, decremented, or dereferenced, but it is assignment compatible with any other pointer type. This is the "universal donor" pointer. Void pointers are used to store addresses when the program does not (yet) know to what the pointer points. (In K&R C this role was usually handled by a `pointer to a char`, but this can confuse the reader and the compiler by implying something that is not yet known.)

Finally, `void` can be used as a cast to indicate that the results of a computation are intentionally being discarded. For example, the following is legal in both C and C++, but it may indicate a problem.

```
int fn(char x);
fn('z');
```

The function `fn()` returns a value in the second line that is being ignored. In such a case, `void` should be used to ensure that no mistake is being made, as in:

```
int fn(char x);
(void)fn('z');
```

volatile and const ANSI C defines the new storage classes `volatile` and `const`. Declaring a variable `volatile` indicates that the variable is subject to change at any time and, therefore, the compiler should make no optimization assumptions about it. This can mean that the variable is a memory mapped I/O device or that it is a global variable accessible from a different task about which the compiler has no knowledge.

In practice, this means that a volatile variable should be loaded from memory every time it is referenced. Often, when the same variable is used many times in a small number of C statements, the compiler will cache the value of the variable in a register rather than load it from memory each time. The compiler does so to avoid unnecessary memory accesses. Declaring a variable `volatile` disables this function.

Consider the following small Turbo C code segment designed to wait for one second. It does so by reading the current global time, in units of clock ticks, directly from lower memory, adding one second (18 clock ticks), and then waiting for the current time stored in lower memory to be equal to that time.

```
waitTime = *currentTimePtr + 18;
while (*currentTimePtr < waitTime);
```

This program may or may not work, depending on what the optimizer does. Once the value of `*currentTime` is loaded into a register in the first line, the compiler might decide not to reload it in the second line. If this happens, the program will never notice that the value is being updated in memory every 1/18th of a second and the loop will become infinite. Declaring `*currentTime` to be `volatile` forces it to be reloaded from memory on each loop, thereby solving the problem.

The `const` declaration is roughly the opposite, implying that the variable is not subject to change at all. The optimizer may make any assumptions it likes about a `const` variable. The user cannot change a `const` variable. A variable declared `const` is not allowed on the left side of an equal sign nor may it be incremented or decremented.

When considering a pointer, either the pointer or the thing pointed at (or both) may have storage class `volatile` or `const`. Neither case is any different from a simple type. Consider the following sample definitions.

```
char *vPtr = "Some string";
char * const cP1; /*constant pointer to a normal string*/
const char * cP2; /*pointer to a constant char string*/

cP1 = vPtr;      /*line 1 - error #1*/
cP2 = vPtr;      /*line 2*/

cP1++;           /*line 3 - error #2*/
cP2++;           /*line 4*/

*cP1 = 'a';      /*line 5*/
*cP2 = 'a';      /*line 6 - error #3*/

vPtr = cP1;      /*line 7*/
vPtr = cP2;      /*line 8 - error #4*/
```

In the above example, `cP1` is a constant pointer to a normal character string. Thus, `cP1` cannot be modified but the characters to which it points can. This explains why lines 1 and 3 are in error and why line 5 is not. The variable `cP2` is a normal pointer to a constant character string. Thus, `cP2` can be modified in lines 2 and 4, but `*cP2` in line 6 cannot be changed.

A pointer to a constant may not be assigned (without a cast) to a normal pointer. This prohibits the user from inadvertently changing the thing pointed at without the compiler being able to detect the change. This explains error 4 on line 8.

As we will see, C++ expands the concept of `const` even further. C++ shares the ANSI C concepts of `volatile` and `const` as well.

Register Variables Declaring a variable to be of the **register** storage class requests that the variable be stored in a register (rather than Random Access Memory) where it can be accessed more rapidly. If the compiler cannot comply, it can ignore the register declaration.

Register variables allow the programmer to assist the compiler in optimizing register usage. If a function uses one variable heavily, declaring it to be `register` might save execution time.

The keyword `register` was part of the original C language but was rarely implemented in DOS-based compilers. Both Turbo C and Turbo C++ can store up to two register variables in the SI and DI registers of the 80x86. Therefore, both of these registers must be saved across function calls. Any function that intends to use either the SI or DI register as a register variable must save the register upon entering the function and restore it upon exiting.

A function argument may also be declared type `register`. For example, the following declaration is legal.

```
unsigned fn(register int a) {
```

Under Turbo C++ a register argument is pushed onto the stack during the function call and loaded into a register when the function starts. Thus the above is functionally equivalent to the following.

```
unsigned fn(int aTemp) {
    register int a = aTemp;
```

However, Borland discourages the use of register variable declarations. The optimizer in the Turbo C++ compiler tends to cache heavily used variables in these registers anyway. Using a register for a specifically declared register variable deprives the compiler of its use for optimization. If the programmer makes a clever selection, the resulting performance will be similar to that achieved by the optimizer. If the choice is not so optimal, the result will be worse.

#pragmas   A new feature of ANSI C was the inclusion of **#pragmas**. The keyword `#pragma,` borrowed from Ada, allows the programmer to affect compilation from within the source program. The ANSI standard does not stipulate any pragmas.

Turbo C 2.0 defined three pragmas: `inline` to indicate inline assembly language, `warning` to enable and disable particular warning messages, and `saveregs` to save the registers when making huge function calls.

To these Turbo C++ has added the `option` pragma which allows the programmer to control the options in effect when the program compiles. Arguments to the `option` pragma are the same switches the programmer would have entered on the command line of the TCC compiler. Using these options, the programmer can control the memory model, the word alignment, and the default sign for characters.

These options have some restrictions. Some switches cannot be set through the `option` pragma. Some switches must be set before any other token is encountered in the source file (i.e., ahead of anything except a comment). A few switches only take effect between function or object declarations. The remaining switches can be set anywhere and take effect immediately.

The switches that can be set via the `option` pragma are listed below. Options marked with an asterisk represent the default condition. Although the -B switch may not be set via `option`, the pragma `inline` has the same effect. If an option as set in the pragma differs from the way it is set in the IDE menu, the pragma takes precedence.

Options that can appear anywhere:

-A	allow ANSI keywords only
* -A- or -AT	allow Turbo C++ keywords
-AK	allow only K&R keywords
-AU	allow only UNIX keywords
-C	enable nested comments
-d	merge duplicate strings
* -d-	do not merge duplicate strings
-gn	stop compilation after n warnings
-jn	stop compilation after n errors
-K	char defaults to unsigned

Introduction to Turbo C++

* -K-	char defaults to signed
-w	display warnings
-w-	do not display warnings
-wxxx	display warning xxx
-w-xxx	do not display warning xxx

Options that can only appear between objects:

-a	align objects to word boundaries
* -a-	align to byte
-b	make enums word sized
* -ff	enable fast floating point
-ff-	strict ANSI floating point
-G	optimize for speed
-G-	optimize for size
* -k	enable standard stack frame
-N	add checks for stack overflow
-O	optimize jumps
* -O-	no jump optimization
-p	use Pascal calling convention
* -p-	use C/C++ calling convention
* -r	store objects in registers
-r-	store objects in RAM
-rd	only store register objects in registers
-v	source code debugging on
-y	line numbers on
-Z	enable register optimization
-1	generate 80186 instructions
* -1-	generate only 8086 instructions
-2	generate 80286 instructions

Options that can only be set before the first token:

-Eassembler	specify assembler to use
* -f	emulate floating point
-f-	disable floating point
-f87	generate 8087 instructions
-f287	generate 80286 instructions
-in	set identifier length to n
-mx	set memory model to x
-npath	set output directory path
-ofilename	output to filename.obj
* -u	underbars on
-u-	underbars off
-zseg	set segment name options

`#pragma startup` and `#pragma exit` allow the programmer to specify functions that are to execute before `main()` begins and after it completes. A priority between 0 and 255 associated with each start-up and exit declaration specifies the order in which they are invoked (functions with a higher priority—lower number—start up earlier and exit later). Priorities greater than 64 are reserved for Turbo C++; the default is 100.

Quiet Changes The ANSI standard contains a few so called **quiet changes**. These are changes in the way certain constructs are interpreted. They are called quiet changes because the same source code may generate different results on older C and ANSI C compilers with neither compiler generating an error or warning.

These changes arise because some pre-ANSI C compilers interpreted these constructs differently. Moving from one pre-ANSI compiler to another exhibited most of these same quiet changes since there was no agreement among compilers before the ANSI standards committee met. Some quiet changes arose from an attempt to clean up aspects of the language.

For example, the original K&R C performed all floating point calculations in double precision because the PDP11 for which C was originally written could perform double precision as quickly as single precision. Many engineering programmers objected to performing all calculations in double precision. The ANSI standard determined that arithmetic between single precision numbers should be performed in single precision. Normally this causes no problem, but if a program somehow depends upon the calculation being performed in double precision, it will fail when compiled under ANSI C without any warning being generated during compilation.

A second quiet change is the difference in interpretation of hexadecimal escape sequences. Prior to Turbo C 2.0, a hex escape character was limited to three digits. The ANSI compatible Turbo C 2.0 makes no such limitation. Therefore, the string "\x0071" would be interpreted as the single character '\x071' under Turbo C 2.0 but as the two characters '\x007' and '1' under Turbo C 1.5 and other pre-ANSI C compilers.

These quiet changes rarely cause problems and are only dangerous because they produce no error messages. Turbo C++, in adhering to the ANSI standard, encounters these same quiet changes. For a complete discussion of quiet changes see "Standard C" written by P. J. Plauger in the February and March 1990 issues of *The C Users Journal*.

From Turbo C to Turbo C++

Although Turbo C++ is a departure from Turbo C, the relationship is unmistakable. Turbo C++ retains the command line version of the compiler as well as the Interactive Development Environment (IDE), but in a more windowed form. In addition, Turbo C++ now supports input from a mouse as well as the keyboard. Following is an overview of the non-language enhancements in Turbo C++.

Interactive Development Environment

The IDE allows programmers to edit, compile, link, and debug from the same environment without the need to move from editor to compiler to debugger. For editing and debugging, the programmer can load more than one file at a time. These are displayed in overlapping windows. Movement between windows is either through function key, menu option, or clicking with the mouse.

The programmer may adjust compilation and linkage by selecting menu options rather than memorizing command line compilation switches. (The compilation switches are still available in TCC.EXE.) Although the option menus have been changed to make them more accessible from the mouse, the options themselves are the same with the addition of a few options that relate specifically to C++.

Turbo C++ has added slider bars on the right and bottom edges as well as **zoom** boxes in the corners for changing the windows to full screen and back and for closing the windows entirely. Command options across the top of the screen, normally accessible by entering Alt- plus the first letter in the menu option, can now be selected by clicking on them. However, in no case is the mouse required.

The addition of a command stack for data entry fields has enhanced the IDE. Now when File Open is selected, a field appears into which the user may enter a file name and a directory listing from which the file may be selected. Entering the down arrow at this point reveals a pushdown stack of the last 10 files the user has edited. This procedure is functionally the same as the Pick option in Turbo C which it replaces, except that this feature extends to all fields that accept typed input.

The interactive debugger in Turbo C++ resembles that in Turbo C. The only additional command is **Inspect**. Unlike the Turbo C Evaluate command, which is still present, Inspect displays not only the value but the type of variable. Inspect is most effective when examining a structure or class object that has many members. The name, type, and value of each member is displayed. Selecting a structure within an inspected structure causes it to be inspected automatically. This gives the debugger a quick overview of composite, often complicated, data elements.

Turbo C++ allows programmers to access other programs from the IDE through a window called the Transfer menu. Much like the DOS shell option, the Transfer menu allows other programs to be executed from within IDE. Transfer is much more convenient than a DOS shell, however. The programmer may assign a hot key for entering the program quickly. In addition, the user may specify the full path to the program along with the arguments to provide when executing. Transfer macros can provide such things as the name of the file being edited and the name of the .EXE created to allow full automation of the Transfer function.

VROOMM

Not all of the non-C++ improvements have been to the IDE. Turbo C++ now includes the **Virtual Run-time Object-Oriented Memory Manager** (**VROOMM**). VROOMM is a sophisticated overlay manager that enables programmers to create programs larger than 640K.

The principle behind overlays is simple. A section of code, such as a function, need only be in RAM when it is actually being executed. Many parts of a program are executed often and must be in memory the entire time that the program is running to avoid reducing performance unacceptably. In addition, the section of code that loads the overlays must stay in RAM as long as the program runs. Most portions of a program, however, are not executed very often. These sections of code can be left on the disk and only loaded into memory when needed. Since these sections overwrite each other in memory as they are loaded, they are known as overlays.

VROOMM not only simplifies greatly the amount of work programmers expend to overlay programs, but also increases program performance with smaller overlays. This increased granularity removes the possibility that the application will load a 50K overlay to execute a 25-line function. Turbo C++ itself uses VROOMM technology to achieve its considerable capabilities and still leave room for user programs.

Support for Assembly Language

Turbo C++ simplifies the job of the assembler programmer as well. Like its predecessors, Turbo C++ supports **pseudo-registers**, intrinsic variable names for the 8086 registers. Turbo C++ also includes interrupt type functions that are called via an INT instruction rather than a CALL. These can be used to generate Terminate-and-Stay Resident programs in Turbo C++ (see Stephen R. Davis, *Turbo C: The Art of Advanced Program Design, Optimization and Debugging* for a discussion of TSRs in C). These two keywords can reduce the amount of assembly language the programmer must write.

For Turbo C++ to provide inline assembly language requires the Borland Turbo Assembler product to generate a .OBJ file, plus a Turbo Pascal-style inline hex facility that does not require a separate assembler. A programmer can also link Turbo C++ modules together with assembly language modules. Chapter 10 examines these Turbo C++ extensions in more detail.

Conclusion

The changes from each version of Turbo C to the next tend to be evolutionary rather than revolutionary. Following this pattern, Turbo C++ includes some noticeable improvements over its older siblings. But, of course, the ++ is the most exciting aspect of Turbo C++ and it is this aspect that we will examine in Chapter 2.

Chapter 2

Using C++

This chapter will survey the features unique to C++. The new constructs will be introduced and discussed. These features will be examined in more detail beginning with Chapter 3.

Classless Primitives

Although the `class` construct is the most important addition of C++, we will start by examining the new features that are not related to `class`.

Strong Typing

The C++ typing rules are similar to those of the current ANSI C and much stronger than those of the original Kernighan and Ritchie C. C++ has also adopted the new function declaration format of ANSI C. Although Turbo C++ 1.0 still accepts the older format for compatibility purposes, new programs should not use it. Other C++ compilers and future versions of Turbo C++ may not support the older style.

To the ANSI C function declaration, C++ adds default arguments that are defined in the function declaration. Consider the following prototype.

```
unsigned fn(int a, int b = 0);
```

This function `fn()` takes two integer arguments, the second of which defaults to 0, and returns an unsigned integer. Thus, given the prototype, the following three calls are functionally equivalent.

```
int i, x, y = 0;

i = fn(x, 0);
i = fn(x, y);
i = fn(x);
```

Several arguments may be defaulted in the same function, but they must be assigned from right to left. The following is not legal.

```
unsigned fn(int a = 0, int b);
```

If a is to be defaulted, then b must have a default value as well.

When a function is called, default arguments are replaced in the same right to left order. Therefore, even though C++ might have compared the types in the following example and determined that the programmer intended the float argument b to be defaulted rather than the integer c, C++ promotes the integer 2 into the float 2.0 and default argument c to 0.

```
unsigned fn(int a, float b = 1.0, int c = 0);

fn(1, 2);
```

In C++ a function declaration `int f()` is taken to be the same as `int f(void)`—a function that takes no arguments. Since `(void)` has the same meaning in both languages, C++ programmers to whom ANSI C compatibility is an issue should use this form. (ANSI C takes `int f()` to be the same as `int f(...)`; ANSI programmers to whom C++ compatibility is an issue should avoid the empty `()` as well.)

A minor difference arises with regard to ellipses arguments. A function declared as `int fn(int a, ...)` takes a single integer argument followed by any number of arguments of any type. In ANSI C, a comma is required between the known arguments and the `....` Early C++, however, did not include the comma. In modern C++, the comma is optional.

Reference Operator

The reference operator in C means **take the address of** as in the following:

```
int   x;           /*define a variable*/
int*  xPtr = &x;   /*define a pointer to same*/
```

While retaining that meaning, C++ has expanded upon the reference operator making it into a new declaration construct as well. Consider the following C++ example.

```
int   x;
int*  xPtr = &x;
int&  xRef = x;
```

We have declared an integer x and a pointer to an integer xPtr and we have set xPtr equal to the address of x so that &x and xPtr refer to the same location. The next line declares a reference to an integer xRef, which is also set to the same address as x.

The variables xPtr and xRef are both aliases for the variable x. Unlike the `pointer to` operator, the reference operator is not part of the type. That is, xPtr is of type `pointer to int`, but xRef is simply of type `int`, not `reference to int`. To assign a second variable y to x using the two aliases, the code is as follows:

```
*xPtr = y;
xRef  = y;
```

The type of xPtr must be changed to integer so that the types of both sides of the assignment operator match. This dereferences the pointer, thus the * preceding the reference. No type conversion is necessary in the second assignment since xRef is already of type `int`. Pointer variables may refer to the same location as a simple type but with a different syntax. However, reference variables refer to the same location with the same syntax, becoming true aliases.

A reference variable must be initialized when declared. A reference variable is not a pointer type. Once a reference variable has been declared, its pointer aspect may no longer be referred to.

Reference variables are often arguments to functions. Consider the following two function declarations.

```
void midPoint1(char s[], char** middlePtrPtr) {
    int i;

    for (i = 0; s[i]; i++);
    *middlePtrPtr = &s[i/2];
}

void midPoint2(char s[], char*& middlePtr) {
    int i;

    for (i = 0; s[i]; i++);
```

```
        middlePtr = &s[i/2];
}
```

Given a string and a pointer, both functions `midPoint()` set the pointer to point to the middle of the string. To change the calling function `midPoint1()` must receive a pointer to the pointer. The pointer to the pointer must be dereferenced to a simple pointer to make the assignment. A reference argument `midPoint2()` can accomplish the same thing with less difficulty for the programmer. (Keeping straight pointers to pointers versus pointers is one of the greatest difficulties of C for beginning programmers.)

The calls to the preceding functions indicate the danger of reference argument types. The call to `midPoint1()` looks like:

```
midPoint1(string, &middlePtr);
```

The call to `midPoint2()` looks like:

```
midPoint2(string, middlePtr);
```

The variable `middlePtr` could, and probably will, return from `midPoint1()` changed because of the `&` operator attached to the argument. However, it is not obvious at all to the C programmer that the same is true of `midPoint2()`. Declaring a reference argument in C++ is equivalent to declaring a `Var` variable in Pascal.

A function not intended to modify the argument should be declared constant as in `midPoint3(char s[], char const* &middlePtr)`. With such a declaration, `midPoint3()` cannot change `*middlePtr` in the function or in the calling function. This regains some of the insulation of pass-by value.

Declaring an argument referential can save a lot of time and space over a value declaration. Consider the following structure.

```
struct BigClass {
    int array[1000];
} oneObject;
```

```
void fn1(BigClass  bc);
void fn2(BigClass& bc);
```

Calling function `fn1()` involves copying the entire 2,000 bytes of `BigClass` onto the calling stack, whereas calling `fn2()` passes only the address of `oneObject`.

A C programmer may be tempted to think of a reference variable as a pointer variable in which the compiler decides when to apply the `*` dereferencing operator. In fact, the following two functions produce identical assembly language even though the types of their arguments are different.

```
int product1(int* i, int* j) {
    int product = *i * *j;
    *i = *j = 0;
    return product;
}

int product2(int& i, int& j) {
    int product = i * j;
    i = j = 0;
    return product;
}
```

It may be easier to consider a reference as an alias without worrying about the assembly language internals. In C++, reference variables provide capabilities not attainable in C.

Declarations Within Blocks

In C++ the position of variable declarations is no longer limited. A variable may be declared almost anywhere within a block. Consider the following C++ `for` loop.

```
for (int i = 0; i < 10; i++)
```

The control variable i is declared within the `for` loop itself.

Variables cannot be declared within most control structures except in the initialization clause of a `for` loop.

For example, the following is not legal.

```
while(int i = 0) {
    //while loop interior
}
```

There are also restrictions on the appearance of declarations in nested `for` loops. The following fragment generates a compiler error on the declaration of j.

```
for (int i = 0; i < 10; i++)
    for (int j = 0; j < 10; j++)   //compiler error
        //remainder of for loop
```

Adding braces to the external `for` loop so that the internal loop appears in a block by itself solves the problem.

```
for (int i = 0; i < 10; i++) {
    for (int j = 0; j < 10; j++)   //no error
        //remainder of for loop
}
```

Once declared, a variable is known throughout the remainder of the block. Variables declared within a `for` loop control structure are available after the `for` loop is completed.

A controversy has arisen over this addition to the language. Proponents of C++ argue that this feature allows the declaration of a variable to appear close to its use so that readers of the program can easily see the type of variable. Opponents maintain that a function is much easier to read when all variables are declared at the beginning. Military specifications for software require that all variable declarations appear in one place.

At least two important reasons have been given for the change. A reference variable must be assigned an alias at the same time it is declared. Placing all such declarations at the beginning of blocks would limit the usefulness of reference variables. In addition, constructors are most useful when they can be called with information that can only be calculated within the function itself. (A full discussion of constructors appears later in this chapter.) My personal preference is to declare variables at the beginning of the block in which they are used unless there is a specific reason not to.

Inline Functions

In C++ a function can be declared to be of storage class **inline**. The definition of an inline function is retained and expanded at each time the function is invoked.

Inline functions replace the preprocessor #define macro capability. There are several reasons for this change. First, macros can generate errors that are difficult to trace. Consider the following macro.

```
#define square(x)  x*x
```

This seemingly straightforward macro fails to generate the desired result in the following case.

```
int y = square(1+2);
```

In this case, y ends up with the value 5 instead of 9. `square()` expands to 1 + 2 * 1 + 2 which equals 5 because multiplication has higher precedence than addition. Consider this case.

```
int x = 2;
int y = square(x++);
```

The resulting x++ * x++ sets x to 4 instead of 3 and y to 6 (2 * 3) instead of the expected 4. The problem of improper association can be solved by proper addition of parentheses in the macro definition, but the second problem cannot.

Defining `square()` as an inline function generates the expected results in both cases.

```
inline int square(int x) {
    return x * x;
}
```

Since they are expanded by the preprocessor, #define macros have no type. Their syntax does not make clear which are function calls and which are macros. The creators of C++ preferred to create a typed capability to replace #defines. Control structures (such as `if`, `for`, etc.) are not allowed in inline functions.

Inline functions should only be used to perform small functions. Large inline functions greatly increase the time required to perform the function itself. A reasonable maximum size for inline functions is 4 or 5 simple lines.

new *and* `delete`

In C, when a user function needed a block of memory of variable length, it called the library function `malloc()` (or `calloc()`) to allocate memory from an area known as the **heap**. When the function finished using the space, the address of the memory area was passed to the library function `free()`. Under C++ the role of `malloc()` and `free()` has been usurped by the keywords `new` and `delete`.

The keyword `new` was introduced to correct several problems with `malloc()`. As a simple function, `malloc()` cannot accept any type information. Input to `malloc()` is a simple integer representing the number of bytes to allocate. Sizes of different types can vary from one system to another. The `sizeof` keyword converts type information into size information. However, `malloc()` is unable to return a pointer to the proper data type; instead it returns the most general pointer it can, `void*`. Then the programmer must recast the returned value into the proper type for assignment. By comparison, as a keyword `new` can accept type and return a pointer to that type without a cast.

Consider the following comparison between `malloc()` and `new`.

```
struct Test {
    int field1, field2;
```

```
} * testPtr;

testPtr = (Test*)malloc(sizeof Test);
testPtr = new Test;
```

More serious problems with `malloc()` arise when memory is to be allocated for user-defined structures. Since `malloc()` is a function, it cannot receive the type information needed to call any constructor defined for that class. (A further discussion of constructors is included later in this chapter.)

The keyword `delete`, analogous to the C library routine `free()`, deallocates heap memory allocated by `new`.

Expanded Role for `const`

In addition to the meanings given `const` in ANSI C, C++ assigns one more. Since a variable defined as `const` is not subject to change, its value is assigned at declaration and, therefore, is known at compile time. A type `const` variable can be used wherever a numerical constant might occur, even as the dimension in an array declaration.

The following is legal in C++.

```
const int arraySize = 10;
char array[arraySize];
```

A `const` variable has a specifically declared type and scope. (Variables of storage class `const` have the same scope as the equivalently declared `static` variable.) Combined with inline functions, `const` eliminates the need for typeless #defines in C++.

Scope Resolution Operator

The scope resolution operator `::` in C++ enables the program to access a variable declared in an outer block even if that variable is obscured by a locally declared variable of the same name. Consider the following program.

```
int a;
void main() {
    int a;

    printf("local a = %d\n",    a);
    printf("global a = %d\n", ::a);
}
```

Within `main()` the global variable `a` is not accessible without the scope resolution operator since any reference to `a` is assumed to apply to the local variable.

The scope resolution operator can also refer to static and obscured members of structures and classes as we will see later.

// Comments

In C++ comments may begin with a // and extend to the end of the line. A new line automatically terminates the comment. This feature eliminates the need to open and close single line comments.

BCPL, the predecessor of C, used // style comments but they were replaced in C. C++ has returned to the BCPL style. Programmers who are more comfortable with the old comment style may continue to use it.

The difference in comment styles is sometimes used to differentiate between C++ and C from within the program. The following expression evaluates to TRUE when compiled with a C++ compiler and FALSE with C.

```
int cPlusPlus = 1 //* */ 2
                ;
```

Turbo C 2.0 and its predecessors ignore the // and evaluate the above expression to 1 / 2;, after removal of the /* */ comment, which truncates to 0. When compiling a C or C++ program, Turbo C++ interprets the // comment and evaluates the expression to 1. The preprocessor symbol __cplusplus, is defined only when the compiler is in C++ mode, thus enabling the program to determine in which mode it is being compiled.

Anonymous Unions

C++ supports unions that are not defined with a type name and are not instantiated directly. These are known as **anonymous unions** since they carry neither a type name nor a variable name. Anonymous unions are often used for type conversions as in the following code segment.

```
void fn() {
    float x = 1.0
    union {
        int i[2];
        float f;
    };

    f = x;              //i now refers to integer
int j=i [0];            //representation of the float x
```

Anonymous unions can also be used with structure definitions as in the following example:

```
struct Test {
    int type;
    union {
        struct TypeX a;
        struct TypeY b;
    };
} test;
```

In this case, a variable of `Test` may contain a `TypeX` or a `TypeY`, the formats of which differ. To save space, the two formats are stored on top of each other within a union. If the union carried the name `inter`, the full name of struct `a` would be `test.inter.a`. In an anonymous union, the full name of `a` is simply `test.a`.

Anonymous unions are used primarily to modify existing code. They enable programmers to alter structure definitions without changing every reference to the structure. However, overlaying structure elements in memory is a process prone to error. C++ offers better ways to achieve the same effect as anonymous unions.

Overloading Functions

In C++ a function's type is as important as its name. Two functions may be given the same name if they can be differentiated by their argument types. Defining two or more functions with the same name is called **function overloading**, since later declarations overload, or overlay, the earlier declarations.

Consider the following program.

```
#include <stdio.h>

void func(char d) {
    printf("Character func (%d)\n", d);
}
void func (int d) {
    printf("Integer func (%d)\n", d);
}
void func () {
    printf("Void func\n");
}

void main() {
    char a = 1; int b = 2;

    func (a);
    func (b);
    func();
}
```

The output from this program appears as follows:

```
Character func (1)
Integer func (2)
Void func
```

This seems reasonable. People have no problem distinguishing between the three declarations of void func(char), void func(int), and void func(void). Strong typing compels the programmer to identify each function completely—C++ merely uses this information.

In Turbo C++, error messages use full function names (for example, fn(char, int)). Otherwise a programmer would not know to which fn() a compiler was referring.

Function overloading allows the programmer to mask petty differences between argument types. For example, in Fortran I always considered it a nuisance to have a SQRT function for single precision arguments, a DSQRT for double precision arguments, and an ISQRT for integer arguments. The programmer should be spared from the need to deal with such trivialities.

In C++ the programmer can define three substantially different square root functions with the following prototypes.

```
int    sqrt(int    i);
float  sqrt(float  f);
double sqrt(double d);
```

Since they are different functions, each can be written optimally for its argument type.

The programmer could define sqrt() in terms of double and let C++ perform the conversion from integer or float. This would be time consuming if many integer square roots were to be performed. Besides, the programmer might define new structure types for which square root is a reasonable operation, such as Complex. C++ cannot convert from a user-defined structure to an intrinsic type without help.

Function overloading can lead to simpler and easier-to-write functions. In C, a function designed to accept non-compatible argument types must resemble the following. The three C++ functions to handle the three cases are easier to write and maintain than the single oversized C function.

```
void flexible(int type, void* argPtr) {
    char*  cPtr;
    int*   iPtr;
    float* fPtr;
```

```
      if (type = = 0) {   /*handle char case here*/
          cPtr = (char*)argPtr;
                .
                .
                .
          return;
      }
      if (type = = 1) {   /*handle int case here*/
          iPtr = (int*)argPtr;
                .
                .
                .
          return;
      }
      if (type = = 2) {   /*handle float case here*/
          fPtr = (float*)argPtr;
                .
                .
                .
          return;
      }
```

Function overloading can also be used to mask previously existing inadequate functions. Suppose a maintenance programmer has to add a new type Complex to an existing program that calls the square root function. Rather than modify the existing function or the code that calls it, the maintenance programmer would write a square root designed to accept the new type. Recompiling the existing modules with the newly overloaded routines would add Complex capability. Adding new functions is generally easier than modifying existing ones.

Function overloading is another reason to replace #define macros with inline functions. Macro definitions are typeless and cannot be overloaded, while inline functions can be.

Classes

Classes are the primary vehicle for implementing data hiding, data abstraction, and inheritance—the very features that make C++ an object-oriented language. In fact, earlier versions of C++ were called "C with Classes." The remaining sections of this chapter deal with classes in C++ and the features that support them.

Classes in C

Classes in C++ are closely related to the `struct` features in C. A C `struct` is a powerful tool for modelling data. Using `struct` the programmer can design data objects that closely describe "real world" objects. For example, a C programmer developing a mailing address data type might come up with something resembling the following:

```
struct Address {
    unsigned    streetNumber;
    char*       streetName;
    char*       cityName;
    char        state[3];    /* extra char for NULL */
    char        zipCode[6];  /* here too */
};
```

Having defined such a structure, the C programmer would then define a set of "access functions" with which to access objects of type `Address`. A set of these access functions is contained in the C module below. A small `main()` function is included to demonstrate how these functions are accessed.

```
#include <string.h>
#include <stdlib.h>

/*Define the structure for an address*/
struct Address {
    unsigned    streetNumber;
```

```c
        char*       streetName;
        char*       cityName;
        char        state[3];
        char        zipCode[6];
};

/*Now define the access functions*/
/*First, create an address*/
void initAddress(struct Address* addressPtr,
                 unsigned sNumber, char* sName,
                 char* cName,      char* stateName,
                 char* zipC) {
    int length;

    addressPtr->streetNumber = sNumber;

    length = strlen(sName) + 1;
    if (addressPtr->streetName = (char*)malloc(length))
        strcpy(addressPtr->streetName, sName);

    length = strlen(cName) + 1;
    if (addressPtr->cityName = (char*)malloc(length))
        strcpy(addressPtr->cityName, cName);

    strncpy(addressPtr->state, stateName, 2);
    addressPtr->state[2] = '\0';

    strncpy(addressPtr->zipCode, zipC, 5);
    addressPtr->zipCode[5] = '\0';
}

/*delete an address*/
void deleteAddress(struct Address *addressPtr) {
    if (addressPtr->streetName)
        free(addressPtr->streetName);
    if (addressPtr->cityName)
```

```c++
        free(addressPtr->cityName);
}
/*fetch the street address as an ASCII string
  (with a space between number and street)*/
void streetAddress(struct Address* addressPtr,
                   char* name) {
    itoa(addressPtr->streetNumber, name, 10);
    strcat(name, " ");
    strcat(name, addressPtr->streetName);
}

/*fetch the city address as a string also*/
void cityAddress(struct Address* addressPtr, char* name){
    *name = '\0';
    strcat(name, addressPtr->cityName);
    strcat(name, ", ");
    strcat(name, addressPtr->state);
    strcat(name, " ");
    strcat(name, addressPtr->zipCode);
}

/*return zip code as a single long*/
unsigned long zipCodeAddress(struct Address* addressPtr){
    return atol(addressPtr->zipCode);
}

void main() {
    struct Address address;
    char buffer[80];

    initAddress(&address, 107, "Rockcrest",
                "Mesquite", "TX", "75401");
    streetAddress(&address, buffer);
    cityAddress(&address, buffer);
    deleteAddress(&address);
}
```

One of these access functions, initAddress(), initializes a new object of type Address. Whenever a new address is created, memory is allocated via malloc() to store the street and city strings. The user must call the initialization function for each object before using it. Since the object allocates memory off of the heap, the programmer must define a destroy function to return the memory with free().

The tendency to define all of the access functions in a single module is an attempt to achieve data encapsulation. Access from other modules to objects of type Address should be through one of the access functions.

Concentration of the access functions narrows the area in which the programmer must look if a problem occurs in the handling of Address objects. Once the program is completed, if the structure of an Address changes, the programmer will know the location of the functions that will have to be changed and retested. However, since C does not limit access to the internals of an object of type Address, the programmer cannot be certain that other modules will not be affected as well.

While it is possible to define structure type Address, it is not possible to "teach" any of the existing functions or operators how to operate on this new type. Each new structure must have a different set of access functions with unique names.

Once a structure such as Address is constructed in C, it is often necessary to derive new structures that are subsets of the original. For example, we might wish to construct a two-part business address consisting of the company's address, plus a mail station or department number representing the address of a person within the company.

Fortunately, it is not necessary to start over in C. A BusinessAddress may contain a simple address as a subset by defining a member object of type Address as follows:

```
struct BusinessAddress {
    unsigned        mailStop;
    unsigned        department;
    struct Address  companyAddr;
};
```

This structure will require a new set of access functions with new names (two functions cannot have the same name in C). Any function designed to deal with an object of type `Address` will have to be modified to call either the `Address`-type functions or the `BusinessAddress`-type functions.

Modifying the `Address` access functions to handle input of either type may obviate the need for changes in the user functions, but it will complicate the access functions considerably. Type fields will have to be added to the `Address` structure definition to allow the access function to distinguish between the two types. Additions of further different address types will require the same types of modifications again.

Fixing `struct` *with* `class`

Let us examine how C++ fixes some of the problems with structures in C. We will start with the encapsulation problem presented by loosely associated access functions.

The access functions can be defined as part of the structure itself. These **member functions** become a part of the structure like member data elements.

Not only is the association between the structure and its access functions more explicit, but parts of the structure can be defined to be accessible only to the member functions. Access to the members of the structure is strictly controlled. Use of the access functions is no longer voluntary.

Since C++ could not change the rules concerning `struct`, without losing C compatibility, C++ defined a new structure type called `class`. Class definitions have the following general format.

```
class ClassName {
  private:
    unsigned privateData;

  public:
    unsigned publicData;
    unsigned readPrivateData();
};
```

I have adopted the naming convention suggested by Borland for Turbo C++: variable names beginning with lowercase letters, class names beginning with capital letters, and #defines in all capitals. Borland suggests that in multiple word variable names all words after the first be capitalized. This is not a requirement of `class`. C++ enforces no convention for naming.

The `readPrivateData()` declaration is a member function also known as a **method**. (The term method stems from the name for similar constructs in other object-oriented languages, such as SmallTalk. The term member function is generally applied only to C++ and similar languages where it seems to describe the way the function is actually defined and used. Most texts, including this one, tend to use the terms interchangeably.)

Classes add the two new keywords: **private** and **public**. Members declared after the `private` keyword are said to be **private members**, those declared after `public` are **public members**. Public members resemble members of a C `struct`—they are accessible to any function. Private members are only accessible to member functions. `Private` and `public` act as toggles; a class may have multiple private and public sections.

Declaring an object of a class type (a process also referred to as "instantiating the class") is the same as declaring an object of a structure type. In C++ use of the keyword `struct` or `class` is not required when declaring a variable but it is still permitted. Thus, the two declarations below are both legal.

```
class ClassName var;
            or
ClassName var;
```

Class members are accessed like structure members:

```
unsigned someValue;
```

```
var.publicData = someValue;   //ok to access public member
```

By extension the member function is called in the same way:

```
someValue = var.readPrivateData();
```

Pointers to class objects use a similar syntax:

```
ClassName* varPtr;

varPtr->publicData = someValue;
someValue = varPtr->readPrivateData();
```

A member function is as much a part of a class object as are its data members. Assume the `var.readPrivateData()` function returns the member `privateData` specific to the instance `var`. If we had three different instances, `var1`, `var2`, and `var3`, each with a different value for `privateData`, the three calls `var1.readPrivateData()`, `var2.readPrivateData()`, and `var3.readPrivateData()` would each return the correct value for its object.

Member functions may be defined within the class definition or separately. For example, `readPrivateData()` could be written as:

```
class ClassName {
  private:
    unsigned privateData;

  public:
    unsigned publicData;
    unsigned readPrivateData() {return privateData;}
};
```

The same function could be defined separately as follows:

```
class ClassName {
  private:
    unsigned privateData;
  public:
    unsigned publicData;
    unsigned readPrivateData();
};
```

```
unsigned ClassName::readPrivateData() {
    return privateData;
}
```

A member function defined within the class definition is assumed to be an inline function subject to the same restrictions as any inline function: limited size and no control structures. The second format is the more common since member functions defined in this manner are not inline functions and have no such restrictions.

The scope operator :: in the second definition tells Turbo C++ to which `readPrivateData()` the programmer is referring. The class to which a function belongs becomes part of its overall description, as does its name or its argument prototype. A single program can define multiple classes, each with a member function of the same name. The compiler can differentiate the functions by class type.

Member access functions such as `readPrivateData()` were another reason for adding inline functions to C++. By making such simple members inline, little overhead is incurred.

Class Address

Our `Address` structure is rewritten below as a C++ class. Again I have included a simple `main()` to demonstrate how the various methods are invoked.

```
#include <string.h>
#include <stdlib.h>

//Define the structure for an address
class Address {
  private:
    unsigned   streetNumber;
    char*      streetName;
    char*      cityName;
    char       state[3];
    char       zipCode[6];
```

```cpp
    public:
      void initAddress(unsigned sNumber, char* sName,
                       char* cName,     char* stateName,
                       char* zipC);

      void deleteAddress() {
          if (streetName)
              delete(streetName);
          if (cityName)
              delete(cityName);
      }

      void streetAddress(char* name) {
          itoa(streetNumber, name, 10);
          strcat(name, " ");
          strcat(name, streetName);
      }

      void cityAddress(char* name) {
          *name = '\0';
          strcat(name, cityName);
          strcat(name, ", ");
          strcat(name, state);
          strcat(name, "  ");
          strcat(name, zipCode);
      }

      unsigned long zipCodeAddress() {
          return atol(zipCode);
      }
};

//Now define the non-inline methods
void Address::initAddress(unsigned sNumber, char* sName,
                          char* cName, char* stateName,
                          char* zipC) {
```

```
        streetNumber = sNumber;

        int length = strlen(sName) + 1;
        if (streetName = new char[length])
            strcpy(streetName, sName);

        length = strlen(cName) + 1;
        if (cityName = new char[length])
            strcpy(cityName, cName);
        strncpy(state, stateName, 2);
        state[2] = '\0';

        strncpy(zipCode, zipC, 5);
        zipCode[5] = '\0';
    }

    void main() {
        Address address;
        char buffer[80];

        address.initAddress(107, "Rockcrest",
                            "Mesquite", "TX", "75401");
        address.streetAddress(buffer);
        address.cityAddress(buffer);
        address.deleteAddress();
    }
```

In the next section, we will examine how C++ has addressed the problem of user-defined initialization functions.

Constructors and Destructors

Generally, an object must be initialized before use. Global variables are automatically initialized to 0, but this value often is not acceptable. In C the function that declares the object assigns a value to each of its members.

Values are assigned either individually or all at once in an initialization statement.

In C++, however, this process is inadequate. To obtain the maximum benefit from encapsulation, most of the data members of a C++ class should be private. The function that declares an object of such a class does not have access to assign initial values to its private members.

C also permits objects to be initialized by defining a function, such as `addressInit()`, and then invoking the function after the object is declared but before it is used. A similar approach can be used in C++ since initialization can be a member function with access to the private members. To facilitate this process, C++ allows the programmer to define a special method known as a **constructor**. A constructor is a special member function that is automatically invoked whenever an object of that type is created.

Format

Constructors always carry the same name as the object itself and have no return type (not even `void`). A constructor for class `Address` might be declared as follows:

```
Address(unsigned number, char* street, char* city,
        char* state, char* zipC);
```

The arguments are passed to the constructor when the variable is created. To invoke the above constructor, an object of type `Address` would be declared as follows:

```
Address myAddr(105, "Rockcrest St.", "Mesquite",
               "TX", "75401");
```

The arguments appearing after `myAddr` serve the same purpose as an initializer list following an equal sign in C.

C++ also allows the programmer to define a member function that is called when an object is destroyed. This method, called a destructor, carries the name of the class preceded with a ~. A destructor has no return type and takes no arguments. The destructor for Address is declared as follows:

```
~Address();
```

Creating and Destroying Objects

The constructor/destructor format is more flexible than the init functions that programmers generate in C, since they are invoked automatically whenever an object is created or destroyed. Global objects and local objects declared static are constructed when a program begins executing but before `main()` gets control. Such objects are destructed when the program terminates as a result of calling `exit()` or returning from `main()`.

An automatic variable (i.e., a variable declared within a function) is constructed whenever the program encounters the declaration for the object (goes into scope) and is destructed whenever the program exits the function (goes out of scope). C++ allows declarations throughout a block because the data needed to construct an object at the beginning of a block may not be known then.

An object allocated off of the heap using `new` is automatically constructed when `new` is called. Such an object is only destructed by explicitly passing the object to `delete`. In contrast, objects allocated with a `malloc()` call are not constructed at all. `malloc()` cannot call a constructor for an existing object because calling the constructor would create a new object. Since `malloc()` does not receive any type information, the function would not know which constructor to invoke.

Consider the following simple program.

```
#include <stdio.h>
#include <string.h>

class Sample {
  private:
    char* name;
  public:
    Sample(char* s) {
```

Using C++

```
            name = new char[strlen(s)+1];
            strcpy(name, s);
            printf("Entering constructor for %s\n", name);
        }
    ~Sample() {
            printf("Entering destructor for %s\n", name);
            delete name;
            name = 0;
        }
};

Sample global1("global #1");

void sillyFn() {
    Sample anotherAuto("function automatic");
    printf ("The function sillyFn\n");
}
void main() {
    Sample auto1("automatic #1");
    printf("The beginning of main()\n");
    sillyFn();
    Sample auto2("automatic #2");
    printf("The remainder of main()\n");
}
Sample global2("global #2");
```

This program generates the following output.

```
Entering constructor for global #1
Entering constructor for global #2
Entering constructor for automatic #1
The beginning of main()
Entering constructor for function automatic
The function sillyFn
Entering destructor for function automatic
Entering constructor for automatic #2
```

```
The remainder of main()
Entering destructor for automatic #2
Entering destructor for automatic #1
Entering destructor for global #2
Entering destructor for global #1
```

The constructor for objects `global1` and `global2` is executed first after which `main()` gets control. The declaration on the first line of `main()` invokes the constructor for `auto1`. The function call to `sillyFn()` constructs the variable `anotherAuto` and then destroys it. The constructor for `auto2` is not invoked until its declaration is encountered in the third line. The destructors for `auto1` and `auto2` are invoked at the closed brace of `main()` followed by the destructors for `global1` and `global2`.

Constructors can be overloaded with different argument types. A single class may have more than one constructor as long as each has a different argument list. When an object is declared, the constructor matching the provided argument list is invoked. Constructors may also have default arguments.

Following is the `Address` class with constructors and a destructor defined.

```
#include <string.h>
#include <stdlib.h>

//Define the structure for an address
class Address {
  private:
    unsigned  streetNumber;
    char*     streetName;
    char*     cityName;
    char      state[3];
    char      zipCode[6];

  public:
    Address(unsigned sNumber, char* sName,
```

```cpp
                    char* cName,      char* stateName,
                char* zipC);

    ~Address() {
        if (streetName)
            delete(streetName);
        if (cityName)
            delete(cityName);
    }

    void streetAddress(char* name) {
        itoa(streetNumber, name, 10);
        strcat(name, " ");
        strcat(name, streetName);
    }

    void cityAddress(char* name) {
        *name = '\0';
        strcat(name, cityName);
        strcat(name, ", ");
        strcat(name, state);
        strcat(name, "  ");
        strcat(name, zipCode);
    }

    unsigned long zipCodeAddress() {
        return atol(zipCode);
    }
};

//Now define the non-inline methods
Address::Address(unsigned sNumber, char* sName,
                char* cName,      char* stateName,
                char* zipC) {
    streetNumber = sNumber;
```

```
        int length = strlen(sName) + 1;
        if (streetName = new char[length])
            strcpy(streetName, sName);

        length = strlen(cName) + 1;
        if (cityName = new char[length])
            strcpy(cityName, cName);

        strncpy(state, stateName, 2);
        state[2] = '\0';

        strncpy(zipCode, zipC, 5);
        zipCode[5] = '\0';
    }

    void main() {
        Address address(107, "Rockcrest",
                        "Mesquite", "TX", "75401");
        char buffer[80];

        address.streetAddress(buffer);
        address.cityAddress(buffer);
    }
```

In the `main()` function the initialization function is called implicitly when `address` is declared. The destructor is invoked automatically when `main()` is exited; it is no longer necessary to call `deleteAddress()`. Single stepping the program will confirm this.

In the next two sections we will examine how C++ addresses the concerns of abstraction and inheritance.

Overloading Operators

Input/output is considered an intrinsic part of languages such as Fortran and Pascal. Having I/O as part of the language allows the compiler to add certain constructs (such as the END= and ERROR= clauses to a WRITE statement in Fortran), but it prohibits the programmer from modifying the basic I/O. If programmers don't care for the way the `Write` statement works in Pascal, they have little opportunity for modification.

In C the I/O statements are members of the library. The programmer can replace `printf()` with another I/O routine. Moving the I/O function from the "language" to the library was one of the attractions of C for programmers.

By the same token, other aspects of the language, previously thought of as intrinsic, can be viewed as function calls. For example, + can be considered a function that takes two arguments (the expressions on either side of the +) and returns a value.

Defining intrinsic operators as functions introduces the same sorts of possibilities as relegating I/O to functions. Since functions may be overloaded by argument type, operators may be overloaded as well.

Operator overloading is a powerful tool, providing a level of data abstraction not available in C. C++ allows the programmer to overload the logical operators (such as !, &&, and | |), the bitwise operators (such as ~, !, and |), the arithmetic operators (such as +, -, *, and /), and the control operators (such as =, [ ], and ( )). Operators that cannot be overloaded are . and ? :, . *, ->*, and : :.

Operator overloading is best used to expand the basic operators to include user-defined types. Suppose we constructed a new class `Complex`. Complex numbers consist of the sum of a "real" number plus an "imaginary" number. An imaginary number is a real number multiplied the square root of -1, commonly referred to as **i**.

The set of real numbers is a subset of the set of complex numbers. Since all of the basic math operators are defined for complex numbers, it would make sense to define the arithmetic operators for the class `Complex`.

Let us examine a method that overloads the "-" operator. (The difference between two complex numbers is equal to the difference between the real parts plus the difference between the imaginary parts.)

```
Complex operator- (Complex& c) {
    return Complex(real - c.real, imag - c.imag);
}
```

In use it appears as:

```
Complex a(1,0), b(0,1), c;

c = a - b;
```

The operator method is invoked as if it had been entered as:

```
c = a.operator-(b);
```

Turbo C++ accepts either format as long as a is an object of a class that has defined the operator.

When the − is encountered, Turbo C++ searches the methods of the left-hand object until it finds the specified operator. It is clear from the syntax that an operator with a single argument corresponds to a binary operator. By extension, an operator with no arguments corresponds to a unary operator. Thus, we could define:

```
Complex operator- () {
    return Complex(-real, -imag);
}
```

This operator is invoked as follows:

```
Complex a, b;

a = -b;
```

which corresponds to:

```
a = b.operator-()
```

An operator method cannot be defined with more than one argument, as there is no mechanism for invoking it. The only trinary operator ? : is not overloadable.

Using C++

We could define several binary `operator-` methods, each with a different argument type. One might accept a `Complex` argument, another a `float` argument, etc. It is not necessary that `operator-` return a `Complex`. The type returned can be different from the type of either argument.

The program below overloads the +, -, *, and / operators for `Complex`, then uses them in some sample, simple equations.

```c++
#include <stdio.h>

//a simple complex number type
class Complex {
  private:
    float real;
    float imag;

  public:
    Complex (void) {
        real = imag = 0;
    }

    Complex (float r, float i = 0) {
        real = r;
        imag = i;
    }

    //define a display method
    void put () {
        printf ("(%.1f,%.1fi)", real, imag);
    }

    //define the simple arithmetic operators
    Complex operator+ (Complex& c) {
        return Complex(real + c.real, imag + c.imag);
    }

    Complex operator- (Complex& c) {
```

```
        return Complex(real - c.real, imag - c.imag);
    }
    Complex operator- () {
        return Complex(-real, imag);
    }

    Complex operator* (Complex& c) {
        return Complex(real * c.real - imag * c.imag,
                       real * c.imag + imag * c.real);
    }

    Complex operator/ (Complex& c) {
        float modulus = c.real * c.real +
                        c.imag * c.imag;
        float newReal = imag * c.imag + real * c.real;
        float newImag = imag * c.real - real * c.imag;
        return Complex(newReal / modulus,
                       newImag / modulus);
    }
};

void main(void) {
    Complex a (2., 3.);
    Complex b (3., 1.);
    Complex c;

    c = a + b;
    a.put(); printf("+"); b.put();
            printf("->"); c.put();printf("\n");
     c = a - b;
    a.put(); printf("-"); b.put();
            printf("->"); c.put(); printf("\n");

    c = b * a;
    b.put(); printf("*"); a.put();
            printf("->"); c.put(); printf("\n");
```

```
        a = c / b;
        c.put(); printf("/"); b.put();
                printf("->"); a.put(); printf("\n");

        a = -Complex(2., 1.);
        printf("-(2.0, 1.0)->"); a.put(); printf("\n");
}
```

The output from this program appears below.

```
(2.0,3.0i)+(3.0,1.0i)->(5.0,4.0i)
(2.0,3.0i)-(3.0,1.0i)->(-1.0,2.0i)
(3.0,1.0i)*(2.0,3.0i)->(3.0,11.0i)
(3.0,11.0i/3.0,1.0i->2.0,3.0i)
-(2.0,1.0)->(-2.0,1.0i)
```

Operator overloading has some limitations. The programmer is not allowed to define any new operators. In addition, the precedence of the operators cannot be changed. The operator * is evaluated before +, even if one is overloaded. The syntax does not allow a distinction to be drawn between pre- and post-increment and decrement.

Nevertheless, the operator overload is a powerful capability. Operators should be overloaded only with functions that are suggested by their "base" definitions.

When used properly, function overloading can greatly simplify the source program and extend source code reusability. Suppose a source code library contained a module of functions written without the class Complex in mind. Normally, such a module would have to be modified or rewritten to include Complex.

By careful definition of the arithmetic operators for the new class in C++, the programmer can recompile the module and reapply it without change. When my module says "a+b" it may be executing a completely different function if a and b are Complex. As long as the functionality is the same, the routines continue to function properly.

Inheritance

In discussing the `Address` class, we noted one final problem. Many types of addresses exist. While most of them have a common base—the company address, the port at which the person is stationed, or the dorm in which the person lives—they all add some extra information.

Starting over each time with the definition of a different address type is labor intensive and obscures the relationship between different types of addresses. Manipulating a dorm address is not entirely different from manipulating a house address.

In our earlier discussion, we noted that C allows the inclusion of the basic `Address` structure within the structure definitions for the other types as a member object. However, each of the new address types is a new structure that is not directly related to `Address`.

Through a mechanism known as inheritance, C++ allows a class to be derived from another class; i.e., the new class can include the old class in such a way that an object of the new class is an object of the old class as well.

For example, consider the following definition of class `BusinessAddress`.

```
class BusinessAddress: public Address {
    unsigned      mailStop;
    unsigned      department;
};
```

This defines `BusinessAddress` as a **publicly derived class** (or **subclass**) of the **base class** (or **superclass**) `Address`.

A subclass inherits all of the members of the superclass, including most methods. Therefore, an object of class `BusinessAddress` includes not only the members mailStop and department, but also `streetNumber`, `streetName`, and the rest.

The public members of the base class remain public in a publicly-derived class. In addition, the derived class can access any public methods of the base class. If the derived class has a member of the same name, the programmer may use the :: operator to specify the "higher" member. The following accesses are legal.

```
class Base {
  private:
    int a;

  public:
    int b;
    void fn1(unsigned x);
    void fn2(unsigned y);
};

class Derived : public Base {
    public:
        void fn2(unsigned x);
};

void Derived::fn2(unsigned x) {
    b = x;
    fn1(x);              //refers to fn1() in Base
    Base::fn2(x);
    ::fn2(x);            //refers to some global fn2()
                         //which is not a class method
}
```

`Derived::fn2()` cannot access the private variable a. Derived classes have no special privileges enabling them to access the private members of other classes, even base classes.

Classes limit access to private data to member functions. If subclasses had access as well, the programmer would have to hunt through the derived classes to find all of the functions that might be responsible for a garbaged private member.

The significance of class inheritance should not be underestimated. A derived class becomes a special case of its base class. An object of class `BusinessAddress` is also an object of class `Address`. Further, an object of type `BusinessAddress` contains all of the data and methods of an `Address`. Thus, a `BusinessAddress` can do anything and store anything that an `Address` can (and probably more).

The implications of this statement are great. First, a function that expects to receive a pointer or a reference to a class can be passed one of its subclasses as well. In addition, an object from a subclass can be included within lists of objects from the superclass. For instance, one could add a business address to a list of addresses without the need to rewrite the functions that handle the list.

Initializing Derived Classes

A derived class may have constructors and destructors. The constructors of a derived class may build upon the constructors of base classes. A new syntax is necessary to invoke the base constructor without creating a new object. Otherwise, invoking the base constructor from within the derived constructor would create a new object rather than initialize the existing object.

```
class Derived : public Base {
  public:
    Derived() : Base() {
        .
        .
        .
```

Invoking the base constructor in this way allows `Base()` to initialize the members of `Derived()` that it has defined. The remainder of the constructor for `Derived()` (after the open brace), initializes only the new members.

A similar situation with member objects is solved in the same way. Examine the following class definition, especially noting its constructor.

```
class TeacherAssistant : public Student {
  private:
    Address studentAddress;

  public:
    TeacherAssistant(char* lastName, char* firstName,
```

```
                      unsigned class,
                      unsigned strNum, char* streetN,
                      char* cityN, char* state,
                      char* zipC) :
      Student(lastName, firstName, class),
      studentAddress(strNum, streetN, cityN, state, zipC){};
```

`TeacherAssistant` not only is a derived class of `Student` (a TA is a special type of student), but also contains a member of class `Address` (TAs have addresses as well).

The call to the `Student()` constructor initializes those fields that `TeacherAssistant` shares with `Student`. The call to `studentAddress()` invokes the constructor to initialize the `Address` fields. The body of the constructor in this case is empty.

Complete `BusinessAddress` Class

The program below implements `BusinessAddress` from the `Address` base we defined earlier. Only the new class definition and a new `main()` are shown since the `Address` class is unchanged.

```
class BusinessAddress : public Address {
  private:
    unsigned mailStop;
    unsigned department;

  public:
    BusinessAddress(unsigned mailS, unsigned dept,
                    unsigned strNum, char* strName,
                    char* cityName, char* stName,
                    char* zipC) : Address(strNum, strName,
                            cityName, stName, zipC)
                    {
                      mailStop = mailS;
                      department = dept;
                    }
```

```
        void deptAddress(char* buffer) {
            char tmp[10];
            strcpy(buffer, "M/S ");
            itoa(mailStop, tmp, 10);
            strcat(buffer, tmp);
            strcat(buffer, ", dept ");
            itoa(department, tmp, 10);
            strcat(buffer, tmp);
        }
};

void main() {
    BusinessAddress address(10, 1220,
                            107, "Rockcrest",
                            "Mesquite", "TX", "75401");
    char buffer[80];

    address.deptAddress(buffer);
    address.streetAddress(buffer);
    address.cityAddress(buffer);
}
```

The business address can access both the `BusinessAddress` member function `deptAddress()` and the two `Address` member functions `streetAddress()` and `cityAddress()`.

Multiple Inheritance

Turbo C++ supports multiple inheritance, which permits a class to inherit from more than one class. Consider the `TeacherAssistant` class again. A TA is not only a student, but also a teacher. Thus, the `TeacherAssistant` class should be able to inherit from class `Teacher` as well as class `Student`. The format for declaring a multi-inheriting `TeacherAssistant` is as follows:

```
class TeacherAssistant : public Student,
                         public Teacher {
```

Similarly, the constructor for `TeacherAssistant` may invoke the constructors for both `Student` and `Teacher` and may access the public members of either class.

When to Use a Derived Class

C++ programmers may be tempted to overuse inheritance of classes. Whether one class should be derived from another or should simply contain another is a reflection of the relationship between the two. Does one class have an "Is a" or a "Has a" relationship with the other? That is, a type that is a special case of another type should be derived. A type that merely has another type should contain the other as a member. For example, a `TeacherAssistant` is a `Student` and, thus, should be derived. However, a `TeacherAssistant` has an `Address`. To build a `TeacherAssistant` class as a subclass of `Address` would only obscure the actual relationship between the two.

Virtual Functions—Polymorphism

When functions were overloaded, the compiler could decide which function was intended by comparing the use with the declaration. If, however, a pointer to a subclass is also a pointer to a superclass, a potential enigma arises. Consider the following:

```
class Base {
  public:
    void aMethod();
};

class Derived: public Base {
  public:
    void aMethod();
};

void fn(Base* basePtr) {
```

```
        basePtr->aMethod();
}
```

To which `aMethod()` does the call in function `fn()` refer? The reference may be to the method `Base::aMethod()`, but this is not necessarily the case. Another function could call `fn()` and pass it a pointer to an object of type `Derived`. In this case `Derived::aMethod()` would be invoked instead. Remember, a `Derived*` is a special instance of `Base*`.

Inheritance may sometimes make it impossible for the compiler to determine which method is meant in a particular call. Ambiguous method calls must be routed through an arbitrator at run-time to determine the proper method to invoke. This is known as **late-binding**.

Late-binding takes time—time that is wasted, in many cases, when no ambiguity exists. To avoid this overhead, C++ introduces the keyword **virtual**. Marking a method `virtual` implies that all calls to that method (and any methods of the same name in publicly derived classes) must go through late-binding. Otherwise, C++ assumes no ambiguity exists and decides what member functions to invoke at compile time (a process known as **early-binding**).

In the preceding program, `Base::aMethod()` would always be invoked. If the class definition were written with `aMethod()` flagged as virtual, however, both methods would be invoked, depending upon the type pointer passed in `basePtr`.

```
#include <stdio.h>

//Declared a base and a subclass with a virtual method
class Base {
  public:
     virtual void vMethod() {printf("    Base\n");}
};
class Derived: public Base {
  public:
     void vMethod() {printf("    Derived\n");}
};

//Now declare a function to invoke the virtual method
```

```
void fn(Base* basePtr) {
    basePtr->vMethod();
}

//Call the three test functions above
void main() {
    Base     base;
    Derived  derived;

    printf(" Base -\n");
    fn(&base);
    printf(" Derived -\n");
    fn(&derived);
}
```

In this program the function `fn()` is declared as accepting a `Base*`. This function is called twice, once passing it a pointer to `Base` and later passing it a pointer to the subclass `Derived`. Executing the program with the `virtual` keyword in place causes late-binding to differentiate between the two classes.

```
Base -
    Base
Derived -
    Derived
```

Removing the `virtual` keyword, recompiling, and reexecuting the program generates the following result.

```
Base -
    Base
Derived -
    Base
```

Now the resolution to the method is made at compile time and the function can no longer distinguish whether it has received a pointer to the base class or to a compatible subclass.

Virtual methods are a direct result of inheritance. Other object-oriented languages assume all functions to be virtual. Thus, invoking a member function is a slightly slower process than invoking a normal function. In C++ the programmer indicates when the compiler should bind late. Classes with no ambiguities do not have to pay this price. Invoking methods of these classes is no slower than invoking any other function.

Stream I/O

As we noted, the ability to overload operators is a powerful tool. Programmers can train C++ to operate on user-defined types.

In C both input and output are handled by library functions with extremely vague prototype declarations—int scanf(const char *, ...) and int printf(const char *, ...). It is impossible to overload either function with a scanf() or a printf() intended for a new type.

C++ introduces a new input/output technique known as **stream I/O**. Rather than write the following:

```
include <stdio.h>

printf("Output = %d, %f\n", integer, real);
scanf("%d", &integer);
```

A C++ programmer might enter something similar to the Pascal Write statement:

```
include <iostream.h>

cout << "Output = " << integer << ", " << real << endl;
cin  >> integer;
```

To use streams the program must include `iostream.h`. Versions of C++ prior to 2.0 used a different form of streams contained in the include file `stream.h`. While Turbo C++ supports this older stream for compatibility purposes, new users of Turbo C++ should use the C++ 2.0 format.

The I/O streams are nothing more than the left and right shift operators overloaded for `istream` and `ostream` classes. Overloaded members of `ostream` exist for all of the "normal" types including `char*`, `int`, and `float`. Since the << operator is left associative, the above output statement is interpreted as:

((((cout << "Output =") << integer) << ", ") << real) << endl;

The object `cout` is of type `ostream` and is connected to the standard output (like `stdout` in C).

The first operator `ostream::operator<< (char*)` outputs the character string to the output stream and returns an object of type `o-stream`. The next operator `ostream::operator<< (int)` outputs an integer to the output stream, returning `ostream`, and so on. Eventually the method `ostream::endl()` outputs a '\n' and flushes output to the standard output file.

Other control methods known as **stream manipulators** replace the formatting characters previously embedded in the `printf()` and `scanf()` control strings. The programmer must include the file `iomanip.h` to access most of these manipulators. To output a floating point number with two digits of precision after the decimal point, the corresponding `printf()` and `ostream` operations are as follows:

```
                //printf approach
                //(include stdio.h)
printf ("float value = %.2f\n", floatValue);

                //streams approach (include
                //iostream.h and iomanip.h)
cout << setprecision(2);
cout << "float value = " << floatValue << endl;
```

Stream manipulators exist to control radix, output field width, precision, and so on.

As with any operator, the user may define versions of `operator<<` and `operator>>` to handle any class. The listing below contains the same definition of Complex that was shown earlier, but now with an `operator<<` defined for `Complex`.

```
#include <iostream.h>

//a simple complex number type
class Complex {
  private:
    float real;
    float imag;

  public:
    Complex (void) {
        real = imag = 0;
    }

    Complex (float r, float i = 0) {
        real = r;
        imag = i;
    }

    //define access methods for Complex
    float realPart () {
        return real;
    }
    float imagPart () {
        return imag;
    }

    //define the simple arithmetic operators
    Complex operator+ (Complex& c) {
        return Complex(real + c.real, imag + c.imag);
```

```
    }

    Complex operator- (Complex& c) {
        return Complex(real - c.real, imag - c.imag);
    }

    Complex operator- () {
        return Complex(-real, - imag);
    }

    Complex operator* (Complex& c) {
        return Complex(real * c.real - imag * c.imag,
                       real * c.imag + imag * c.real);
    }

    Complex operator/ (Complex& c) {
        float modulus = c.real * c.real +
                        c.imag * c.imag;
        float newReal = imag * c.imag + real * c.real;
        float newImag = imag * c.real - real * c.imag;
        return Complex(newReal / modulus,
                       newImag / modulus);
    }
};

//Define an output operator for class complex
ostream& operator<< (ostream& s, Complex& c) {
    s << "(" << c.realPart() << ","
            << c.imagPart() << "i)";
    return s;
}

void main(void) {
    Complex a (2., 3.);
    Complex b (3., 1.);
    Complex c;
```

```
    c = a + b;
    cout << a << "+" << b << "->" << c << endl;

    c = a - b;
    cout << a << "-" << b << "->" << c << endl;

    c = b * a;
    cout << b << "*" << a << "->" << c << endl;

    a = c / b;
    cout << c << "/" << b << "->" << a << endl;

    a = Complex(2., 1.);
    cout << "-" << a << "->" << -a << endl;
}
```

When executed, this program generates the same results as the earlier version, with some minor format differences.

```
(2,3i)+(3,1i)->(5,4i)
(2,3i)-(3,1i)->(-1,2i)
(3,1i)*(2,3i)->(3,11i)
(3,11i)/(3,1i)->(2,3i)
-(2,1i)->(-2,-1i)
```

Compare in particular the `main()` function of the two and the format of the output.

Stream I/O has been described as simply "a better I/O" method. In many ways, stream input/output is more clumsy than that which it replaces. The major advantages of stream I/O are that it can be overloaded for user-defined types and it is type safe. (Unlike `printf()`, stream I/O does not allow a user to pass a `float` and mistakenly display it as a `char`.) Programs that continue to use `printf()` will not be able to abstract the output of class objects.

Conclusion

The inventors of C++ intended it to be upwardly compatible with C so that the new language would spare programmers the shock of adapting to a new paradigm all at once. To take proper advantage of object-oriented programming, the programmer must embrace a new paradigm. Its compatibility might make the C++ conversion that much more difficult.

However, C++ is the standard-bearer for real-time object-oriented programming. I hope this overview has explained some of the Whys as well as the Whats of Turbo C++. The chapters that follow will provide in-depth examinations of the features outlined herein.

Chapter 3

The Classless Primitives

The Classless Primitives

With this chapter we begin an analysis of the C++ features introduced in Chapter 2. C++ and ANSI C borrow heavily from each other in areas of the language not related to classes. While much of this chapter is new with regard to the older K&R standard, readers familiar with ANSI C on the PC will be able to skim rapidly to Chapter 4.

Strong Typing

C++ encourages the programmer to declare the types of all objects—simple variables, functions, or class objects. The type of each object is compared with its original declaration each time it is used.

Declaring Simple Objects

A simple variable is declared by indicating an optional storage class, then the type followed by the name of the variable.

The legal storage classes and their meanings follow.

extern—known to all modules throughout the program; often called globals. Both variables and functions may be declared extern.

static—known within the module. Both variables and functions may be declared static.

auto—known within a block, such as a function. Only variables within a block may be declared `auto`. These variables are allocated when entering the block and deallocated when exiting the block.

register—similar to `auto` except that the variable is stored in a register rather than RAM. If the compiler cannot accommodate the request, it may treat a `register` declaration the same as an `auto` declaration.

The default storage class for objects declared at the module level is global. The default for variables declared within functions is auto. Thus, in the following example `xyz` is a global character, `abc` is an automatic long integer, and `def` is a static array of floats.

```
signed char xyz;
void fn() {
    long int abc;
    static float def[10];
```

Integer and character variables may be declared signed or unsigned. The default for long, int and char is signed. The default for char can be changed to unsigned via the Options/Compiler/Code Generation/Unsigned chars menu item or the -K command line switch. In addition, integer variables may be declared long or short and double may be defined long. The sizes of each type and their respective ranges are listed in Table 3–1.

Table 3–1   Range and Sizes of Intrinsic Types

Storage Type	Width [bits]	Range
char	8	
unsigned		0 - 255
signed		-128 - 127
int		
<normal>	16	
unsigned		0 - 65535
signed		-32768 - 32767
short	16	
unsigned		0 - 65535
signed		-32768 - 32767
long	32	
unsigned		0 - 4,294,967,295
signed		-2,147,483,648 - 2,147,483,647
float	32	3.4E-38 - 3.4E38
double		
<normal>	64	1.7E-308 - 1.7E308
long	80	1.1E-4932 - 1.1E4932

The long double type is a result of the 80-bit word size of the Intel 80x87 Numerical Coprocessor. This 80-bit floating point is compatible with, but not a part of, the IEEE standard for floating point numbers. Calculations in this extended format are extremely fast and accurate on machines equipped with the 80x87.

Variables may also be declared `const` or `volatile`. `const` variables are not subject to change. Simple `const`s may only be assigned a value when declared. The values of `const` variables may be used as indexes in declaring arrays. `const` members may be initialized from the constructor as follows:

```
struct X {
  const i;
  X() : i(1) {}
};
```

The scope of a `const` variable defaults to static because its establishment cannot be deferred to link time if its value is to be used at compile time. The programmer may give a `const` variable global scope by declaring it `extern const`. However, an `extern const` cannot be used in subscripts or any place where its value must be known at compile time. In this respect, Turbo C++ treats an `extern const` like a `const` in ANSI C.

A `volatile` variable may be changed by sources external to the program. For example, a memory-mapped I/O device may be declared `volatile` to preclude Turbo C++ from caching its value in a register.

The `volatile` and `const` specifications have particular meaning for class member functions. A `volatile` object may only invoke `volatile` methods. Similarly, a `const` object may only invoke `const` methods. Calling a normal method from a `const` or `volatile` object generates a warning. A member function declared `const` may not change any of the members of its class object. A single method may be declared both `volatile` and `const`.

```
struct Test {
    int data;

    void aNormalMethod();
    void aVolatileMethod() volatile;
    void aConstMethod() const;
```

```
};

void Test::aConstMethod() const {
    data = 1;                       //generates an error
};

void main() {
    volatile Test volObj;
          Test normalObj;

    volObj.aNormalMethod();        //generates a warning
    volObj.aVolatileMethod();      //access here is ok

    normalObj.aNormalMethod();     //both here are okay
    normalObj.aVolatileMethod();
}
```

The member function `aConstMethod()` cannot change the member data since it is declared `const`. Accessing the member function `aNormalMethod()` from the volatile object `volObj` generates a compiler warning. No warning is generated when accessing `aVolatileMethod()` from the volatile object nor is any warning generated accessing either function from the non-volatile `normalObj`.

Functions should be declared in terms of the return type as well as the type of argument. A function is declared when it is defined; however, in a prototype declaration a function can be declared without being defined.

```
int fun1(char c);     //accept a character, returns int
void fun2(int i);     //accept an int, returns nothing
float fun3();         //accept nothing, returns float
```

A function may use an ellipsis to indicate that the type and number of arguments is not known.

```
int fun4(int a, ...);  //accepts an int followed by any
                       //number of any type of arguments,
```

```
                        //returns int
void fun5(...);         //accepts any arguments,
                        //returns nothing
```

The prototype declaration only states the type and number of arguments; variable names may differ from the eventual definition or may be omitted entirely. The following is a legal prototype declaration.

```
void tuneRadio(double, int, char);
```

Compare the preceding statement with the following more readable prototype declaration of the same function.

```
void tuneRadio(double frequency,
               int outputGain,
               char modulationCode);
```

Function prototypes may declare default argument values. The following function may be called with two or three arguments.

```
int ascii2Int(char* numberString, int radix=10);
```

This function may be invoked equivalently as either `ascii2Int("123", 10)` or `ascii2Int("123")`.

Default arguments are not limited to constants. A variable can be specified as long as it is defined at the point of the declaration. Local variables can only appear as defaults in local declarations.

```
int globalValue;
void ascii2Int(char* numberString,
               int radix = globalValue);

void main() {
    globalValue = 16;
    ascii2Int(numberString);
}
```

Here the second argument to `ascii2Int()` defaults to the value of `globalValue` at the time the call is made. One argument cannot make reference to another since it is not defined at the time of the declaration.

```
void fn(int arg1, int arg2 = arg1);   //compiler error
```

Two default declarations cannot appear in the same scope even if they specify the same value. Thus, the next function definition shown is in error.

```
void fn(int arg1, int arg2 = 0);

void fn(int arg1, int arg2 = 0) {
    //function definition
}
```

Multiple default declarations can appear if they are in different scopes, however. The following is legal.

```
void fn(int, int = 0);

void localFn() {
    void fn(int, int = 1);         //different default

    fn(1);
}

void otherFn() {
    fn(1);                         //uses global declaration
}
```

The call to `fn()` in the function `localFn()` uses the local declaration, resulting in a call of `fn(1, 1)`. Without a local declaration for `fn()`, the call in `otherFn()` uses the global declaration resulting in a call of `fn(1, 0)`.

This restricted scope also allows different defaults to be declared in different functions.

```cpp
void testFn(int, int = 3);

void func1() {
    int localVar = 1;
    void testFn(int, int = localVar);

    testFn(1);          //results in testFn(1, localVar);
}

void func2() {
    void testFn(int, int = 2);

    testFn(1);          //results in testFn(1, 2);
}

void func3() {
    testFn(1);          //results in testFn(1, 3);
}
```

Typed Expressions

Every expression in C++ has a value and a type. The following expression is clearly of type integer.

```cpp
int a, b;
a + b;
```

Less clear, however, is that the following expression is also of type integer (`const int`, actually).

```cpp
5 + 7;
```

A fixed point constant may be decimal (e.g., 5), octal (e.g., 005), or hexadecimal (e.g., 0x005). The type of a constant is determined by the following rules:

- a constant ending with an l or L is `long int`
- a constant ending with a u or U is `unsigned`
- a single character enclosed in single quotes is `char`
- two characters enclosed in single quotes is `int`

Otherwise, the constant is of the smallest type that can accommodate it; the order of types is `int`, `unsigned int`, `long int`, and `unsigned long int`. Decimal constants skip the `unsigned int` step.

A constant is not a fixed point if it contains a decimal point, appears in exponential notation (e.g., 5e2 = 500), or ends with the suffix f or F. Such constants are `float` if they end in an f or F or `long double` if they end with an l or L. Otherwise, they are `double`.

Expressions involving operands of differing types may be used as long as Turbo C++ can convert the two operands into a common type for which the operation is defined. To evaluate the type of an expression, first convert `char`, `enum`, and `short` to `int`. Then convert the operator of lower precedence type to the higher precedence type. The order is as follows:

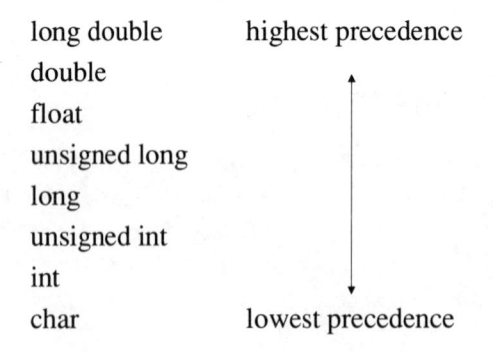

long double	highest precedence
double	
float	
unsigned long	
long	
unsigned int	
int	
char	lowest precedence

For example, adding an `int` to a `long` results in a type `long`.

The preceding types are assignment compatible with potential loss of data when moving from a higher precedence expression to a lower precedence storage object. For example:

```
float x = 2.5;
int i = x;           //loses the .5
float y = i;         //no problem here
```

The programmer may change the type of an expression by applying a **cast**. In C++ casts have two forms. Both of the following expressions cast the floating point variable x into an integer.

```
float x;
int i;

i = (int)x;            //C format
i = int(x);            //newer format
```

These rules may lead to some unexpected results for the novice (e.g., the sum of two characters is an integer), but they do remove some of the peculiarities of K&R C. For example, the sum of two floats is now a float and not a double.

Addressing in the 80x86 Processor Family

The original K&R C assumed that all pointers are essentially alike; that is, the format of all addresses is the same, no matter what type of object is pointed at.

On the 80x86 class of processors, upon which the PC is based, this assumption is essentially true. A pointer to a char is identical to a pointer to a class instance or any other type of object. In addition, the Intel family of processors does not restrict multiple byte objects to even byte addresses.

The 80x86 processors use a **segmented memory model**, which requires some explanation. Most modern processors implement logical-to-physical mapping along with some form of memory protection. A **logical address** is an address that the software sees, while a **physical address** is an address that external hardware to the CPU sees. When supported by a capable operating system, each program is assigned several ranges of physical memory, known as **segments**. Attempts by the program to access memory outside of these assigned areas generate a trap by the CPU which can be handled by the operating system. The offending program is generally terminated.

Memory protection is an effective debugging tool that is all but required on multiprogramming systems. Programs generally only attempt to access memory outside of their boundaries when they contain an errant pointer or when they have run amok. Trapping the program at the first illegal access directs the programmer close to the source of the problem. Allowing a defective program to continue not only makes finding the problem more difficult, but generally causes the system to crash.

A processor can implement memory protection in several ways. One of the most common is **paged memory**. In this approach a logical address is divided into two parts: the **page selector** and the **page offset**. The page selector is a pointer to a table of addresses within the processor called the **page table**. Let us assume a 16-bit physical address and a 16-bit logical address with the upper 8 bits used as the page selector, as shown in Figure 3–1.

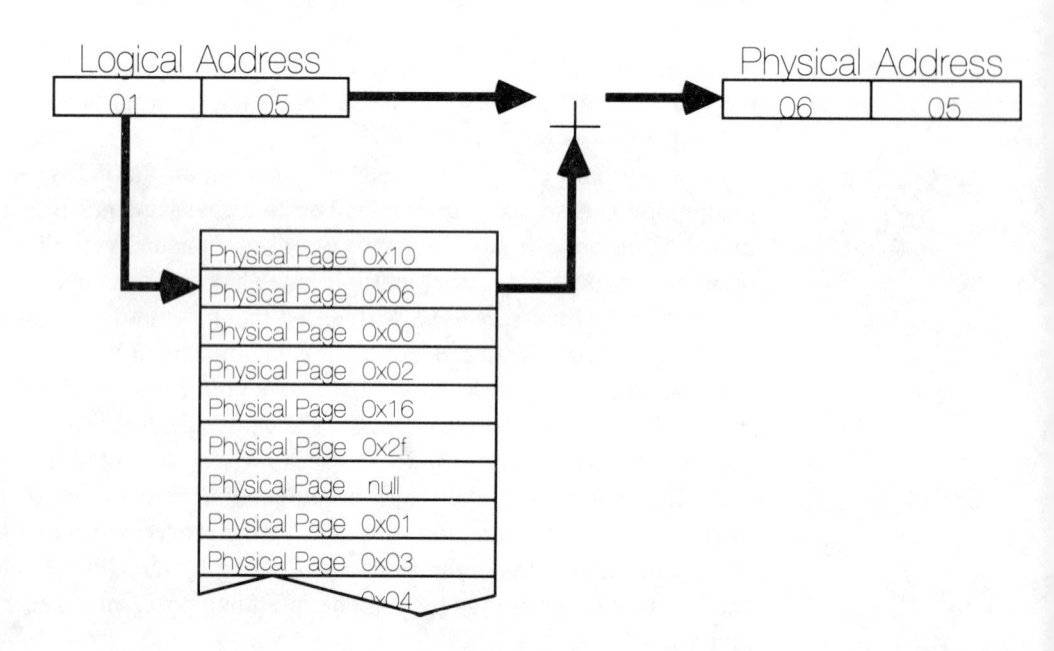

Figure 3–1 Logical to Physical Conversion in Paged Memory

In this example, the logical address 0x0105 would result in a page selector of 0x01, which converts to a 0x06. When added to the page offset of 0x05, a physical address of 0x0605 results.

The page table can also include memory protection bits. Thus, our page 0x01 may be marked as read-only. Attempts to write to this location would generate a memory protection fault. A page may be marked as not being present in RAM at all. Attempting to access such a location would generate a "not present" fault, which the operating system would answer by loading that page somewhere in physical memory and placing its physical address in the page table. This function is known as virtual memory, since not all of a program's memory pages need to be in RAM at one time, giving the program the appearance of using more RAM than actually exists in the system.

(A good analogy to virtual memory is a police inquiry in a small office. Several witnesses have facts about different aspects of the case, but they cannot all fit into the office at once. As the investigation begins, the first witnesses are summoned. Occasionally the needed witness is not in the office, but is just outside in the waiting room. When this occurs, a new witness is summoned and another is asked to leave to allow room for the incoming informant.)

When developing the replacement for the 8080, the Intel designers wanted to implement some form of memory management including support for protection and virtual memory. The designers decided not to exceed 16 bits for the internal registers. However, this would result in a 64K logical address space, too small a limit even for that time.

Logical addresses were divided into two parts: a **segment register** and a **segment offset**. The segment register effectively became the page selector while the 16-bit address contained within a register or instruction served as the page offset. (Other differences between the paged memory and segmented memory models are not germane to this discussion.)

The 8086 has four segment registers: the code segment to generate instruction addresses, the data segment for data addresses, the stack segment for stack addresses, and the extra segment for special block copy instructions. An instruction to load or store a memory address may specify any of the four segments. In the absence of specific instructions, all address instructions use one of the defaults. Memory cannot be accessed without going through one of the segment registers. The 80286 was the first processor to use segment registers to support memory management, including virtual memory and memory protection.

A C++ address may specify both segment and offset, a so-called **far address**, or it may contain only the offset portion, a **near address**. A near address is assumed to be an offset within the default segment. A near variable is relegated to the program's default data segment for global and static variables and to the stack segment for auto variables. A global variable declared far is assigned to its own segment. Automatic variables cannot be declared far since they must all be on a single stack. Register variables can be neither near nor far since they are not stored in memory. All of the functions declared far within a single module go into the same far segment.

```
int near x;
int far y;
void far fn();
```

Some readers who have programmed in C on the 8086 may never have declared an object near or far because Turbo C++ provides six sets of defaults called the **compiler model**. These defaults are accessible via the Option/Compiler/Code Generation/Model menu option (the -m switch on the command line version). The names and meanings of the different compiler models are listed in Table 3–2.

Table 3–2 Compile Models in Turbo C++

Model	*Switch*	*Function*	*Data*
Tiny	-mt	near	near (CS == DS)
Small	-ms	near	near (CS != DS)
Medium	-mm	far	near
Compact	-mc	near	far
Large	-ml	far	far
Huge	-mh	far	far

If the small compilation model is in effect, all global variables and functions default to near with the two kept in separate segments.

The tiny model is a rarely used memory model in which the code segment and data segment are equal and no far declarations appear anywhere in the program. Executable .EXE files generated under the tiny model may be converted into .COM files using the EXE2BIN utility provided with older versions of DOS.

Notice that the large and huge memory models appear in Table 3–2 as identical. In both models, functions default to far with each module assigned its own code segment. In the large model, all modules share a single data segment, while in the huge model, each module is assigned its own data segment.

What are the relative advantages of near and far addresses? The offset portion of addresses is only 16 bits wide. A program that uses only near addresses may not exceed 64K of data for global and static variables, plus 64K of code for functions, plus 64K of stack for automatic and dynamically declared objects. While this is enough space for many programs, it is not sufficient for modern applications.

Accessing a far address takes more computer time than accessing a near address, however. The CPU must load up not only 16 bits of segment offset, but also an additional 16 bits of segment register for each access.

I compiled the following sieve of Eratosthenes C program under the small model. Executing 1,000 iterations required 55 seconds.

```
#include <stdio.h>
#include <stdlib.h>

#define TRUE 1
#define FALSE 0
#define ITER 1000
#define SIZE 8190

/*define our Boolean sieve*/
char flags [SIZE+1];

/*Main - the sieve program*/
void main () {
    int i,k;
    int iter, count;
```

```
        printf ("%d iterations. "
                "Hit enter and start stop watch\n", ITER);
        getchar ();
        printf ("Start...");

        for (iter = 1; iter <= ITER; iter++) {

            /*clear the prime number count and set
              "multiples array" to all true*/
            count = 0;
            for (i = 0; i <= SIZE; i++)
                flags[i] = TRUE;

            /*if the "multiples array" flag is TRUE
              for this number then this number
              is a prime; count it and then clear the
              flags for all of the multiples of this
              number*/
            for (i = 2; i <= SIZE; i++)
                if (flags[i]) {
                    for ( k = i + i; k <= SIZE; k += i )
                        flags[k] = FALSE;
                    count++;
                }
        }

        printf ("stop!\n\n%d primes\n", count);
}
```

I then changed the declaration of the heavily used `flags` array as follows:

```
char flags [SIZE+1];    ->    char far flags [SIZE+1];
```

Recompiling and executing the program resulted in an execution time of 66 seconds for 1,000 iterations. Changing the declaration of one array decreased performance by 20 percent.

Far declarations allow programs to access larger memory areas. The following declarations will not compile together.

```
char array1[40000L];
char array1[40000L];
```

Two 40K arrays obviously cannot fit into a single 64K segment. Changing the declarations to far forces each array into its own segment. As a result, the following declarations compile properly.

```
char far array1[40000L];
char far array2[40000L];
```

It is legal to compile a far or near declaration under any of the compiler models except tiny.

Declaring Pointers in C++

Declaring a pointer can be a confusing process in C. Although elegant in its consistency, the syntax of complex pointer declarations can seem torturous. Review for a moment the following pointer declarations.

```
int * simplePtr;
void * voidPtr;
char * arrayOfPtrs[10];
char (* ptrToArray)[10];

int (* funcPtr)(char);

int far * farPtr;
int near * (far * complexPtr)(char*);
```

The first two declarations allocate a pointer to an integer, `simplePtr`, and a pointer to a void, `voidPtr`. As with addresses, pointers need not be declared near or far. The default pointer type matches the default address type for the current compilation model. If object addresses default to far, pointers to objects default to far as well.

The next two statements in the preceding sample define, first, an array of pointers to characters and, second, a pointer to an array of characters.

In the fifth declaration the variable `funcPtr` is defined as a pointer to a function that accepts a character and returns an integer. As with functions, pointers to functions should be fully prototyped—specifying the return type as well as the types of all arguments.

The variable `farPtr` is a far version of the near integer pointer `simplePtr`. The last example, `complexPtr`, declares a far pointer to a function that accepts a default pointer to a character and returns a near pointer to an integer.

In use, these variables closely resemble their declarations.

```
int func(char);
int * far complexFunc(char*);

void main() {
    int w;
    simplePtr = &w;
    *simplePtr = 1;

    char x;
    arrayOfPtrs[0] = &x;
    *arrayOfPtrs[0] = '2';
    char y[10];
    ptrToArray = &y;
    (*ptrToArray)[2] = '3';

    funcPtr = func;    //store address of function
    (*funcPtr)('4');

    farPtr = (int far *)simplePtr;
    *farPtr = 5;

    complexPtr = complexFunc;
```

```
        int near * z = (* complexPtr)(&x);//address may be...
                * z = 6;         //...stored and used or...
        *(*complexPtr)(&x) = 6; //...just used directly

        int array[10];     //defining an array...
        array[7] = 7;
        *(array + 7) = 7; //...also defines a pointer
}
```

In case 3 the parentheses are necessary to evaluate the pointer before the index. Otherwise, this case would be indistinguishable from case 2.

In the first line of case 4, the address of the function `func()` is stored in the location `funcPtr`. A function name without parentheses is taken to be the address of the function (`&func()` would mean the address of the object returned by `func()`). The second line calls the function pointed at by `funcPtr`, passing the character '4'. Here the parentheses force evaluation of the pointer before the function call is performed.

The dereferencing of a pointer to a function may be left implicit when the pointer is used in a call. The function pointed at by `funcPtr` can be called as follows:

```
funcPtr('4');           //equivalent to (*funcPtr)('4');
```

Case 6 also calls a function indirectly. The address of the function `complexFunc()` is stored into `complexPtr` in the first line. In the second line, the function pointed at by `complexPtr` is invoked, passing the address of the variable `x` and storing the resulting pointer in variable `z`. In the third line a 6 is stored in the integer pointed at by `z`. The final line performs the same operation in one step without using the intermediate `z`. In complex function pointer declarations the call should be broken into two steps as shown with variable `z`.

Case 7 indicates that a direct relationship exists between declaring an array and a pointer. The array name without the subscript is the address of the first element. Performing addition with a pointer is similar to indexing an array as long as neither operator is overloaded.

Pointers may be assigned to each other if they are assignment compatible or specifically recast. To use the newer format for a pointer cast, a `typedef` must be defined.

```
int* intPtr;
char* charPtr;
typedef char* CharPtr;

charPtr = intPtr;           //not legal without cast
charPtr = (char*)intPtr;    //C cast is still legal
charPtr = char*(intPtr);    //not a legal cast
charPtr = CharPtr(intPtr);  //C++ cast using typedef
```

A far pointer may not be assigned to a near pointer. Recasting a far pointer to a near pointer is legal but results in the segment portion of the address being truncated.

```
char far farChar;
char near nearChar;

void main() {
    char far *  farPtr = &farChar;
    char near * nearPtr = &nearChar;

    farPtr  = nearPtr;               //legal
    nearPtr = farPtr;                //compiler error
    nearPtr = (char near *)farPtr;   //legal but dangerous
}
```

When mixing far and default sized pointers, the programmer must make sure that the sizes of all assignments match. For example, the following code fragment will only compile under the compact, large or huge memory models where data pointers default to far.

```
char far farChar;
char*    defaultPtr = &farChar;
```

Under the small and medium models, `defaultPtr` defaults to a near pointer which cannot contain the larger far address of `farChar`.

The same problem arises when passing addresses to functions. For example, the following fragment will not compile under the near data memory models.

```
void charFn(char*);
char far farString[80];

charFn(farString);
```

This is not serious for fully prototyped C++ functions. As long as all modules are compiled using the same compiler model, the error will be caught by Turbo C++. This problem is not caught, however, for external C functions to which the program links, such as the functions which make up the Turbo C++ Run Time Library.

An address explicitly declared either near or far should never be passed to such a function unless the programmer can be sure of the size of pointer expected. For example, the following program fragment will only execute properly under the compact, large or huge memory models.

```
#include <string.h>

char far farSource[80];
char far farDestination[80];

strcpy(farDestination, farSource);
```

The programmer should use conditional compilation to guarantee the compiler model as in the following example.

```
#ifndef __LARGE__
    #error Must be compiled under Large Memory Model
#endif

#include <string.h>
```

```
char* far farSource;
char* far farDestination;

strcpy(farDestination, farSource);
```

The label __LARGE__ is only defined when the large compilation model is in effect. The compiler directive `#error` forces compilation to stop with an error message. Other labels are defined for the different compiler models.

Pointers and Defaults

Arguments to functions may be assigned default values. Although the default is not part of the type, it may be listed in the prototype declaration. The default type may be part of the declaration of a function pointer as well. When assigning the address of a function to a function pointer, the argument types must match, but not the default. The default is applied when the function is invoked.

```
void fn1(int, int),    (*f1)(int, int = 0);
void fn2(int, int = 0), (*f2)(int, int);

main() {
    f1 = fn1;
    fn1(1)              //illegal - no default for fn()
    (*f1)(1);           //no compiler error here

    f2 = fn2;
    fn2(2);             //this is okay
    (*f2)(2);           //but not here
}
```

In the above example, `f1` and `fn2()` are assigned default values while `f2` and `fn1()` are not. Since the default is not part of the type, `fn1` and `fn2` are assignment compatible with both `f1` and `f2`. The variable `f2` does not have a default argument even when it points to the function `fn2()`.

Tentative Declarations

Declaring a pointer to a user-defined object is essentially the same process as declaring a pointer to an intrinsic object type.

```
struct A {
    int a;
    char b;
} * anObjectPtr;
```

However, sometimes it is impossible to define a structure before referring to it. Take, for example, the following structure definitions.

```
struct A {
    struct B * bPtr;
};

struct B {
    struct A * aPtr;
};
```

Referring to structure A within the definition of B is fine, but referring to structure B within A is not. The structure B has not been defined at that point. Reversing the order of the structure definitions would only reverse the problem.

C++ allows the programmer to insert a **tentative declaration** to serve notice of the programmer's intent to define an object of that name. The tentative declaration does not define an object. The following segment compiles properly.

```
struct A;   struct B;   //tentative declarations
struct A {
    struct B * bPtr;
```

```
};

struct B {
    struct A * aPtr;
};
```

Void Pointers

Void pointers cannot be dereferenced nor can they be incremented or decremented since nothing is known about the size of the objects to which they point.

A `void*` is a repository for pointers of an as yet unknown type. Any pointer type can be assigned to a `void*`. In C++, a `void*` can be assigned to another pointer type only with the proper cast.

```
typedef int* intPtr;

void fn() {
    int* x;              //any other pointer type
    void* y;

    y = x;               //legal without cast
    x = (int*)y;
    x = intPtr(y);
}
```

Huge Objects

The segmented architecture of the 80x86 family limits pointer arithmetic to the segment offset portion of an address. Since the offset is only 16 bits wide, arithmetic on a pointer cannot increase it by more than 64K, nence the limit on the size of an array. This limit is true for both near and far objects.

To allow arrays larger than 64K, Turbo C++ defines a third type of address known as huge. Huge addresses appear in memory like far pointers;

however, every time a huge object is accessed, Turbo C++ generates a call to an internal function to calculate a new segment along with a new offset.

Both global objects and pointers may be declared huge; auto and static objects may not. In the following example, all of the declarations are legal except for `notAllowed`.

```
char huge  hugeArray[100000L];
char huge* hugePtr1;
void fn() {
    char huge notAllowed;      //compiler error
    char huge* hugePtr2;
}
```

Huge is never the default.

While huge pointers allow data structures to exceed 64K, the calls which must be made considerably increase the required access time. For example, declaring the flags array huge in the Sieve benchmark as follows:

```
char huge flags [SIZE+1];
```

increased the execution time to 345 seconds, 420 percent longer than the far pointer time, and 525 percent longer than the near pointer time! Huge pointers are only effective for arrays that are accessed seldom or for applications where execution time is not a concern.

Reference Operator

The unary reference operator `&` in C is used to take the address of its argument. C++ expands the role of the reference operator to include declarations. Declaring a variable a reference to another variable defines an alias.

```
int  object;
int& objectRef = object;
```

In this example, `object` is a simple integer. The variable `objectRef` is an alias of `object`.

In use, the reference is not a part of the type. Thus, `objectRef` is of type `int`. At the machine language level, `objectRef` contains the address of `object`. However, C++ automatically dereferences the `objectRef` when used.

Since a reference variable has the same type as its alias, the "address part" of a reference variable cannot be accessed. For example:

```
int   i, j, k;
int&  iRef = i;         //est. iRef as alias for i
int*  iPtr;


iRef =  j;              //same as i = j;
iPtr = &iRef;           //same as iPtr = &i;
iRef = &k;              //illegal - type mismatch
```

The first declaration assigns `j` to the location pointed at by `iRef` (which is `i`). In the second assignment, taking the address of a reference variable returns the address of the aliased variable, in this case `i`.

The third assignment is wrong since `iRef` is of type `int` whereas `&k` is of type `int*`. The alias for a referential variable can only be established when it is declared. The following declaration is illegal.

```
int& iRef;
```

It establishes a referential variable with no alias and no way of assigning one later on.

Reference variables can facilitate the programmer's work with pointer variables. The following declaration allocates space from the heap for an object of class `MyClass` and associates it with a reference object.

```
MyClass   classObj;
MyClass&  classRef = *new MyClass;

classRef.aMember;
classRef.aMethod();
```

In use `classRef` resembles a variable declared on the stack, such as `classObj`, except that the destructor for `classRef` is not automatically invoked as it goes out of scope. This is also true for pointers to class objects.

Arguments to functions can be declared referential.

```
void fn(MyClass& argRef) {
    argRef.aMember = 1;
}
void main() {
    MyClass anInstance;

    fn(anInstance);
```

In the example the variable `argRef` becomes an alias for `anInstance`. This brings two potential advantages: First, changes made to the object within the function `fn()` remain after the function returns. In addition, passing large structures by value can take a lot of stack space and waste a lot of time. In the following code segment, space for the object `largeObject` must be allocated twice, as it is first declared and then as a separate copy is passed to `fn()`.

```
void main() {
    LargeClass largeObject;
    void fn(LargeClass);

    fn(largeObject);
}
```

Changing the declaration of `fn()` to `fn(LargeClass&)` reduces the time and space required to call the function by passing just the address of the single copy of `largeObject`. If `fn()` has no intention of changing the object passed to it, some protection can be achieved by redeclaring the function `fn(const LargeClass&)`. This retains the speed advantage while not allowing `fn()` to change the object.

All of these capabilities are available in C via pointer variables. With pointer variables the programmer must decide when to dereference the pointer with a *. With reference types, C++ performs the dereferencing automatically.

Reference Types

Since a reference variable is an address, reference declarations share many of the properties of pointer declarations. Consider the following declarations.

```
void fn() {
    int a;
    int const &  b = a;

    //b = 20;    //this is illegal since b is const

    int c;
    int volatile & d = c;

    int e;
    int far& f = e;
}
```

In each case, the declarations have the same effect as the corresponding pointer declaration. The object b is a constant alias. It is illegal to attempt to assign b a value. The `volatile` reference keeps the compiler from caching multiple access to d in a register. (The compiler can still cache c, as it is not `volatile`.)

The last line of the example declares f to be a far reference to the variable e. Turbo C++ stores both the segment and offset of &e into the alias f. The size of a reference variable defaults to the same size as the corresponding pointer.

Reference can be made to other than simple types as well. Notice the declarations in the following small function.

```
void fn() {
    int   a;
    int* aPtr = &a;
    int* & aPtrRef1 = aPtr;
```

```
    int* & aPtrRef2 = &a;

    *aPtrRef1 = 1;
    *aPtrRef2 = 2;
}
```

Here `aPtrRef1` and `aPtrRef2` are references to pointers. They may be used identically to the aliased pointer. This declaration is not very useful in practice. However, a similar declaration allows reference variables to avoid pointers to pointers when calling functions.

```
void fn(int* & aPtr) {
    aPtr = new int;   //aPtr retains new value in caller
```

The change to the variable `aPtr` in this function is retained in the calling function.

Functions with Referential Arguments

Since the reference operator is not part of the type, it cannot be used to differentiate a function. Therefore, the following declarations are ambiguous.

```
void fn(int   x);
void fn(int& x);
```

No construct exists to determine which one of these `fn()`s is applicable to any particular call. The assembly language for calling these two functions is considerably different, however. In the first case the value of x is pushed on the stack (pass by value), whereas in the second the address of x is pushed (pass by reference).

When the arguments are structures, the differences become more pronounced. Consider the following small program.

```
#include <stdio.h>
struct X {
    int a;
    int b;
```

```
        X() {
            printf("Default constructor\n");
            a = b = 0;
        }
        X(X& x) {
            printf("C-I constructor\n");
            a = x.a;
            b = x.b;
        }
};

void fn1(X x) {
    printf("In fn1\n");
}

void fn2(X& x) {
    printf("In fn2\n");
}

void main() {
    X sample;

    fn1(sample);
    fn2(sample);
}
```

This program generates the following output.

```
Default constructor
C-I constructor
In fn1
In fn2
```

The default constructor is invoked when `sample` is instantiated in main(). The two messages from the functions are clear as they are called. A C-I constructor is used to make copies of objects. Why is the C-I constructor message before invoking `fn1()` but not before `fn2()`?

The function `fn1()` passes its arguments by value. Thus, the C-I constructor was used to copy the object `sample` into a new X object on the call stack. For `fn2()` the address of the object `sample` was pushed. For large or complicated objects, declaring arguments referential can save CPU time and space by allocating and copying objects onto the caller's stack.

Referential Functions

Functions may also be declared referential. The following example declaration is adapted from the Chapter 11 example program.

```
unsigned far& screen(unsigned xloc, unsigned yloc) {
    static unsigned (far* screenMatrix)[25][80] =
         (unsigned (far*)[25][80])MK_FP(0xB800,0x0000);
    return   (*screenMatrix)[yloc][xloc];
}
void putText(unsigned xloc, unsigned yloc,
             char color, char symbol){
    unsigned fullChar = ((unsigned)color << 8) + symbol;
    screen(xloc, yloc) = fullChar;            //ref#1
}
char getText(unsigned xloc, unsigned yloc){
    return (char)(screen(xloc, yloc) & 0xff); //ref#2
}
```

The function `screen()` is declared `unsigned&`. This function calculates the address of the screen location (xloc,yloc) on a CGA, EGA, or VGA display in text mode (replace the 0xB800 with a 0xB000 for a monochrome display). The `xloc` corresponds to the display column, the `yloc` corresponds to the row. The far declarations indicate that a 32-bit address is required to reach video memory.

A function declared an alias for a location may appear on either the left side of an equal sign, as in reference #1, or on the right side, as in reference #2.

In reference #1, the function `putText()` stores a symbol and color pair into the screen location (xloc, yloc). This has the effect of writing the symbol to the screen at that location and with that color. The `getText()` function of reference #2 reads the screen at location (xloc, yloc).

`screen()` could have been declared `unsigned*` to achieve virtually the same effect. References in `putText()` and `getText()` would then include the dereferencing `*` in the proper places.

With functions that return a structure, considerable differences arise between referential and non-referential functions. This problem is discussed in Chapter 6.

Passing Constants as Referential Arguments

The following is permitted, but may not produce the expected result.

```
void fn(int& x) {
    x = 5;
}

void main() {
  const int y = 10;

  fn(y);
}
```

The call to `fn()` does not change the value of `y`. Instead, Turbo C++ stores the value 10 in a local temporary whose address gets passed.

The process is more obvious in the following program.

```
void increment(int& x) {
    x++;
}
```

The Classless Primitives

```
void increment(int* x) {
    (*x)++;
}

void main() {
    int value = 0;

    //these two calls generate exactly the same code
    increment (value);      //calls first  increment()
    increment (&value);     //calls second increment()

    increment (value+1);    //increments temporary
//  increment (&(value+1)); //illegal
}
```

The assembly language generated by the two increment () functions and the first two calls is identical. In the second pair of calls the call to increment (), with its implicit reference to the address of value+1, passes the address of a local temporary variable containing the new value, which is then incremented. The variable value is not effected. However, the second call, containing an explicit reference to the address of value+1, generates a compiler error.

The same results can be expected from operators implemented as functions with referential arguments. For example, the following nonsensical structure generates no error.

```
cin >> (a + b);
```

The sum of a and b is stored in a local temporary that is then used to store the results from standard input. The temporary is not accessible to the programmer.

Declaring Variables Within Blocks

C allows a group of statements within a function to be set off in a separate block by enclosing them in a { } pair. Like functions, blocks may contain variable declarations before any executable statements with the block. Such variables go into scope at the opening brace and go out of scope at the closing brace. Space on the stack for automatic variables is allocated only during the time they are in scope. Blocks carry no name and may not be called like a function.

```
void fn(int a, int b) { //legal C function also
    b = a * a;

    {                   //start a new block
        int c;          //with its own variables
        for (c = 0; c < 10; c++)
            b -= a;     //can still access outer variables
    }                   //c no longer accessible here
}
```

C++ allows variables to be declared anywhere within a block. Space for a variable is allocated when the block is entered, no matter where the variable is declared within the block. The constructor for the variable is called at the point of the declaration. A variable cannot be accessed until it has been declared.

Turbo C++ permits multiple declarations of a variable. The following program "declares" y five times.

```
#include <stdio.h>

struct Int {
    int a;
    Int () {
        printf("Default constructor\n");
        a = 0;}
};

void main() {
    int x;
```

The Classless Primitives

```
        for (x = 0; x < 5; x++) {
            Int y;
        }
    }
```

This program generates the following results.

```
Default constructor
Default constructor
Default constructor
Default constructor
Default constructor
```

Although the constructor is invoked five times, space on the stack is allocated only once. Each call to the constructor resets the same y.

The destructor for a simple object is invoked at the closing brace of the block in which it is defined. For constructors that involve calls to `new`, the programmer must delete the pointer at the end of the block. Invoking a constructor multiple times can result in loss of memory if the constructor contains a call to `new`. The programmer should prevent a `break` or `cont` from avoiding the `delete` or memory will be lost as well.

C++ constructs that might avoid a declaration, such as a `goto` or `if` statement around a declaration, generate error warnings in Turbo C++. The program may `goto` around a variable declaration at the beginning of a block in C, but if there is no constructor this has no effect.

The following works, but has a different meaning than expected.

```
if (x == y) {
    MyClass z;
    //other statements
}
```

Object z is declared conditionally within a conditional block. If the condition is true, the constructor is invoked after the open brace and the destructor ~MyClass is invoked at the close brace. The variable z is not accessible outside of the { } block.

Inline Functions

An inline function definition resembles a normal function definition. The difference is that an inline function reference is expanded in place instead of generating a function call.

```
inline int square(int x) {
    return x * x;
}
```

Member functions may be declared using the inline keyword or by defining the function within the structure definition. In the class below, both of the print methods are inline.

```
struct X {
    void print1() { cout << "this is inline" << endl; }
    void print2();
};

inline void X::print2() {
    cout << "so is this" << endl;
}
```

Inline functions have several advantages over the #define macros. Inline functions are not expanded by the preprocessor into code that the programmer can neither see nor evaluate. Inline functions are fully typed and may be overloaded.

Efficiency Considerations

Compared with normal functions (what Borland calls **outline functions**), inline functions avoid the instructions normally used to set up and make the call. When the function `square()` (see Inline Functions) is not inline, it compiles into the following six instructions. (I have added comments to explain what the instructions are doing.)

The Classless Primitives

```
PUSH    BP                      ;SET UP STACK FRAME
MOV     BP,SP

MOV     AX,[BP+4]               ;X * X
IMUL    AX,[BP+4]

POP     BP                      ;TEAR DOWN STACK FRAME
RET
```

Calling the function generates another five instructions.

```
                                ;y = square(x);
MOV     AX,[BP-4]               ;GET X
PUSH    AX                      ;PUSH IT AS ARGUMENT
CALL    _SQUARE                 ;MAKE THE CALL
POP     CX                      ;RESTORE THE STACK
MOV     [BP-2],AX               ;STORE THE RESULTS
```

Thus, to execute `square()` as an outline function requires eleven instructions. When recompiled as an inline function, invoking `square()` is reduced to the following three instructions.

```
                                ;y = square(x);
MOV     AX,[BP-4]               ;GET X
IMUL    AX,[BP-4]               ;MULTIPLY IT TIMES X
MOV     [BP-2],AX               ;STORE RESULTS IN Y
```

To get an idea of the performance difference inline functions can make, I wrote and timed the following program.

```
inline void count1(unsigned long &i) {
    i++;
}

void count2(unsigned long &i) {
    i++;
```

```
}

void main() {
    unsigned long i;

    for (i = 0; i < 1000000ul;)    //first straight
        i++;

    for (i = 0; i < 1000000ul;)    //now inline
        count1(i);

    for (i = 0; i < 1000000ul;)    //now outline
        count2(i);
}
```

The inline function `count1()` is an optimal candidate for inlining because of its small size. Timing each of the loops produced the following results.

case	time[sec]
loop #1 inline code	3.0
loop #2 inline function	2.9
loop #3 outline function	6.3

If we assume 0.2-second accuracy, then loops #1 and #2 generated identical results, as we would expect. Loop #3, by comparison, displayed a 110 percent increase over the times of the first two loops.

The overhead for setting up and returning from an inline function is not determined by the size of the function. The **relative** time advantage for inline functions diminishes as the complexity of the function increases. To demonstrate this, I increased the complexity of `count1()` and `count2()` to the following and retimed the loops. These functions still return i+1.

```
inline void count1(unsigned long &i) {
    unsigned long j;
```

```
    j = i * 4;
    i = (j >> 2) + 1;
}
```

Of course, these functions were considerably slower than their simpler counterparts. The **relative** times for each loop are of interest here.

case	time[sec]
loop #1 inline code	14.1
loop #2 inline function	14.1
loop #3 outline function	18.4

A modest increase in complexity reduced the penalty of an outline function to 30 percent over its inline counterpart. Further increases in complexity diminish the advantage until it becomes immeasurable. A good rule of thumb for the maximum size of an inline function is three or four C++ statements.

Problems with Inline Functions

Inline functions are not an unconditional boon. Space is one problem. A large inline function used several times will increase the size of the executable. Counting the number of times a normal function is invoked to determine the cost in size is a straightforward process. Not so easy is determining the number of times an inline constructor or destructor is invoked. As we will see in Chapter 6, constructors may be invoked in some less than obvious situations.

This problem is exacerbated when constructing objects of derived classes. A constructor of a derived class invokes the constructors of each base and all contained classes. If all the constructors are defined as inline, the overall inline expansion can become quite large.

Further, inline functions cannot be single-stepped in the debugger. An inline function single steps like a single C++ line. (Inline functions are forced outline by the Option/Compile/C++/Outline menu option.) The impact of inlining's problems is most apparent in larger functions.

Inline functions also have drawbacks not related to size. Arguments to inline functions are referential even when they appear to be pass-by value; i.e., if an inline function calls a function with a referential argument. Consider the following example.

```
int changeArg(int& i2);
inline int noChange(int i1) {
    return changeArg(i1);
}
```

The function `noChange()` alters its argument because the function `changeArg()`, into which it expands, alters its argument.

Several C++ constructs cannot be accommodated in an inline function. These are outlined in the next section.

When Inline is Outline

Constructs that C++ cannot accommodate in an inline function are "outlined." That is, C++ automatically converts the construct into a non-inline function. The C++ standard specifies that this function should be static; however, the early versions of Turbo C++ left it global.

Since an inline function cannot contain a loop, the following function is automatically outlined.

```
inline int loop(int a) {
    int i = 1;
    for (; --a;)
        i *= a;
    return i;
}
```

Curiously, an inline function that calls itself recursively results in the creation of both inline and outline versions of the same function! Consider the following `factorial()` function.

```cpp
inline int factorial(int x) {
    if (x > 1)
        return x * factorial(x-1);
    else
        return 1;
}
void main() {
    int x = 3;
    int y = factorial(x);
    printf("x = %d, x! = %d\n", x, y);
}
```

`factorial()` is expanded inline on line 2 of `main()`. The call within the inline expansion is not expanded, however, and calls a conventional, outline version of `factorial()`. (This is simply C++'s attempt to make sense out of what probably should be declared a programmer error.)

Similarly, attempting to take the address of an inline function results in in-line schizophrenia. The function is expanded inline when called directly, but an outline version is invoked when the function is called indirectly.

```cpp
inline int max(int a, int b) {
    if (a > b)
        return a;
    else
        return b;
}

void main() {
    int i = 1, j = 2, k;
    k = max(i, j);   //calls inline version

    int (*f)(int,int);
    f = max;
    k = (*f)(i, j);  //calls outline version
}
```

Turbo C++ can handle certain other conditions which cause automatic outlining in the AT&T `cfront` translator. These include:

- multiple returns
- local array declarations
- nested calls from another inline function
- being called from a previously defined inline function

A future C++ standard may require that such functions be outlined.

The `new` and `delete` Keywords

The `new` and `delete` keywords replace `malloc()` and `free()`. `new` accepts a type as its argument and returns a pointer to an object of that type allocated off of the heap (or a Null if insufficient heap space is present). For example:

```
MyClass* objectPtr =  new MyClass;
MyClass& object    = *new MyClass;
```

The argument to `new` may be an array. The following allocates a pointer to an array of ten integers. Compare it with the corresponding `malloc()` call.

```
int* iPtr1 = new int[10];
int* iPtr2 = (int*)malloc(10 * sizeof int);
```

Since `new` returns the proper type, it does not need the recast required by `malloc()`.

Unlike auto, global or static arrays, the range of the left-most subscript passed to `new` does not have to be known at compile time.

Consider, for example, an array that is to contain names of people. If the programmer uses an auto array for the names, the array must be of fixed length. If it is too short, many names will be truncated to the consternation of the people listed. If the length of the array is too long, memory space will be wasted resulting in fewer names being stored.

By allocating memory off the heap to handle the names, the programmer can give a different length array to each person. In this way no arbitrary limit is established and little memory is wasted. The following short code segment will save a copy of a name.

```
char* newName = new char[strlen(oldName) + 1];
if (newName)
    strcpy(newName, oldName);
```

The program first counts the number of characters in `oldName` and adds one to cover the null at the end. Then a block of memory of the exact size is allocated.

When the problem is expanded to an unknown number of names of unknown length the dynamic solution becomes more attractive. With dynamic memory the programmer does not need to decide beforehand how many blocks to allocate.

Unlike `malloc()`, `new` automatically invokes the corresponding constructor for the object allocated.

```
MyClass* objectPtr1 = new MyClass(1, "My Name", 0);
MyClass* objectPtr2 = new MyClass;
```

The first object, `*objectPtr1`, is initialized with the constructor `MyClass(int, char*, int)`. The second object, `*objectPtr2`, is created with the default constructor, `MyClass()`. An object allocated with `malloc()` cannot be initialized with a constructor. When declaring arrays of objects, the default constructor is invoked on each element of the array.

`delete` performs the inverse operation, returning the space occupied by the object to the heap. The argument to `delete` is a pointer to an object. Pointers to objects do not automatically invoke a destructor when they go out of scope. The programmer should call `delete` explicitly.

To remove an array of objects, `delete` must be informed of the number of objects in the array using the following syntax.

```
MyClass* objectPtr[10] = new MyClass[10];

delete [10]objectPtr;
```

The relationship of `new` and `delete` to constructors will be discussed again in later chapters. Chapter 6 will cover how `new` is implemented.

Conclusion

The features discussed in this chapter fall into the category of language enhancements. Other than inline functions, and the `new` and `delete` keywords, many of these features have already been added to the ANSI C standard.

We'll continue in Chapter 4 by examining a feature unique to C++, the overloading of functions.

Chapter 4

Overloading Functions

Overloading Functions

A function definition in C++ includes the function name and the type of each argument. A function `fn(int)` may be defined even though a function `fn(char)` already exists. Giving two functions the same name but different arguments and different definitions is called function overloading. Although overloaded functions may have the same name, by virtue of their different input data requirements they are not considered related.

The inclusion of data types in the identification of functions requires their inclusion in error messages generated by the Turbo C++ compiler and linker. Turbo C++ does not inform the programmer of a missing semicolon in function `fn()`, for example. The message indicates in which `fn()`, such as `fn(int)`, the error occurs.

Differentiating Functions

C++ can differentiate functions by the storage type and/or the number of arguments. In the following small program the functions `fn(int)`, `fn(int, int)`, and `fn(char)` are all different.

```
#include <iostream.h>

void fn(int a) {
    cout << "fn(int) called with " << a << endl;
}
void fn(int a, int b) {
    cout << "fn(int, int) called with " << a
         << " and " << b <<endl;
}
void fn(char a) {
    cout << "fn(char) called with " << a << endl;
}
void main() {
    int i = 1, j = 2;
    char c = 'a';

    fn(i);              //call fn(int)
```

```
        fn(i, j);         //call fn(int, int)
        fn(c);            //call fn(char)
}
```

Running the program generates the following output.

```
fn(int) called with 1
fn(int, int) called with 1 and 2
fn(char) called with a
```

Whether the arguments are signed or unsigned is considered part of the function's type as well. Consider the following simple program.

```
#include <iostream.h>

void fn(signed i) {
    cout << "Signed value = " << i << endl;
}
void fn(unsigned i) {
    cout << "Unsigned value = " << i << endl;
}
void main() {
    fn(1);
    fn(2u);

    fn(0x7fff);
    fn(0x8000);
}
```

The first two calls to `fn()` are straightforward: 1 is a signed integer while 2u is unsigned. In the next two calls, the constant 0x7fff also defaults to a signed integer. Since 0x8000 cannot be accommodated in a signed integer, Turbo C++ interprets it as an unsigned integer. The results follow.

```
Signed value = 1
Unsigned value = 2
```

```
Signed value = 32767
Unsigned value = 32768
```

Pointers can be differentiated from their non-pointer counterparts. C++ has no problem distinguishing between the following two functions.

```
void fn(int   a);
void fn(int* aPtr);
```

Different pointer types can be identified as well, including pointers to different user-defined types.

```
void fn(int*  aPtr);
void fn(char* bPtr);
```

Function prototypes cannot be distinguished by the names of their arguments. The following prototypes are identical.

```
void fn(int a);
void fn(int b);
```

The names of the arguments are place holders. A function `fn(int a)` may be invoked as `fn(anotherInt)` as long as `anotherInt` is an integer. The names used in the prototype declaration are ignored by the compiler.

C++ does not differentiate functions by their return type. The following declarations are ambiguous and would not be allowed in the same program.

```
float fn(int a);
int   fn(int a);
void  fn(int a);
```

The type of each argument of a function is easier to determine than its return type. Each argument must be declared, which establishes its type. The return type of a function must be inferred from its use. Given the preceding declarations, it is difficult to determine which `fn()` is meant by the following:

```
int i;
fn(i);                  //what is the return type?
```

One might guess `void fn(int)`, but this is not necessarily so. A user may invoke an integer function and discard the results. Consider another possibility.

```
int i;
float x = fn(i);
```

The reader might conclude that the above function call refers to `float fn(int)`. However, a programmer may assign an integer to a float in which case `int fn(int)` would be possible.

Arguments also cannot be distinguished by reference type. The following two function declarations cannot be differentiated in use.

```
void fn(int  a);
void fn(int& a);
```

Turbo C++ can read the `&` operator and treat the two functions differently because the assembly language that Turbo C++ generates for `int&` differs from that for an `int` argument. The problem arises when the functions are used.

```
int i;
fn(i);                  //pass by value or reference?
```

Turbo C++ cannot determine which function is to be invoked. For this reason `&` is not considered part of an object's type. Both of the above functions are of type `fn(int)`.

C++ cannot differentiate functions by the default value of their arguments. Default values can cause other overloading problems as well. Consider the following code segment.

```
void fn(int a);
void fn(int a, int b = 0);

fn(1, 2)            //clearly refers to fn(int, int)
fn(1);              //which one does this invoke?
```

The first reference is to `fn(int,int)`. The second reference is ambiguous, however. Is the programmer trying to call `fn(1)` or `fn(1,0)`? In this case, Turbo C++ does not generate an error when the declarations are made. The error appears when the programmer attempts to make use of the default in the second call.

Turbo C++ cannot differentiate pointers by their nearness or farness. The following two definitions would not be allowed in the same program.

```
void putAddr(int near* cPtr) {
    cout << hex;
    cout << "Address = 0x" << FP_OFF(cPtr) << endl;
}

void putAddr(int far* cPtr) {
    cout << hex;
    cout << "Address = 0x" << FP_SEG(cPtr) <<
                    ":" << FP_OFF(cPtr) << endl;
}
```

Since a near address can easily be promoted to a far address, Turbo C++ considers the two preceding functions indistinguishable. (This may be an oversight in early versions of Turbo C++, as near and far are pointer properties limited to 8086 family processors and are not a part of the original AT&T C++ definition.)

Function declarations containing ellipses can cause overloading difficulties as well. Consider the following three function declarations.

```
void fn(char a, ...);
void fn(int* a, ...);
void fn(int* a, int b);
```

The first two declarations are unambiguous. The type of the first argument can be compared with the other declarations to determine which to use. The third declaration, however, is ambiguous with the second. Would entering `fn(aPtr, b)` be an attempt to refer specifically to the third function or to the second with the second argument falling under the ellipses? A function `fn(...)` cannot be overloaded at all.

Typesafe Linking

Overloading is not limited to functions defined in the same module. The function a programmer is attempting to overload may be in a different module. Consider the following possible configuration for a three-module program.

```
Module A -
  defines:
    void func1()
    int  func2()
    void fn(int)

Module B -
  defines:
    void fn(char*)
    char* func3()

Module C -
  calls
    func2()
    func3()
    fn(char*)
```

During the compilation of module C, Turbo C++ finds three calls to functions in other modules. The compiler does not know where these functions will be located in the eventual executable so it marks the name and location of the call in the .OBJ file. During the **link step** (also known as the **bind step**), the Turbo Linker (or the linker built into the Turbo C++

IDE) combines all of the .OBJ files and matches up the function definitions with the function calls.

When the time comes to fill in the address for the `fn(char*)` call, a problem arises. Two functions `fn()` exist. Pascal, Basic, and C did not support function overloading, so there is no field in the .OBJ file to indicate the argument types. The linker does not have enough information to determine which `fn()` module C intends.

The most direct solution would be to change the linker by adding fields to the .OBJ file and extra checks in the linker code. Two arguments go against this approach, however. First, the format of .OBJ files is standard. It would be rash for one company to abandon such a widely accepted standard. Second, C++ was originally implemented as a translator that generated C code. Adding a field to the .OBJ file was not an option.

The C++ and Turbo C++ solution is to change the name of each function within the .OBJ file to indicate the number and types of arguments. This is known as **type safe linking** since it guarantees that the way a function is declared in one module is the same as the way it is defined in another.

The following list includes some of the more common naming conventions used by Turbo C++ to construct a type safe function name.

Format of a type safe name:

`[@class name]@function_name$q<argument suffixes>[S]`

- class name prefix only for member functions
- an argument suffix for each argument. Each argument may have an amplifier followed by a mandatory type.
- S, if present, indicates static function

suffixes:

type:

v   - void
zc - character
i   - integer
s   - short int

l   - long int
f   - float
d   - double
e   - ellipses

amplifier:
w   - const
x   - volatile
p   - near pointer
n   - far pointer
r   - near reference
m   - far reference

Consider the type safe names resulting from the following function declarations. Remember that the return type is not a part of the type safe name.

```
this function:              generates:
fn()                        ->  @fn$qv
fn(int)                     ->  @fn$qi
fn(float*)                  ->  @fn$qpf
fn(char*, int&)             ->  @fn$qpzcri
fn(int const* volatile)     ->  @fn$qwpxi
static X::fn(float*)        ->  @X@fn$qpfS
```

The rules for constructors and operators rely on artificial operator function names to indicate which operator is being overloaded.

Ironically, given that type safe linking was introduced to avoid changes in the linker, the Turbo Linker (and Turbo Debugger) have been changed to read the type safe names. Consider the following small program.

```
int max(int x, int y) {
    return (x>y) ? x : y;
}
int min(int x, int y) {
```

Overloading Functions

```
        return (x>y) ? y : x;
}

void main() {
    int i = 0, j = 1;

    i = max(i, j);
}
```

The following is a small section of the load map generated by compiling and linking this program.

```
0000:0239 idle   max(int,int)
0000:024B idle   min(int,int)
0000:0260        _main
0000:0289 idle   _atexit
0000:02AE        _exit
0000:02D1        _fflush
```

Standard C functions such as _main and _exit, which do not carry type safe names, continue to appear with a prepended underscore and without argument information. The max() and min() function names appear without underscore and with the argument type and number listed.

The TLINK which was delivered with Turbo C 2.0 was written before Turbo C++ and Borland's support for type safe linking. Linking the same Turbo C++ object files and libraries with this version of TLINK generates a different load map. The same small segment follows.

```
0000:0239        @MAX$QII
0000:024B        @MIN$QII
0000:0260        _MAIN
0000:0277        _ATEXIT
0000:029C        _EXIT
0000:02BF        _FFLUSH
```

`_main` and `_exit` are the same (other than appearing in upper case and at slightly different addresses). However, `max()` and `min()` are barely recognizable with their type safe names of `@max$qii` and `@min$qii`.

The Turbo Linker has undergone some changes with Turbo C++ to make argument information in the .OBJ files more accessible to the programmers. It is worth noting that because type safe linking was implemented without changes to the .OBJ files, the older TLINK produces essentially the same executable program as the newer version.

Linking C++ with C Modules

A major design goal of C++ was compatibility with existing C programs, including object and library files. Thus, a device was necessary to disable the type safe naming of functions.

C++ provides the `extern "C" {}` directive to disable type safe naming. The braces may enclose any number of source code statements. Any function declarations within the braces are named using C conventions. Thus, `printf()` should be prototyped as follows:

```
extern "C" {
    int printf(const char*, ...);
}
```

Entire include files can be enclosed within `extern "C"` braces.

```
extern "C" {
    #include <stdio.h>
}
```

Standard Turbo C++ include files already contain `extern "C"` declarations. Include files associated with libraries generated from a C compiler (such as those delivered with commercial windowing packages) must be declared `extern"C"`, however, in order to link properly.

Overloading Functions
133

To reenable type safe naming within an `extern "C"` range, the programmer may designate an `extern "C++"{}` region. The preceding program may be redesignated as follows.

```
extern "C" {
    int max(int x, int y) {
        return (x>y) ? x : y;
    }

    extern "C++" {
        int min(int x, int y) {
            return (x>y) ? y : x;
        }
    }

    void main() {
        int i = 0, j = 1;

        i = max(i, j);
    }
}
```

Recompiling and linking the program results in the following load map segment.

```
0000:0239 idle   _max
0000:024B idle   min(int,int)
0000:0260        _main
0000:0277 idle   _atexit
0000:029C        _exit
0000:02BF        _fflush
```

Now `max()` appears with a C name while `min()` appears with its type information.

The `extern` braces do not define a new block. Neither is the scope of variables declared within extern braces. `extern "C"` does not affect the compiler in any way other than type safe naming. Specifically, it does not attempt to inform the compiler that the code segment within the braces is not C++ and should be compiled using C rules.

Functions declared within an `extern "C"` region should not be overloaded. Without the type information, the linker cannot determine which function should be linked with which call.

Declaring `extern "C"` prototypes is useful for functions written in other languages. For example, a programmer can include an assembly level module during the link step. Assembly functions must have prototypes within the C++ module. While each assembly function can be assigned the proper type safe name to match its arguments, it is easier to assign the assembly functions C names (by prepending an underscore) and encase their prototypes in an `extern C` directive. Linking assembly language routines will be discussed in depth in Chapter 10.

Conclusion

As a strongly typed language, C++ can determine, unambiguously, the type of a given expression without simply defaulting all expressions to either `int` or `double`, as was the case with K&R C. We have seen how C++ allows programmers the flexibility of differentiating between functions by the types of their arguments, allowing the best solution for each type argument.

In Chapters 5 through 9 we will begin looking at different aspects of object classes in C++.

Chapter 5

Classes

The introduction of classes is the single most important improvement in C++. Classes allow the programmer to define new object types in a way only partially supported by the `struct` keyword in C. This chapter will examine the details of the class structure.

Organization of Classes

A C++ `struct/class` format may have two types of members: data and functions, also known as methods. Both are instantiated with each object declaration of that structure type. In the following definition, the structure `Sample` has two members: the integer variable `memberVariable` and the method `memberFunction()`.

```
struct Sample {
  int   memberVariable;
  void memberFunction(int);
};

Sample x, y, z;

x.memberVariable = 1;
y.memberFunction(2);
```

Both `memberVariable` and `memberFunction()` are defined for each new object, `x, y` and `z`. The fully qualified names for these members include both the object and the class name, as in `x.Sample::memberVariable` or `y.Sample::memberFunction()`. When the class is known, it is rarely necessary to include the class name, leaving the shortened names of the members `x.memberVariable` and `y.memberFunction()` as shown.

Members of a C++ structure may have either public or private scope. A public member of a class object is accessible to any function that has the object in scope. A private member is only accessible to other members of the class.

The keywords `public` and `private` act as toggles to control the scope of class members. Members declared after one of these keywords are of that scope. The default scope for `struct` is `public`. The default scope for `class` is private. Consider the following example.

```
struct S1 {
    int firstMember;   //members are public
    int secondMember;
};

class C1 {
  public:
    int firstMember;   //public here too
    int secondMember;
};

struct S2 {
  private:
    int firstMember;   //this struct's members are private
    int secondMember;
};

class C2 {
    int firstMember;   //these members private too
    int secondMember;
};
```

The structure `S1` is identical to the class `C1` in that all members are public; the structure `S2` is identical to the class `C2` with all members private. The only difference between a class and a structure is the default scope of its members.

A private member of a class is not accessible to the methods of a derived class. The keyword `protected` declares a member private to the current class and any publicly derived classes. Consider the following example.

```
class Base {
  private:
```

```
    int privValue;
  protected:
    int protValue;
};
class Derived : public Base {
  public:
    void anyMethod {
        privValue = 0;   //error - not accessible
        protValue = 1;   //no error here
    }
};

void fn() {
    Derived x;
    x.privValue = 0;   //error - not accessible
    x.protValue = 1;   //error - not accessible either
}
```

Although defaults exist, the preferred style in Turbo C++ is to declare the scope of all class members. Programmers can use `class` and `struct` interchangeably. Programs are easier to read if the composite objects are declared classes when they contain features that are not part of a C structure (i.e., methods or protected or private member variables). Otherwise, the objects should be declared structures.

The details of class storage within Turbo C++ is a Borland trade secret. It is helpful, however, to see how a C++ class looks when implemented in C. The following explanation was developed by Eric White in the February 1990 issue of *C Users Journal*.

Consider the following class definition.

```
class Window {
  public:
    int width, height;
    int cursorXLoc, cursorYLoc;

    void setCursorPos(int newX, int newY);
```

```
        void writeToWindow(char* string, int xLoc, int yLoc);
        void clearWindow(char color);
};
```

One might start with the following:

```
struct Window {
    int width, height;
    int cursorXLoc, cursorYLoc;

    void (*setCursorPos)(int newX, int newY);
    void (*writeToWindow)(char* string, int xLoc, int yLoc);
    void (*clearWindow)(char color);
};
```

The member variables appear as conventional structure members. The methods appear as pointers to functions. The functions are defined separately and their addresses are assigned to the pointers. Declaring and using an object of type `Window` can be carried out as follows:

```
//prototypes for Window methods
void setCursorPosFn(int, int);
void writeToWindowFn(char*, int, int);
void clearWindowFn(char);

//declare a Window object
struct Window aWin = {0, 0, 0, 0,      //member data
                      setCursorFn,     //method addresses
                      writeToWindowFn,
                      clearWindowFn};

aWin.width  = 20;        //access data members
aWin.height = 10;
(*aWin.clearWindow)(WHITE);  //invoking a method
```

Classes

Considerable overhead would result from the preceding program if many objects of type `Window` were declared because each object contains the same pointers to the same functions. A `sizeof` result would also be misleading because it would include the pointers to each of the methods. Since C++ structures should work with existing C modules, a higher construct must be defined, which gives the resulting C code the following basic appearance.

```
struct ClassDefinition {
    struct ClassData    *d;
    struct ClassMethods *m;
};

struct WindowData {
    int width, height;
    int cursorXLoc, cursorYLoc;
} wd;
struct WindowMethods {
    void (*setCursorPos)(int newX, int newY);
    void (*writeToWindow)(char* string, int xLoc, int yLoc);
    void (*clearWindow)(char color);
} wm = {setCursorPosFn, writeToWindowFn, clearWindowFn};

struct ClassDefinition Window = {&wd, &wm};
```

In this approach, a new object of type `ClassDefinition` is declared for each definition of a new class. This object consists of a pointer to the data structure and a pointer to a list of the methods. Whenever an object of type `Window` is declared, a new structure `WindowData` must be allocated to contain the object's data memory. All objects of type `WindowData` can share the same structure `WindowMethods` containing the class methods.

What is this?

The internal organization of a class object shows how Turbo C++ knows which function to invoke when a method is referenced. When the programmer invokes a method such as aWin.clearWindow(), Turbo C++ infers the Window:: from the type aWin and calls the function Window::clearWindow().

Consider the following:

```
Window aWin;
Window anotherWin;

aWin.setCursorPos(40, 15);
```

Invoking aWin.setCursorPos() alters the cursor position of aWin but has no effect on anotherWin. The function Window::setCursorPos() must know with which object it is being invoked.

Every non-static method of a class receives a hidden first argument containing the address of the object on which to operate. The hidden pointer does not appear in the argument list and is known within the function as this.

Assume that setCursorPos() is defined as follows:

```
void Window::setCursorPos(int xLoc, int yLoc) {
    cursorXLoc = xLoc;
    cursorYLoc = yLoc;
    writeToWindow("", xLoc, yLoc);
}
```

Here, this is of type Window* and points to either aWin or another-Win, depending upon how it is called. this is used whenever a method references a member of its own object. Explicit use of this is allowed but usually not necessary since it is the default for the "current" object. The preceding function could have been defined as follows:

```
void Window::setCursorPos(/*Window* this,*/
                          int xLoc, int yLoc) {
    this->cursorXLoc = xLoc;
    this->cursorYLoc = yLoc;
    this->writeToWindow("", xLoc, yLoc);
}
```

A reference by a member of object A to a member of object B must specify the object B explicitly. Consider the following:

```
//position cursor in another window similar to its
//position in the current window
void Window::trackCursor (Window& otherWindow) {
    otherWindow.setCursorPos(cursorXLoc, cursorYLoc);
}
```

Referring to `setCursorPos()` without any object would call `this->setCursorPos()`.

Explicit use of `this` is required when the method must return the address of the object being operated upon. This is also the case when the method must set a global pointer to the address of the current object, for example, when adding the object to a list of some type. Consider the following partial implementation of a linked list class.

```
class List {
  private:
    List* next;
  public:
    void addObject(List* before) {
        next         = before->next;
        before->next = this;
    }
};
```

In the second line of `addObject()`, the variable `before->next` needs to point to the current object which is only available via `this`.

A method has access not only to its own private members (those pointed at by `this`), but also to the private members of other objects of the same class. Class protection is on a class basis, not an object basis.

`this` is accessible from the Turbo C++ debugger. Inspecting `this` from the Debug menu can be helpful when setting breakpoints or single-stepping through member functions. An inspected `this` displays the current object address and its class whenever the program is stopped within a member of any class. Outside of a member function, `this` is undefined. Setting a debug Watch or leaving the Inspect window open on `this` can also help in keeping track of where the program is.

Under the AT&T `cfront` C++ translator, `this` could be an lvalue (i.e., allowed on the left side of an assignment operator). Assigning a value to `this` had the effect of moving the object to a new address. This device was used to define variable-sized objects or to allocate objects off of a user-defined heap.

Assigning values to `this` is not recommended under Turbo C++ as it does not move an object permanently. (In fact, it causes the IDE to crash.) Turbo C++ generates a compiler warning whenever `this` appears on the left side of an equal sign. Most effects that could have been achieved by changing `this` can be realized in a more controlled fashion by overloading the `new` operator for the class type.

Arrays of Class Objects

Arrays of class structures can be declared in Turbo C++. When such an array is instantiated, the default or void constructor (with no arguments) is invoked on each element, beginning with the index 0 element and working its way towards the end. Upon exit, the destructor is invoked on each element of the array.

Arrays of objects can be allocated from the heap using the `new` call. For example, allocating an array of ten objects of type `Sample` appears as follows:

```
Sample* x = new Sample[10];
```

Classes

Notice that x is of type `Sample*`, corresponding to the type of a simple array. (Given an array declaration `int y[]`, the variable y is of type `int*`.) However, when `delete` is invoked to destruct the objects pointed at by x, a problem arises.

```
delete x;
```

Since x is declared as a pointer to a single object, C++ does not know that `*x` is an array of objects. The programmer must tell delete how many objects are to be destructed using the following format.

```
delete [10]x;
```

The following program allocates two arrays, one off the stack and the other off the heap, and then destroys them both. Output statements in the constructor and destructor allow the reader to follow the process.

```
#include <iostream.h>

    class Sample {
  public:
    Sample() {
        cout << hex;
        cout << "Void constructor for " << this << endl;
    }
    ~Sample() {
        cout << "Destructor for " << this << endl;
    }
};

void main() {
    Sample x[5];
    Sample *y = new Sample[5];

    delete [5]y;
}
```

Executing this program generated the following output.

```
Void constructor for 0x8f97ffec  <- Sample x[5]
Void constructor for 0x8f97ffee
Void constructor for 0x8f97fff0
Void constructor for 0x8f97fff2
Void constructor for 0x8f97fff4
Void constructor for 0x8f970ddc  <- y = new Sample[5]
Void constructor for 0x8f970dde
Void constructor for 0x8f970de0
Void constructor for 0x8f970de2
Void constructor for 0x8f970de4
Destructor for 0x8f970ddc        <- delete [5]y;
Destructor for 0x8f970dde
Destructor for 0x8f970de0
Destructor for 0x8f970de2
Destructor for 0x8f970de4
Destructor for 0x8f97ffec        <- exit from main()
Destructor for 0x8f97ffee
Destructor for 0x8f97fff0
Destructor for 0x8f97fff2
Destructor for 0x8f97fff4
```

The first five addresses constructed increment by two bytes each time, corresponding to the size of Sample. The next five increment in a different address range, because they were allocated from the heap via new. The five elements from the heap are destructed in the delete [5]y call followed by the array x, which is destructed automatically upon exiting main(). Turbo C++ does not need to be told the number of statically declared x objects to destruct.

To maintain compatibility, C++ allows arrays of structure objects to be initialized with a conventional C initialization statement provided that no constructors are defined.

```
class Sample {
  private:
```

```
    int a;
    int b;
    int c;

  public:
    void aMethod();
};
Sample y[] = {{1, 2, 3}, {4, 5, 6}, {7, 8, 9}};
Sample z[2][3][2] = {
                      { { {0, 0, 0}, {0, 0, 1} },
                        { {0, 1, 0}, {0, 1, 1} },
                        { {0, 2, 0}, {0, 2, 1} } },

                      { { {1, 0, 0}, {1, 0, 1} },
                        { {1, 1, 0}, {1, 1, 1} },
                        { {1, 2, 0}, {1, 2, 1} } }
                                                   };
```

The values for each class usually appear in braces separated by commas. Each level of grouping above class object is usually also enclosed in braces. For example, the single dimensional array `y` consists of the three class objects `y[0]`, `y[1]` and `y[2]`. The three-dimensional array `z`, however, consists of twelve objects grouped into three levels. To facilitate reading of the initializer, I assigned the values to correspond to the z index.

Pointers to Class Members

Pointers to class members must include the storage class and the class type. Examine the following class definitions and pointer assignments.

```
class Sample {
  public:
    int aMember;
    void aMethod(int);
```

```
};

void fn() {
  Sample x;
  Sample* y = &x;

  int z = 1;
  int* intPtr;
  void (* fnPtr)(int);

  intPtr = &x.aMember;   //allowed
  intPtr = &y->aMember;
  *intPtr = z;
  fnPtr  = x.aMethod;    //not allowed
  (*fnPtr)(z);           //no good either
}
```

The two pointer assignments to `intPtr` and `fnPtr` represent a certain asymmetry in C++. The first address assignment is allowed as long as `aMember` is accessible to the function (`fn()` is a member function or `aMember` is public).

The function address assignment is not allowed, however, because `fnPtr` was declared a pointer to a normal function and not to a member function. When `(*fnPtr)()` is called, Turbo C++ does not recognize it as a member function and does not push the address of an object as the hidden argument. A member function would have no `this` and would not know to which object the caller was attempting to refer. To fully describe a pointer to a member function `aMethod()`, the following syntax must be used.

```
void fn() {
  Sample x;
  Sample* y = &x;

  int z = 1;
  void (Sample::* fnPtr)(int);
```

```
    fnPtr   = Sample::aMethod;//address of method
    (x.*fnPtr)(z);             //invoke method
    (y->*fnPtr)(z);
}
```

The declaration defines `fnPtr` as a pointer to a member function of the class `Sample` that takes an integer argument and returns nothing. To invoke the method pointer the programmer must indicate the object as well as the fact that the method is being invoked indirectly. Hence, the `(x.*fnPtr)()` syntax. The `.*` and `->*` operators were added to C++ 2.0 to handle pointers to member functions.

So why adopt one syntax for pointers to class member variables and another for member functions? The extra class information is not needed to access the member variable but is required to invoke the member function. The object's address is figured into the address of the member variable when it is returned. (In addition, if we refer back to our organization of member functions, `aMethod` is not in the same address space as `aMember`.)

A more compelling reason for the two formats is historical. The syntax for taking the address of member variables in C is long established and must be supported. However, the same syntax can be used with member variables that was used for member functions. The following is legal C++.

```
void fn() {
  Sample x;
  Sample* y = &x;

  int z = 1;
  int Sample::* intPtr;

  intPtr = &S::aMember;
  x.*intPtr  = z;
  y->*intPtr = z;
}
```

Not only does this syntax resemble that used for member functions, but it also allows increased flexibility. The pointer `intPtr` is no longer an address but an offset within the class which is not resolved until the address of the object is known. Consider the following small function to copy an array from one object to another of the same type.

```
struct Sample {
    int sizeOf;
    int aMember[10];
};

void fn(Sample& a, Sample& b) {
  int Sample::* x;

  x = &Sample::sizeOf;
  for (int i = 0; i < (a.sizeOf + 1); i++, x++)
      b.*x = a.*x;
}
```

The same effect can be achieved here by using an index.

The address of a class member can only be taken when the function has access to it. If a member variable or function cannot be accessed, its address cannot be taken. This was not true in early versions of Turbo C++ that could access any member indirectly by taking its address.

Static Class Members

The default storage class for variables declared within functions is `auto`. The scope of auto variables is limited to the function in which they are declared. The space for an auto variable is reallocated each time the function is invoked and deallocated when the function returns. An initialized auto variable is reinitialized on each subsequent call.

```
void fn() {
    int x = 1;

    x++;
```

Classes

In the preceding example, a local copy of x is assigned the value 1 each time fn() is invoked. Even though x is incremented, the local copy is lost when the function returns.

A variable declared static within a function retains its value from one calling of the function to the next. In the following code segment the static variable counter records the number of times the function is called. After initializing the counter to zero when the program begins, each call to fn() increments the counter.

```
void fn() {
    static int counter = 0;
    counter++;
```

Static variables are stored with global variables, not on the stack. Thus, the address of a static variable declared within a function differs from the addresses of automatic variables declared around it.

To prevent static variables declared in different functions from interfering with each other, C gives static variables local scope. Declaring a global variable or a function static causes the variable's scope to become local so that it is not known outside of the module.

Members of a class may also be declared static. A static member variable retains the same value for all objects. Therefore, static member variables cannot be stored with other class members. As with static variables within functions, the address of a static member variable is not related to the address of the objects of its class. Static members exist once for all objects of a class.

A static member variable may be initialized explicitly as follows:

```
class Sample {
  private:
    static int objectCount; //cannot assign value here

  public:
    Sample() { objectCount++;} //okay here...
};

int Sample::objectCount = 0;   //...or here
```

A static member cannot be initialized within the class definition. However, a static member can be assigned a value by any function that has access to it—for example, a constructor. The preceding sample shows one of the common uses for static member variables. The class constructor uses the static `objectCount` to record the number of times the function is called.

By analogy with static member variables, a static member function is not associated with any particular object. Static methods have no `this` pointer. In the following example the address of s is not evaluated to invoke the function `s.fn()`.

```
class Sample {
  private:
    int privateData;

  public:
    static void fn();
};

void main() {
    Sample s;

    s.fn();
```

All that is necessary for Turbo C++ to invoke the member function `fn()` is the type of s. A static member function may be invoked using the class name as in `Sample::fn()`.

Notice that s is not evaluated even if it is a function call. In the following example the function `getSAddr()` is not called. The return type of the function is used to infer the class.

```
Sample* getSAddr();

getSAddr()->fn();
```

Since a static member function has no `this` pointer, member variables cannot be referred to without specifying the object as well. Therefore, the above function `fn()` could not be defined as follows:

```
Sample::fn() {
    privateData = 1;   //not allowed; no this
}
```

A static function can refer to static member variables. A static function may also refer to the private members of the class. For example, `fn()` could be modified as follows:

```
Sample::fn(Sample& s) {
  s.privateData = 1;
}
```

The absence of a `this` pointer is counterintuitive, especially when the function is invoked with an object. That is, even if invoked as `a.fn()`, `fn()` has no knowledge of a other than its class type.

In practice, member functions are declared static only when they must be invoked without a particular object in mind. For example, `operator new()` and `operator delete()` are automatically static. Clearly new cannot be invoked with an object since no object yet exists when it is invoked!

Enumeration Members

Pascal was the first language to popularize enumerated types. In C an enumeration declares a series of integer constants as follows:

```
enum daysOfTheWeek {sun, mon, tues,
                    wed, thur, fri,
                    sat, holiday = -1};

enum daysOfTheWeek today;
```

The enumeration type `daysOfTheWeek` has eight members. The value of the first member defaults to zero and each successive member defaults to one more than its predecessor. However, an assignment can appear anywhere within the enumeration to change the sequence. Two enumerated constants may have the same value.

`today` is declared to be of the enumerated type `daysOfTheWeek`. In C++ the keyword `enum` is optional here.

In C the preceding declaration has roughly the same effect as the following:

```
const int sun   = 0;
const int mon   = 1;
const int tues  = 2;
const int wed   = 3;
const int thur  = 4;
const int fri   = 5;
const int sat   = 6;
const int holiday = -1;

int today;
```

In C++, however, the type checking is more stringent. A variable of an enumerated type should only be assigned another variable of the same type or one of the enumerated constants. The expression

```
today = fri;
```

is legal, but the expression

```
today = 5;
```

is not, even though it has the same effect. Under Turbo C++ this statement generates a warning.

An enumerated type can be declared within a structure or class. The effect is the same as if static variables were declared at the position of the `enum` and initialized with the appropriate values. If the enumerated type `daysOfTheWeek` was declared within the private section of a class

Date, then functions outside of the class could not access it or any of the enumerated constants. If the enumerated type daysOfTheWeek is declared within a public section of Date, then non-member functions must refer to enumerated constants by their fully qualified names, such as Date::mon, Date::tues, etc.

Friends of Classes

The restriction that only member functions have access to private members is sometimes too rigid. Sometimes non-member functions need to be able to access private members of a class. C++ enables programmers to grant access to private members through the keyword friend.

The following class Sample has the private member privateData, which can only be accessed by its method aMethod(), and the declared friend function aFriend().

```
class Sample {
    friend void aFriend(Sample&, int);
  private:
    int privateData;

  public:
    void aMethod(int);
};
```

The definitions for the two functions differ only slightly.

```
void Sample::aMethod(int x) {
    privateData = x;
}

void aFriend(Sample& s, int x) {
    s.privateData = x;
}
```

Notice that aMethod() is declared a member of Sample whereas aFriend() is not. As a member function, aMethod() has a this pointer. Since aFriend() does not have a `this` pointer, the programmer must include the address of the object to be operated on in the argument list.

The friend declaration must occur within a class. A function may not grant friendship to itself. In the preceding example, the friend declaration had to be part of the definition of Sample. The programmer who wrote Sample granted the special privileges, not the programmer of aFriend().

Other types of functions may be friends as well. A method of one class can be named friend to another class, for example.

```
class Class2;

class Class1 {
  private:
    int privateData;

  public:
    void aMethod(Class2&);
};
class Class2 {
    friend void Class1::aMethod(Class2&);
  private:
    int privateData;

  public:
    void aMethod(int);
};

void Class1::aMethod(Class2& x) {
    x.privateData = privateData;
}
```

Notice that Class1::aMethod() has access to the private data of both Class1, via the `this` pointer, and Class2, via the specifically passed argument x. Notice also that the class Class2 is declared in the first line without being defined. `Class2` must be declared before it can be used in the declaration of `Class1::aMethod()`.

As with other member functions, the friend privilege may be extended to member operators. In fact, operators can be implemented as friends rather than members.

Friends are not limited to functions. A class may be a friend of another class. Declaring another class to be a friend is equivalent to declaring all of its member functions friends.

So the question arises as to which functions should be implemented as friends and which as members. Except for the case of friend operators, which we will address in more detail, neither option presents a clear advantage. Some general rules can be drawn, however.

A function that modifies a member variable should be declared a method. That way, if anything goes wrong with any data in the structure, the problem should be easier to locate.

A function never has to be a friend. Given enough access methods, a function can always be written without requiring extra rights.

Friend functions allow the programmer to draw a balance with encapsulation. If access functions demand too much overhead, a function can be given the right to access all of the elements of a class directly. While not protected, such a function is neither slower nor more difficult to write than a C function that accesses a C structure.

Unions

Unions may be used to decode bit formats but in general their use should be avoided. Overlaying data that are mutually exclusive is almost always a bad idea. The amount of memory saved does not make up for the debugging problems caused by this practice.

All members of a union must be public. A union can specify an initializer only for the first member as in the following example.

```
union {
    int     a;
    float   b;
    char    c;
} x = 1;
```

The initializer here is for x.a. None may be specified for x.b or x.c.

Named unions can have member functions, including constructors, that may help in clearing up the conversion process as shown in the following program.

```cpp
#include <iostream.h>
#include <iomanip.h>   //get the manipulators

union X {
    int a[2];
    float b;

    X(int i, int j)    {a[1] = i;
                        a[0] = j;}
    X(float x)         {b    = x;}
    float* asFloat()   {return &b;}
    int*   asInt()     {return a;}
};

void main() {
    X first (0x4123, 0x0000);

    cout << hex << setw(4) << setprecision(2);
    cout << "first: int = " << first.asInt()[0] << ", "
                            << first.asInt()[1] << "; "
                            <<*first.asFloat()   << endl;
    X second(1.0);
    cout << "secnd: int = " << second.asInt()[0] << ", "
                            << second.asInt()[1] << "; "
                            <<*second.asFloat()  << endl;
}
```

The preceding program generates the following output.

```
first: int = 0, 4123; 10.19
secnd: int = 0, 3f80; 1
```

Anonymous unions may not have member functions. No syntax exists for handling functions that are members of an unnamed type. Unions cannot inherit a class nor can they be inherited.

Conclusion

The structure is the primary mechanism of data abstraction in C. With the advances in C++, `struct` and `class` structures have become powerful tools for describing real-world objects.

Chapter 6

Constructors and Destructors

A programmer-defined class may contain multiple special member functions known as **constructors** and a single member function known as a **destructor.** Constructors are invoked automatically by C++ to initialize an object when it is created and its memory space is allocated. Destructors are invoked from C++ to disassemble the object when its memory space is deallocated.

The rules for constructing and destructing each of the storage classes are as follows:

auto—constructed when the declaration is encountered; destructed when the block in which it is defined is exited

static and global—constructed at the beginning of the program before `main()` and destructed once at the end

heap objects—constructed with `new` and destructed with `delete`

ANSI C allows an object to be declared repeatedly as long as subsequent declarations do not conflict with earlier ones. While C++ allows a class to be declared more than once, accumulated declarations are not supported because C++ cannot determine when to invoke the constructor.

Constructors

Constructors carry the same name as the class for which they are defined and have no return type (not even `void`). Constructors may, however, have arguments. Although constructors have no return type, they implicitly return a pointer to the object they have just constructed. An implicit `return this;` occurs at the end of every constructor.

Constructors are only used to construct new objects. Declaring a pointer or a reference to an object does not invoke the constructor. The constructor is invoked separately for each element in an array of class objects.

A constructor is inline if it is defined within the class or declared using the `inline` keyword. The following shows the same constructor defined once within the class and once separately.

```
class Id1 {
  public:
    char* lastName;
    char* firstName;
    Id1() {              //define within class
        lastName = (char*)0;
        firstName = (char*)0;
    }
};

class Id2 {
  public:
    char* lastName;
    char* firstName;
    Id2();
};

Id2::Id2() {             //define separately
   lastName = (char*)0;
   firstName = (char*)0;
}
```

Constructors are subject to the same overloading rules as other functions. A single class may have multiple constructors as long as no two have the same argument types.

The Default Constructors

The default constructor has no (a `void`) argument. The default constructor is used when an object is declared without initialization data. Consider, for example, the following:

```
#include <iostream.h>

class Id {
  public:
```

```
    char* lastName;
    char* firstName;

    Id() { cout << "Initializing default" << endl;
        lastName = (char*)0;
        firstName = (char*)0;
    }
};

Id globalName;
void main() {
    cout << "Entering main" << endl;
    Id aName;
    cout << "Exiting main" << endl;
}
```

Executing this program generates the following output.

```
Initializing default   <--for globalName
Entering main
Initializing default   <--for aName
Exiting main
```

The default constructor is invoked for the global variable `globalName` before execution begins in `main()`. The default constructor for the automatic `aName` is called when the variable is declared.

Without a default constructor, no objects could be declared without initial values. If no constructor is declared for a class, Turbo C++ assigns a default constructor. If any other constructor exists for a class, the programmer should define a default constructor as well.

Constructors are not inherited from a base class. A constructor may invoke the constructors of any base classes plus any objects contained therein. Otherwise, default constructors for base and contained classes are invoked automatically.

Other Constructors

Other constructor types are differentiated by their argument types. These arguments correspond to the value assigned at creation. Expanding the preceding program for different initialization values results in the following:

```
#include <iostream.h>

class Id {
  public:
    char* lastName;
    char* firstName;
    Id() {
            cout << "Initializing default" << endl;
            lastName = (char*)0;
            firstName = (char*)0;
         }
    Id(char* lName) {
            cout << "Initializing " << lName << endl;
            lastName = lName;
            firstName = (char*)0;
         }
    Id(char* lName, char* fName) {
            cout << "Initializing " << fName <<
                            " " << lName << endl;
            lastName = lName;
            firstName = fName;
         }
};

void main() {
    Id dummyName;
    Id lastNameOnly1 = "Smith";
    Id lastNameOnly2("Jones");
    Id fullName("Smith", "Nancy");
    Id arrayName[5] = {"One", "Two", "Three", "Four"};
}
```

Constructors and Destructors

Executing this program produces the following:

```
Initializing default    <- dummyName
Initializing Smith      <- lastNameOnly1
Initializing Jones      <- lastNameOnly2
Initializing Nancy Smith <- fullName
Initializing One        <- arrayName
Initializing Two
Initializing Three
Initializing Four
Initializing default
```

Notice how the constructors are invoked. The variable `dummyName`, appearing without an initial value, invokes the default constructor.

The object `lastNameOnly1` uses the C-like initialization of an equal sign followed by a single value. This form is retained in C++ for compatibility although it has several problems: (1) no more than a single argument can be passed; (2) the relationship between this format and the constructor is not obvious; and (3) the equal sign might cause confusion with an assignment. In this case the equal sign represents initialization and not assignment.

The initialization of `lastNameOnly2` demonstrates the new C++ format. The C++ syntax can be expanded to include more than one argument, as shown with the `fullName` declaration. The newer format allows any number of initialization values to be passed.

If the new initialization format could extend "backward" to include void initialization lists, the statement might resemble the following:

```
Id lastNameOnly2("Jones");
Id noInitialName();
```

However, this conflicts with the declaration of a function. The preceding example does not declare `noInitialName` to be an object of type `Id` with no initialization data, but rather a function that returns an object of type `Id` by value.

The new initialization format does not expand to include the declaration of arrays. The initialization of `arrayName` must revert to the equal sign format. Each object is constructed with the next sequential element of the array until the initialization array is depleted. Remaining elements are initialized with the default constructor.

As with other functions, constructors may have default arguments. The preceding class could have been defined as follows:

```
class Id {
  public:
    char* lastName;
    char* firstName;
    Id() {
         cout << "Initializing default" << endl;
         lastName = (char*)0;
         firstName = (char*)0;
    }
    Id(char* lName, char* fName = (char*)0) {
         cout << "Initializing " << fName <<
                          " " << lName << endl;
         lastName = lName;
         firstName = fName;
    }
};
```

Both `Id(char*)` and `Id(char*, char*)` can be handled by the constructor `Id(char*, char* = 0)`. However, `Id(char* = 0, char* = 0)` can never assume the responsibilities of the default constructor. The default constructor must have a void argument list specifically.

Class Constants

Constructors can be invoked to create constants as well. (Class constants are sometimes called anonymous objects since they have no object name.) The following code segment uses the Complex class developed earlier.

```
Complex {
  private:
```

```
    int real, imag;
  public:
    Complex();
    Complex(int, int = 0);
};
Complex c1(1, 2);          //declaration #1
Complex c2;                //declaration #2

c2 = c1 + Complex(3, 4);   //declaration #3
c2 = c1 + Complex(5);      //declaration #4
```

The first declaration initializes the `Complex` object c1 to (1,2i). The second defaults c2 to (0,0i). The next two lines construct a constant of type const Complex using the Complex(int, int = 0) constructor. The first const has the value (3,4i) and the second the value (5,0i).

The latter declaration effectively converts the integer 5 into the Complex (5,0i). Thus, defining a constructor for Complex with a single int argument provides a coercion path from an integer to a complex. We could have entered the following:

```
c2 = c1 + 5;
```

Turbo C++ first looks for operator+(Complex, int). Not finding it, Turbo C++ attempts to coerce either argument into something it can use. Since operator+(Complex, Complex) is defined, Turbo C++ uses the Complex(int, int = 0) constructor to convert the int into a Complex, then applies the addition operator to the result.

The Copy-Initializer Constructors

A constructor may have almost any type of argument. A constructor may even be an object of the class itself. Such a constructor has the following prototype.

```
MyClass::MyClass(MyClass&);
```

This constructor builds a new object by copying data out of an old object. Used to copy or initialize an object from another object, this constructor is called a *copy-initializer constructor*, which is sometimes shortened to *c-i constructor*.

The copy-initializer constructor for our `Id` class looks like the following:

```
Id::Id(Id& s) {
    cout << "Copying " << s.firstName <<
            " " << s.lastName  << endl;
    lastName  = s.lastName;
    firstName = s.firstName;
}
```

Each of the two fields that make up `Id` are copied from the source to the destination object.

The copy-initializer constructor is as important as the default constructor. The c-i constructor is used by C++ any time it needs to a copy an object, something that happens more often than many novice programmers expect.

If the programmer does not define the c-i constructor for a class, Turbo C++ will. The default copy-initialization constructor performs a member-by-member copy of each field from the source to the destination object. This ensures that any `operator()` or c-i constructors which may have been defined for the member fields are used.

Initializing an Object with Another Object of the Same Class

This is the initializer portion of the c-i constructor. Given the preceding c-i constructor definition, the following `main()` program

```
void main() {
    Id fullName("Smith", "Nancy");
    Id newObject1 = fullName;
    Id newObject2(fullName);
}
```

generates the following:

```
Initializing Nancy Smith
Copying Nancy Smith
Copying Nancy Smith
```

The first call to the `Id(char*, char*)` constructor generates the "Initializing..." message. The next two calls invoke copy-initialization directly, either by using the C-style equal sign or the C++ format.

Passing an Object by Value   When an object is passed to a function by value, the object must be copied onto the argument stack. For a simple object, this is a simple operation.

```
int square(int z) {
    return z * z;
}

void fn() {
    int x = 1;

    x = square(x);
}
```

The z to which the function `square()` refers is not the same object to which `fn()` refers. The call to `square(x)` passes the contents of x (in this case, one). While `square()` receives the contents of x, it is housed in a different location.

For a class object, the process is essentially the same. Consider the following call to the friend function `printNames()`.

```
void printNames(Id n) {
    cout << "Print Names function:" << endl;
    cout << "First name = " << n.firstName << endl;
    cout << "Last name = "  << n.lastName  << endl;
}

void main() {
```

```
        Id fullName("Smith", "Nancy");

        cout << "printNames(fullName)" << endl;
        printNames(fullName);
}
```

The object `fullName` is constructed locally to `fn()` using the `Id(char*, char*)` constructor. The call to `printNames()` copies `fullName` onto the stack (pass by value) with the copy-initializer constructor. Thus, the output from this program is as follows:

```
Initializing Nancy Smith   <- building fullName
printNames(fullName)       <- calling printNames
Copying Nancy Smith        <- make copy of fullName
Print Names function:      <- function executes
First name = Nancy
Last name = Smith
```

If the print function is changed to `printNames(Id&)`, only the address of the existing object is passed (pass by reference). Executing the print function

```
void printNames(Id& n) {
    cout << "Print Names function:" << endl;
    cout << "First name = " << n.firstName << endl;
    cout << "Last name = "  << n.lastName  << endl;
}

void main() {
    Id fullName("Smith", "Nancy");

    cout << "printNames(fullName)" << endl;
    printNames(fullName);
}
```

generates the following:

```
Initializing Nancy Smith   <-building fullName
printNames(fullName)       <-calling printNames
Print Names function:      <-function executes
First name = Nancy
Last name = Smith
```

Notice that the copy-initializer is not called in this case. Declaring the arguments referential avoids the copy process by passing the address of the existing object. Declaring the function `printNames(Id*)` would also avoid calling the copy-initializer constructor but would require changes in the way the function is written.

If we declared the copy-initializer constructor as `Id(Id)`, the copy-initializer would require a copy-initializer just to call itself! The AT&T specificaton disallows a constructor of this type. Compiling the preceding program with this constructor would result in the misleading error message: `Fatal 44: Out of memory in function xxxx`. A fatal error message normally indicates a problem with the compiler and is more serious than a simple error. Adding more memory does not help.

The compiler is in an infinite loop. When the `printNames()` function references the c-i constructor by passing by value, the c-i constructor itself references the c-i constructor by passing by value and so on. This compiler loop consumes more and more memory until none is left and the compilation is halted.

The argument to the c-i constructor *must* be of type `Id` but cannot be pass by value because it could throw the compiler into an infinite loop. A constructor of type `Id(Id*)` can exist, of course, but since its argument is not of type `Id`, it would not be invoked to copy an `Id` object.

Returning an Object by Value In principle, returning an object by value is the same as passing an argument by value. Consider the following:

```
MyClass fn();
MyClass anObject = fn();
```

The function `fn()` returns an object of type `MyClass` which is then copied into `anObject` using the copy-initializer constructor. Making the case more complicated, we see that the copy-initializer is still invoked.

```
MyClass fn();
MyClass anObject;
anObject = fn();
```

To understand how the copy-initializer is involved, we must know what is going on inside `fn()`. Let us consider the simplest possible `fn()`.

```
MyClass globalObject;

MyClass fn() {
    return globalObject;
}
```

Here `fn()` returns the object `globalObject`. Since the function returns by value, it is not the object itself but a copy of `globalObject` that `fn()` returns. The return must generate a call to the copy-initializer constructor to create a copy of `globalObject`.

Declaring `fn()` either `MyClass&` or `MyClass*` alleviates the call to the copy-initializer. In either case `fn()` returns the address of the existing object rather than creating a new one. The `MyClass*` case is more obvious.

```
MyClass globalObject;
MyClass* fn() {
    return &globalObject;
}
```

The following class investigates the differences between the three return types more fully.

```
#include <iostream.h>

struct S {
  int a[10];

    S() {cout << "Default constructor" << endl;}
```

Constructors and Destructors

```
    S(S& s) {cout << "C-I constructor" << endl;}

    S& operator=(S& s) {
        cout << "Assignment operator" << endl;
        return s;
    }
};

S& fn1() {
    return *new S;
}

S fn2() {
    return *new S;
}

S* fn3() {
    return new S;
}

void main() {
    cout << "S s1, &s2 = *new S;" << endl;
    S s1, &s2 = *new S;
    cout << "S* sPtr = &s1;" << endl;
    S* sPtr = &s1;

    cout << "s1 = s2;" << endl;
    s1 = s2;
    cout << "s1 = fn1();" << endl;
    s1 = fn1();

    cout << "s1 = fn2();" << endl;
    s1 = fn2();

    cout << "s1 = *sPtr;" << endl;
    s1 = *sPtr;
```

```
        cout << "s1 = *fn3();" << endl;
        s1 = *fn3();
}
```

The extra output statements in `main()` keep track of which statements generate which calls. The `operator=()` method prints out whenever assignment is being made. The output from executing this program follows:

```
S s1, &s2 = *new S;
Default constructor
Default constructor
S* sPtr = &s1;
s1 = s2;
Assignment operator
s1 = fn1();
Default constructor
Assignment operator
s1 = fn2();
Default constructor
C-I constructor
Assignment operator
s1 = *sPtr;
Assignment operator
s1 = *fn3();
Default constructor
Assignment operator
```

Declaring the objects `s1` and `s2` invokes the default constructor. Since `sPtr` points to an existing object, its declaration does not invoke any constructor nor does it invoke `operator=()` because, even with an equal sign, initialization is not assignment.

The assignment of `s2` to `s1` is for comparison with the `fn1()` call that follows. The `new` call within `fn1()` invokes the default constructor to create a new object. The resulting object is returned to the calling routine by reference and assigned to `s1`, hence the following:

```
s1 = s2;
Assignment operator
s1 = fn1();
Default constructor    <- create a new object
Assignment operator    <- assign to s1
```

The function `fn2()` returns its object by value. After invoking the default constructor to build a local object, `fn2()` calls the copy-initializer constructor to copy the object onto the stack upon returning. This generates the extra line before the assignment operator.

```
s1 = fn2();
Default constructor    <-create a new object
C-I constructor        <-return a copy to caller
Assignment operator    <-assign to s1
```

The output from the `S* fn3()` case is identical to that from `S& fn1()`. Assignment with a simple pointer to an object is performed first for comparison.

```
s1 = *sPtr;
Assignment operator
s1 = *fn3();
Default constructor    <- create a new object
Assignment operator    <- assign to s1
```

The function `fn3()` returns the address of an object. In `main()`, the object pointed at by the address returned is assigned to `s1`.

A Look Under the Hood Analyzing the assembly language generated from compiling test modules gives the programmer a better understanding of what is being done. (Readers not interested in the assembly language generated by Turbo C++ may want to turn to the next section.)

The assembly language generated by `fn1()`, once stripped of debugger information, appears as follows:

```
S& fn1() {
    return *new S;
}
```

produces:

```
PUSH BP                 ;SET UP STACK FRAME
MOV  BP,SP

PUSH 0                  ;MORE ON THIS LATER
CALL S::S()             ;CALL CONSTRUCTOR TO CREATE OBJECT
POP  CX

POP  BP                 ;PULL DOWN STACK FRAME
RET                     ;RETURN WITH OBJECT ADDRESS IN AX
```

After setting up the standard stack frame, `fn1()` invokes the default constructor to build a new object. `fn1()` returns the address of the new object in AX to the caller, `main()`. The assembly language produced by `fn3()` is the same since it, too, returns the address of a newly created object. The assembly language for `fn2()` shows the extra call to the copy-initializer constructor.

```
S fn2() {
    return *new S;
}
```

produces:

```
PUSH BP                 ;SET UP STANDARD STACK
MOV  BP,SP

PUSH 0                  ;CREATE A NEW OBJECT
CALL S::S()
POP  CX
PUSH AX                 ;PASS ITS ADDRESS
```

Constructors and Destructors

```
PUSH  [BP+4]              ;PLUS THE FIRST ARGUMENT TO FN2()
CALL  S::S(S&)            ;TO THE COPY CONSTRUCTOR
POP   CX
POP   CX


POP   BP                  ;THEN RETURN
RET
```

Again, `fn2()` sets up the standard stack frame, then calls the default constructor to build a new object. The address of the new object is passed along with the first argument to `fn2()` to the c-i constructor. This seems odd since `fn2()` has no first argument.

The function `fn2()` must return a copy of the object it creates to the calling function. The copy could not be made to a global object since this is not reentrant. Memory for the copy cannot be allocated from `fn2()`'s stack like a normal auto variable because `fn2()` must relinquish its stack before returning. Before the calling routine can copy the object to its own stack area, an interrupt might occur which would overwrite the data.

Room for the copy must be allocated before `fn2()` is called. The address of this area is then passed to `fn2()` as a hidden first argument that `fn2()` uses as a receptacle for the return object. The calling sequence in `main()` reveals this process.

```
s1 = fn2();
```

produces:

```
PUSH  DS                  ;PASS FAR ADDRESS OF...
LEA   AX,[BP-40]          ;...TEMPORARY OBJECT...
PUSH  AX
CALL  FN2                 ;...TO FN2()
POP   CX
POP   CX


LEA   AX,[BP-40]          ;PASS NEAR ADDRESS OF...
PUSH  AX                  ;...TEMPORARY OBJECT...
```

```
LEA     AX,[BP-20]          ;...AND NEAR ADDRESS OF...
PUSH    AX                  ;...S1...
CALL    S::OPERATOR=        ;...TO THE ASSIGNMENT OPERATOR
POP     CX
POP     CX
```

A far address is passed for the temporary object instead of the smaller near address because the hidden argument is not declared. Without a declaration, Turbo C++ does not know how large the pointer must be. Turbo C++ assumes the worst case and passes both offset and segment. In the next call, the argument to `operator=()` is declared as a near reference (by default) and Turbo C++ passes only the offset portion.

If `fn2()` were a method of S, instead of a friend, the address of an object would also be passed as the hidden `this` argument. Thus, a member function may have two hidden arguments.

Constructing Member Objects

A class object may contain objects of other classes. The constructor for any member object is invoked before the open brace of the constructor as in the following:

```
struct LineSegment {
    Complex fromPoint;
    Complex toPoint;
    float   magnitude;
    int     color;

    LineSegment(Complex& from, Complex& to, int c)
            : fromPoint(from), toPoint(to)
            {
                magnitude = 0;
                color     = c;
            }
};
```

Constructors and Destructors 181

The class `LineSegment` defines a beginning and an end point— both of which are `Complex`—as well as a color, and a magnitude. The objects `fromPoint` and `toPoint` are initialized using the copy-initializer constructor.

All classes must have a copy-initializer constructor. If one is not specifically defined, C++ provides one. This rule includes intrinsic types; otherwise, the following would require the definition of some special case.

```
int a = 1;
int b = a;
```

The following equivalent form is legal as well.

```
int c(a);
```

The copy-initializer constructor for intrinsic types can also be invoked from a constructor. Thus, the previous constructor can be written as follows:

```
LineSegment(Complex& from, Complex& to, int c)
        : fromPoint(from), toPoint(to),
          magnitude(0), color(c) {}
```

The constructors for `magnitude` and `color` must be specified before the open brace. To do so after the open brace would construct new `float` and `int` objects.

One might erroneously assume that the following constructor invokes the default constructor for `magnitude` and the copy-initializer constructor for `color`.

```
LineSegment(Complex& from, Complex& to, int c)
        : fromPoint(from), toPoint(to),
          magnitude, color = c {}
```

The older C initialization format is not allowed in this context. A value must be specified.

Constructors and `new`

Constructors must work with the keyword `new` when allocating objects from the heap. This relationship works both ways: a constructor may invoke `new` and `new` may invoke a constructor.

Calling `new` from a Constructor

Depending upon its use, the `Id` class we discussed earlier may have a serious problem. Consider, the following function using an `Id` constructor.

```
Id& fn() {
    const char c[] = {"Jones"};

    return Id(c);
}
```

The array `c` is allocated from the `fn()` stack. The constructor for `Id`, which copies the address of the initialization string into the local pointer variable, is left with a bogus address once the program returns from `fn()`. A somewhat slower, but more universal implementation of the constructors for `Id` is as follows:

```
#include <iostream.h>
#include <string.h>

class Id {
  public:
    char* lastName;
    char* firstName;
    Id() {
        cout << "Initializing default" << endl;
        lastName = (char*)0;
        firstName = (char*)0;
    }
    Id(char* lName) {
```

```cpp
            cout << "Initializing " << lName << endl;
            lastName = new char[strlen(lName) + 1];
            if (lastName)
                strcpy(lastName, lName);
            firstName = (char*)0;
    }
    Id(char* lName, char* fName) {
            cout << "Initializing " << fName <<
                                " " << lName << endl;
            lastName = new char[strlen(lName) + 1];
            if (lastName)
                strcpy(lastName, lName);
            firstName = new char[strlen(fName) + 1];
            if (firstName)
                strcpy(firstName, fName);
        }
    Id(Id& s) {
            cout << "Copying " << s.firstName <<
                        " " << s.lastName  << endl;
            lastName = firstName = (char*)0;
            if (s.lastName) {
                lastName = new char[strlen(s.lastName)+1];
                if (lastName)
                    strcpy(lastName, s.lastName);
            }
            if (s.firstName) {
                firstName = new char[strlen(s.firstName)+1];
                if (firstName)
                    strcpy(firstName, s.firstName);
            }
        }

    Id& operator=(Id& s) {
            lastName = new char[strlen(s.lastName) + 1];
            if (lastName)
                strcpy(lastName, s.lastName);
```

```
            firstName = new char[strlen(s.firstName) + 1];
            if (firstName)
                strcpy(firstName, s.firstName);
            return *this;
        }

        ~Id() {
            cout << "Destroying "
                << (firstName ? firstName : "<default>")
                << " "
                << (lastName  ? lastName  : "<default>")
                << endl;
            if (lastName) {
                delete lastName;
                lastName = (char*)0;
            }
            if (firstName) {
                delete firstName;
                firstName = (char*)0;
            }
        }
};

void main() {
    Id dummyName;
    Id lastNameOnly1 = "Smith";
    Id lastNameOnly2("Jones");
    Id fullName("Smith", "Nancy");
    Id arrayName[5] = {"One", "Two", "Three", "Four"};
}
```

This program generates the following:

```
Initializing default
Initializing Smith
Initializing Jones
```

```
Initializing Nancy Smith
Initializing One
Initializing Two
Initializing Three
Initializing Four
Initializing default
Destroying <default> One
Destroying <default> Two
Destroying <default> Three
Destroying <default> Four
Destroying <default> <default>
Destroying Nancy Smith
Destroying <default> Jones
Destroying <default> Smith
Destroying <default> <default>
```

The new `Id` class appears to work like the earlier `Id`. However, instead of storing a pointer, the new class uses `new` to allocate a block of heap memory to which it copies each initialization string. With its memory off the heap, the class can handle any length name whether the string passed to the constructor is in temporary storage or not.

Memory allocated from the heap must eventually be returned or a net loss of memory will occur. Building a constructor which includes a call to `new` necessitates the inclusion of a destructor with a call to `delete` to restore the memory.

Two good programming practices are built into the `Id` class. Every return from `new` should be checked for 0, as in the constructors of `Id`; `new` returns a 0 when it cannot honor a memory request. In addition, the destructor should always reset a pointer to null (0) after deleting the memory to which it points. If an object were somehow to be destructed twice, the second call to the destructor would have no negative effect because `delete` ignores null addresses.

The copy-initializer constructor is important for classes that allocate memory from the heap. The Turbo C++ c-i constructor, which performs a member-by-member copy, is not satisfactory. Consider the following:

```
Id name1("Davis", "Stephen");
Id name2 = name1;
```

The constructor for `Id` allocates two blocks of memory and assigns them to the objects `name1.lastName` and `name1.firstName`. The default copy-initializer constructor copies the contents of these pointers into `name2` in line 2. When `name1` is destructed, `~Id()` returns the memory stored in `name1.lastName` and `name1.firstName` to the heap via a call to `delete`. When `~Id()` destructs `name2`, it attempts to delete the same memory blocks again, resulting in corruption of heap memory and a probable system crash.

The copy-initializer for `Id` allocates separate memory areas for the new object and copies the contents of the old object into the new areas. Even though the two objects contain the same data, they do not share memory. Destructing one of the objects does not affect the other's memory areas. A similar problem with the assignment of one object to another is solved with a user-defined `operator=()` the same way.

The rule of thumb is that if the constructors of a class allocate memory from the heap via `new` or `malloc()`, the programmer must provide a destructor, a copy-initializer constructor, and an `operator=()`.

Calling a Constructor from new

We have seen how a class object may be allocated from the heap directly by invoking a default constructor as in the following:

```
Id& anObject = *new Id;
```

Initialization data can be provided as well.

```
Id& anObject = *new Id("Dissinger", "Leroy");
```

Thus, not only can a constructor invoke `new` to allocate memory for member objects, but `new` can invoke a constructor as well. We can compare this to a more static case to see the pattern.

```
void fn() {
   Id  object1("Struthers", "Sally");
   Id& object2 = *new Id("Southerland", "Donald");
```

In the case of `object1`, C++ allocates a fixed amount of space on the stack when the function is entered. `Id(char*, char*)` is called passing the address of the newly allocated object as its `this` pointer. The `this` returned by the constructor is discarded.

The dynamic `object2` is allocated enough memory by `new` to contain an object of type `Id`. The address returned from `new` is passed as `this` to the `Id(char*, char*)` constructor. Having initialized the object, the constructor returns `this` which is assigned to the reference object `object2`. `Id&` and `Id*` do not invoke a constructor; they declare pointers to objects, not objects themselves. It is the `new Id()` that invokes the constructor.

The internal details are slightly more complicated. In the case of `object2`, the constructor is invoked with a `this` pointer of 0. Finding the `this` pointer null, the constructor calls the `operator new()` function to allocate space for the object. The address returned from the `operator new()` call is what the constructor returns.

Destructors

A destructor carries the name of the class for which it is defined with a ~ added to the front. The ~ is a universal symbol for NOT, which leads to the logical representation of a destructor as a ~constructor.

A destructor must have a void argument list and has no return type (not even void). Since destructors have no arguments, they may not be overloaded. Only one (or no) destructor may be defined for a given class.

Invoking Destructors

Destructors are almost never explicitly invoked. They are invoked automatically by C++ when an object goes out of scope. Automatic (and register) objects go out of scope when the program exits the block in which they are defined. Global and static variables go out of scope when the program exits.

A program may exit by returning from `main()` or by calling the `exit()` function. Calling `exit()` invokes any exit routines plus the destructors for any globally defined objects. `exit()` does not destruct any automatic variables that are active. A bug in early versions of Turbo C++ often caused no destructors to be invoked, global or otherwise, when a program terminated via `exit()`.

Abnormal terminations caused by calling `abort()` or `_exit()` or by internal traps do not invoke any exit routines, including destructors. Objects pointed at do not go out of scope when the pointer does. Therefore, the destructor is not automatically invoked when a pointer or a reference variable goes out of scope. If the pointer points to another object, the memory is destructed when that object goes out of scope. If the pointer addresses a block of memory returned from `new`, the program must invoke `delete` to restore it to the heap.

In the same way that `new` automatically invokes a constructor, `delete` automatically invokes the destructor for a class. That similarity extends into the generated assembly code. All destructors contain a hidden first argument and a hidden call to `operator delete()`. The argument passed tells the destructor what type of object is being destroyed. If it is a pointer to heap memory, the destructor calls `operator delete()` as the last step before returning.

A destructor can be invoked directly. However, the call must be fully qualified as follows:

```
Object anObject;
Object* anObjectPtr = new Object;

anObject.Object::~Object();
anObjectPtr->Object::~Object();
```

The full qualification avoids potentially confusing the C++ parser. Normally `~fn()` would mean "complement the return value from `fn()`". Fully qualifying the name places the tilde as part of the function name. Assigning existing symbols additional meanings frequently results in confusion.

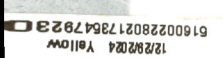

Invoking the destructor explicitly on a pointer does not automatically call `delete`. If the pointer refers to heap memory, that memory is lost until the program calls `delete`, which destructs the memory area a second time, or the program terminates.

Destructing Member Objects

Unlike constructors, destructors for member objects are not explicitly called by the parent destructor. When an object goes out of scope, any member objects also go out of scope. We can build a `Container` class to hold an `Object` class, as in the following:

```
#include <iostream.h>

class Object {
  private:
    char* name;
  public:
    Object(char* n) { name = n; }
   ~Object() {
        cout << "Destructor invoked for "
             << name << endl;
    }
};

class Container {
  private:
    Object one;
    Object two;

  public:
    Container() : one("One"), two("Two") {}
   ~Container() {
        cout << "Destructor for Container" << endl;
    }
};
```

```
Container anObject;
void main() {
}
```

This program generates the following output.

```
Destructor for Container
Destructor invoked for Two
Destructor invoked for One
```

The constructor for `Container` explicitly invokes the constructor for `Object` to initialize the two member objects so that instantiating `anObject` constructs `anObject.one` and `anObject.two`. The destructor makes no reference to the destructor for the member objects. The destructor for these is invoked immediately after the destructor for the `Container` class. If `Container` had no destructor, the destructors for the two members would still be invoked.

Virtual Destructors

A pointer to a publicly derived class also points to its base class. This can result in confusion about which destructor to invoke. Consider the following class definitions.

```
struct Base {
    ~Base(){}
};

struct Derived : public Base {
    ~Derived(){}
};
```

Now assume that a function is defined as follows:

```
void fn(Base* bPtr) {
    delete bPtr;
}
```

The definitions are written so that C++ invokes `~Base()`, whether the object pointed at by `bPtr` is of type `Base*` or of type `Derived*`. By declaring `~Base()` to be virtual as in the following definition, `fn()` invokes the proper destructor for the type of object pointed at.

```
struct Base {
    virtual ~Base(){}
};
```

This rule applies to linked lists or arrays of different types. Suppose that objects of type `Base` and `Derived` are mixed in a linked list. Once the linked list has served its purpose, a single function can make its way through the list, deleting each object. If the destructors have been declared virtual, the proper destructor is invoked for each object.

It would make no sense to declare a constructor virtual. When a constructor is invoked, the object does not yet exist and so cannot be of either a derived or base type. An object is given a type through the declaration/construction process.

Initializing Other Types of Objects

Often a module must initialize other types of objects before execution of the main program and after its termination. A windowing package might need to set the video mode, a database package might create or open a file, and almost any package might need to open and read a configuration file.

The approach used in other languages is to define an initialization function that `main()` calls immediately after starting and a termination function called just prior to returning. This method has several limitations. First, the process intrudes upon the encapsulation of C++. A self-contained solution would be better than calls to initialization functions to `main()`. Second, a C++ program can exit anywhere by calling the `exit()` library function. Finding and inserting a call to an exit function before each potential termination point is problematic. The risk of missing an exit point or of a maintenance programmer adding a new exit path without calling the proper exit routines is high.

Executing Before or After main()

The C++ alternatives to the preceding approach are outlined below.

Global Constructors   The most straightforward approach is to define a dummy class associated with the device or file that requires initialization. An object of the dummy class is declared globally only once within the package. The constructor for a globally declared object executes prior to main() gaining control and therefore acts as the start-up function. Similarly, the dummy class destructor is executed as part of the program's exit procedure.

C++ does not limit constructors and destructors to processing the data within an object. In fact, such a dummy class probably would not contain any data.

In programs with multiple packages, each package may define its own dummy class. The order of execution of the constructors is the same as the order of inclusion at link time. The order of execution of the destructors is the reverse of the order of execution of the constructors when the program started.

atexit()   Adding a call to an initialization function is not nearly as problematic as adding calls to the termination function in all the proper places. ANSI C defines a solution to the exit problem in the atexit() library function. This solution also applies in C++.

The prototype type for atexit() is as follows:

```
extern "C" {
    int atexit(void (*fn)(void));
}
```

The input to atexit() is the address of a function that accepts nothing and returns nothing. This function executes when the program exits. The return from atexit() indicates whether the "installation" was successful. If more than one atexit() function is declared, they are executed in the reverse order of their declaration. The following simple C (or C++) program.

Constructors and Destructors

```
#include <stdio.h>    /*prototype for atexit()*/
#include <stdlib.h>

void exitFn1(void) {
    printf("Exit function #1 called\n");
}

void exitFn2(void) {
    printf("Exit function #2 called\n");
}

void main(void) {
    atexit(exitFn1);  /*post the exit functions*/
    atexit(exitFn2);

    printf("Program terminating\n");
}
```

generates the following output.

```
Program terminating
Exit function #2 called
Exit function #1 called
```

Up to 32 `atexit()` functions may be declared in one program.

Start-up and Exit Pragmas Start-up and exit pragmas are unique to Turbo C++ and therefore are not nearly as portable as the two previous solutions. However, the pragmas allow a priority to be assigned to each function to determine the order in which the initialization routines are executed.

```
#pragma startup startFn1 80
#pragma startup startFn2
#pragma exit     exitFn   80
```

Priorities range from a high of 0 to a low of 255; the default priority is 100. Initialization routines with higher priority execute first. For exit routines, the order of execution is reversed: low priority routines execute first and higher priority routines later. Turbo C++ reserves the priority range 0 to 63 for its own modules and suggests that programmers not use these.

The following program shows the startup and exit pragmas in use.

```
#include <iostream.h>

//first the program prototypes (must precede the
//pragmas themselves)
void MoreImportant();
void LessImportant();

//define startup and exit functions
#pragma startup MoreImportant 100
#pragma exit    MoreImportant 100

#pragma startup LessImportant 110
#pragma exit    LessImportant 110

//define the functions themselves
void MoreImportant() {
    cout << "More important" << endl;
}
void LessImportant() {
    cout << "Less important" << endl;
}

//execute a 'dummy' program
void main() {
    cout << "In main" << endl;
}
```

Output from this program is as follows:

```
More important
Less important
In main
Less important
More important
```

Order of Execution

When different types of start-up and exit functions are defined within the same program, the order of execution is as follows:

1. the Turbo C++ pragma start-up functions beginning with priority 0 and ending with priority 63. This includes the constructors for globally declared variables, which are called in the order they appear in the program
2. the user pragma start-up functions beginning with priority 64 and ending with the priority 255, irrespective of the order of declaration; among start-up functions with the same priority, the order of declaration
3. the main program
4. `atexit()` functions declared within the program in the reverse order of their declaration
5. pragma exit functions starting with the lowest priority and proceeding toward the highest priority
6. destructors in the reverse order in which the corresponding constructors were invoked

Termination functions are only invoked in programs that terminate either by returning from `main()` or by calling the `exit()` library routine. Programs that terminate abnormally, either via the `_exit()` or `abort()` library calls, do not invoke the terminating routines.

Conclusion

The constructors and destructor of a class are special methods of any class definition. Their proper definition can lead to enhanced data abstraction and encapsulation. These properties can also be enhanced by clever definition and use of overloaded operators, which is covered in the next chapter.

Chapter 7

Overloading Operators

Overloading Operators

Most programming languages define a set of operators to handle operations such as addition, subtraction, and multiplication. In earlier languages these operators were considered intrinsic; their syntax was fixed and rigidly prescribed. The programmer could accept the operators provided or not, but could not change them. Additional features had to be handled by subroutines.

As languages have progressed, the set of immutable, intrinsic operators has become smaller and their syntax more general. Languages such as Ada have taken this to its logical conclusion by declaring all operators to be functions with a different calling syntax. When a language such as Ada sees the following:

```
int a, b;
a + b;
```

it does not necessarily "know" what + means. It searches through a library for a function +(int,int) that can used to interpret the line.

In C, except for the I/O functions, all operators are intrinsic and not modifiable by the programmer. However, most operators can be used in many different constructs with essentially the same meaning.

C++ treats operators as partially intrinsic and partially modifiable. Operations on C++-defined types are intrinsic; i.e., the programmer cannot influence what the addition of an integer to an integer means. The programmer may, however, define any existing operator (such as addition) for a newly created class. The definition of an operator appears identical to the definition of a function with a special name. A unary member operator may be defined as follows:

```
struct MyClass {
MyClass operator@();
};
```

where @ represents any legal operator to be defined. Unary member operators have no explicit arguments. The single argument is the object itself. In use, a unary operator appears as follows:

```
MyClass object;

@object
```

which is interpreted by C++ as

```
MyClass object;
object.operator@()
```

This latter format clarifies the relationship between the object and the operator function. In fact, the programmer may use this wordier syntax to invoke the operator if desired.

The syntax for a binary member operator is similar.

```
MyClass {
MyClass operator@(MyClass a);
};

MyClass obj1, obj2;

obj1 @ obj2;
```

is interpreted by C++ as

```
obj1.operator@(obj2)
```

Here @ represents any valid C++ operator. Although `operator@()` returns an object of class `MyClass` in these examples, it could return any other type desired.

The overloading of operators for different argument types is similar to the overloading of other functions. The C++ programmer may define a function `fn(int)` that has no relation to the function `fn(float)`. Even in C, the operators `+(int, int)` and `+(float, float)` bear little similarity to each other in their implementation. Adding an integer to another integer generates little more than an ADD 8086 assembly instruction. Adding two floating points generates anywhere from inline 8087 instructions to a call to the floating point emulation library.

C++ Operators

In C++ new operators cannot be defined. Programmers may define what existing operators mean when applied to new types. The precedence or associativity of existing operators also cannot be redefined. These are listed in Table 7–1.

Table 7–1 The Precedence and Associativity for C++ Operators

Operator	Associativity
higher precedence	
( ) [ ] -> : : .	Left to right
! ~ - (unary)	Right to left
++(preincrement) --(predecrement)	Right to left
& (address of) * (dereference)	Right to left
(typecast)	Right to left
sizeof new delete	Right to left
+ -(binary)	Left to right
++ (postincrement)	Right to left
-- (postdecrement)	Right to left
.* ->*	Left to right
* (multiply) / %	Left to right
+ -	Left to right
<< >>	Left to right
< <= > >=	Left to right
== !=	Left to right
& (arithmetic AND)	Left to right
^	Left to right
|	Left to right

	&&	Left to right
	||	Left to right
	?: (conditional expression)	Right to left
	= *= /= %= += -= &= ^= |= <<= >>=	Right to left Right to left
		Left to right

lower
precedence

Higher precedence operators are evaluated first in the absence of other groupings. The expression a + b * c is interpreted as a + (b * c) because the precedence of * is higher than that of +. For operators with the same precedence, associativity (also known as binding) determines the grouping. Thus, a + b + c is interpreted as (a + b) + c because + associates from left to right.

The order of evaluation of the individual terms is not specified and cannot be made specific by parenthetical groupings. For example, in the expression a + b + c, the order in which a, b and c are evaluated is not specified.

Some operators are also lvalues. These include all of the forms of assignment, subscript, dereference (*), preincrement, predecrement, conditional (?:), and comma operators. Different forms of assignment are considered different operators and overload separately.

Programmers learning C++ may not perceive some of these operators as operators at all. For example, a programmer may have considered fn() to be simply the way one calls a function fn; however, the C++ programmer interprets this as applying the () operator to the fn object.

C++ does not allow all operators to be overloaded. The non-overloadable operators are ., the member operator ::, the scope operator .* and ->*, the member pointer operators and ?:, the trinary or conditional operator. The first four operators are too basic to allow overloading.

The conditional operator is not overloadable because of its semantic peculiarities; i.e., it is not an operator of the right arguments on the left argument, and depending upon the value of the first argument, either the second or the third argument is not evaluated. This would be very difficult to implement as an overloading function.

There is one other peculiar feature of ?:. In C++, the conditional is an lvalue. Thus, the following is legal.

```
int a, b, c;

(c ? a : b) = 1;
```

To achieve the same affect in C, the programmer must revert to pointer manipulation.

```
*(c ? &a : &b) = 1;
```

Overloading such an operator probably obscures more than simplifies.

The current syntax of C++ does not allow any distinction to be drawn between preincrement and postincrement (or predecrement and postdecrement). Thus, while the programmer may define `operator++()` (or `operator--()`), there is no difference between `++myObject` and `myObject++`.

The following definition syntax has been proposed to differentiate the two.

```
operator++()    -> preincrement
operator++(int) -> postincrement
```

However, Turbo C++ 1.0 does not support this obvious kludge and it is doubtful that such syntax will become part of any future C++ standard.

The C++ programmer should be careful about overloading even the more conventional operators. Consider, for example, the comma operator. While conceptually not very difficult, overloading the comma operator function may lead to considerable reader confusion as in `1+2,anObject,4`.

Finally, a default assignment operator is provided for classes that do not have their own `operator=()`. Like the default copy-initializer constructor, the default assignment operator performs a member-by-member assignment to ensure that assignment operators defined for member objects are used. In the following example,

```
#include <iostream>

struct LimitedRange {
```

```
    int maxX;
    int x;

    LimitedRange(int val, int maxVal {
       x = val;
       maxX = maxVal;
    }
    LimitedRange& operator=(LimitedRange& s) {
       x = s.x;
       if (x > maxX) {
          cout << "Max val exceeded" << endl;
          x = maxX;
       }
       return *this;
    }
};
struct LargeClass {
   LimitedRange anObj;

   LargeClass(int aVal, int maxVal :
      anObj(aVal, maxVal {}
};
void main() {
   LargeClass largeVal (1, 15);
   LargeClass smallVal (0, 5);

   smallVal = largeVal;
}
```

the assignment of `largeVal` to `smallVal` invokes the function `LimitedRange::operator=()` even though no assignment is defined for `LargeClass`.

Friend Operators Versus Member Operators

Defining overload operators as member functions directly associates the operator with the class for which it is defined. Member operators also have

Overloading Operators

access control. An operator declared in the private section of a class definition is available to other member functions but not to the general public. This effectively removes from general use any default definition for this operator.

For example, if a class does not define `operator=()`, C++ provides a default member-by-member assignment operator similar to the default copy-initializer. However, by declaring an `operator=()` in the private section, the programmer can prevent other modules from placing an object of that class on the left side of an assignment.

Operators can be implemented as non-member functions as well. The format of a non-member operator is similar to that for a member.

```
MyClass operator@(MyClass a);            //unary
MyClass operator@(MyClass a1, MyClass a2); //binary

@a            //equivalent to operator@(a)
a1 @ a2       //equivalent to operator@(a1, a2)
```

The non-member operator declaration always has one more explicit argument than the equivalent member version because the member operator is always passed a hidden `this` which points to the first argument of the operator. For the non-member operator, both arguments must be included specifically.

Let us consider one of the operators defined for `Complex` in Chapter 2. As a method, the binary and unary `operator-()` operators are as follows:

```
class Complex {
  private:
    float real;
    float imag;

  public:
    Complex(void) {
      real = imag = 0;
    }
```

```
        Complex(float r, float i = 0) {
           real = r;
           imag = i;
        }

        Complex operator-(Complex& c);
        Complex operator-();
};

//binary minus
Complex Complex::operator-(Complex& c) {
    return Complex(real - c.real, imag - c.imag);
}
//unary minus
Complex Complex::operator-() {
    return Complex(-real, imag);
}
```

As a non-member, `operator-()` does not have access to the private members `real` and `imag`. One solution is to provide access methods as in the following:

```
class Complex {
   private:
      float real;
      float imag;

   public:
      Complex(void) {
         real = imag = 0;
      }

      Complex(float r, float i = 0) {
         real = r;
         imag = i;
      }
```

Overloading Operators

```
        //define access methods for Complex
        float realPart() {
          return real;
        }
        float imagPart() {
          return imag;
        }
};

Complex operator-(Complex& c1, Complex& c2) {
    return Complex(c1.realPart() - c2.realPart(),
                   c1.imagPart() - c2.imagPart());
}

Complex operator-(Complex& c) {
    return Complex(-c.realPart(), c.imagPart());
}
```

Another more common solution is to make the operators friends of the class to avoid the necessity of access routines.

```
class Complex {
      friend Complex operator-(Complex&);
      friend Complex operator-(Complex&, Complex&);
    private:
      float real;
      float imag;

    public:
      Complex(void) {
        real = imag = 0;
      }

      Complex(float r, float i = 0) {
        real = r;
        imag = i;
```

```
        }
    };

    Complex operator-(Complex& c1, Complex& c2) {
        return Complex(c1.real - c2.real,
                       c1.real - c2.imag);
    }

    Complex operator-(Complex& c) {
        return Complex(-c.real, c.imag);
    }
```

Non-member operators are often called friend operators since they are generally declared as friends to give them access to the private sections of a class. In any case, operators defined for a new class must be intimately knowledgeable of the class. However, the syntax does not require a non-member operator to be a friend function.

To examine the difference between the two formats, let us consider a sample problem. Given the preceding definition of `Complex`, suppose we enter the following:

```
float a;
Complex b;

b - a;          //expression #1
a - b;          //expression #2
```

The first expression attempts to subtract a `float` from a `Complex`. Since neither `Complex::operator-(float)` nor `operator-(Complex, float)` is defined, Turbo C++ cannot understand what is meant. To find out, Turbo C++ attempts to find a coercion path that will generate something it does understand.

By using the `Complex(float, float=0)` constructor, Turbo C++ can create a `Complex` out of the `float`. It can use this either by searching the members of `Complex` to find the member operator `Complex::operator-(Complex)` for the method case or by searching

Overloading Operators 209

the non-member operators to find `operator-(Complex, Complex)` for the non-method case.

Thus, the first expression is evaluated properly for both the method and non-method case. However, the second expression is not processed the same for both cases. Let us consider the member case first.

Since a is now the left-hand object, Turbo C++ searches the member operators of its class, `float`, for a match with `float::operator-(Complex)`. When no mention of any `Complex` arguments occurs in this list, Turbo C++ then looks for any non-member operators that might help. Since there are none, the second expression cannot be evaluated. The coercion path from `float` to `Complex` does not help here, since Turbo C++ never searches the members of `Complex`. It could evaluate the expression if a coercion path existed from `Complex` to `float`. In that instance Turbo C++ would coerce b into a `float` which it would then evaluate as `float::operator-(float)`.

In the case of the non-member operator, however, the second expression is evaluated in the same way as the first. Turbo C++ searches the member operators of `float`. It then searches the non-member operators where it finds `operator-(Complex, Complex)` as before.

Implementing a binary operator as a method instructs the right-hand argument to be applied to the left-hand argument; the operation is defined only in terms of the left-hand argument. By implementing a binary operator as a non-member, the programmer focuses on the operation. Both arguments are essentially equal in importance in the sense that reversing the arguments results in an expression that still has meaning.

Coercion Operators

In the above discussion we noted that if C++ knew how to coerce `Complex` into `float`, it would have been able to parse the second expression. Constructors are an implicit conversion of a type into the current class type. Consider the following class definitions.

```
struct A; struct B;
struct A {
    int a;
```

```
    A(int i) {a = i;}
    A(B b);
};

struct B {
   int b;
   B(int i) {b = i;}
   B(A a);
};

A::A(B b) { a = b.b;}
B::B(A a) { b = a.a;}

void main() {
   A a = 1;
   B b = 2;

   a = b;      //convert from type B to type A
   b = a;      //convert in other direction
}
```

By adding constructors that accept an object of the other's class, objects of type A can be converted into objects of type B and vice versa.

To add a converter to `Complex` without modifying `float`, C++ allows the programmer to define coercion operators. These operators must be written as unary member operators.

Following is the coercion operator from `Complex` to `float`. The remainder of the `Complex` class definition is identical to the previous examples.

```
class Complex {
   operator float() {
      return real;
   }
         .        //continue with remainder of class
         .
         .
```

Overloading Operators

In use, the coercion operator appears as follows:

```
void main(void) {
  Complex a (2., 3.);
  float b;

  b = float(a);      //expression #1
  b = a;             //expression #2
  b = a * 2.0;       //expression #3
  b = 2.0 * a;       //expression #4
}
```

In the first expression, the coercion operator is specifically applied to convert a into a `float`. In the second line, the call to the coercion operator is implied. In the third and fourth expressions, the conversion is implied as well.

The last two expressions appear to be identical. When using member operators, however, they are not. In expression three, `2.0` is first converted to a `Complex`, which is multiplied with a using the member `operator*(Complex)`. The result is converted back to a `float` using the coercion operator and then is stored into b.

In the fourth expression, Turbo C++ cannot find a multiplication operator that applies as long as a remains `Complex`. Therefore, Turbo C++ converts a into a `float` and then performs simple floating point multiplication and assignment.

Programmers must be careful about providing coercion paths, both in the form of constructors and operators, between different types. If constructed properly, the preceding expressions 3 and 4 should produce the same result.

Coercion paths can be established between pointer types or between a pointer type and a non-pointer type. Consider the following:

```
#include <iostream.h>

struct A {
  unsigned a;
```

```
    A(int i) {a = i;}
    operator A* () {
      return this;
    }
};
void print (A *ptr) {
  cout << ptr->>a << endl;
}

void main() {
  A a = 1;
  A* aPtr = &a;

  aPtr = a;     //hey, wait a minute!
  print(aPtr);
  print(a);
}
```

Class A contains a coercion operator from `A*` to A. Thus, while the declarations of `a` and `aPtr` in function `main()` appear quite normal, the assignment of `a` to `aPtr` does not. Even stranger is the `print(a)` call. In both cases, Turbo C++ invokes the coercion path provided from an object of class A to a pointer to an object of class A.

Virtual Arrays

A **virtual array** is an array that appears to be in normal RAM but is not. These arrays are stored in other devices, such as disk files, extended memory, or EMS expanded memory. Although accessing them is much slower than conventional arrays, virtual arrays allow access to very large amounts of memory.

A file in DOS can be as large as 32 MB. Therefore, a correctly constructed virtual array also could be as large as 32 MB. Conventional arrays cannot exceed 64K. Huge arrays can be considerably larger but still come out of the 640K DOS area.

Overloading Operators

When designed carefully, programs can construct virtual arrays that appear conventional by overloading certain operators.

Virtual File Array

Take a simple array, `c[i]`, and consider what would be required to implement a virtual character array so that `c[i]` actually referred to a character in a file on the disk.

Referencing an array is a two-part process. The index and the base address of the array are used to calculate the address of the field. That address is either read from, if `c[i]` is on the right-hand side of an assignment, or written to, if c[i] is on the left. We can build a virtual array capable of handling the following:

```
char s;
FileArray c;

c[i] = 'a';
s = c[i];
```

The overloading of `FileArray::operator[]()` can be used to calculate the location of the character. Since `[]` appears on both sides of the equal sign, we cannot know whether to read or write at that point.

The assignment operator `FileArray::operator=()` is only accessed when data is being written into the virtual array. The assignment operator `char::operator=()` is utilized in the second expression for the read, which we cannot overload. However, before `c[i]` can be assigned to the character, its type must be changed. Therefore, we can use the coercion `FileArray::char()` to perform the read function.

The resulting file virtual array is as follows:

```
//Make a file array type. An object of class FileArray
//can be referenced like a character array (except,
//of course, it has no address):
// c = f[i]; reads the i'th character from the file
// f[i] = c; writes the i'th character to the file
```

```cpp
//

#include <fstream.h>
#include <stdlib.h>

class FileArray : public fstream {
  private:
    streampos filePtr;//the current file location
    void operator&() {}

  public:
    FileArray(char* fName) :
      fstream(fName, ios::in | ios::out) {}
    FileArray& operator[] (unsigned x);
    FileArray& operator= (char c);   //write to the file
    operator char();                 //read from the file
};

FileArray& FileArray::operator[] (unsigned x) {
  filePtr = streampos(x);
  return *this;
}


FileArray& FileArray::operator= (char c) {
  seekp(filePtr, ios::beg);
  write(&c, 1);
  flush();
  return *this;
}

FileArray::operator char() {
  char c;

  seekg(filePtr, ios::beg);
  read(&c, 1);
  return c;
}
```

Including `fstream.h` gives the program access to the stream file library which includes the functions in the list that follows. This will be discussed more fully in Chapter 9.

seekp()	seek for write
seekg()	seek for read
write()	write at the current write location
read()	read at the current read location
flush()	flush the output stream

In addition, this include file defines the class `fstream`, which is inherited by `FileArray`, to describe a file on the disk and the type `streampos`, which can hold the location in a file. `Streampos` is `typedefed` as a `long int`.

The constructor for `VirtArray` opens the file to which the array is to be assigned. The `operator[]()` saves the location that the program is attempting to access. The `operator=()` writes to the location last saved by `operator[]()`; this handles the `c[i] = s;` case. The read path is handled by `operator char()` which reads the character pointed at by the last `operator[]()`; this handles the `s = c[i];` case.

In use, the above virtual array appears as follows:

```
int main() {
  char ch;
  unsigned i;

  FileArray f1("d:\\copy.bat");
  if (!f1)
    abort();

  //First write something out to the file
  for (i = 0; i < 10; i++) {
    ch = 'A' + i;
    f1[i] = ch;
    cout << ch;
  }
```

```
    cout < endl;

    //Now read it back
    for (i = 0; i < 10; i++) {
      ch = f1[i];
      cout << ch;//can say: cout << char(f1[i]);
    }
    cout << endl;
}
```

This program opens an object of f1 of type `FileArray` and assigns it to the file `copy.bat` in the root directory of drive d. The double backslashes are interpreted as a single backslash in a C character string. The `operator!()` is overloaded in `fstream.h` to check for an error in the last file operation.

If no error occurs upon the opening, the program proceeds to write the first 10 letters of the alphabet, then prints them to the screen. Notice that `iostream.h` is not needed to access the stream operators since `fstream.h` already does so. Finally, the program enters a loop to read the 10 characters out of the array and output them to screen. Output from the program is quite simple.

ABCDEFGHIJ
ABCDEFGHIJ

Although far from bulletproof, `FileArray` does contain some protection. Since the elements of a virtual array have no address in RAM, a private `operator&()` is defined. Being private, its presence precludes functions from taking the address of a `FileArray` element.

Virtual EMS Array

Another type of virtual array is stored in Expanded Memory Specification (EMS) memory. This section describes a virtual array class `EMSArray`.

Although a complete discussion of EMS memory is out of the scope of this book, a short description will suffice. EMS memory is paged RAM.

The EMS driver establishes a 64K page frame in an unused area above 640K. This page frame is divided into four 16K slots. 16K pages are mapped into and out of these slots via calls to the EMS driver. All calls to the EMS driver are through interrupt 0x67.

Version 4.0 of the EMS defines room for up to 32 MB of memory although few, if any, EMS boards support this much. Still, it is not uncommon for PCs to be equipped with several megabytes of EMS memory that is not directly accessible to their DOS programs.

EMS memory is normally implemented via hardware on a specially equipped EMS memory board. Mapping pages on EMS memory is very fast (< 50 microseconds). PCs equipped with an 80386 or 80486 CPU may install a device driver that uses the mapping registers of the processor to emulate EMS memory. While not as fast as external hardware, the mapping times of these drivers are quite respectable ($\approx$150 microseconds). These mapping times are much faster than the tens to hundreds of milliseconds required to access a disk file. While a virtual EMS array may not be quite as large as a virtual file array, it is much faster.

The implementation of `EMSArray` starts with a module that contains the functions needed to manipulate EMS memory. The include file for this module follows:

```
#include <dos.h>

//these globals are used throughout the program
const unsigned EMSInt = 0x67;
const unsigned pageSize = 0x4000;

//first define an often used inline function
inline unsigned EMSCall(unsigned EMSCallNum, REGS& reg) {
    reg.h.ah = EMSCallNum;
    int86(EMSInt, &reg, &reg);
    return (unsigned)reg.h.ah;
}

//prototype declarations for the EMS package
void far* EMSPresent(void);
```

```
        void far* EMSSlotAddr(unsigned slotnum);
        unsigned EMSStatus(void);
        unsigned EMSPageCount(void);

        //the EMS class definition
        class EMS {
            friend void far* EMSPresent(void);
            friend void far* EMSSlotAddr(unsigned);
          private:
            unsigned handle;
            unsigned noPages;
            static unsigned frameSegment;

          public:
            //allocate and unallocate the EMS handle
            EMS (unsigned pageCount);
            ~EMS ();

            //map the memory area in
            unsigned map (unsigned page, unsigned frameSlot);

            //check on an object's status
            unsigned status();
        };
```

The four general purpose functions provide most of the access to the EMS memory. The function `EMSPresent()` checks to make sure that an EMS driver is installed. If it is not, it returns zero. If EMS memory is installed, the function returns the address of the page frame in upper memory. This function must be invoked before any of the others, even if the program is sure that EMS memory is available.

The function `EMSSlotAddr()` accepts a slot number in the range of 0 through 3 and returns its far address. The `EMSStatus()` function queries the hardware status, and `EMSPageCount()` reports the number of available 16K pages.

Overloading Operators

The `EMS` class contains the information necessary to describe an EMS object. Its constructor allocates the requested number of pages. The destructor restores these pages to the EMS driver. The method `map()` maps a page into the specified page frame slot while the method `status()` returns the software status.

The implementation of these functions is as follows:

```
#include "ems.hpp"

//--------Implementation of the EMS methods---------
MS::EMS (unsigned pageCount) {
    REGS regs;

    //first set to "none values"
    handle = 0xffff;
    noPages = 0;

    //if EMS memory not present, give up now
    if (EMSPresent() = = 0)
        return;

    //otherwise allocate that many from EMS handler
    regs.x.bx = pageCount;
    if (EMSCall(0x43, regs) = = 0) //if okay...
        handle = regs.x.dx;         //...save handle
        noPages = pageCount;
    }
}

EMS::~EMS () {
   union REGS regs;

   //give the EMS member back (if we have any)
   if ((regs.x.dx = handle) != 0xffff)
      EMSCall(0x45, regs);
}
```

```c
//map the specified page into the specified frameslot
//   return a 0 if successful
unsigned EMS::map (unsigned page, unsigned frameSlot) {
  union REGS regs;

  regs.x.bx = page;
  regs.h.al = (char)frameSlot;
  if ((regs.x.dx = handle) == 0xffff)
    return 0xffff;
  return EMSCall(0x44, regs);
}

unsigned EMS::status() {
  if (handle == 0xffff)
    return 0xffff;
  return EMSStatus();
}

//--------Implementation of the general functions---------
//EMSPresent - return a 0 if EMS handler is present;
//        otherwise, return the page frame address
void far* EMSPresent(void) {
  REGS regs;
  SREGS sregs;
  const char EMSName[] = "EMMXXXX0";
  struct EMSHandler {
    char padding [0x0a];
    char name [9];
  } far* EMSPtr;

  //get the address of the EMS handler (with 0 offset)
  regs.h.al = EMSInt;
  regs.h.ah = 0x35; //get interrupt address
  int86x (0x21, &regs, &regs, &sregs);
  EMSPtr = (EMSHandler far*)MK_FP(sregs.es, 0);
```

```c
    //now check for the name of the EMS handler
    for (int i = 0; i < 8; i++)
      if (EMSPtr->name[i] != EMSName[i])
        return (void*)0;

    //okay, it's there
    if (EMSCall(0x41, regs))
      return (void*)0;
    EMS::frameSegment = regs.x.bx;
    return EMSSlotAddr(0);  //return pageframe addr
}

//EMSSlotAddr - given a frame slot number,
//              calculate its address.
void far* EMSSlotAddr (unsigned slotnum) {
  const unsigned frameOffsets[] = {0x0000,
                                   0x4000,
                                   0x8000,
                                   0xC000};
    if (slotnum > 3)
  return 0;
    return MK_FP(EMS::frameSegment,
                 frameOffsets[slotnum]);
}

//EMSStatus - return the status of the EMS handler
unsigned EMSStatus (void) {
    REGS regs;

    return EMSCall(0x40, regs);
}

//EMS_pagecount - return unallocated page count
unsigned EMSPageCount (void) {
    REGS regs;
```

```
        if (EMSCall(0x42, regs))
    return 0;
        return regs.x.bx;
}
```

My implementation of EMSArray is as follows:

```
//Implement a EMS-Virtual Array (similar to the
//File Virtual array)
// Each subsequent array occupies its own single
// page frame slot so that up to a maximum of 4
// arrays may be accommodated simultaneously.

#include "EMS.HPP"

struct DataBlock;

class EmsArray {
  private:
    unsigned    emsStatus;
    int         frameSlot;
    char far*   slotAddr;
    unsigned    currentPage;
    EMS*        ems;
    long        noBlocks;
    unsigned    blockSize;
    unsigned    noPages;
    static int  framesInUse[4];

    void operator&(EmsArray& v) {} //grant no access

  public:
    enum emsStatus {okay = 0,
                    noEMSDriver,
                    noFreeSlot,
                    notEnoughEMS,
```

Overloading Operators

```
                        EMSFailure,
                        outOfRange,
                        uninitialized,
                        readFail };

    EmsArray (long no_blocks, unsigned block_size);
    ~EmsArray ();
    DataBlock& operator[] (long blockNum);
    unsigned status();
};
int EmsArray::framesInUse[4] = {0, 0, 0, 0};

EmsArray::EmsArray (long noBlks, unsigned blockSz) {
    //first make sure that EMS is even present
    frameSlot = -1;
    if (!EMSPresent()) {
      emsStatus = noEMSDriver;
      return;
    }

    //find a free slot in the EMS page frame
    for (int i = 0; i < 4; i++)
       if (framesInUse[i] = = 0)
          frameSlot = i;
    if (frameSlot = = -1) {
      emsStatus = noFreeSlot;
      return;
    }
    framesInUse[frameSlot] = 1;
    slotAddr = (char far*)EMSSlotAddr(frameSlot);

    //calculate the number of pages
    blockSize = blockSz;
    noBlocks = noBlks;
    noPages = ((blockSize*noBlocks)+pageSize-1)/pageSize;
    currentPage = -1;
```

```cpp
        //and then go allocate the necessary EMS memory
        if (noPages > EMSPageCount()) {
          emsStatus = notEnoughEMS;
          return;
        }
        ems = new EMS(noPages);
        emsStatus = okay;
        if (ems->status()) {
          emsStatus = uninitialized;
          framesInUse[frameSlot] = 0;
        }
}

EmsArray::~EmsArray() {
    delete ems;//restore the EMS memory
    framesInUse[frameSlot] = 0;//free the page frame slot
    emsStatus = uninitialized; //clear the status
}

//Status - simply return the last status
unsigned EmsArray::status() {
    return emsStatus;
}

//Operator[] - return the (address of the) record
DataBlock& EmsArray::operator[] (long blockNum){
    //calculate the page within EMS
    //and the offset within the frame
    long recordOffset   = blockNum * blockSize;
    unsigned page       = recordOffset / pageSize;
    unsigned pageOffset = recordOffset % pageSize;

    //if this page is not already mapped in, map it
    emsStatus = okay;
    if (page != currentPage)
       if (page > noPages)
```

```
            emsStatus = outOfRange;
        else
            if (ems->map(page, frameSlot))
                emsStatus = readFail;

    //then return the address of the offset
    //within the page frame slot
    if (emsStatus = = okay)
        currentPage = page;
    return (DataBlock&)slotAddr[pageOffset];
}
```

The constructor for EMSArray is invoked with two arguments: the number of blocks and the size of each block. The program first checks for the presence of EMS memory. If EMS is present, it searches for an empty page frame slot to assign to the object. A different page frame slot is assigned to each EMSArray object by using the static array framesInUse. Although this procedure simplifies the code, it limits to four the number of EMSArray objects that can be active at one time.

A more efficient implementation of this class of EMSArray might minimize the number of page mappings by caching pages in all four slots. This can be difficult if several EMSArray objects are active. Our approach reduces the possibility of conflict for assignments such as the following:

```
EMSArray x(1000), y(1000);
x[i] = y[i];
```

Once a slot is found, the constructor attempts to allocate the required number of blocks. If no EMS memory is present, the program will not run. Even if EMS is present, executing the program under the Turbo C++ IDE is problematic. If TC is started with the /e switch, most of EMS memory will already be claimed by TC. Even without the /e switch, Turbo C++ seems to hinder application programs attempting to access EMS memory.

Turbo C++ defaults to using EMS memory even without the /e switch, unless the defaults have been changed from the installation program TCINST. The destructor for EMSArray returns the memory and marks the page frame slot as available again.

The key to `EMSArray` lies in the `operator[]()`. Separate methods are not required to perform the read and write operations as in the `FileArray` case. `operator[]()` can appear on either side of an assignment. The data itself is stored in objects of the class `DataBlock`.

The `operator[]()` accepts the index of the `DataBlock` entry to address and converts the block number into a page number and page offset. This maps the page into its assigned page frame slot and calculates the address of the block within that slot. The operator verifies that the specified block is in directly addressable memory and returns its address.

In use, `EMSArray` appears as follows:

```
#include <stdio.h>
#include <conio.h>

//...insert EMSArray code here...

//DataBlock can be defined by the user to contain
//any type of data desired
struct DataBlock{
   int a;
   operator int() {
      return a;
   }
   DataBlock& operator= (int v) {
      a = v;
      return *this;
   }
};

void main() {
   DataBlock d;
   EmsArray x(30000L, sizeof d);
   if (x.status() != EmsArray::okay) {
      printf("Error allocating x = %d\n", x.status());
   return;
}
```

Overloading Operators

```
EmsArray y(30000L, sizeof d);
if (y.status() != EmsArray::okay) {
  printf("Error allocating y = %d\n", y.status());
  return;
}
unsigned variable;
int index, oldValue, newValue;

for (;;) {
  printf("Enter 0 for x or 1 for y followed "
         "by index and new value:");
  scanf("%d %d %d", &variable, &index, &newValue);

  if (variable > 1) break;

  if (!variable) {
      oldValue = x[index];
      x[index] = newValue;
  } else {
      oldValue = y[index];
      y[index] = newValue;
  }
  printf("%c[%d] was %d, is %d\n",
      (variable ? 'y' : 'x'), index,
      oldValue, newValue);
  }
}
```

This program allocates two `EMSArrays`, each containing 30,000 `DataBlock` entries. The user may specify the object and the index followed by a new value, thus enabling the user to assign values across the range of indices. The user may exceed the upper index limit up to the end of the last EMS page.

Output from this program is particularly interesting when an extra output statement is added to `EMS::map()` to note each time a new EMS page is mapped into one of the page frame slots.

```
Enter 0 for x or 1 for y followed by index and new
value:0 0 0            <- x[0] = 0
EMS::map(0, 3)         <- map block 0 into slot 3
x[0] was 26956, is 0

Enter 0 for x or 1 for y followed by index and new
value:0 0 0            <- x[0] = 0
x[0] was 0, is 0

Enter 0 for x or 1 for y followed by index and new
value:1 0 0            <- y[0] = 0
EMS::map(0, 2)         <- map block 0 into slot 2
y[0] was 2675, is 0

Enter 0 for x or 1 for y followed by index and new
value:0 29999 29999    <- x[29999] = 29999
EMS::map(3, 3)         <- map block 3 into slot 3
x[29999] was 2283, is 29999

Enter 0 for x or 1 for y followed by index and new
value:0 0 0            <- x[0] = 0
EMS::map(0, 3)         <- map block 0 into slot 3
x[0] was 0, is 0

Enter 0 for x or 1 for y followed by index and new
value:2 0 0            <- exit
```

Accessing `x[0]` the first time maps block 0 into slot 3. This is because x, being the first instance of `EMSArray`, is assigned the last page frame slot. The next reference to the `x[0]` causes no remapping since the proper map is already present.

Accessing `y[0]` maps block 0 (a different block 0 than the one used for x) into slot 2, which as the next available slot was assigned to y. The next access of `x[29999]` forces a new block into slot 3, so that the next reference to `x[0]` must remap block 0 again.

By using different page frame slots, the programmer could enter `y[0] = x[10000]`. Though there is nothing in the code to prevent it, the programmer should not enter `x[0] = x[10000]` since the two elements would attempt to map two different blocks into the same page frame slot.

Although the two instances of `EMSArray` above are only 64K in length, the above code has been tested with virtual arrays up to one megabyte long. Since every access involves a call to `operator[]()`, this virtual array is slower than a real array. The speed can be enhanced if consecutive accesses are clustered in the same block, rather than skipping back and forth randomly causing a large number of repagings. For applications in which size is everything and speed is of secondary importance, virtual arrays allow the programmer access to tremendous amounts of data.

Overloading `new` and `delete`

As discussed in Chapter 6, the keyword `new` does little more than invoke an `operator new()` from within the constructor. This operator may be overloaded for any given class. Thus, while `new` is neither a function nor an operator and therefore is not overloadable, the operator upon which it relies is. Programmers may also provide an `operator delete()` member operator, which effectively overloads `delete`.

Like `malloc()`, `operator new()` is a general purpose routine that can allocate blocks of memory from the heap and return them in any order. This ability costs the program both memory and speed. Typically, all objects of the same class are of the same size. A programmer can gain some efficiency by building an `operator new()` to allocate fixed size blocks.

We have seen how constructors can be used to allocate virtual objects that are stored either on the disk or in EMS expanded memory. If the programmer cannot overload `new`, the simulation is incomplete. In this case the programmer could overload `operator new()` to allocate a swap file or a block of expanded memory. Overloading `operator new()` can also be used to generate variable sized structures. Before overloading `operator new()` was allowed, this could only be accomplished by the trick of assigning values to `this`, which is dangerous and illegal in Turbo C++.

Simple `operator new()`

The arguments to `void* operator new(size_t)` are not what one might expect given the flexibility of `new`. The keyword `new` can accept a class name and return a pointer to that class. Operators must have fixed arguments. The `size_t` argument specifies the number of bytes to allocate. The return `void*` is the address of the memory block allocated.

An `operator new()` that only allocates blocks of a single class may ignore the `size_t` argument. However, the `new` and `delete` operators follow the normal rules of inheritance. A single `operator new()` might be called upon to allocate objects for different subclasses, which are normally larger.

By the same token, `void delete(void*, size_t)` receives a pointer to the block to return and an indication of its size. The first argument is of type `void*` since `operator delete()` cannot ascertain the type. It may be passed the address of the class for which it is defined or of any subclass of that class. The `size_t` argument is necessary (but optional) here to tell the program the exact size of block to return.

Both `operator new()` and `operator delete()` are static, whether declared so or not, since they have no `this` object.

In practice, overloading `new` and `delete` is done as follows:

```
#include <iostream.h>
#include <string.h>

struct Block {
    char name[20];
} block;

class Test {
  private:
    char name[20];
  public:
    Test(char* n) {
      cout << "Constructing " << n << endl;
      strncpy(name, n, sizeof name);
      name[sizeof name] = '\0';
```

Overloading Operators

```
    }
    ~Test() {
      cout << "Destructing " << name << endl;
    }
    void* operator new(size_t sz) {
      cout << "New, size = " << sz << endl;
      return (void*)&block;
    }
    void operator delete(void* ptr, size_t s) {
      Block* bPtr = (Block*)ptr;
      cout << "Deleting " << bPtr->name
           << ", size = " << s << endl;
    };
};

void main() {
    cout << "\nTest* y = new Test(Heap Variable);"
         << endl;
    Test* y = new Test("New Variable");

    cout << "\ndelete y;" << endl;
    delete y;
}
```

This sample program generates the following output.

```
Test* y = new Test(Heap Variable);
New, size = 20
Constructing New Variable

delete y;
Destructing New Variable
Deleting New Variable, size = 20
```

Here, `operator new()` returns the address of a single block of the proper size. A more sophisticated `operator new()` might allocate from an array or a linked list of blocks. The matching `operator delete()` must mark or otherwise return the blocks for reuse.

If the request for memory cannot be granted, `operator new()` must return a 0. Seeing a null, the constructor will terminate without taking action. The application program can detect this same null, realize that the object has not been allocated, and take whatever action is necessary. Returning an invalid address will lead to a difficult to find crash.

When an `operator new()` and/or `operator delete()` has been defined for a class, the default functions can still be accessed by invoking the keywords as `::new` and `::delete`. This is demonstrated in the following program example.

```
#include <iostream>

void* global = (void*)x1234;      //marker value
struct Class {
   Class() {
      cout << "Entering default constructor" << endl;
   }

   void* operator new(size_t sz {
      cout << "Invoked Class new()" << endl;
      return global;
   }

   void operator delete(void *ptr) {
      cout << "Invoked Class delete()" << endl;
   }
};

void main() {
   Class* ptr;

   cout << "Use defined new and delete" << endl;
   ptr = new Class;                 //Note A
   cout << "ptr = " << (void*)ptr << endl;
```

Overloading Operators

```
    delete(ptr);

    cout << "\nRevert to default new and delete: << endl;
    ptr = ::new Class;                    //Note B
    cout << "ptr = " << (void*)ptr << endl;
    ::delete(ptr);
}
```

The `operator new()` and `operator delete()` for class `Class` do nothing more than output a message. In addition, the `operator new()` returns a marker value to the caller:

```
Use defined new and delete
Invoked Class new()
Entering default constructor
ptr = 0x1234
Invoked Class delete()

Revert to default new and delete
Entering default constructor
ptr = 0x1f0a0004
```

The line marked `Note A` invokes the default constructor to create an object of type `Class`. This constructor, in turn, calls the `operator new()` defined for `Class`. The `delete` that follows invokes `Class::operator delete()` as well.

The line marked `Note B` invokes the default constructor, which then calls the default `::operator new()`. The subsequent `::delete` calls the default `::operator delete()`.

Compound `operator new()`

A programmer might wish to invoke a different `new` on separate objects of the same type. To have more than one `new`, `operator new()` may be provided with any number of arguments after the initial `size_t` argument.

The arguments are passed to new by including a parenthetical pair immediately after the new keyword.

```
//format of operator new()
void* operator new(size_t s, int i, char*);

//format of corresponding new
char buffer[80];
Test* tPtr = new (1, buffer) Test("Test Pointer");
```

Thus, the size of the object being allocated is tacked onto the beginning of the argument string immediately following new. The resulting arguments are used to find a matching operator new(). Any type of arguments can be passed to new, but only a few types truly make sense.

A programmer might want to have different heap areas from which to allocate blocks. Assume, for example, that Test had a subclass FinalTest that was larger than Test. The programmer might allocate objects of type Test from one area and objects of type FinalTest from another. Differentiating by the different size of the objects would not be very portable.

Although there are different types of operator new(), there is only one type of operator delete(). When the object is allocated, the program knows everything. Information of all sorts can be passed in arguments to new. When the object is deallocated, however, little beyond the object's address is known. The information as to how the block was allocated is stored within the block itself.

The following program shows the previous Test class expanded to support several different types of new. A storageType member has been added to the structure to tell delete how to return the memory allocated by the different new types.

```
#include <iostream.h>
#include <string.h>

struct Block {
    int storageType;
    char name[20];
```

Overloading Operators

```
} block;

class Test {
  private:
    int storageType;
    char name[20];
  public:
    Test(char* n) {
      cout << "Constructing " << n << endl;
      strncpy(name, n, sizeof name);
      name[sizeof name] = '\0';
    }
    ~Test() {
      cout << "Destructing " << name << endl;
    }
    void* operator new(size_t sz) {
      cout << "New, size = " << sz << endl;
      block.storageType = 0;
      return (void*)&block;
    }
    void* operator new(size_t sz, Block* ptr) {
      cout << "New(Block* ptr), size = "
        << sz << endl;
      ptr->storageType = 1;
      return (void*)ptr;
    }
    void* operator new(size_t sz, Block* ptr, int sT) {
      cout << "New(Block* ptr), size = "
        << sz << endl;
      ptr->storageType = sT;
        return (void*)ptr;
    }
    void operator delete(void* ptr, size_t s) {
      Block* bPtr = (Block*)ptr;
      cout << "Deleting " << bPtr->name
        << "; type = " << bPtr->storageType
```

```cpp
              << ", size = " << s << endl;
    };
};

struct Final : public Test {
    int moreData;
    Final(char* n) : Test(n) {}
};

void main() {
    cout << "\nTest* x = new Test(Test);"
         << endl;
    Test* x = new Test("Test");

    cout << "\ndelete x;" << endl;
    delete x;

    cout << "\nTest* y = new(&Block) Test(Type 1 Test)"
         << endl;
    Block b1;
    Test* y = new(&b1) Test("Type 1 Test");

    cout << "\ndelete y;" << endl;
    delete y;

    cout <<
      "\nFinal* z=new(&Block, 2) Final(Type 2 Final)"
         << endl;
    Block b2;
    Final* z = new(&b2, 2) Final("Type 2 Final");

    cout << "\ndelete z;" << endl;
    delete z;
}
```

Executing this program generates the following output.

```
Test* x = new Test(Test);
New, size = 22
Constructing Test

delete x;
Destructing Test
Deleting Test; type = 0, size = 22

Test* y = new(&Block) Test(Type 1 Test)
New(Block* ptr), size = 22
Constructing Type 1 Test

delete y;
Destructing Type 1 Test
Deleting Type 1 Test; type = 1, size = 22

Final* z=new(&Block, 2) Final(Type 2 Final)
New(Block* ptr), size = 24
Constructing Type 2 Final

delete z;
Destructing Type 2 Final
Deleting Type 2 Final; type = 2, size = 24
```

Variable Sized Structures

One of the most common uses for overloading operator new() is the creation of variable sized objects. Consider the following program.

```
#include <stdlib.h>

struct S {
    int size;
    int data[1];
```

```
        void* operator new(size_t s, int actualSize) {
            S* sPtr = (S*)malloc(actualSize + sizeof(S));
            if (sPtr)
                sPtr->size = actualSize;
            return (void*)sPtr;
        }
    };

    void main() {
        S* sPtr = new (50 * sizeof(int)) S;

        for (int i = 0; i < 50; i++)
            sPtr->data[i] = i;

        delete sPtr;
    }
```

Class S defines two fields. The size field is followed by an array ostensibly with only one element. The purpose is to define a class whose size is not known until execution. We need to tell new how large to make the structure as an argument. The data array is meant to be of variable size. Declaring the array positions it as a place holder.

Also defined is an operator new(size_t, int) to allocate space for objects of class S. The second argument, actualSize, is the actual size to create the object. The operator allocates the requested memory from the heap using malloc(). The size of the object is stored in the size field for use by subsequent routines. Since operator new() defaults to static, size cannot be accessed directly. Therefore, operator new() must save the value returned from malloc() in a local pointer for use in accessing class members.

Since operator new() allocates memory using malloc(), a new operator delete() is not needed because the default returns heap memory by calling free(). The need to allocate structures of different lengths is not uncommon. This procedure is especially useful in creating a base class for other classes of variable length. The earlier method of assigning to the `this` object is dangerous and does not work in Turbo C++. The technique described in this chapter is straightforward and safe.

Conclusion

When used improperly, the overloading of operators for new classes can lead to code that is very difficult to read. There is a national contest held for C programmers called the National Obfuscated C Code contest. Awards are given every year for the the most difficult to read programs (most of the programs are intended to be difficult to read, although there is a special category for unintentionally complex programs). I do not believe that an Obfuscated C++ Code contest will ever become popular, since C++ provides too many ways to make a program completely unreadable.

By the same token, when properly written, overloaded operators can greatly enhance both the readability of programs and the reusability of existing algorithms.

Chapter 8

Class Inheritance

Class Inheritance

C++ would be severely limited if it could not pass all of the user-defined features for a class on to more detailed descendant classes. In this chapter we will examine the aspects of C++ that allow inheritance of features by one class from another.

The sample classes in this chapter are quite small and should be considered merely representative. Fully developed classes in real-world applications may contain several kilobytes of code and extend over many pages of listings. Presenting real-world classes here would needlessly add pages of coding.

Simple Inheritance

One class may inherit the members of another class. The class that donates its members is known as the **base class**. The class that receives the donation is called the **derived class**. The name of the base class is listed immediately after the name of the derived class and before the open brace as in the following declaration of Level1.

```
class Level0 {
   private:
      int a;
   protected:
      int b;
   public:
      int c;
      void f0();
};

class Level1 : public Level0 {
   private:
      int d;
   protected:
      int e;
   public:
      int f;
```

```
        void f1();
};
```

In this case, the derived class `Level1` inherits the members of the base class `Level0`. The new class contains all of the members of the older class plus any additional members it defines.

Access to Inherited Members

A private member is only accessible to members and friends of its class, whereas a public member is accessible to all. Private members of a base class are not accessible to derived classes. If this were not so, programmers could access private members of a class by implementing functions as member functions of a new derived class.

A programmer may want to allow derived classes to access certain members. To avoid having to declare these members public, C++ provides a third category of accessibility called **protected**. Protected members are not accessible to the general public, but they are accessible to members of derived classes.

A class may be publicly or privately inherited. The different types of inheritance affect only the default accessibility of the base class members in the derived class. The rules are shown in Table 8–1.

Table 8–1 Inheritance of Accessibility in C++

Inheritance Accessibility	Accessibility In Base Class	Accessibility In Derived Class
public	public	public
	protected	protected
	private	private
private	public	private
	protected	private
	private	private

Class Inheritance

The default, however, is private. Good programming style dictates that inheritance accessibility always be specified. A publicly inherited member retains the same accessibility that it had in its base class. In the following code segment, only the specified accesses are legal.

```
class Level1a : public Level0 {
   private:
      int d;
   protected:
      int e;
   public:
      int f;
      void f1();
};

//General function - has access only to public members
void fn() {
     Level0 l0;
     Level1a  l1;

     l0.c = 1;   //public member
     l0.f0();

     l1.c = 1;   //public members of Level0 are
                 //public in Level1a
     l1.f = 2;
     l1.f0();
     l1.f1();
}

//Member functions
void Level0::f0() {
     a = 1;     //has access to all of Level0
     b = 2;
     c = 3;
}
```

```
void Level1a::f1() {
    b = 1;      //does not have access to a
    c = 2;

    d = 3;      //has access to all of Level1a
    e = 4;
    f = 5;
    f0();
}
```

In the following private derivations, `l1.c` and `l1.f0()` are no longer accessible to the general function `fn()`, since they are now private, even though `l0.c` and `l0.f0()` remain accessible. The accessibility of the members to the member functions `f0()` and `f1()` remains the same.

```
class Level1b : private Level0 {
  private:
    int d;
  protected:
    int e;
  public:
    int f;
    void f1();
};

class Level1c : Level0 { //identical to Level1b
  private:
    int d;
  protected:
    int e;
  public:
    int f;
    void f1();
};

//General function
```

Class Inheritance

```
void fn() {
    Level0 l0;
    Level1b l1;

    l0.c = 1;
    l0.f0();

    l1.f = 1;          //no longer has access to l1.c or l1.f0()
    l1.f1();
}
```

A derived class can change the accessibility of base class members individually. However, a derived class cannot grant itself access to a member that it would not have if the class had been publicly derived.

```
class Level1d : private Level0 {
  public:
    Level0::c;      //specifically declare c public
    int f;
    int f1();
};

                    //General function
void fn() {
    Level0 l0;
    Level1d l1;

    l0.c = 1;
    l0.f0();

    l1.c = 1;       //c is now accessible, though f0
                    //still is not
    l1.f = 2;
    l1.f1();
}
```

By declaring `Level1d` privately derived, the default changes the accessibility of c from public to private. By specifically declaring c public, however, the default can be overridden, rendering `l1.c` accessible to the general function `fn()`. `Level1d` cannot grant itself access to a, which is already private in the base class.

Constructors for Derived Classes

Constructors for base classes are invoked in the same manner as the constructors for contained classes. The call appears immediately after the name of the derived class constructor and before the open brace.

```
class Level0 {
   private:
      int a;
   protected:
      int b;
   public:
      int c;
      void f0();

      Level0(int v0) {
         a = b = c = v0;
      }
};

class Level1 : public Level0 {
   private:
      int d;
   protected:
      int e;
   public:
      int f;
      void f1();

      Level1(int v0, int v1) : Level0(v0) {
```

```
        d = e = f = v1;
    }
};

//General function
void fn() {
    Level0 l0(1);
    Level1 l1(1, 2);
}
```

A constructor for a derived class may initialize the protected and public members of a base class without calling the constructor. C++ calls the default base class constructor if the constructor for the derived class does not do so.

In early versions of C++, which only supported single inheritance, the name of the base class did not appear in the constructor call. Version 2.0 supports this anachronism, although it is considered bad style and generates a warning under Turbo C++. The following generates the same result as the preceding constructor definition.

```
Level1(int v0, int v1) : (v0) { //defaults to Level0(v0)
    d = e = f = v1;
}
```

Constructors for contained objects may be invoked on the same line as the constructor for the base class. The following constructor for Level1 is equivalent to the previous two.

```
Level1(int v0, int v1) : Level0(v0),d(v1),e(v1),f(v1) {}
```

Derived Versus Containing Classes

Let us compare derived classes with a class Level1 that contains, rather than inherits, an object of class Level0. I will call these **containing classes**.

```
class Level1 {
    public:
        Level0 l0;

    private:
        int d;
    protected:
        int e;
    public:
        int f;
        void f1();
};

//Non-privileged functions
void fn() {
    Level1 l1;

    l1.l0.c = 1;
    l1.f = 2;
    l1.l0.f0();
    l1.f1();
}

//Member function
void Level1::f1() {
    l0.c = 1;
    d = 2;
    e = 3;
    f = 4;
    l0.f0();
}
```

If we were to examine memory, the containing class Level1 would appear identical to the derived class Level1. The first few words of both would be occupied by the Level0 members of a, b, and c. The accessibility of the class members is similar, as well. Level0::a is not accessible to the members of `Level1` while `Level0::c` is. The protected member, `Level0::b`, is no longer accessible to the containing class.

The primary difference between a derived class and a containing class is the manner in which inherited elements are accessed. Every time an element of `Level0` is accessed, it is specifically noted, as in `l0.c`, `l0.f0()`, etc. The derived class references these same members, as if they were its own members, which they are.

A derived class adopts the members of its base class. A container class merely provides members of the other class a place to stay. Every access to members of the containing class reminds the programmer that it is separate from the derived class.

Subclasses

All members of a base class are retained with the same accessibility in a publicly derived class. To highlight this relationship, a publicly derived class is also known as a **subclass**, its base class is sometimes referred to as a **superclass**.

In the following example, an object of class `SubClass` can take the place of an object of class `Base` and a `SubClass*` can be provided where a `Base*` is required. An object of class `SubClass` is also an object of class `Base`.

```
#include <iostream.h>
#include <string.h>

struct Base {
    char name[20];

    Base(char* n) {
      strncpy(name, n, 20);
      name[19] = '\0'; //make sure string terminated
    }
    void print() {
      cout << "This is the base class member="
          << name
```

```
            << endl;
    }
};

struct SubClass : public Base {
    SubClass(char* n) : Base(n) {}
};

void fn(Base& aBaseRef) {
  cout << "From within fn():";
  aBaseRef.print();
}

void main() {
  SubClass aSubClassObj("aSubClassObj");

  Base& aBaseRef = aSubClassObj;
  aBaseRef.print();         //case #1

  Base* aBasePtr = &aSubClassObj;
  aBasePtr->print();        //case #2
  fn(aSubClassObj);         //case #3
}
```

The reverse is not true, however. A base class is not a subclass. Thus, the following addition to the preceeding program is not legal and would generate a compiler error.

```
Base aBaseObj("aBaseObj");
SubClass* aSubClassPtr = &aBaseObj;
```

A subclass contains every member of a superclass, but it may contain members that the superclass does not. A function that expects to access one of the extra members would fail if it were passed a pointer to the base class.

Class Inheritance

A pointer to a base class can be cast into a pointer to a subclass. In that case the programmer affirms that the pointer references a subclass object. The programmer may also provide a coercion path from the base object to a pointer to the subclass as in the following:

```
struct SubClass;
struct Base {
    operator SubClass*() {
      return (SubClass*)this;
    }
    //remainder of base class definition
```

This is not a very safe practice because C++ may make the conversion without your knowing. Subsequent attempts to access a member unique to `SubClass` will prove disastrous. The danger can be mitigated by the addition of a signature field to accurately identify the type of object.

```
struct SubClass;
struct Base {
    int signature;
    char name[20];

    Base(char* n) {
      signature = 1;
      strncpy(name, n, 20);
      name[19] = '\0';
    }
    operator SubClass*() {
      if (signature != 2)
        abort();
      return (SubClass*)this;
    }
    void print() {
      cout << "This is the base class member="
           << name
           << endl;
```

```
        }
};

struct SubClass : public Base {
    SubClass(char* n) : Base(n) { signature = 2; }
};
```

The signature field resembles the field used to determine the type of `operator delete()` to invoke.

A privately derived class is not a subclass of the base class since not all of the members of the base class are accessible from the derived object. A function expecting to access a public member may, in fact, not have access to the same member in the derived class. Therefore, a privately derived class cannot replace a base class object.

Linked List Examples

The singly linked list is second only to the array in popularity as a data structure. Not surprisingly, the linked list class has become a popular base class on which to build other classes. Let us examine an implementation of a circular `LinkedList` class.

Implementation of any base class consists of two parts: the .HPP include file and the .CPP source code file. The include file portion defines the class structure along with the names and arguments of any members in the class. The include file will be incorporated by any modules that reference the class members.

The include file for `LinkedList`, labeled SLIST.HPP, follows:

```
#ifndef SLIST_HPP
#define SLIST_HPP

//The single linked list class with associated methods
class LinkedList {
  private:
        LinkedList* nextPtr;     //link to next element
  public:
        LinkedList();
     LinkedList*   next();
```

```
    LinkedList*   previous();
    int           addAfter(LinkedList* prevMemberPtr);
    int           remove();
    int           removeNext();
};
#endif
```

The `#if/#endif` combination avoids compiler errors in the event that the include file is included twice in the same module. The only data member, `nextPtr`, points to the next object in the linked list.

The member functions of `LinkedList` are reasonably straightforward. The `next()` function returns the address of the next member of the list. `previous()` returns the address of the previous member. Since a singly linked list has no backward pointer, the `previous()` function must travel around the circular list to reach its predecessor. The remaining three methods add and remove entries from the list.

The implementation of these member functions is included in the module SLIST.CPP that follows:

```
#include "slist.hpp"

//------Implement the SLIST methods----------
LinkedList::LinkedList() {
    nextPtr = this;
}

LinkedList* LinkedList::next() {
    return nextPtr;
}

LinkedList* LinkedList::previous() {
    LinkedList* memberPtr;

    memberPtr = nextPtr;
    while (memberPtr->nextPtr != this)
      memberPtr = memberPtr->nextPtr;
```

```
        return memberPtr;
}

int LinkedList::addAfter(LinkedList* prevMemberPtr) {
    nextPtr              = prevMemberPtr->nextPtr;
    prevMemberPtr->nextPtr = this;
    return 0;
}

int LinkedList::remove() {
    LinkedList* prevMemberPtr;

    prevMemberPtr = previous();
    return prevMemberPtr->removeNext();
}

int LinkedList::removeNext() {
    LinkedList* nextMemberPtr = nextPtr;
    nextPtr = nextMemberPtr->nextPtr;
    nextMemberPtr->nextPtr = 0;
    return 0;
}
```

Once compiled, `SLIST.OBJ` must be linked with any program that uses the `LinkedList` class. This is normally done by building a project file as described in the Turbo C++ *User's Guide*.

The following program implements a student record class for calculating the GPA and standing of university students.

```
#include <iostream.h>
#include <iomanip.h>
#include <string.h>
#include "slist.hpp"

//-------General purpose field store functions---
inline void storeCharField(char* target, char* source,
```

Class Inheritance

```
            int length) {
    strncpy(target, source, length);
    target[length-1] = '\0';
}

//-------Student class--------------------------
LinkedList keystone;
class Student : public LinkedList {
  private:
    float GPA;
    int totalHours;
    int creditHours;
    int hoursRequired;

  public:
    char lastName[40];
    char firstName[40];
    char middleI[2];
    long ssNumber;

  public:
    Student() : LinkedList() {
       lastName[0] = firstName[0] = middleI[0] = '\0';
    }

    Student(char* ln, char* fn,
        char mi, int hoursReq) {
      storeCharField(lastName, ln, 40);
      storeCharField(middleI, &mi, 2);
      storeCharField(firstName, fn, 40);
      hoursRequired = hoursReq;
      GPA = 0;
      creditHours = totalHours = 0;

      addAfter(&keystone);
    }
```

```cpp
    static Student* studentStart() {
      return (Student*)&keystone;
    }

    float studentGPA() {
      return GPA;
    }
    void studentNewGPA(float grade, int hours) {
      if (grade > 4.0 || grade < 0.0)
         return;

      GPA = (GPA * totalHours + grade * hours) /
            (totalHours + hours);
      totalHours += hours;
      if (grade > 1.0)
        creditHours += hours;
    }

    void studentList() {
      cout << firstName << " " << lastName;
    }
    char* studentPassing() {
      return (studentGPA() > 1.5) ?
          "Passing" : "Failing";
    }
};

//-------General purpose status routine----------
void displayStudentList() {
    Student* studentPtr = Student::studentStart();

    for(;;) {
      studentPtr = (Student*)studentPtr->next();
      if (studentPtr == Student::studentStart())
        break;
      cout << studentPtr->studentPassing()
```

```
            << " " << setprecision(2)
            << studentPtr->studentGPA()
            << " ";
        studentPtr->studentList();
        cout << endl;
    }
}
```

The `keystone` entry declared immediately before `Student` serves as the head record for the circular list—both initiating and terminating the list. The `keystone` is the only member that is not a `Student` and that cannot be removed from the list. The constructor for `Student` links all subsequent records of class `Student` to the list starting at `keystone`.

The access method `studentStart()` returns the first student in the list. This method is declared statically so that no object is needed to call it. The access method `studentGPA()` returns the GPA of the student. The method `studentList()` prints the name of the student saved when the object was created.

The `studentNewGPA()` function adjusts the student's current GPA, weighted by the total number of class hours completed, with the grades made in the most recent classes, weighted by the class hours. The method `studentPassing()` compares the student's GPA with what is considered passing and returns a "Pass" or "Fail".

The non-member display function links through and displays each entry in the linked list using the `studentList()` method. Display begins at the next record after the keystone record, which is returned by `studentStart()`, and continues until the keystone record is encountered again.

An example of output from `displayStudentList()` follows.

```
Failing 1.33 Spencer Dissinger
Passing 1.85 Jeff Larson
Passing 2.85 Stephen Davis
```

The program that reads in the student records is not included here for brevity.

Polymorphism

A subclass may contain a method of the same name as the base class. Returning to our previous example, `SubClass` may contain its own print method.

```
struct SubClass : public Base {
    SubClass(char* n) : Base(n) {}

    void print() {
      cout << "This is the subclass member="
           << name
           << endl;
    }
};

void main() {
    Base aBaseObject;
    SubClass aSubClassObject;
}
```

Reference to `print()` defaults to the lowest level method that applies. Thus, `aBaseObject.print()` refers to `Base::print()`, whereas `aSubClassObject.print()` refers to `SubClass::print()`. A program may call a different method by specifying the fully qualified name, e.g., `aSubClassObject.Base::print()`. A subclass method may refer to a base class method in the same way. However, a program could not refer to `aBaseObject.SubClass::print()` since `SubClass::print()` is not a method of `Base`.

If a subclass overlays a base class method with a new definition, a problem may arise. Consider what defining this new `print()` method does to our old function `fn()`.

```
void fn(Base& aBaseRef) {
  cout << "From within fn():";
```

```
    aBaseRef.print();
}
```

The object `aBaseRef` is specifically declared as being of class `Base`. The reference to `aBaseRef.print()` always refers to the method `Base::print()`, but a subclass object can take the place of a base class object. Thus, `fn()` could be called as either `fn(aSubClassObject)` or `fn(aBaseClassObject)`. The call to `print()`, then, should invoke the method `SubClass::print()`.

Using a single call to refer to different methods depending upon the type of the object passed, not the declared type, is called **polymorphism**. To support polymorphism, a language must decide at execution which member function to invoke by examining the type of object in a process known as **late-binding**. The normal practice of determining the method to call during compilation is called **early-binding**.

Pure object-oriented languages are completely polymorphic. That is, all functions are bound late. As a hybrid language, however, C++ is only partially so. Late-binding slows down execution performance. Whenever a polymorphic function is called, the program must perform extra memory references. The designers of C++ did not want C++ programs to go through this process on every function call when in most cases there is no ambiguity. C++ leaves the use of late-binding up to the programmer. The default is early-binding, even if an ambiguity exists.

Therefore, the way that the class definitions are written, `fn()` always calls `Base::print()`. No late-binding is performed. Adding the keyword `virtual` to the method definition makes it polymorphic.

```
virtual void print() {
    cout << "This is the base class member="
        << name
        << endl;
}
```

Calls to `virtual print()` are bound late.

A virtual function may not be static. Without an object, Turbo C++ could not perform late-binding.

Declaring a method virtual automatically makes methods of the same name in subclasses virtual.

If the method of the same name in the subclass accepts different arguments, there is no polymorphism. Consider the following:

```
#include <iostream.h>

struct Base {
    virtual void print() {
      cout << "This is a base class object" << endl;
    }
};

struct SubClass : public Base {
    virtual void print(char* c) {
      cout << "This is subclass object " << c << endl;
    }
};
void fn(Base& obj) {
    obj.print();
    obj.print("Relative object");   //compile error #1
}

void main() {
    SubClass aSubClass;

    aSubClass.print();              //compile error #2
    aSubClass.print("aSubClass");

    fn(aSubClass);
}
```

Both `Base` and `SubClass` contain a method `print()`; however, the two functions do not have the same arguments. C++ will not allow what it is sure is a call to `Base::print()` to be made with the wrong argument types, so it generates a compile error. A similar situation occurs later with the apparent call to `SubClass::print()`.

The `isA()` Method

If the rules for processing a subclass object differ from those for a base class object, the preferred technique is to overload the base class method with a new definition. This may be inconvenient, especially when the function has been implemented as a non-member. In such cases, the function needs to know exactly what type of object it is dealing with.

To solve this problem, the programmer may define an indentification method commonly called `isA()`. This virtual method returns a constant unique to each subclass type. Consider the following non-member version of `print()`.

```cpp
#include <iostream/h>

struct Base {
  enum ClassType {BASE, SUBCLASS};
  virtual ClassType isA() { return BASE; }
};
struct SubClass : public Base {
  virtual ClassType isA() { return BASE; }
};

void print (Base& obj) {
   if (obj.isA() == Base::BASE)
       cout << "This is a base class object\n";
   else
     if (obj.isA() == Base::SUBCLASS)
         cout << "This is a subclass object\n";
     else
         cout << "This is an unknown object type\n";
}

void fn(Base& obj) {
```

```
    print (obj) {
}
void main () {
  Base       aBaseClass;
  SubClass aSubClass;

  fn(aBaseClass);
  fn(aSubClass);
}
```

Executing this program generates the following results.

```
This is a base class object
This is a subclass object
```

Another Linked List Example

The linked list `Student` example discussed earlier has a serious limitation. There are several different types of students. Some of these different student types have similar data (e.g., undergraduate and graduate), but some student types are quite different (e.g., undergraduate and student faculty).

Consider the following definitions of `Graduate` and `Faculty-Student` based upon the `Student` class derived earlier.

```
#include <iostream.h>
#include <iomanip.h>
#include <string.h>
#include "slist.hpp"

//-------General purpose field store functions---
inline void storeCharField(char* target, char* source,
                           int length) {
    strncpy(target, source, length);
    target[length-1] = '\0';
}
```

Class Inheritance

```cpp
//-------General student class-------------------
LinkedList keystone;
class Student : public LinkedList {
  private:
    float GPA;
    int totalHours;
    int creditHours;
    int hoursRequired;

  public:
    char lastName[40];
    char firstName[40];
    char middleI[2];
    long ssNumber;

  public:
    Student() : LinkedList() {
       lastName[0] = firstName[0] = middleI[0] = '\0';
    }

    Student(char* ln, char* fn,
            char mi, int hoursReq) {
      storeCharField(lastName, ln, 40);
      storeCharField(middleI, &mi, 2);
      storeCharField(firstName, fn, 40);
      hoursRequired = hoursReq;
      GPA = 0;
      creditHours = totalHours = 0;

      addAfter(&keystone);
    }

    static Student* studentStart() {
      return (Student*)&keystone;
    }
```

```
    float studentGPA() {
      return GPA;
    }
    void studentNewGPA(float grade, int hours) {
      if (grade > 4.0 || grade < 0.0)
        return;

      GPA = (GPA * totalHours + grade * hours) /
            (totalHours + hours);
      totalHours += hours;
      if (grade > 1.0)
        creditHours += hours;
    }

    virtual void studentList() {
      cout << firstName << " " << lastName;
    }
    virtual char* studentPassing() {
      return (studentGPA() > 1.5) ?"Passing" :
                                   "Failing";
    }
};

//-------Graduate students----------------------
class Graduate : public Student {
  private:
    char prevDegree[4];

  public:
    Graduate (char* ln, char* fn,
      char mi, int hoursReq, char* pd) :
      Student (ln, fn, mi, hoursReq) {
      storeCharField(prevDegree, pd, 4);
    }
    virtual void studentList() {
      cout << firstName << " " << lastName
```

```cpp
              << ", " << prevDegree;
        }
        virtual char* studentPassing() {
          return (studentGPA() > 3.0) ? "Passing" :
                                        "Failing";
        }
};
//-------Faculty students---------------------
class FacultyStudent : public Student {
    private:
        char degree[4];
        char title[20];

    public:
        FacultyStudent (char* ln, char* fn, char mi,
          int hoursReq, char* pd, char* t) :
          Student (ln, fn, mi, hoursReq) {
          storeCharField(degree, pd, 4);
          storeCharField(title, t, 20);
        }
        virtual void studentList() {
          cout << title << " "
               << firstName << " " << lastName
               << ", " << degree;
        }
        virtual char* studentPassing() {
          return (studentGPA() > 2.5) ?"Passing" :
                                        "Not passing";
        }
};

//-------General purpose status routine----------
void displayStudentList() {
    Student* studentPtr = Student::studentStart();

    for(;;) {
```

```
        studentPtr = (Student*)studentPtr->next();
        if (studentPtr = = Student::studentStart())
          break;
        cout<< studentPtr->studentPassing()//virtual call
            << " " << setprecision(2)
            << studentPtr->studentGPA()
            << " ";
        studentPtr->studentList();           //virtual call
        cout << endl;
    }
}
```

The `Student` class definition is basically unchanged except for declaring the `studentList()` and `studentPassing()` methods to be virtual. The subclasses `Graduate` and `FacultyStudent` were added because the titles for Undergraduate, Graduate, and Faculty and the rules for passing differ among the three. The constructors for `Graduate` and `FacultyStudent` are added to include both a previous degree and title. Undergraduates are assumed to have no previous degree and both undergraduate and graduate students are assumed to have no titles. Since all of these groups invoke the constructor for `Student`, they are added to the same linked list of students.

The `displayStudentList()` function remains unchanged. However, the calls to `studentPassing()` and `studentList()` are now bound late as a result of being declared virtual. As the function processes the heterogenous linked list of students, it calls the member function that matches the type of object being processed. Output from this function, showing the three display types, is as follows:

```
Passing 3.38 Professor Kinsey Davis, PhD
Passing 3.27 Jenny Davis, MA
Passing 2.92 Stephen Davis
```

Abstract Classes

An **abstract class** is a class that contains at least one **pure virtual member function**. A pure virtual member function is a virtual function to which a **pure specifier** has been added, and is a member function for which the programmer does not intend to provide an implementation. It is declared as follows:

```
class Employee {
   private:
      char name[40];
   public:
      Employee(char* n);
      virtual void* promote() = 0; //a pure virtual
                                   //function
};
```

An abstract class may not be instantiated. Thus, the following generates a compile error.

```
Employee s("My Name");
```

However, a program may declare a pointer to an abstract class, so the following is legal.

```
Employee* sPtr;
```

Members of an abstract class can be inherited. Once all of the pure virtual methods of a class have been overlayed by non-pure virtual methods, the class is no longer abstract. In the following, the class Secretary may be instantiated because the promote() function has been overlayed with a new meaning.

```
class Secretary : public Employee {
   private:
      int moreData;
```

```
    public:
       Secretary(char* n) : Employee(n) {}
       virtual void* promote();
};
Secretary sec("Another Name");
```

The address of the `Secretary` object may be passed to a function expecting an `Employee`.

```
void fn(Employee*);
Secretary sec("Another Name");
```

```
fn(&sec);
```

Abstract classes are useful in establishing class hierarchies. For example, it may be known that all employees should belong to a subclass of `Employee`. Since different employees have different promotion cycles, each subclass should have its own `promote()` method. By declaring `promote()` pure virtual, the designer of the `Employee` class is requiring the developer of a subclass to write a `promote()` method before implementing any derived class of `Employee`.

Multiple Inheritance

In Turbo C++, a class may inherit from more than one class. Thus, unless we are prepared to make `Faculty` a subclass of `Student` or vice versa, then `FacultyStudent` should be able to inherit from two base classes simultaneously.

Using Multiple Inheritance

The format for deriving a class from multiple base classes is similar to deriving from a single base class.

```
class SubClass : public Base1, private Base2 {
    //remainder of class definition
}
```

Any number of base classes can be listed, each separated by a comma. No base class can be directly inherited more than once. Each base class can be inherited publicly or privately; the default is private.

When classes could only inherit a single class, the order of execution of constructors was not rigidly specified. With the advent of multiple inheritance, the order of construction became very important. The order is as follows:

1. the constructors for any virtual base class; if more than one is present, they are constructed in the order in which they are inherited (virtual classes are discussed in the next section)
2. the constructors for non-virtual base classes in the order in which they are inherited
3. the constructors for any member classes

Consider the following:

```
#include <iostream.h>

struct Base1 {
    Base1() { cout << "Constructing Base1" << endl; }
};
struct Base2 {
    Base2() { cout << "Constructing Base2" << endl; }
};
struct Base3 {
    Base3() { cout << "Constructing Base3" << endl; }
};
struct Base4 {
    Base4() { cout << "Constructing Base4" << endl; }
};

struct Derived : private Base1,
```

```
                private Base2,
                private Base3 {
    Base4 anObject;
    Derived() {}
};
void main() {
    Derived anObject;
}
```

Executing this program generates the following results.

```
Constructing Base1
Constructing Base2
Constructing Base3
Constructing Base4
```

Adding specific calls with a different order to the constructor for `Derived` and reexecuting the program does not change the output.

```
struct Derived :  private Base1,
                  private Base2,
                  private Base3 {
    Base4 anObject;
    Derived() : anObject(), Base3(), Base2(), Base1() {}
};
```

Changing the order in which the classes are inherited does alter the output. Declaring `Derived` as follows:

```
struct Derived :  private Base3,
                  private Base2,
                  private Base1 {
    Base4 anObject;
    Derived() : anObject(), Base1(), Base2(), Base3() {}
};
```

generates the following output.

```
Constructing Base3
Constructing Base2
Constructing Base1
Constructing Base4
```

The destructors are invoked in the inverse order of the constructors.

Implementing Multiple Inheritance

Multiple inheritance is a recent addition to C++. This is due as much to implementation difficulties as to conceptual arguments. Let us examine a few of these problems.

Ambiguous Objects   With a multiply derived class, it is possible that one class could inherit two objects of the same name, as in the following:

```
struct Base1 {
    int object;
};
struct Base2 {
    int object;
};
class Derived : public Base1, public Base2 {
} d;
```

Here there are two members d.object, one inherited from Base1 and the other from Base2. It is therefore illegal to refer simply to d.object; however, it is possible to differentiate between the two by qualifying the member with its full name. In our example, the programmer must refer to d.Base1::object or d.Base2::object.

The same problem exists with respect to member functions. In this case another solution may be used.

```
struct Base1 {
    void fn();
};
struct Base2 {
    void fn();
};
class Derived : public Base1, public Base2 {
    void fn() { Base1::fn(); Base2::fn();}
} d;
```

Here, calling d.fn() invokes both functions without the need to specify further. If this is not what the programmer intended, the members' explicit names may be specified.

Name ambiguity is the reason a class may not inherit the same class twice, as in the following:

```
struct Base {
    int object;
    void f();
};
class Derived : public Base, public Base {
    //remainder of class definition
} d;
```

Here two members are named d.object. Unlike the previous examples, there is no way to specify one or the other since d.Base::object is still ambiguous. Any reference to d.object or d.f() would be illegal. This problem can be avoided by inheriting through an intermediate class, as in the following:

```
struct Base {
  int object;
  void f();
};
class FirstBase : public Base {};
class SecondBase : public Base {};
```

```
class Derived : public FirstBase, public SecondBase {
  //remainder of class definition
} d;
```

The programmer can differentiate between the two copies of `object` by referring to either `FirstBase::object` or `SecondBase::object`.

Ambiguous Classes The intermediate class solution introduces another problem. An ambiguity can arise when casting a pointer from one class to another. Given the previous class definitions, consider the following program.

```
void main() {
    Derived d;
    Derived* dPtr = &d;
    Base* b;

    b = (Base*)dPtr; //compiler error - ambiguous cast
}
```

When the programmer attempts to cast a `Derived*` into a `Base*`, a compiler error is generated because Turbo C++ does not know whether to convert the pointer into a `FirstBase::Base*` or `SecondBase::Base*`. Since there is nothing in the expression to indicate which, Turbo C++ disallows the cast.

Obviously this is true whether the cast is explicit as it is or implicit as in the following:

```
void main() {
    Derived d;
    Derived* dPtr = &d;
    void fn(Base*);

    Base* bPtr = dPtr;//same as above with implicit cast
    fn(dPtr);         //same here
```

```
        d.f();          //ditto - which f()?
}
```

The call to `fn()` is not allowed because Turbo C++ cannot decide which `d.Base::object` to pass. The call to `d.f()` is also ambiguous. A pointer to a subclass can be used wherever a pointer to a superclass is required as long as Turbo C++ can determine to which superclass object the reference is made. To remove the ambiguity, the programmer must cast to a class from which the complete cast is no longer ambiguous.

```
b = (Base*)(FirstBase*)dPtr;    //explicit cast
b = (FirstBase*)dPtr;           //cast beyond ambiguity

fn((Base*)(SecondBase*)dPtr);   //same applies
fn((SecondBase*)dPtr);

((FirstBase*)dPtr)->f();        //same again
```

Casting the `&d` to a `FirstBase*` makes the subsequent cast to `Base*` unambiguous. Turbo C++ now knows the programmer wants the address of `FirstBase::object`. Once the pointer has been cast to a `FirstBase*`, the second cast to `Base*` is implicit and unambiguous. Without the ambiguity, Turbo C++ can figure out how to get from the subclass to the superclass. The same is true with the call to `fn()` and the call to `Base::f()`.

Base Class Addresses   A basic problem arises from the way in which a derived class is laid out in memory. One of the key reasons a pointer to a subclass could pass as a pointer to a superclass was that the superclass appeared first in the subclass. Consider the following simple class inheritance.

```
struct Base {
    int a;
    float b;
    void f1();
```

```
};
struct Derived : public Base {
    int c;
} object;
```

If we were to examine the layout of an object of class `Derived` in memory—using the Inspect debugger command, for example—we would see something akin to Figure 8-1.

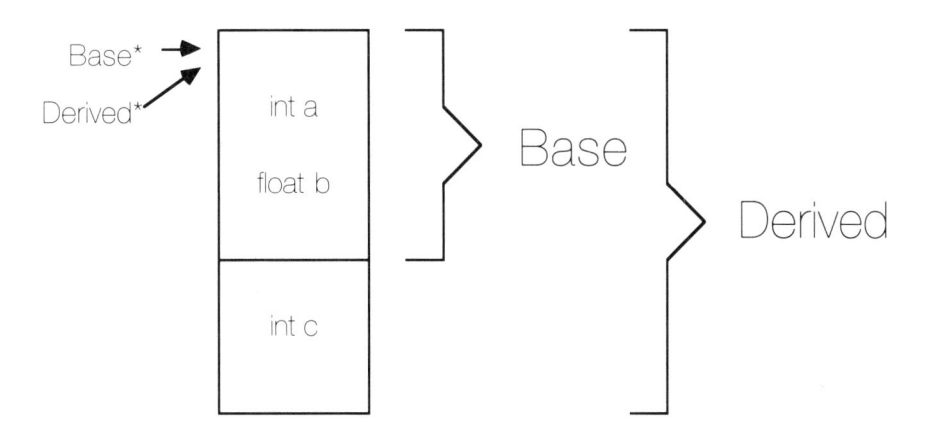

Figure 8-1 Memory Layout of a Simply Derived Class

If a `Derived*` is passed to a function that expects a `Base*`, no confusion arises. A `Derived` is a `Base` up to the end of the `Base` portion. The same is true if `object.f1()` is invoked. The `this` pointer that is passed has the same value irrespective of what type it has. But with a multi-inherited class `Derived`, the same cannot be said.

```
struct Base1 {
    int a;
    float b;
```

```
        void f1();
};
struct Base2 {
    int c;
    float d;
    void f2();
};
struct Derived : public Base1, public Base2 {
    int e;
} object;
```

Its layout in memory resembles Figure 8–2.

The `Base2` class is no longer stored at the beginning of the class `Derived`. If we pass a `Derived*` to a function expecting a `Base1*`, no problem arises. However, if we call a function expecting a `Base2*`, the address is no longer correct.

To correct the address, C++ must add the offset of the `Base2` class within `Derived` to the address of the `Derived::object` to make it point to the `Base2` portion. This same correction must be made on every pointer cast from a `Derived*` into a `Base2*`, including the hidden `this` pointer passed to member functions of `Base2`.

```
Derived object;

object.f2()//address of object must be
           //adjusted before passing to f2()
```

By the same token, C++ must apply the modification in the opposite direction when casting from `Base2*` to `Derived*`.

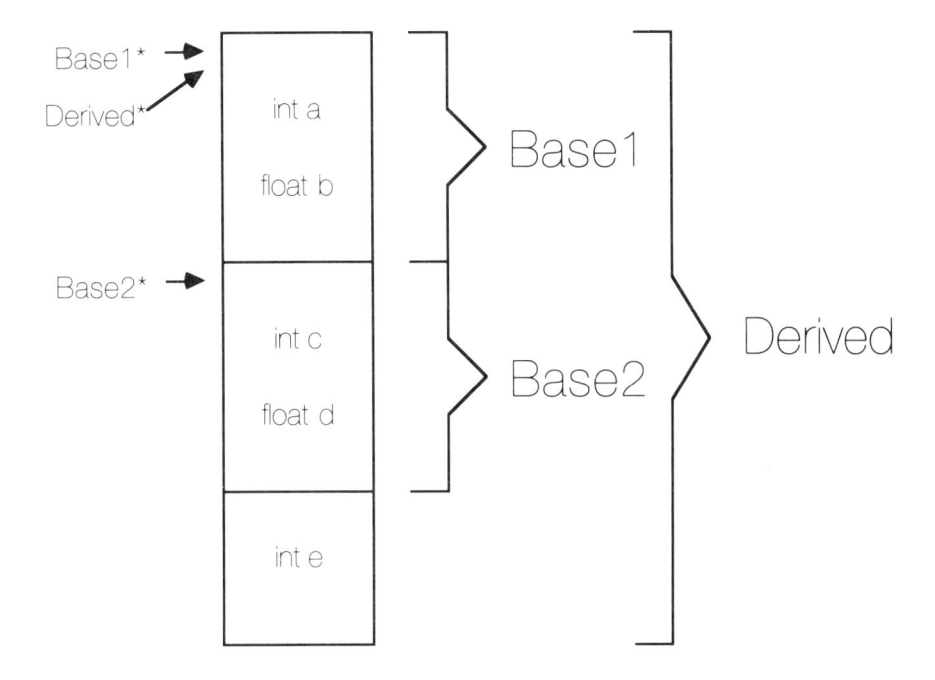

Figure 8–2 Memory Layout of a Multiply Derived Class

Doubly Linked Lists

Lists may be linked singly or doubly. In singly linked lists each element contains a single pointer to the next member in the list. Removing an entry chosen randomly in a singly linked list is difficult because the program must circumnavigate the entire list to find the element immediately preceding the element to be deleted.

As shown in Figure 8–3, doubly linked lists contain two pointers, one to the next member in the list and the other to the previous member. Removing an element from a doubly linked list is quicker since both neighbors are known immediately.

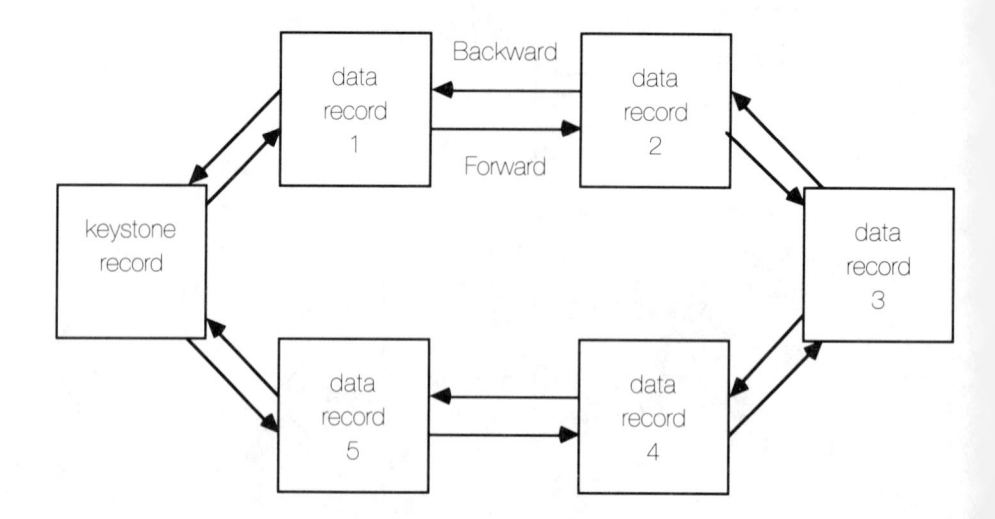

Figure 8-3 A Doubly Linked Circular List

A doubly linked list can be viewed as two singly linked lists linking the same elements, one in the forward direction and the other in the backward direction. In fact, a doubly linked class can be implemented from two class objects in a singly linked list.

Containing Class Solution The experienced C programmer will recognize that the solution to this problem is to define a `DLinkedList` class containing two objects of type `LinkedList`, being careful to give them names indicative of their respective roles. The following is such a solution.

```
#include <stddef.h>
#include "slist.hpp"

//Define a doubly linked list as two singly linked lists
class DLinkedList {
```

```cpp
    private:
       LinkedList nextp;    //link to next element
       LinkedList prevp;    //link to previous element

    public:
                     DLinkedList() : nextp(), prevp() {}
       DLinkedList*  next();
       DLinkedList*  prev();
       int           addAfter(DLinkedList* prevMember);
       int           remove();
};

DLinkedList* DLinkedList::next() {
    char* temp = (char*)nextp.next();
    int offset = offsetof(DLinkedList, nextp);
    return (DLinkedList*)(temp - offset);
}

DLinkedList* DLinkedList::prev() {
    char* temp = (char*)prevp.next();
    int offset = offsetof(DLinkedList, prevp);
    return (DLinkedList*)(temp - offset);
}

int DLinkedList::addAfter(DLinkedList* prevMember) {
    DLinkedList* nextMember = prevMember->next();

    nextp.addAfter(&prevMember->nextp);
    prevp.addAfter(&nextMember->prevp);
    return 0;
}
int DLinkeList::remove() {
    DLinkedList* prevMember = prev();
    DLinkedList* nextMember = next();
```

```
        prevMember->nextp.removeNext();
        nextMember->prevp.removeNext();
        return 0;
}
```

The class `DLinkedList` implements the same set of member functions that were present in the singly linked `LinkedList` class. Most functions consist of two `LinkedList` calls, one for the forward pointer and the other for the backward pointer.

One problem arises in the `next()` method. Calling `nextp.next()` returns the address of the next `LinkedList::nextp` object. To convert this to the address of the overall object, the offset of `nextp` within `DLinkedList` must be subtracted using the variable `offset`. The `offsetof()` macro was added by ANSI C to return the offset of a member within a structure.

The `prev()` member function has the same problem. Calling `prevp.next()` returns the address of the next `LinkedList::prevp` object. The same offset correction must be applied to render the address of the `DLinkedList` object itself.

The subtracting of offsets is identical to the type of conversions C++ performs when casting a subclass pointer into a base class pointer. When written as a containing class, these corrections must be applied manually.

Multiple Inheritance Solution One could argue that a doubly linked list does not have two singly linked lists but **is** two singly linked lists. Thus, it would be preferable to implement `DLinkedList` as a derived class of two `LinkedList` classes.

To avoid ambiguity `LinkedList` must be inherited through two different classes, in this case `Forward` and `Bakward` (the peculiar spelling was chosen just to give it the same number of letters as its counterpart). This implementation follows:

```
#include <stddef.h>
#include "slist.hpp"
```

Class Inheritance

```cpp
class DLinkedList;
struct Forward : public LinkedList {};
struct Bakward : public LinkedList {};

class DLinkedList : public Forward,
                    public Bakward {
  public:
                     DLinkedList() : Forward(),
                     Bakward() {}
    DLinkedList*     next();
    DLinkedList*     prev();
    int              addAfter(DLinkedList* prevMember);
    int              remove();
};

//C++ makes the conversions from Forward* and
//Bakward* to DLinkedList* and back to make these work
DLinkedList* next() {
    return (DLinkedList*)Forward::next();
}
DLinkedList* prev() {
    return (DLinkedList*)Bakward::next();
}

int DLinkedList::addAfter(DLinkedList* prevMember) {
    DLinkedList* nextMember = prevMember->next();

    //cannot cast from DLinkedList* to LinkedList*
    //as this is ambiguous; MUST go through the
    //intermediate of specifying either Forward* or
    //Bakward* to allow C++ to make the corrections;
    //you can double cast as follows:
    //  (LinkedList*)(Forward*)prevMember
```

```cpp
        Forward* prevFMem = (Forward*)prevMember;
        Bakward* nextBMem = (Bakward*)nextMember;

        Forward::addAfter(prevFMem);
        Bakward::addAfter(nextBMem);
        return 0;
    }

    int DLinkedList::remove() {
        DLinkedList* prevMember = prev();
        DLinkedList* nextMember = next();

        prevMember->Forward::removeNext();
        nextMember->Bakward::removeNext();
        return 0;
    }
```

Let us compare this multi-inherited version of `DLinkedList` with the previous containing version.

Notice how the methods `next()` and `prev()` have simplified. However, if we were to compare the assembly language generated by these functions with the previous version we would find that they are almost identical! When casting from a `Forward*` or `Bakward*` to a `DLinkedList*`, C++ automatically makes the offset corrections that one has to make manually in the containing class version.

A new problem springs up in the member function `addAfter()`. The argument to `LinkedList::addAfter()` is of type `LinkedList*`. `prevMember` and `nextMember` are of type `DLinkedList*` and cannot be cast directly to `LinkedList*`. Converting to `Forward*` or `Bakward*` and then to `LinkedList*` avoids the ambiguity.

Virtual Inheritance

In the following example, the class `Derived` inherits two copies of the class `Base`, one via the class `FirstBase` and the other from class `SecondBase`.

```
struct Base {
    int object;
};
struct FirstBase : public Base{
    int a;
};
struct SecondBase : public Base{
    float b;
};

class Derived : public First Base, public Second Base {
    long dObject;
};
```

The memory layout of an object of class `Derived` resembles Figure 8-4.

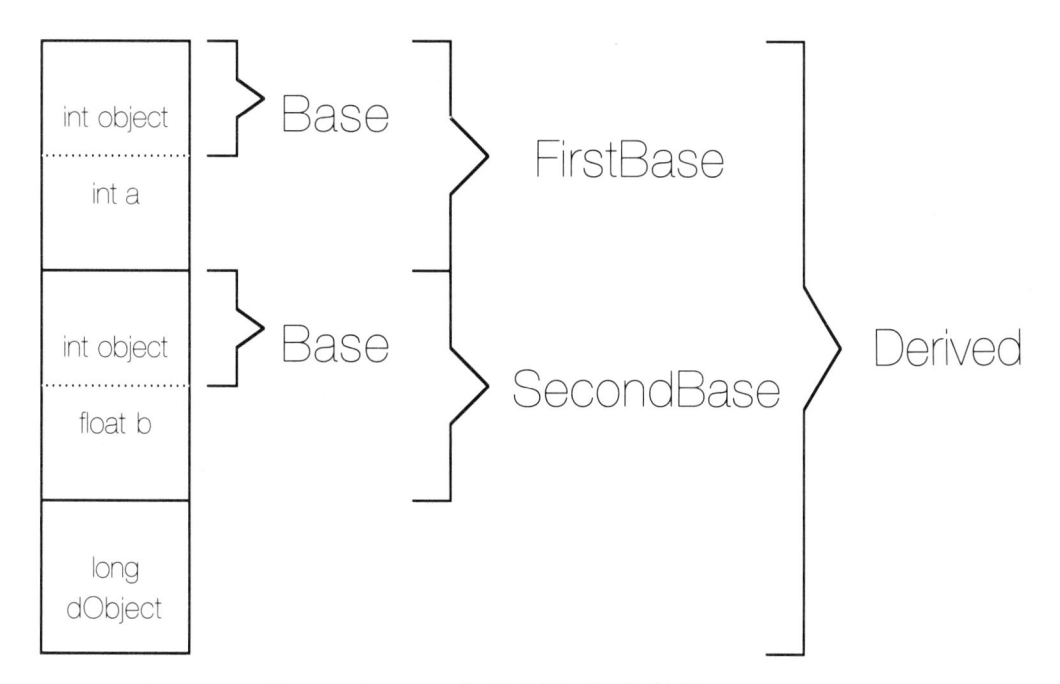

Figure 8-4 Memory Layout of a Multiply Derived Class

To allow a single copy of Base to be inherited in such cases, C++ allows the inclusion of the `virtual` keyword with the inheritance command. The program could be rewritten as follows:

```
struct Base {
     int object;
};
struct FirstBase : virtual public Base{
     int a;
};
struct SecondBase : virtual public Base{
     float b;
};

class Derived : virtual public First Base,
                virtual public Second Base {
     long dObject;
};
```

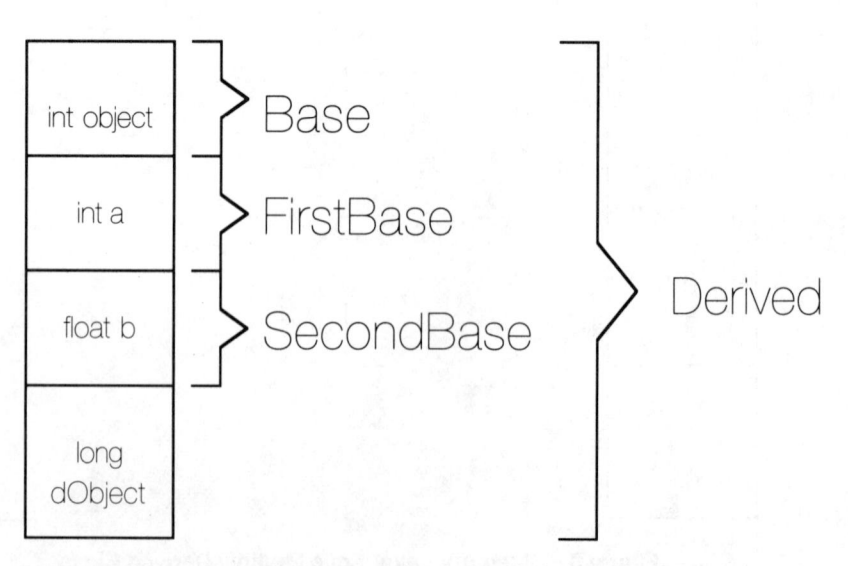

Figure 8–5 Memory Layout of a Virtual Multiply Inherited Class

This modification changes the appearance in memory of an object of class Derived as shown in Figure 8–5.

Now only a single copy of Base exists.

Conclusion

We have now discussed all of the intrinsic language features of C++. Input and output in C++ are handled by a set of functions implemented primarily as a set of overloaded friend operators. We will examine this I/O package in the next chapter.

Chapter 9

Stream Input/Output

When used for output, the left-shift operator is known as the **inserter**. The recipient of output data is called the **sink**. When used for input, the right-shift operator is called the **extractor**; it inputs data from a **source**. The most common sink and source are the display monitor and keyboard, respectively.

Conventional C I/O

In C++ parlance, conventional C I/O is called **stdio** because the `stdio.h` file contains the prototypes for `printf()`, `scanf()`, and their associated functions. Stdio enables a programmer to output a reasonably complex line with a few cryptic symbols. Being ANSI C compatible, Turbo C++ supports stdio.

Balanced against the concise format of stdio is a total lack of type checking. The prototypes of `printf()` and `scanf()` are almost completely wide open. Mistakes in `printf()` calls generally produce incorrect output. Mistakes on the `scanf()` side are harder to trace and more common.

Without more restrictive prototype definitions, overloading `printf()` for different user types is not possible. Therefore, `printf()` cannot output user-defined classes. Further, stdio is not adequately buffered. In many implementations, each call to `fprintf()` results in at least one disk access. The stdio mechanism is tied to the concept of files. Although it includes in-core I/O with `sprintf()` and `sscanf()`, stdio cannot be expanded to other types of sinks and sources.

Older C++ Streams

In response to these problems, C++ introduced the concept of **streams**. The first attempt at a stream solution was not entirely successful. C++ Version 1.x streams did not support the full range of file operators (in particular, seek). Early streams also provided only limited format control.

While Turbo C++ supports 1.x streams, Borland strongly recommends against their use. Since most readers are learning C++ for the first time, 1.x streams are not presented in this book.

C++ 2.0 Streams

Version 2.0 of C++ introduced a new implementation of streams, which I will call **iostreams** after the `iostream.h` file which contains the prototype and operator definitions. Iostreams have several advantages over stdio.

First, iostreams can be extended. The insertion and extraction operators may be overloaded for new types. This ability is critical if large blocks of source code are to be reused with newly created data types. In addition, iostreams are fully buffered. Individual I/O statements do not generate disk accesses until complete sectors of information have been accumulated.

Inserter output collects in an output hopper. When the hopper is full or when the program specifically requests it, the hopper is flushed to the sink file, as shown in Figure 9–1.

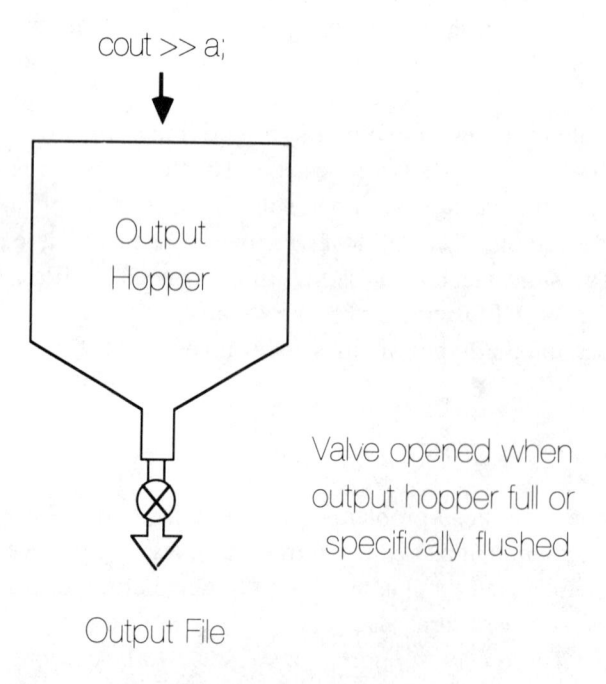

Figure 9–1 Buffering of Output Stream

Stream Input/Output

Similarly, C++ associates an input hopper with the source file when it is opened. When the first request for input is made, the extractor finds the hopper empty. The extractor reads a complete block into the hopper and extracts the first field. In the case of a keyboard source, a block consists of data up to the NewLine character. Further extractor calls read subsequent fields from the hopper until the data is exhausted, at which point the extractor returns to the source file for more data, as shown in Figure 9–2.

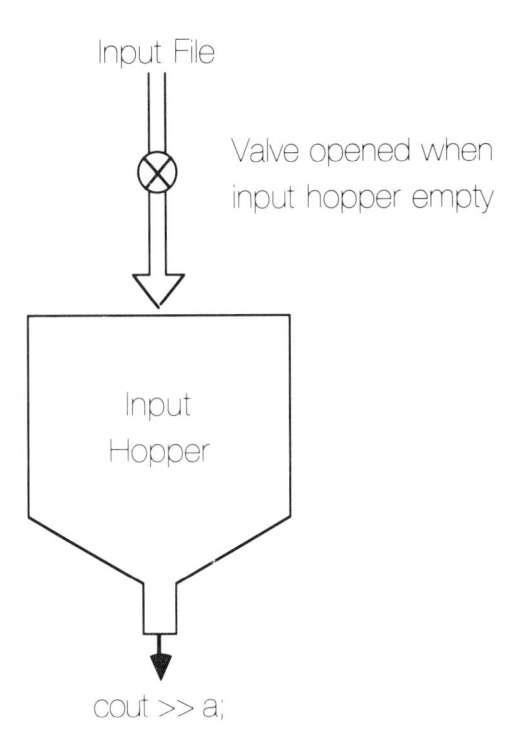

Figure 9–2 Buffering of Input Stream

Buffering increases performance significantly for small transactions by reducing the number of disk transactions.

Iostreams do have some disadvantages, however. Data cannot be accessed directly in the buffers. Instead, the data must be copied into local buffers where they can be assigned a proper type.

A more serious problem is the clumsiness of outputting complex lines. Compare the following two statements that generate the same output.

```
#include <stdio.h>
#include <iostream.h>

int a = 1;
float b = 2.0;
long c = 3L;
char d[] = "this is a string";

printf("a = %d, b = %f, c = %ld, d = %s\n", a, b, c, d);
cout << "a = "   << a
     << ", b = " << b
     << ", c= "  << c
     << ", d = " << d
     << "\n";
```

The chaining of insertion operations is possible because of the binding of << and because `operator<<()` is of type `ostream`. Thus, the preceding iostream sequence is interpreted as if written:

```
(((cout << "a = ") << a) << ", b = ")... and so on
```

The first expression, `cout << "a = "`, inserts the string into the ostream cout. Then cout is returned and used to evaluate the next expression, `cout << a`, which also returns `cout`, and so on.

The chaining of operations gives iostream I/O the look and feel of Pascal. Experienced C programmers may prefer `printf()`. Most people, however, find the iostream format more readable.

Iostreams do not provide as much control or conciseness as `printf()`. What control exists, however, is accessible to user-defined inserters and extractors.

Inserters

The iostream inserter is the << operator overloaded for the `ostream` class as its left argument. Thus, in the following:

```
int i;
ostream j;

i << 2;            //left shift i two bits
j << 2;            //insert a 2 to ostream j
```

the integer variable `i` is left-shifted two bits while in the second line a 2 is inserted in the `ostream` variable `j`.

The insertion operator retains the same precedence and binding as left-shift. This precedence is lower than most other operators so that most expressions have the expected result when inserted.

```
cout << c[i];      //same as cout << (c[i]);
cout << 1 + 2;     //same as cout << 3;
cout << 2 * 3;     //same as cout << 6;
cout << i++;       //same as cout << (i++);
```

Consider what is wrong with the following:

```
int a = 0x1234;

cout << a ? 1 : 0;    //same as (cout << a) ? 1 : 0;
```

A novice C++ programmer might expect a 1 or a 0 to be output. Instead a 4660, the decimal equivalent of 0x1234, appears.

Most incorrect bindings are caught by the compiler. The following line generates a compiler error since `operator&()` is not defined for `ostream`.

```
cout << a & 0xff;     //same as (cout << a) & 0xff;
```

No matter what the operator precedence, unexpected associations can be avoided by placing parentheses around expressions within an insertion operator.

Another class of errors arises when the same object appears twice in a single output expression. Consider the following:

```
#include <iostream.h>

void main() {
    int i = 1;

    cout << "I = "            << i++
         << ", I now equals " << i++
         << endl;
}
```

The output from this expression is as follows:

```
I = 2, I now equals 1
```

The increment operator has a higher priority than the inserter; thus, both increments are evaluated before any insertions are made. The order of evaluation is not specified by the ANSI standard. In this example, Turbo C++ evaluates the right-most `i++` first.

An object can be duplicated implicitly with the same erroneous results, as in the following:

```
#include <iostream.h>

int globalVariable;
int fn(int i) {
    globalVariable = i;
    return i;
}

void main() {
```

```
    globalVariable = 1;
    cout << "globalVariable = "   << globalVariable
         << ", fn = "              << fn(2)
         << ", globalVariable = " << globalVariable
         << endl;
}
```

The function `fn()` modifies the object `globalVariable`. Including `globalVariable` and `fn()` in a single output stream generates the following result.

```
globalVariable = 2, fn = 2, globalVariable = 1
```

A variable that is subject to change should not appear more than once in a single output stream. Dividing the single output stream into multiple expressions, each with a single reference to the modified variable, solves the problem as in the following example.

```
#include <iostream.h>

void main() {
    int i = 1;
    cout << "I = "              << i++;
    cout << ", I now equals " << i++
         << endl;
}
```

This program generates the expected output.

```
I = 1, I now equals 2
```

Inserter Types

The `iostream.h` include file must define several versions of `operator<<()`, one for each intrinsic type that may be inserted. Inserters exist for `char`, `signed` and `unsigned` `short`, `signed` and `unsigned` int, signed and unsigned long, float, double, long double, char*, and void*.

Notice the two different pointer type inserters. The char* inserter outputs null-terminated strings. The void* inserter prints out the value of an address. Since void* is the universal recipient, all pointer types not covered by the char* inserter are cast to void*.

```
#include <iostream.h>

void main() {
    int a = 1;
    float b = 2.0;
    int*   aPtr = &a;
    float* bPtr = &b;
    char*  cPtr = "this is a string";

    cout << "aPtr = " << aPtr << "\n";
    cout << "bPtr = " << bPtr << "\n";
    cout << "cPtr = " << cPtr << "\n";
}
```

Executing this program segment generates the following output.

```
aPtr = 0x8f5afff4
bPtr = 0x8f5afff0
cPtr = this is a string
```

The programmer may use a cast to change the inserter. For example, changing the last line in the preceding program to

```
cout << "cPtr = " << (void*)cPtr << "\n";
```

generates the following output.

```
aPtr = 0x8f5afff4
bPtr = 0x8f5afff0
cPtr = 0x8f5a00ac
```

Changing the inserter is especially useful with many older string functions that are of type `int`. In K&R C, `char` was not an evaluation type, so many older functions that return a character are declared type `int`. If inserted without a cast, the output of such a function displays as a number, not a character. To display the character, a cast is needed as in the following example.

```
cout << (char)getch();
```

Casts should also be used when an operator might have changed the type of the expression as in the following:

```
cout << (char)('A' + i - 1); //insert ordinal character
```

For i equals 1, the programmer should see 'A' not 65 (the decimal equivalent of 'A').

Format Control

The `ostream` class has several members that control the formatting of output from inserters. Format control consists of storing values in the member variables. Subsequent inserter calls read the values and act accordingly. Control members may be set through member functions or through **manipulators**.

The format control flags are stored in the `ios` class member `x_flags`. The different flags defined in the enumerated type contained in `ios` are as follows:

```
enum {
    skipws    = 0x0001, //skip whitespace on input
    left      = 0x0002, //left-adjust output
    right     = 0x0004, //right-adjust output
```

```
    internal   = 0x0008,  //padding after sign or base
    dec        = 0x0010,  //decimal conversion
    oct        = 0x0020,  //octal conversion
    hex        = 0x0040,  //hexidecimal conversion
    showbase   = 0x0080,  //use base indicator on output
    showpoint  = 0x0100,  //force decimal point (on float)
    uppercase  = 0x0200,  //upper-case hex output
    showpos    = 0x0400,  //add '+' to positive integers
    scientific = 0x0800,  //use 1.2345E2 floating notation
    fixed      = 0x1000,  //use 123.45 floating notation
    unitbuf    = 0x2000,  //flush all streams after <<
    stdio      = 0x4000   //flush stdout, stderr after <<
};
```

These flags may be set using either the `flags()` or `setf()` member functions. The function `flags(long)` allows the programmer to store the x_flags field. The function `flags()` returns the current value of the flags. The following lines clear the `skipws` flag and then set the uppercase flag.

```
cout.flags(cout.flags() & ~ios::skipws);
cout.flags(cout.flags() | ios::uppercase);
```

The function `setf()` is more sophisticated and also has several versions. The most common version accepts two long arguments. The second argument specifies the flag to be set while the first specifies its value. The following two lines are equivalent to the preceding lines of code.

```
cout.setf(             0, ios::skipws);
cout.setf(ios::uppercase, ios::uppercase);
```

The first call sets the flag `skipws` to 0, while the second sets the uppercase flag to uppercase (i.e., sets the flag).

Not all of the format fields are independent. Only one of the base flags dec, oct, or hex should be set at a time. To aid in setting fields that are mutually exclusive, iostreams.h defines three constants for use with setf().

```
basefield = dec|oct|hex
adjustfield = left|right|internal
floatfield = scientific|fixed
```

To set the base to decimal, the programmer would enter the following:

```
cout.setf(ios::dec, ios::basefield);
```

While setting the decimal flag, the preceding call simultaneously clears the octal and hexidecimal flags.

The two other versions of the setf() function are easier to read. The function setf(long) sets a particular flag, while the function unsetf(long) clears it. Therefore, the earlier two function calls could be coded as follows:

```
cout.unsetf(ios::skipws);
cout.setf(ios::uppercase);
```

Consider the following example of format control using format flags. The program outputs the number 16 in three different formats: decimal, octal, and hexidecimal, with and without format shown and in lower- and uppercase.

```
#include <iostream.h>
void main() {
    cout.setf(ios::dec, ios::basefield);
    cout << "16 = " << 16 << endl;
    cout.setf(ios::oct, ios::basefield);
    cout << "16 = " << 16 << endl;
    cout.setf(ios::hex, ios::basefield);
    cout << "16 = " << 16 << endl;
```

```
        cout << "Can show base along with number\n";
        cout.setf(ios::showbase);
        cout.setf(ios::dec, ios::basefield);
        cout << "16 = " << 16 << endl;
        cout.setf(ios::oct, ios::basefield);
        cout << "16 = " << 16 << endl;
        cout.setf(ios::hex, ios::basefield);
        cout << "16 = " << 16 << endl;

        cout << "Can have uppercase too\n";
        cout.setf(ios::uppercase);
        cout << "10 = " << 10 << endl;

        cout << "For mixed case do it yourself\n";
        cout.unsetf(ios::showbase);
        cout << "10 = " << "0x" << 10 << endl;
}
```

The output from this program is as follows:

```
16 = 16
16 = 20
16 = 10
Can show base along with number
16 = 16
16 = 020
16 = 0x10
Can have uppercase too
10 = 0XA
For mixed case do it yourself
10 = 0xA
```

The class `ios` also defines the format control fields `x_width`, `x_precision`, and `x_fill`. The width setting specifies the smallest output field width. The `width(int)` member function sets the width while returning the old setting. The `width()` member function returns

Stream Input/Output

the current width setting without changing it. A setting of zero implies that the inserter should use the minimum number of characters required. A larger value forces the inserter to pad the field to the specified size. The inserter does not truncate to fit the width.

In the following small program, a is output twice: first with a width of 0, then with a width of 10.

```
#include <iostream.h>

void main() {
    int a = 123;

    cout << "a = (" << a << ")\n";

    cout << "a = (";
    cout.width(10);
    cout << a << ")\n";

    cout << cout.width();
}
```

The output from this program appears as follows:

```
a = (123)
a = (         123)
0
```

The call to width() must appear immediately before the field that it affects. The width resets to zero after each output field, as the final line demonstrates.

The precision setting x_precision, which may be read with the precision() method and adjusted with the precision(int) method, determines the maximum number of digits to be displayed or read after the decimal point. The fill character x_fill specifies the character to use when filling an output field to the minimum width. The default is a space, but may be changed using the `fill()` method.

More convenient than member functions are manipulators that are inserted directly into the output stream. For example, converting the previous example to use the `setw()` manipulator instead of the `width()` function results in the following:

```
cout << "a = (" << setw(10) << a << ")\n";
```

Since manipulators are coded "in stream", they are generally easier to use. The include files `iostream.h` and `iomanip.h` define the manipulators listed in Table 9–1.

Table 9–1   C++ I/O Stream Manipulators

Manipulator	Type	Class Action
dec	i/o	set decimal conversion base flag
hex	i/o	set hex conversion base flag
oct	i/o	set octal conversion base flag
setbase(int)	o	set conversion base
ws	i	extract whitespace
ends	o	insert a terminal null
endl	o	insert newline and flush stream
flush	o	flush output stream
resetiosflags(long)	i/o	clear specified flags
setiosflags(long)	i/o	set specified flags
setfill(int)	i/o	set fill character
setprecision(int)	i/o	set floating point precision
setw(int)	i/o	set field width

Manipulators marked with an 'o' apply to fields used by inserters, those marked with an 'i' effect only extractor fields. Manipulators marked 'i/o' apply to both inserters and extractors.

Stream Input/Output

The direct member function equivalents of some manipulators included in Table 9–1 are as follows:

```
ios s;

s<<resetiosflags(i)   is equivalent to  s.unsetf(i)
s<<setiosflags(i)           "      "    s.setf(i)
s<<setfill(i)               "      "    s.fill(i)
s<<setprecision(i)          "      "    s.precision(i)
s<<setw(i)                  "      "    s.width(i)
```

Thus, invoking the `setiosflags()` manipulator is equivalent to calling the `setf(long)` member function.

Buffering

The C++ programmer should be aware that iostream I/O is buffered. A string inserted to `cout` does not appear on the display until the output buffer has been flushed.

Two manipulators can be used to flush the output buffer. The `flush` manipulator simply flushes any output to the file or display. The `endl` tacks on a NewLine before flushing the buffer. Adding either of these manipulators to the end of calls is good practice, especially if the output text is to be seen immediately, as in the following:

```
cout << "Process takes 10 minutes; be patient" << endl;
```

If this statement remained in the output buffer, the user would not see the message until **after** 10 minutes had expired and further output was attempted.

Output should also be flushed when prompting for input, as in the following:

```
char userName[80];

cout << "Enter your name:" << flush;
cin  >> userName;
```

This is so common and such a likely source of error that C++ has safeguards. An input stream may be **tied** to an output stream via the member `istream::tie` of type `ostream*`. Whenever the program extracts from the `istream`, the extractor flushes the `ostream` pointed at by `tie`.

The standard input stream `cin` is tied to the standard output stream `cout`. Therefore, the call to `flush` in the preceding example is unnecessary because the subsequent call to the `cin` extractor would automatically flush any output pending to `cout`.

Sometimes this is inconvenient or inefficient, however. For example, in the following segment, tying `cin` to `cout` would substantially reduce the program's performance.

```
char c;
while (cin >> c)
    cout << c;
```

With `cout` tied to `cin`, each call to the extractor flushes the inserter, effectively disabling any buffering of output. In such a case, `cout` can be untied from `cin` for greater efficiency using the `tie()` member function, as in the following:

```
char c;
cin.tie(0);            //untie cin from cout
while (cin >> c)
    cout << c;
```

Custom Inserters

To build an inserter for a user-defined class, the programmer must define the operator function `operator<<(ostream&, MyClass&)` as follows:

```
#include <iostream.h>

class MyClass {
```

```
        friend ostream& operator<<(ostream&, MyClass&);
    private:
        int i;
        int j;
    public:
        MyClass(int a1, int a2) : i(a1), j(a2) {}
};

ostream& operator<<(ostream& o, MyClass& mc) {
    o << "(" << mc.i << "," << mc.j << ")";
    return o;
};
```

The inserter must be written as a non-member function because the user's class is the right-hand argument, not the left. Programmers should never modify the class `ostream` to add a member `operator<<(MyClass&)`.

A user-defined insert should follow the format control fields when they apply. In our example most of the control fields are transparent; however, our constructor should not ignore the field width. The width in effect when the `MyClass` inserter is invoked should be evenly divided between the two integers (minus three for the parentheses and comma). A better solution would be the following:

```
#include <iostream.h>
#include <iomanip.h>

class MyClass {
        friend ostream& operator<<(ostream&, MyClass&);
    private:
        int i;
        int j;
    public:
        MyClass(int a1, int a2) : i(a1), j(a2) {}
};
```

```cpp
ostream& operator<<(ostream& o, MyClass& mc) {
    int w = o.width();
    w = (w - 3) / 2;       //divide width evenly
    w = (w > 0) ? w : 0;   //no negative widths
    o << setw(0) << "("    //reset width for '('
      << setw(w) << mc.i   //set it for 'i'
      << ","
      << setw(w) << mc.j   //set it again for 'j'
      << ")";
    return o;
};

void main() {
  MyClass o1(1,2);

  cout << "MyClass o1 = " << setw(20) << o1 << "\n";
}
```

This program generates the desired results.

```
MyClass o1 = (          1,          2)
```

In this inserter the width must be reset before inserting " (", but not before " , " or ") " since the previous insertion already zeroed it.

A user-defined inserter does not have to be of type `ostream&` or return the `ostream` input object. Unless it does so, however, the inserter cannot be chained with other inserters in a compound output command.

Custom Manipulators with Restricted Argument Types

The programmer may also define custom manipulators. Such manipulators can set flags for user-defined inserters and extractors in the same way that the C++-provided manipulators set flags in `ios` for the standard stream operators.

Manipulators that take no arguments are not difficult to write. The following manipulator inserts a tab into the output stream.

```
#include <iostream.h>

ostream& tab(ostream& o) {
    return o << '\t';
}

void main() {
    int a = 123;

    cout << "a = (" << tab << a << ")\n";
}
```

Study the preceding code segment to determine what a simple manipulator is and how the program works.

A simple manipulator is the address of a function declared `fn(ostream&)`. The include file `iostream.h` defines a special inserter that accepts the address of such a function. The inserter, declared `ostream& operator<<(ostream&, (*)(ostream&))`, simply calls the function.

The preceding output expression is evaluated as follows: First, any expressions of precedence higher than `<<` are calculated. Then the expression `cout << "a = ("` is evaluated using the standard `char*` inserter. Next, the expression `cout << tab` is evaluated using the special inserter that calls the function `tab()`. Evaluation then continues as normal. A separate set of operators exists for manipulators declared `fn(ios&)`.

Writing manipulators that take arguments (complex manipulators) is more difficult. Consider the following example using the complex manipulator `setprecision()`.

```
cout << a << setprecision(2) << b;
```

The function call to `setprecision()` occurs before any of the insertion operations since the precedence of `()` is higher than `<<`. However, the manipulator `setprecision()` should set the precision only after the inserter has output variable a. Thus, the `setprecision()` call cannot set the precision itself. Instead, it must return something that can be "found" later by a specially designed inserter and used to set the precision before inserting the variable b, as requested.

The include file `iomanip.h` contains special support for manipulators that accept either a single `int` or a single `long` argument. It defines `setprecision()` as follows:

```
// set the floating-point precision to n digits
smanip_int setprecision(int _n);
```

The function `setprecision()` returns an object of class `smanip_int`. The constructor for `smanip_int` stores the address of a function and its integer argument in this object. The sequence in evaluating the above output stream is as follows:

1) The expressions, a, b, and `setprecision()` are evaluated; the function returns an object of type `smanip_int`.
2) The inserter `cout << float` is invoked on the result of expression a at the old precision setting.
3) The inserter `cout << smanip_int` is invoked on the object returned by `setprecision()`. This inserter calls the function address stored in the object. The function sets the precision.
4) The inserter `cout << float` is invoked on the result of expression b at the new precision setting.

The sequence is shown graphically in Figure 9–3.

The programmer can use the pattern established in `iomanip.h` to define new manipulators with either a single `int` or a single `long` argument. In the following program, the user-defined manipulator `setFlag()` stores a value into `globalFlag` by using the constructor for `smanip_int` to save the address of the function `ios& doIt(ios&, int)` and its integer argument. The inserter subsequently calls the function `doIt()` which changes the value of `globalFlag`.

```
#include <iostream.h>
#include <iomanip.h>

int globalFlag;
```

Stream Input/Output

```
ios& doIt (ios& s, int flag) {
    cout << "\nChanging globalFlag to " << flag << endl;
    globalFlag = flag;
    return s;
}
smanip_int setFlag(int flag) {
    cout << "\nBuilding smanip_int(doIt,"
         << flag << ")\n";
    smanip_int object(doIt, flag);
    return object;
}

void main() {
    cout << "Reset flag,"      << setFlag(0);
    cout << " flag = "          << globalFlag
         << endl;

    cout << "Now set it to 2," << setFlag(2);
    cout << " flag = "          << globalFlag
         << endl;
};
```

Extra I/O statements have been added to demonstrate the order in which the functions are invoked.

```
Building smanip_int(doIt,0)
Reset flag,
Changing globalFlag to 0
 flag = 0

Building smanip_int(doIt,2)
Now set it to 2,
Changing globalFlag to 2
 flag = 2
```

```
cout << a << setprecision(2) << b;
```

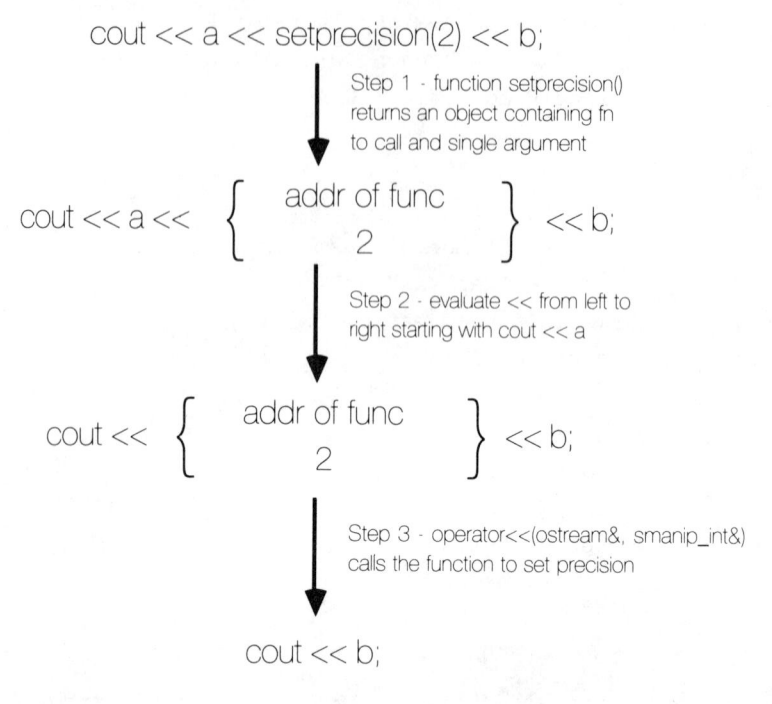

Step 1 - function setprecision() returns an object containing fn to call and single argument

```
cout << a << { addr of func
                    2        } << b;
```

Step 2 - evaluate << from left to right starting with cout << a

```
cout << { addr of func
              2        } << b;
```

Step 3 - operator<<(ostream&, smanip_int&) calls the function to set precision

```
cout << b;
```

Step 4 - evaluate << using new precision

Figure 9–3 Evaluation of Integer Manipulator

We can now add meaningful manipulators to our earlier example, `My-Class`. In the following program, the manipulators `iOnly` and `jAlso` control the display of `i` and `j` by setting and clearing the static member `MyClass::iOnly`. The third manipulator `permWidth(int)` establishes a default field width.

```
#include <iostream.h>
#include <iomanip.h>

class MyClass {
    friend ostream& operator<<(ostream&, MyClass&);
  private:
    int i;
```

Stream Input/Output

```cpp
        int j;
    public:
        static int iOnly;
        static int fieldWidth;
        MyClass(int a1, int a2) : i(a1), j(a2) {
            iOnly = fieldWidth = 0;
        }
};

ostream& operator<<(ostream& o, MyClass& mc) {
    int w = o.width(); //start with the specified width
    if (w == 0)        //if its zero...
        w = MyClass::fieldWidth; //...use the default

    w = (w - 2);
    w = (w > 0) ? w : 0;

    //either output (i) or (i,j) depending on iOnly flag
    if (MyClass::iOnly) {
        o << setw(0) << "("
          << setw(w) << mc.i
                    << ")";
    } else {
        w /= 2;
        o << setw(0) << "("
          << setw(w) << mc.i
                    << ","
          << setw(w) << mc.j
                    << ")";
    }
    return o;
};

//define a set of manipulators to set and clear
//the iOnly flag
ostream& iOnly(ostream& s) {
```

```cpp
        MyClass::iOnly = 1;
        return s;
}
ostream& jAlso(ostream& s) {
        MyClass::iOnly = 0;
        return s;
}

//now a manipulator to set width for all MyClass objects
ios& doIt(ios& s, int width) {
        MyClass::fieldWidth = width;
        return s;
}
smanip_int permWidth(int width) {
        smanip_int object(doIt, width);
        return object;
}

void main() {
    MyClass o1(1,2);

     cout <<
       "Set the default field width to 20 and output o1\n";
     cout << "MyClass o1 = " << permWidth(20)
          << o1 << "\n";

     cout << "Do it again to make sures its permanent\n";
     cout << "MyClass o1 = " << o1 << "\n";

     cout <<
       "Override the default width to 10 with setw()\n";
     cout << "MyClass o1 = " << setw(10)
          << o1 << "\n";


     cout << "Now try with iOnly set\n";
```

```
        cout << "MyClass o1 = " << iOnly
             << o1 << "\n";

        cout << "Put iOnly back to 0\n";
        cout << "MyClass o1 = " << jAlso
             << o1 << "\n";
}
```

The main program in this case demonstrates the manipulators and the improved inserter.

```
Set the default field width to 20 and output o1
MyClass o1 = (          1,          2)
Do it again to make sures its permanent
MyClass o1 = (          1,          2)
Override the default width to 10 with setw()
MyClass o1 = (    1,    2)
Now try with iOnly set
MyClass o1 = (                    1)
Put iOnly back to 0
MyClass o1 = (          1,          2)
```

Custom Manipulators with General Argument Types

The `smanip_int` and `smanip_long` manipulator classes outlined in `iomanip.h` are well written. A user-defined manipulator based on one of these classes will work in almost any application.

To build manipulators that accept other argument types a programmer may follow the pattern established by `smanip_int` and `smanip_long` to generate other `smanip_` types, or write a custom class for the manipulator. Designing a manipulator that will work for all subclasses of `ios` is difficult, but is more straightforward and easier to maintain than the `smanip` method.

Consider the following example in which `setDivider(char, int)` enables the programmer to determine the number and type of characters to use as a divider between entries `i` and `j` for the class `MyClass`.

```cpp
class CustomManip {
    friend ostream& operator<<(ostream&, CustomManip&);
  private:
    char divider;
    char noTimes;
  public:
    CustomManip(char d, int n) {
        divider = d;
        noTimes = n;
    }
    void changeDivider() {
        MyClass::divider = divider;
        MyClass::numOfTimes = noTimes;
    }
};

ostream& operator<<(ostream& s, CustomManip& cm) {
    cm.changeDivider();
    return s;
}
CustomManip setDivider(char d = ';', int count = 1) {
    return CustomManip(d, count);
}
```

The manipulator is called with up to two arguments. The first argument specifies the character to use as a divider and defaults to ';'. The second argument specifies the number of times the character should appear and defaults to 1. In use, the new manipulator appears as follows:

```cpp
MyClass o1;

cout << "o1 = " << setDivider('-', 1) << o1;
```

The preceding line calls the function `setDivider()` which constructs an object of class `CustomManip` to temporarily save both arguments. The character inserter outputs the string "o1 = ". The next <<

inserts the `CustomManip` object returned by `setDivider()` into the output stream `cout`. This inserter invokes the method `changeDivider()` which retrieves the arguments saved in the temporary `CustomManip` object. The arguments are stored in the `MyClass` members `divider` and `numOfTimes`, which control the output of the inserter for `MyClass`.

The complete program, including additions to implement the variable divider, and a new `main()` program, is as follows:

```cpp
#include <iostream.h>
#include <iomanip.h>

class MyClass {
    friend ostream& operator<<(ostream&, MyClass&);
  private:
    int i;
    int j;
  public:
    static int iOnly;
    static int fieldWidth;
    static char divider;
    static int  numOfTimes;

    MyClass(int a1, int a2) : i(a1), j(a2) {
        iOnly = fieldWidth = 0;
        divider = ';';
        numOfTimes = 1;
    }
};

ostream& operator<<(ostream& o, MyClass& mc) {
    int w = o.width(); //start with the specified width
    if (w == 0)        //if its zero...
        w = MyClass::fieldWidth; //...use default width

    w = (w - 2);
    w = (w > 0) ? w : 0;
```

```cpp
        //either output (i) or (i,j) depending on iOnly flag
        if (MyClass::iOnly) {
            o << setw(0) << "("
              << setw(w) << mc.i
                        << ")";
        } else {
            w = (w - MyClass::numOfTimes) / 2;
            w = (w > 0) ? w : 0;
            o << setw(0) << "(" << setw(w) << mc.i;

            for (int i = MyClass::numOfTimes; i > 0; i--)
                o << MyClass::divider;

            o << setw(w) << mc.j << ")";
        }
        return o;
};

//define a set of manipulators to set and clear
//the iOnly flag
ostream& iOnly(ostream& s) {
    MyClass::iOnly = 1;
    return s;
}
ostream& jAlso(ostream& s) {
    MyClass::iOnly = 0;
    return s;
}

//now a manipulator to set width for all MyClass objects
ios& doIt(ios& s, int width) {
    MyClass::fieldWidth = width;
    return s;
}
smanip_int permWidth(int width) {
    smanip_int object(doIt, width);
```

Stream Input/Output

```
        return object;
}

//and another to set the divider
class CustomManip {
    friend ostream& operator<<(ostream&, CustomManip&);
  private:
    char divider;
    char noTimes;
  public:
    CustomManip(char d, int n) {
        divider = d;
        noTimes = n;
    }
    void changeDivider() {
        MyClass::divider = divider;
        MyClass::numOfTimes = noTimes;
    }
};

ostream& operator<<(ostream& s, CustomManip& cm) {
    cm.changeDivider();
    return s;
}
CustomManip setDivider(char d = ';', int count = 1) {
    return CustomManip(d, count);
}

void main() {
    MyClass o1(1,2), o2(3,4);

    cout << "O1 with default divider\n";
    cout << "MyClass o1 = " << o1 << "\n\n";

    cout << "Now try divider = ###\n";
    cout << "MyClass o1 = " << setDivider('#', 3)
```

```
              << o1 << "\n\n";

    cout << "Try two dividers in the same line\n";
    cout << "MyClass o1 = "  << setDivider('-', 2) << o1
         << ", MyClass o2 = " << setDivider('@', 2) << o2
         << "\n\n";

    cout << "Now set it back to default\n";
    cout << setDivider();
    cout << "MyClass o1 = " << o1 << endl;
}
```

The output from this program is as follows:

```
O1 with default divider
MyClass o1 = (1;2)

Now try divider = ###
MyClass o1 = (1###2)

Try two dividers in the same line
MyClass o1 = (1--2), MyClass o2 = (3@@4)

Now set it back to default
MyClass o1 = (1;2)
```

While it is preferable to use the classes provided for `int` and `long` arguments in `iomanip.h`, manipulators can be built to handle any argument types.

Extractors

Standard extractors are defined in `iostream.h` in the same manner as inserters for the intrinsic types. Consider, for example, the following extractions.

```
#include <iostream.h>

void main(void) {
    char    a;
    int     b;
    long    c;
    float   d;

    cin >> a;           //read a single character
    cin >> b;           //read an integer
    cin >> c;           //read a long integer
    cin >> d;           //read a float
}
```

Extractors fall into three categories: integral, floating point, and character. The first two are collectively known as numeric extractors.

By default, all extractors ignore leading white space. Numeric extractors begin with the first non-whitespace character and continue until the first non-numeric character. Numeric characters are not limited to digits. An e may be a numeric character to a floating point extractor, since it may represent the beginning of the exponent portion of the number.

If the first character is non-numeric, the extractor returns a 0 and sets the `failbit` in the error state for the input stream. For example, the sequence 123%456 would be extracted by an integer extractor as 123 followed by a zero and an error.

Extraction does not begin from the keyboard until the user enters a return, at which point the extractor reads the line into the input buffer. The extractor does not return to the keyboard for further input until the contents of the buffer have been exhausted. The following input line

1 2 3 4

is equivalent to

1
2

3
4

Extractors are left-associative and return their left operand, the `istream` object. Extractors can be chained. Doing so has no effect on the way extractions are performed.

Integer extractors are affected by the base or radix in the same way that inserters are.

```
int a, b, c;

cin >> dec >> a;
cin >> oct >> b;
cin >> hex >> c;
```

Given the input string 16 20 10, all three variables would be set to the same value. The three numbers could also be entered as 16 020 0x10, but this is not necessary.

A change in the input radix without a corresponding change in the output radix can generate unexpected output. Consider the following program segment.

```
int a;

cin >> hex >> a;
cout << a;
```

If the user enters a 10, the output would appear as 16. In hexidecimal mode the extractor for `cin` interprets 10 as 0x10. Since the `cout` output stream is in decimal mode, the inserter displays decimal 16.

If the `skipws` flag is set, which is the default, the `char*` extractor skips the leading white space and extracts characters until the next white space is encountered. With the flag cleared, the white space remains at the beginning of the string.

The `char*` extractor will not transfer more characters to the buffer than the number specified in the `x_width` field of the input stream. A `setw()` prior to a character string extraction protects the program from input buffer overflow. For example, the following program segments will not overflow the `buffer` array.

```
#include <iostream.h>
#include <iomanip.h>

void main() {
    char buffer[10];

    cin >> setw(10) >> buffer;
    cout << buffer;
}
```

This program generates the following output.

```
123456789012345678901234567890   <-- input string
123456789                        <-- resulting output
```

The output string terminates after the ninth ASCII character to leave space for the terminating null.

Custom Extractors

The rules for writing an extractor are the same as for an inserter. The format for input numbers is similar to that for output. The input object must be broken down into its constituent parts.

An object of class `MyClass` consists of an opening parenthesis, the member `i`, an optional divider, the member `j`, and a closing parenthesis. The programmer should verify each of these format items to insure that the program is in synch with the input stream.

The following is a sample extractor for `MyClass`.

```
istream& operator>>(istream& i, MyClass& mc) {
    char border;
    int count;
```

```
        //save time; if error on istream, just quit
        mc.i = mc.j = 0;
        if (i.bad())
            return i;

        //start with opening brace
        i >> border;
        if (border != '(') {
            i.clear(ios::failbit|i.rdstate());
            return i;
        }

        //now read the first term
        i >> mc.i;

        //if second term to be included, read it too
        if (!mc.iOnly) {
            //start with divider
            for (count = mc.numOfTimes; count > 0; count--) {
                i >> border;
                if (border != mc.divider) {
                    i.clear(ios::failbit|i.rdstate());
                    return i;
                }
            }

            //now the second term
            i >> mc.j;
        }

        //finally the closed brace
        i >> border;
        if (border != ')')
            i.clear(ios::failbit|i.rdstate());
        return i;
    }
```

Stream Input/Output

The first test in the extractor is to save time. Error bits set in the input stream state impede extraction, so the extractor quits immediately to save time. To continue would set the **failbit.**

The next few lines extract a single character and test to confirm that it is the open parenthesis as expected. If it is not, the extractor sets the failbit in the input stream and exits. The character extractor ignores white space.

Each subsequent block extracts the next portion of the `MyClass` object. This extractor is sensitive to the `iOnly` and `divider` fields. If the divider were set to `&&`, the user would be expected to enter `&&` for the object to be accepted.

The complete `MyClass` class with a small program to demonstrate the extractor follows:

```
#include <iostream.h>
#include <iomanip.h>

class MyClass {
    friend istream& operator>>(istream&, MyClass&);
    friend ostream& operator<<(ostream&, MyClass&);
  private:
    int i;
    int j;
  public:
    static int iOnly;
    static int fieldWidth;
    static char divider;
    static int  numOfTimes;

    MyClass(int a1, int a2) : i(a1), j(a2) {
        iOnly = fieldWidth = 0;
        divider = ';';
        numOfTimes = 1;
    }
};

istream& operator>>(istream& i, MyClass& mc) {
```

```
    char border;
    int  count;

    //save time; if error on istream, just quit
    mc.i = mc.j = 0;
    if (i.bad())
        return i;

    //start with opening brace
    i >> border;
    if (border != '(') {
        i.clear(ios::failbit|i.rdstate());
        return i;
    }

    //now read the first term
    i >> mc.i;

    //if second term to be included, read it too
    if (!mc.iOnly) {
        //start with divider
        for (count = mc.numOfTimes; count > 0; count--) {
            i >> border;
            if (border != mc.divider) {
                i.clear(ios::failbit|i.rdstate());
                return i;
            }
        }

        //now the second term
        i >> mc.j;
    }

    //finally the closed brace
    i >> border;
    if (border != ')')
```

Stream Input/Output

```
            i.clear(ios::failbit|i.rdstate());
        return i;
}

ostream& operator<<(ostream& o, MyClass& mc) {
        int w = o.width();
        if (w == 0)
            w = MyClass::fieldWidth;

        w = (w - 2);
        w = (w > 0) ? w : 0;

        //either output (i) or (i,j) depending on iOnly flag
        if (MyClass::iOnly) {
            o << setw(0) << "("
              << setw(w) << mc.i
                        << ")";
        } else {
            w = (w - MyClass::numOfTimes) / 2;
            w = (w > 0) ? w : 0;
            o << setw(0) << "(" << setw(w) << mc.i;

            for (int i = MyClass::numOfTimes; i > 0; i--)
                o << MyClass::divider;

            o << setw(w) << mc.j << ")";
        }
        return o;
};

//define a set of manipulators to set and clear
//the iOnly flag for both istream and ostream
ios& iOnly(ios& s) {
    MyClass::iOnly = 1;
    return s;
}
```

```cpp
ios& jAlso(ios& s) {
    MyClass::iOnly = 0;
    return s;
}

//now a manipulator to set width for all MyClass objects
ios& doIt(ios& s, int width) {
    MyClass::fieldWidth = width;
    return s;
}
smanip_int permWidth(int width) {
    smanip_int object(doIt, width);
    return object;
}

//and another to set the divider character
class CustomManip {
  private:
    char divider;
    int  noTimes;
  public:
    CustomManip(char d, int n) {
        divider = d;
        noTimes = n;
    }
    void changeDivider() {
        MyClass::divider = divider;
        MyClass::numOfTimes = noTimes;
    }
};

ostream& operator<<(ostream& s, CustomManip& cm) {
    cm.changeDivider();
    return s;
}
istream& operator>>(istream& s, CustomManip& cm) {
```

Stream Input/Output

```
        cm.changeDivider();
        return s;
}

CustomManip setDivider(char d = ';', int count = 1) {
        return CustomManip(d, count);
}

void main() {
    MyClass o1(0,0);

    cout << "O1 with default divider:" << endl;
    cin  >> o1;
    cout << "MyClass o1 = "    << o1
         << ", error state = " << cin.rdstate()
         << "\n\n";

    cout << "Now try divider = ###" << endl;
    cin  >> setDivider('#', 3) >> o1;

    cout << setDivider()
         << "MyClass o1 = "    << o1
         << ", error state = " << cin.rdstate()
         << "\n\n";

    cout << "Finally, with iOnly set" << endl;
    cin  >> iOnly >> o1;
    cout << jAlso
         << "MyClass o1 = "    << o1
         << ", error state = " << cin.rdstate()
         << "\n\n";
}
```

Neither the `MyClass` class nor its inserter has been changed. The `setDivider()` manipulator is unchanged except for the addition of a

`CustomManip` extractor which permits the divider to be changed during input as well as output.

Manipulators built with `iomanip.h`, such as `permWidth()`, may be used with either inserters or extractors. To be usable with either `istream` or `ostream` objects, the `iOnly` and `jAlso` manipulators must be changed to type `ios`, a base class for both.

The output from a sample run of this program follows:

```
O1 with default divider:
(1;2)                   <-- user input
MyClass o1 = (1;2), error state = 0

Now try divider = ###
(3###4)                 <-- user input
MyClass o1 = (3;4), error state = 0

Finally, with iOnly set
(5)                     <-- user input
MyClass o1 = (5;0), error state = 0
```

Entering any format other than the one prescribed, such as the wrong divider, renders the remainder of the object and all subsequent objects 0.

Input/Output to Files

As we have seen, C++ automatically opens several streams at program start. These are listed in Table 9–2.

Table 9–2 Standard ios objects

Object	*stdio Equivalent*	*Purpose*
cin	stdin	standard input
cout	stdout	standard output
cerr	stderr	standard error (unbuffered)
clog		standard error (buffered)

The input stream `cin` reads from the standard input file—normally, the keyboard. The C equivalent is `stdin`. The stream `cout` outputs to standard output, which defaults to the display (`stdout`). The streams `cerr` and `clog` both output to standard error, which also defaults to the display (`stderr`). All four may be redirected to different files using the <, >, and |> rerouting commands on the program command line.

C++ offers two error streams: one unbuffered, the other buffered. Buffering error messages is not always a good idea. Usually not enough errors occur to affect output efficiency. Error messages should be output as soon as possible to avoid losing them in the event of a crash. The stream `cerr` is an unbuffered version of the standard error stream.

Buffering of the error stream does make sense when the programmer expects standard output to be rerouted to a file. Then output can be sent to the standard error device, which also points to the display and is not normally rerouted. The buffered stream `clog` is available for this function.

User Files

For user-defined files, C++ provides the classes `fstream`, `ifstream`, and `ofstream`, which are derived from `iostream`, `istream`, and `ostream`, respectively. These classes contain objects of class `filebuf`, which is derived from `streambuf`, to handle the buffering of the file I/O. The class descriptions are contained in the include file `fstream.h`, which also includes `iostream.h`.

All three of the file stream classes provide constructors to open stream objects and associate them with files. The most used constructors for these classes are declared as follows:

```
ifstream(const char*, int = ios::in,
                     int = filebuf::openprot);
ofstream(const char*, int = ios::out,
                     int = filebuf::openprot);
fstream (const char*, int,
                     int = filebuf::openprot);
```

In all three, the first argument represents the name of the file to open. The following program reads integers from file `source` and writes them out to file `sink`. The program terminates when the end of file is encountered in the source file.

```
#include <fstream.h>
#include <stdlib.h>

void main() {
    ifstream source("source");
    if (!source) {
        cerr << "error opening source\n";
        abort();
    }
    ofstream sink("sink");
    if (!sink) {
        cerr << "error opening sink\n";
        abort();
    }

    int number;
    for (;;) {
        source >> number;
        if (source.eof())
            break;
        sink   << number;
    }
};
```

The operator ! is overloaded for streams to return a nonzero if an error has occurred and to return a zero if there are no errors.

The second argument to the stream constructors is an integer field made up of the ORing of flags of type `enum ios::open_mode` to indicate the mode to use when opening the file. The list of other flags follows. Notice that `ifstream` defaults to an input file while `ofstream` defaults to an output file. Since `fstream` has no default, the programmer must specify the open mode for objects of type `fstream`.

```
enum ios::open_mode {
    in        = 0x01,   //open for reading
    out       = 0x02,   //open for writing
    ate       = 0x04,   //seek to eof upon open
    app       = 0x08,   //append: all additions at eof
    trunc     = 0x10,   //truncate if already exists
    nocreate  = 0x20,   //no open if file doesn't exist
    noreplace = 0x40,   //no open if file already exists
    binary    = 0x80    //binary (not text) file
};
```

To prevent the destination file from being created if it did not already exist in the above program, the programmer would change the constructor call to the following:

```
ofstream sink("sink", ios::out|ios::nocreate);
```

If the second argument is to be specified, the `ios::in` and/or `ios::out` flag must also be specified, as it is no longer assumed. Objects of class `fstream` can be opened for simultaneous input and output.

The final argument to the constructor is the protection, which is a static member of `filebuf`.

When a stream object is opened with the default constructor, an object is created, but no file is opened. Before use, the object must be associated with a file using the `open()` member function. The arguments to `open()` are the same as those of the normal constructor. Thus, the preceding source file could have been opened as follows:

```
ifstream source;
source.open("source");
if (!source) {
            //remainder of program
```

In addition, we might have written the second example as follows:

```
ofstream sink;
sink.open("sink", ios::out|ios::nocreate);
```

The member `close()` closes an object. An object may be opened and closed repeatedly.

Seeking Within a Stream

The type `streampos` defined within `iostream.h` holds the location of the read or write pointer within a file stream. Two stream methods can be used to report on the location of the pointer. The method `tellg()` reports the location of the get pointer (the next location to read), while the `tellp()` method reports the location of the put pointer (the next location to write). The following expression saves the current write position.

```
//declaration
ofstream sink("sink");

//later on in the program
streampos sinkPos = sink.tellp().
```

The methods `seekg()` and `seekp()` reposition the stream pointers to a `streampos`. Two variants of these methods exist: one for absolute positioning and the other for relative positioning.

```
sink.seekp(sinkPos);         //return to saved location

sink.seekp(-10, ios::curr);  //move to 10 bytes before
                             //current position
sink.seekp( 10, ios::beg);   //move to 10 bytes after
                             //beginning of file
sink.seekp(-10, ios::end);   //move to 10 bytes before
                             //end of file
```

Stream Input/Output

The seek methods were demonstrated as part of the Virtual File Array in Chapter 6.

Tying Streams

An input stream object may be tied to an output stream object with the `tie()` member function as in the following:

```
#include <fstream.h>

void main() {
    ifstream inp("from_file");
    ofstream out("out_file");

    inp.tie(&out);
}
```

Subsequent read requests from `inp` will automatically flush any buffered output to the file `out_file`.

Pointers to Streams

Most programs accept input from the file specified in the command line or from standard input if no file name is present. The standard predefined stream objects are declared to allow assignment to a different stream. A better approach is to use pointers to streams.

Consider the following program.

```
#include <fstream.h>
#include <iomanip.h>

void main(int argc, char* argv[]) {
    istream* input = &cin;
    char buffer[80];
```

```
        if (argc = = 2)
            input = new ifstream(argv[1]);

        while (!input->eof()) {
            (*input) >> setw(80) >> buffer;
            cout << buffer;
        }
}
```

The pointer `input` is first assigned the address of the standard input stream `cin`. The program uses `input` to read in character strings and insert them into standard output. If an argument is provided, however, the program assumes that it is the name of a file and a new `ifstream` object is opened on that file. The address of the new object is stored into `input` so that subsequent input comes from the new file instead of standard input.

Using pointers to streams simplifies the job of redirecting both input and output in a program.

Handling Errors in Streams

Errors during I/O operations on stream objects are retained in an error state member of the class `ios`. Bits are set within this state field to specify the nature of the error. The error flags are defined as follows:

```
enum ios::io_state {
    goodbit  = 0x00,   //no bit set: all is ok
    eofbit   = 0x01,   //pointer at end of file
    failbit  = 0x02,   //last I/O operation failed
    badbit   = 0x04,   //invalid operation attempted
    hardfail = 0x80    //unrecoverable error
};
```

Once an error occurs, subsequent inserter and extractor requests to that stream are ignored until the error flags are cleared. In this way, errors are passed back to the caller. An error within a function may be ignored until detected by the calling function.

Several methods are available to query and manipulate the stream error state. When `operator!()` is applied to a stream object, a nonzero is returned if `failbit`, `badbit`, or `hardfail` are set. The function `operator void*()` returns a zero if `failbit`, `badbit`, or `hardfail` are set and a nonzero otherwise. This provides an alternative means of checking an object for error, as in the following:

```
ifstream source("source");
int value;

if (source)              //is there an error on source?
    return               //return if no error
//error code here


// OR //

if (source >> value)    //was the operator successful?
    return;             //return if no error
//error code
```

In the first example, Turbo C++ converts the type `ifstream` into a type `void*` using the supplied operator in order to make sense of the conditional. If `operator void*()` returns a zero, then one of the error flags is set; otherwise, no error has occurred.

The second example takes the same principle one step further. The `operator >>(ifstream, int)` returns an object of type `ifstream`, which is then converted to `void*`. If `operator void*()` returns a zero here, it does not mean that an error occurred in the extraction. The error could have occurred earlier.

This is particularly true in a compound extraction or insertion. Consider the following:

```
if (cout << a << b << c)
    return;            //okay
//error code here
```

If the expression evaluates to zero, the final insertion `cout << c` is not necessarily in error. Any of the insertion operations could have generated the error.

More explicit error methods are defined for stream classes, as follows:

```
int rdstate()    //returns current state
int good()       //returns a nonzero if state
                 //equals goodbit
int eof()        //returns a nonzero if eofbit set
int bad()        //returns a nonzero if badbit or
                 //hardfail set
int fail()       //returns a nonzero if failbit or bad()
void clear(int = 0); //set error bits except hardfail
```

The method `clear()` is most often used to clear the error state after an error has been acknowledged, but it can be used to set the error state as well.

```
ofstream output(outputFileName);

if (!output) {
    //take corrective action

    //now clear the error flags
    output.clear();
}

if (someUserFunction(output)) {
    //function did not work, set fail flag
    output.clear(ios::failbit|output.rdstate());
}
```

The first call to `clear()` in the preceding example clears the error flags since the default argument is zero. The second call to `clear()` adds the `failbit` flag to any error bits already set.

Other Stream Methods

The class `ostream` includes several member functions that can be used instead of overloaded stream operators. The output method `put()` is roughly equivalent to the character inserter `operator<<(char)`. For larger blocks of data, the programmer may use the member function `write()`.

```
char singleByte;
char buffer[numberOfBytes];

cout.put(singleByte);
cout.write(buffer, numberOfBytes);
```

Both of the preceding functions perform no formatting and ignore the formatting flags, making them most useful for binary data. Both functions also return an object of type `ostream` so they may be placed directly into a conditional to check for error.

Similarly, the `istream` class includes two methods for reading individual or blocks of characters: the `get()` and `read()` functions. Both are used to input raw binary data. No formatting is performed. While the character extractor skips leading white space, `get()` does not. In addition, `get()` and `read()` are not tied. Performing a `cin.get()` does not automatically flush any pending output to `cout`.

```
char singleByte;
char buffer[numberOfBytes];

cin.get(singleByte);
cin.read(buffer, numberOfBytes);
```

Both methods return `istream`, so they may appear in conditionals.

Mixing I/O with `stdio`

Since `stdio` is unbuffered, the programmer must be careful when mixing inserter output and `stdio` output in the same program. The `printf()` output tends to "race ahead" of the inserter output resulting in garbled output.

To handle this problem, flush the output stream before sending `stdio` output to the same file. The programmer can also unbuffer stream output by calling the method `ios::sync_with_stdio()`. While this handles the `stdio` problem, it levies a significant performance penalty.

Incore I/O

The classes `istrstream` and `ostrstream`, defined in `strstream.h`, perform insertions and extractions on buffers in memory. The constructor for `istrstream` accepts the address of a buffer of type `char*`. To read from a fixed buffer, the programmer might enter the following:

```
char* numPtr = "1";
istrstream input(numPtr);
int i;

input >> i;
```

However, reading a numerical command line argument using the array of buffers `argv` is much more common.

```
#include <strstream.h>

void main(int argc, char* argv[]) {
    int i;
    istrstream input(argv[1]);

    input >> i;
    cout << i;
}
```

An `istrstream` constant can also be created by calling the constructor anonymously. This is particularly useful when reading an array of pointers to character strings. The following program reads all of the command line arguments into an integer array.

```
#include <strstream.h>

void main(int argc, char* argv[]) {
    int* array = new int[argc];

    for (int count = 1; count < argc; count++)
        istrstream(argv[count]) >> array[count - 1];
}
```

Insertion into RAM is similar except that the constructor for `ostrstream` requires a second integer argument to specify the length of the buffer. The inserter will not store outside the bounds specified in the constructor.

```
#include <strstream.h>

void main(void) {
    int   i;
    char buffer[80];

    ostrstream output(buffer, sizeof buffer);
    output << "i = " << i << ";\n" << ends;

    cout << buffer;
}
```

The `ostrstream` inserter does not add a null at the end of the generated ASCII string. The programmer must invoke the manipulator `ends` to do so.

The final inserter in the program displays the string accumulated in `buffer`. The output from this program is as follows:

```
i = 10;
```

Conclusion

Turbo C++ provides the programmer with capabilities beyond those specified in the C++ language standard, including a powerful overlay manager. Chapter 10 examines these features in detail.

Chapter 10

Turbo C++ Advanced Features

Let us examine some of the advanced features of Turbo C++ that are not derived from C++.

Virtual Run-time Object-oriented Memory Manager

The **Virtual Run-time Object-oriented Memory Manager**, known as **VROOMM**, is Borland's new overlay manager. Overlaying is a technique used to squeeze a large amount of code into a small memory area.

When the CPU is executing a set of instructions, the other instructions that make up the program need not be loaded into internal memory. When the program completes the currently loaded instructions, the program loads new segments into memory, overwriting the no longer needed instructions.

In the extreme, only the instruction being executed needs to be memory resident; however, if the set of memory resident instructions is too small, an excessive time penalty will arise as the program stops to reload code from disk after every instruction.

A program does not flow evenly from the open brace of `main()` to its close brace. Loops often cause the program to cycle over the same instructions multiple times before continuing. Loops can be explicit, as in the case of a `for` loop, or implicit, as when the user repeatedly enters the same command. For example, in a word processor, "insert character" functions are executed more often than any other.

If a lengthy loop is contained within a single overlay, the time required to load the overlay is small compared to the time required to complete the loop. Overlays containing often-executed code sections are retained in memory as much as possible to avoid reloading them. The performance of an overlaid program approximates that of the same program when not overlaid except that its memory requirements are significantly smaller.

Conventional Overlay Systems

In conventional overlay arrangements, the programmer is responsible for organizing functions into overlays. The programmer can define multiple overlay areas, but each is assigned a fixed RAM address. Each overlay is assigned to a single overlay area.

Since the linker knows the address of each overlay and the area to which each overlay belongs, the program can calculate the RAM address of every overlaid function at link time. To load an overlay, the program reads the overlay directly into its assigned area. No address conversions are necessary.

In less well developed systems, the programmer must code the calls to perform the overlay loads. The programmer must make sure that an overlaid function is in memory before calling it. In slightly more advanced systems, the compiler generates extra code to perform the overlay loads automatically. That is, the program might code a call to `fn()`. Noting that `fn()` is in the first overlay for area A, typically known as overlay A1, the compiler would add a call `loadOverlay(A1)` immediately before the call to `fn()`. Loading an overlay that is already loaded has no effect.

Even in this improved system, the programmer must make sure that a function can be loaded into memory. Since several overlays often share the same area, it is easy to build conflicts into the system. Take, for example, the program in Figure 10–1 with three overlays A1, A2, and A3 sharing a single overlay area A. Before the function `f()` can call a function `fa()` in overlay A1, the program loads overlay.

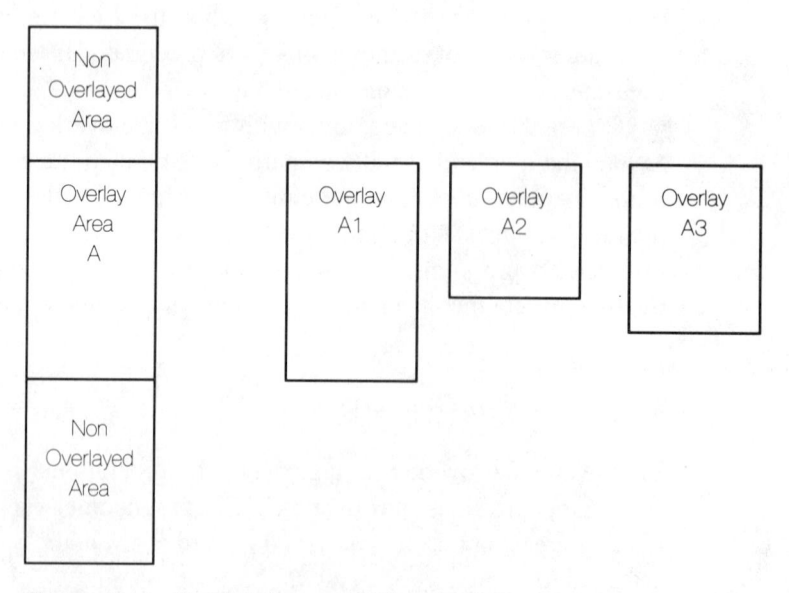

Figure 10–1 Overlay Area with Three Overlays

Suppose that `fa()` attempts to call a function `fb()` in overlay A2. Nothing about the function's prototype would discourage the programmer from making this call, but the procedure would be very difficult to perform.

In order to call `fb()`, the overlay loaded must load overlay A2, thus overwriting A1. When complete, `fb()` cannot return without reloading overlay A1 containing the calling function `fa()`.

No problem arises if both `fa()` and `fb()` are in the same overlay or if they occupy different overlay areas. In older systems the programmer was required to work out the different function interactions and to organize the overlays so that each was accessible through every possible path.

In a small system, determining all of the ways in which overlay functions can call each other is a manageable task. In a larger system, however, the task is quite difficult. A system that has been structured to avoid such conflicts is very difficult to change.

Suppose that `fa()` does not call `fc()` in the original system. No problem arises when `fa()` is put into overlay A1 and `fc()` is stored in A3. Sometime later, however, if a call to `fc()` is added to `fa()`, the maintenance programmer may find the system crashes upon returning from `fc()`. If the overlay structure is not properly documented, the programmer will have to undertake a complete analysis of the program to determine how the overlays should be reorganized in order to avoid the conflict and not introduce new ones.

This problem can be prevented if all calls from one overlaid function to another are performed through an intermediate overlay controlling function. For example, when the programmer codes a call to `fc()`, the compiler replaces this with a call such as `loadOverlay(A3, fc)`. The function `fc()` returns to the function `loadOverlay()` in order to reload the overlay A1 before returning to `fc()`. This process is depicted in Figure 10–2.

As the sophistication of conventional overlay systems increases, so does the overhead. While the most basic overlay system places a considerable burden upon the programmer by requiring that calls to `loadOverlay()` be coded explicitly, the operating overhead may be minimized. Calls to `loadOverlay()` are only included where they are needed. When the calls are generated automatically by the compiler, the overhead of unnecessary calls is added. The intermediate function solution adds another layer of overhead by effectively adding a call to `loadOverlay()` to both the function call and the function return.

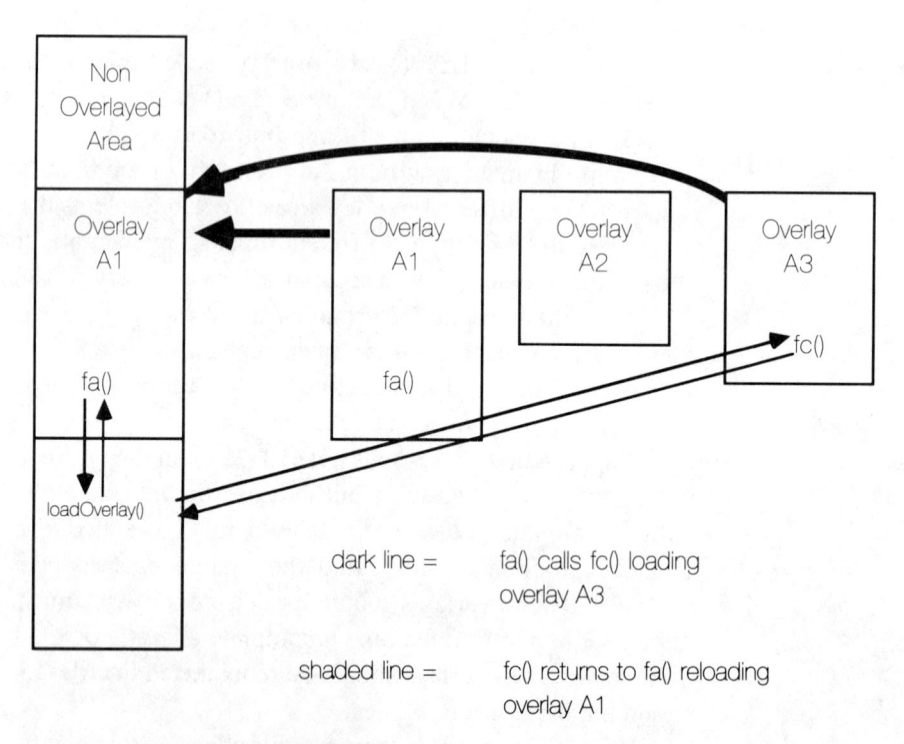

Figure 10-2 Calling `fc()` from `fa()` via `loadOverlay()`

dark line = fa() calls fc() loading overlay A3

shaded line = fc() returns to fa() reloading overlay A1

VROOMM System

The VROOMM overlay system avoids the lockout problems associated with fixed overlay area approaches by not limiting an overlay to a single area. That is, when `f()` calls `fa()` in overlay 1 (it is no longer correct to refer to this as A1), VROOMM allocates space for the overlay from the beginning of the overlay area. If `fa()` were to call `fb()` in overlay 2, VROOMM would allocate space starting with the end of overlay 1.

Once control is passed from `fb()` back to `fa()`, overlay 2 stays in memory. The chances are good that function `fb()` will be needed again in the near future. Such references do not require the overlay to be reloaded until the overlay space is needed by another function and the function is flushed.

To keep track of which overlays are loaded, VROOMM assigns each overlaid function a five-byte field in non-overlaid memory. At the beginning of each of these VROOMM cells, Turbo C++ stores an INT 0x3F, which is a call to the overlay loader. The remainder of the cell contains the offset of the function within its overlay.

If we use as our example functions fa(), fb(), and fc() in overlays 1, 2, and 3, memory begins as shown in Figure 10–3.

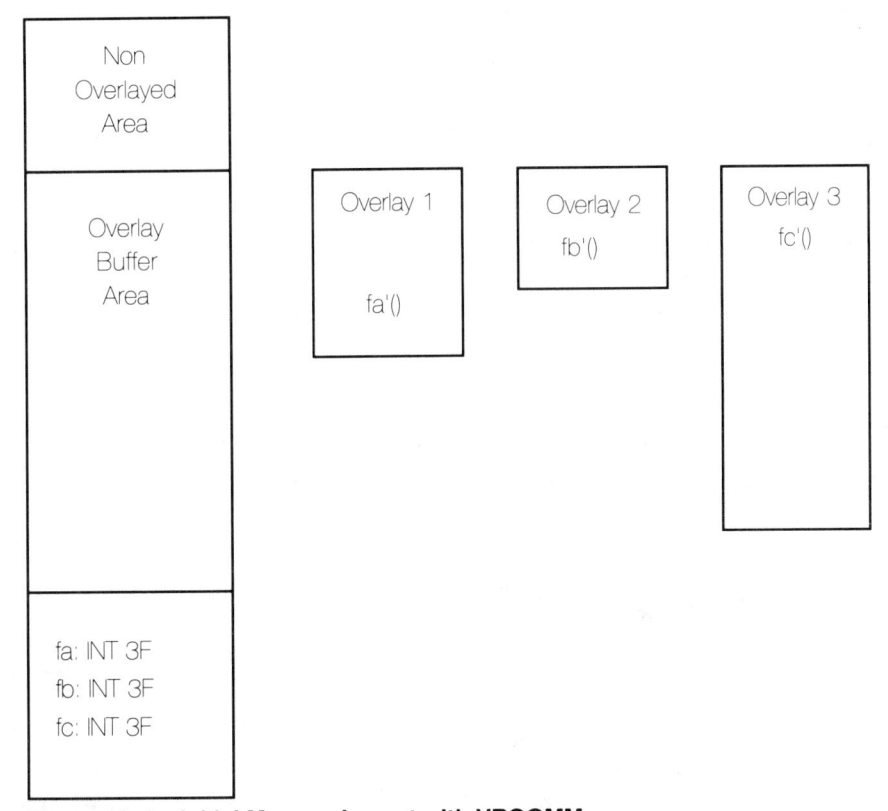

Figure 10–3 Initial Memory Layout with VROOMM

When f() calls fa(), the overlay loader is invoked. The loader loads fa() into the beginning of the overlay area and stores a far jump in the cell in place of the INT 0x3F as shown in Figure 10–4.

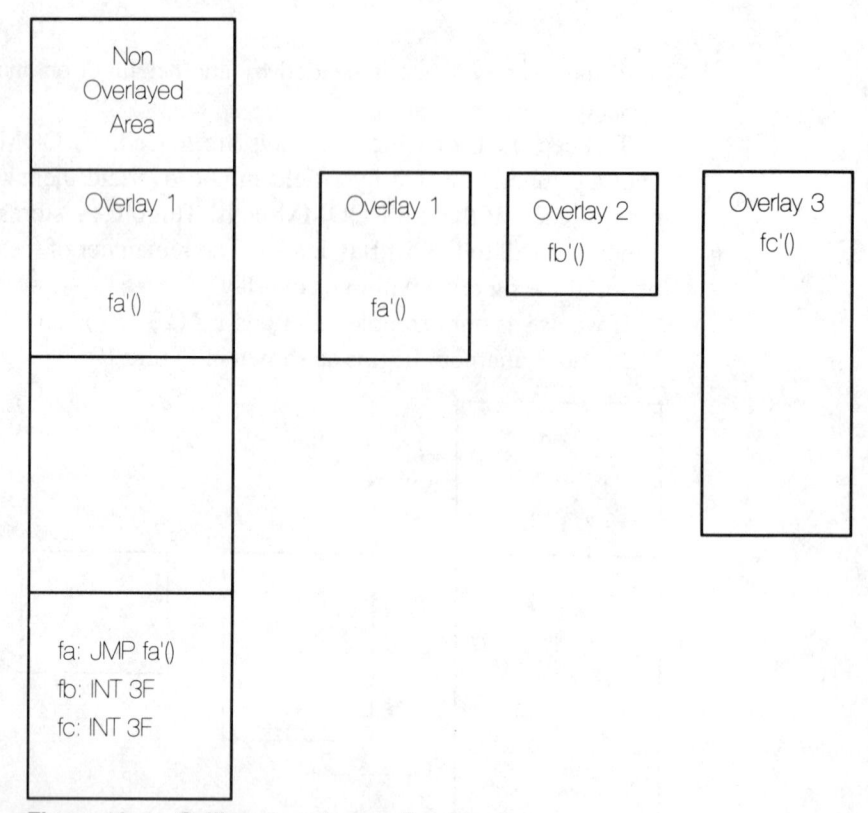

```
┌─────────────┐
│    Non      │
│  Overlayed  │
│    Area     │
├─────────────┤                ┌──────────┐ ┌──────────┐
│  Overlay 1  │   ┌──────────┐ │Overlay 2 │ │Overlay 3 │
│             │   │Overlay 1 │ │  fb'()   │ │  fc'()   │
│   fa'()     │   │   fa'()  │ │          │ │          │
│             │   └──────────┘ └──────────┘ │          │
├─────────────┤                             │          │
│             │                             │          │
│             │                             │          │
│             │                             └──────────┘
│             │
├─────────────┤
│fa: JMP fa'()│
│fb: INT 3F   │
│fc: INT 3F   │
└─────────────┘
```

Figure 10–4 Calling `fa()` Loads Overlay 1

As long as overlay 1 stays in memory, subsequent calls to the `fa()` cell jump directly to the function. If function `f()` now calls the `fb()` cell, the overlay loader is invoked again resulting in the situation depicted in Figure 10–5.

As before, calling the `fc()` cell invokes the overlay loader. In order to create sufficient room for oversized overlay 3, the loader flushes overlays 1 and 2. When the overlay is flushed, the `INT 0x3F` is stored back into the cells for `fa()` and `fb()`. This is shown in Figure 10–6.

Overlays in VROOMM are based upon compilation modules. Functions defined within a single module are included in the same overlay. Calling any one of these functions loads all of them into memory and sets all of their cells to long jumps. Calls within a module do not go through the function cell.

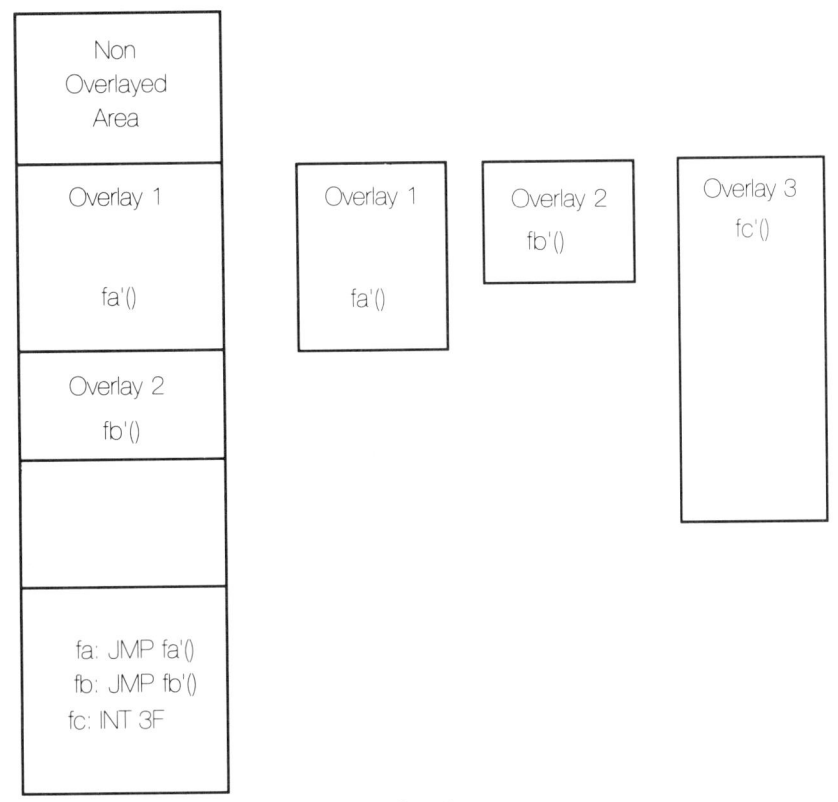

Figure 10-5 Calling fb() Loads Overlay 2

Using VROOMM

To overlay modules, all of the modules that make up the program must be compiled with the Overlay Support flag in the Options/Compiler/Code Generation menu of the IDE or with the -Y switch of the command line version. The programmer indicates which modules to overlay by setting the Overlay flag in the Options menu of the Project file. When using the command line version, use the -Yo switch before the modules you plan to overlay. Overlaying is only supported in the Medium, Large, and Huge compile models.

When using VROOMM the programmer must make sure that moving from one overlay to another does not result in thrashing. Consider the following example function fa().

```
for (i = 0; i < 100; i++ )
    fb();
```

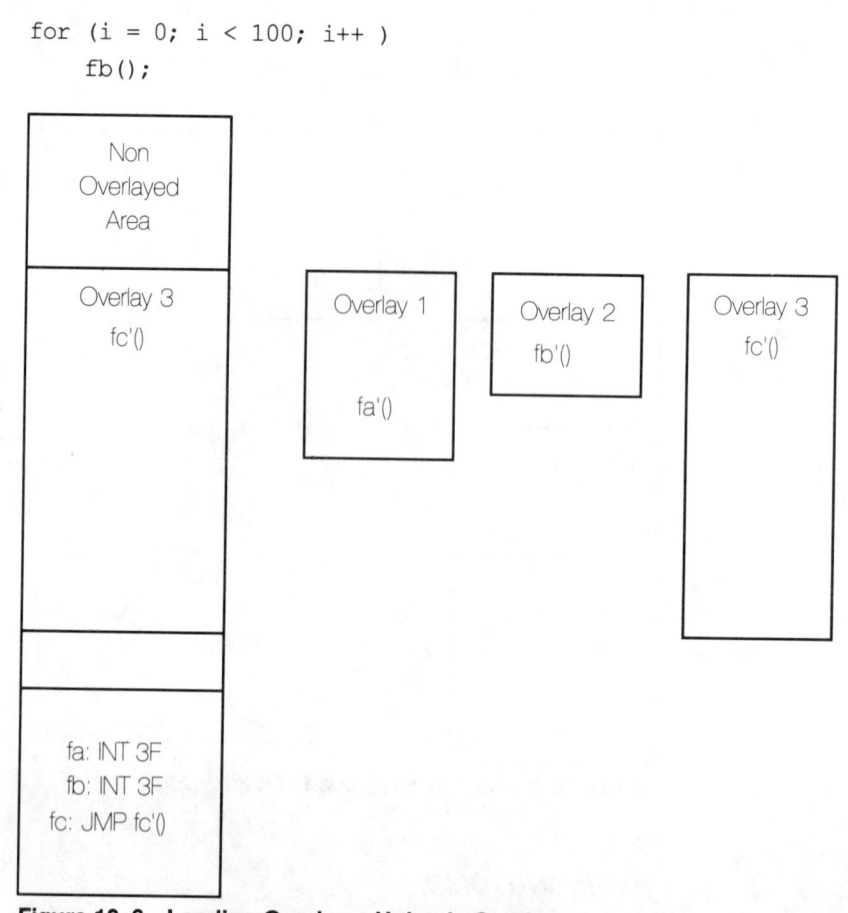

```
Non
Overlayed
Area
```

```
Overlay 3
fc'()
```

```
Overlay 1
fa'()
```

```
Overlay 2
fb'()
```

```
Overlay 3
fc'()
```

```
fa: INT 3F
fb: INT 3F
fc: JMP fc'()
```

Figure 10-6 Loading Overlay 3 Unloads Overlays 1 and 2

When function `fb()` is called the first time, VROOMM loads it into memory. The next time through the loop `fb()` does not need to be reloaded. However, the following might cause trouble if `fb()` and `fc()` were not defined in the same module.

```
for (i = 0; i < 100; i++ ) {
    fb();
    fc();
}
```

Once `fb()` returns, the overlay containing `fc()` must be loaded. If the overlay buffer is not large enough to hold both, the `fb()` overlay is flushed. As soon as `fc()` returns, however, VROOMM must reload `fb()`, flushing `fc()`. In this example, VROOMM performs some 200 overlay loads. This is known as **overlay thrashing.** Since the program can fulfill all requests, no error is generated. However, thrashing reduces system performance to a crawl.

A programmer might suspect thrashing when the program executes unexpectedly slowly. If the program executes well when it is not overlaid or if it previously ran well but slowed down after the addition of a few extra function calls, thrashing may be occuring. Thrashing can be verified by forcing VROOMM to use the disk. Since a disk is so much slower, disk thrashing will reduce performance even further and a flurry of disk activity will give further visual evidence of thrashing. Eliminating thrashing is generally a matter of increasing the overlay buffer area until it can accommodate all of the critical overlays simultaneously or reorganizing the functions that call each other repetitively into the same overlays.

The first time that an overlay is loaded, VROOMM reads it from the .EXE executable file. Normally when an overlay is flushed, its area is marked as available. However, if either Expanded or Extended Memory is available, VROOMM can swap the overlay into the expanded memory. Since reading memory areas is faster than reading from disk, the overhead of loading the overlay subsequently will be greatly reduced.

Passing an EMS handle to the function `_OvrInitEms()` instructs VROOMM to use the EMS memory as an overlay swap area. Passing a zero handle causes `_OvrInitEms()` to request memory of its own from the EMS handler. A return of zero indicates success.

```
int far _OvrInitEms(unsigned emsHandle,
                    unsigned emsFirst,    //first EMS page
                    unsigned emsPages);   //# of EMS pages
```

An essentially identical function `_OvrInitExt()` allocates extended memory for overlay loader use. The prototype for this function is as follows:

```
int far _OvrInitExt(unsigned long extStart,
                    unsigned long extLength);
```

Here `extStart` is the address of the beginning of extended memory (this should have been declared `void * far extStart`) while `extLength` is its length. Prototypes for both of the above functions are contained in the include file DOS.H as long as Turbo C++ is selected from the Options/Compile/Source menu; in other words, as long as `_STDC_` is not defined.

Several global variables are also defined. The variable `ovrbuffer` can be used to increase the size of the overlay area from its default of twice the size of the largest overlay. If sufficient memory is available, this function can reduce thrashing by keeping more overlays loaded simultaneously.

The global `_OvrSize` appears to contain the calculated size of the overlay area in paragraphs. In addition, `_OvrTrapCount` contains the number of times that overlays have been loaded. This can be useful in detecting a thrashing condition. Both of these calls must be specifically prototyped, as they are not contained in any include file. Both `_Ovrbuffer` and `_OvrSize` are in paragraphs.

```
extern unsigned far _OvrSize;
extern unsigned far _OvrTrapCount;
```

The TC.EXE and TCC.EXE of Turbo C++ were created with VROOMM. The effect is quite noticeable in the IDE. Many operations, such as bringing down a new command window, cause otherwise unexplained disk activity, depending upon how much time has elapsed since the operation was last performed. The code to perform that operation may no longer be in RAM when the option is selected. Executing TC.EXE with the /e or /x switch allows the IDE to use expanded or extended memory respectively. (Turbo C defaults to EMS memory unless this has been disabled with TCINST.)

Since access to extended memory is problematic, Borland also provides the /rx switch, which allows a RAM disk built in extended memory to be used to hold overlay files. Even though slightly slower, accessing overlays on a RAM disk is less prone to error than accessing extended memory directly.

Inline Assembly Language

No compiler can generate machine code as efficiently as a skilled assembly language programmer. A programmer can cache a value in a register for use in some calculation several instructions away. An experienced programmer can also determine when a particular machine instruction exists to solve the problem at hand in just a few clock cycles. Compilers can only perform these optimizations with difficulty. If the compiler spends too much time seeking register optimizations, the compilation time increases uncomfortably. Adding too much code to examine applications for odd CPU instructions makes the compiler large and unwieldy.

Programmers familiar with assembly language may be tempted to drop down to the machine level to improve upon what Turbo C++ can accomplish. One should not take this path too quickly. First, remember the adage: "90 percent of the time is spent on 10 percent of the code or less." Let us look again at the Sieve of Eratosthenes benchmark.

```
//The Sieve of Eratosthenes Prime Number Program
//  adapted from  Byte Magazine, January 1983.

#include <stdio.h>
#include <stdlib.h>

#define TRUE  1
#define FALSE 0
#define ITER  1000
#define SIZE  8190

//define our Boolean sieve
char flags [SIZE+1];

//Main - the sieve program
void main () {
    int i,k;
    int iter, count;
```

```
    printf ("%d iterations. "
            "Hit enter and start stop watch\n", ITER);
    getchar ();
    printf ("Start...");

    for (iter = 1; iter <= ITER; iter++) {
        count = 0;

        //initialize flags to TRUE
        for (i = 0; i <= SIZE; i++)             //Note A
            flags[i] = TRUE;

        //now search for primes
        for (i = 2; i <= SIZE; i++)             //Note B
            if (flags[i]) {
                //found a prime - cancel multiples
                for ( k = i + i; k <= SIZE; k += i )
                    flags[k] = FALSE;
                count++;
            }
    }

    printf ("stop!\n\n%d primes\n", count);
}
```

A closer look at this program reveals that it spends most of its time in the two loops marked Note A and Note B. By applying the Turbo Profiler to the program, I determined that more than 92 percent of the program's time is spent in these two areas.

Attempts to streamline the program outside of the two loops would be fruitless. Even if the time spent outside the loops was reduced by 50 percent, no more than a 4 percent difference in the overall execution time of the program would result. If, however, the efficiency of the two loops was improved by even 25 percent—a much more achievable sum—the program would finish 23 percent faster.

Rewriting the two loops in assembly language immediately would be a mistake. We should first examine the program to see if there are some efficiencies we can add in C++. Making improvements to the algorithm in C++ is much easier than making changes in the relatively confusing machine language. It has often been said, one should optimize the algorithm before optimizing the code.

Notice that the second loop begins with 2. The loop then marks out and searches for all subsequent even numbers. However, 2 is the only even number that is also prime. Thus, changing the loops as follows generates the same results.

```
    for (iter = 1; iter <= ITER; iter++) {
count = 1;    //assume 2 is prime

//initialize flags here
for (i = 3; i <= SIZE; i += 2)
    flags[i] = TRUE;

//search for primes
for (i = 3; i <= SIZE; i += 2)
    if (flags[i]) {
        //found a prime - cancel multiples
        for ( k = i + i; k <= SIZE; k += i )
            flags[k] = FALSE;
        count++;

    }
}
```

Here `count` starts with 1 since 2 is prime. From then on only the odd numbers are examined. This change reduces the execution time by almost 30 percent.

Once all improvement possibilities at the C++ level have been exhausted, a programmer may then recode the most critical sections of a program in assembly language. Let us examine the ways that Turbo C++ makes this job easier.

Pseudo-registers and `geninterrupt()`

Several features of Turbo C++ allow programmers access to the machine level from C++ itself. For example, Turbo C++ defines an intrinsic variable name for each register. The pseudo-registers bear the name of the 80x86 register in uppercase with an underscore attached to the front. These are shown in Table 10–1.

Table 10–1   Turbo C++ Pseudo-registers.

8-bit registers	16-bit registers	Pseudo-registers
_AL	_AX	general purpose registers
_AH		
_BL	_BX	
_BH		
_CL	_CX	
_CH		
_DL	_DX	
_DH		
	_CS	segment registers
	_DS	
	_SS	
	_ES	
	_SP	stack pointer
	_BP	stack base pointer
	_SI	source registers
	_DI	destination register
	_FLAGS	processor flags

With the pseudo-register, the programmer can avoid mundane assembly language additions as in the following:

```
_AX = 1;    //same as MOV AX,#1
```

While pseudo-registers can reduce the size or complexity of assembly language sections, there are only a few cases where accessing the registers directly is of much use without adding machine instructions as well. One of these is in combination with geninterrupt().

When calling an interrupt routine from C++, the preferred method is the int86() library routine or one of its variants such as int86x() or bios(). The int86() function appears as follows:

```
#include <dos.h>
REGS reg;

reg.h.ah = callNumber;
reg.x.dx = someOtherValue;
int86(interruptNumber, &reg, &reg);
```

The union REGS is defined in the include file DOS.H as follows:

```
struct WORDREGS {
    unsigned int  ax, bx, cx, dx, si, di, cflag, flags;
};

struct BYTEREGS {
    unsigned char al, ah, bl, bh, cl, ch, dl, dh;
};

union REGS    {
    struct WORDREGS x;
    struct BYTEREGS h;
};
```

A variable is defined for every register. Since each of the registers AX, BX, CX, and DX can be accessed either as single 16-bit values or as two 8-bit values, the two structures BYTEREGS and WORDREGS overlap in the REGS union.

The registers to the interrupt are pulled out of the source REGS structure in the int86() function before performing the interrupt. Upon returning from the interrupt, the registers are stored back into the target `REGS` structure before returning. The source and target can be the same structure.

The following function instructs the BIOS to read the screen pixel from page 0, row R, and column C. The function assumes the screen is in graphics mode.

```
char readPixel(unsigned R, unsigned C) {
    REGS reg;

    reg.h.ah = 0x0d;     //read pixel function
    reg.h.bh = 0x00;     //page number 0
    reg.x.cx = R;
    reg.x.dx = C;
    int86(0x10, &reg, &reg);
    return reg.h.al;
}
```

Interrupt `0x10` calls the video-handling portion of the BIOS routines. Service call `0x0D` is the Read Pixel function. The color of the pixel is returned in the `AL` register. Programmers interested in researching the BIOS calls are referred to *CBIOS for IBM PS/2 Computers and Compatibles* (Reading, Mass.: Addison-Wesley, 1989).

The programmer can address registers `AX` through `DX` as either a single register or two half-registers. Therefore, the following:

```
reg.x.ax = 0x0102;
```

is the same as

```
reg.h.al = 0x01;
reg.h.ah = 0x02
```

The register `AL` assumes the first byte of `AX`, and `AH` the second.

Handling registers as members of a union adds a certain level of overhead. This may be avoided by using the `geninterrupt()` macro, which codes an interrupt instruction directly inline. The programmer uses the pseudo-registers to initialize the registers before performing the interrupt call. For example, the previous `int86()` example could be coded using `geninterrupt()` as follows:

```
char readPixel(unsigned R, unsigned C) {
    _AH = 0x0d;    //read pixel function
    _BH = 0x00;    //page number 0
    _CX = R;
    _DX = C;
    geninterrupt(0x10);
    return _AL;
}
```

One must be careful when using `geninterrupt()`, however. Just because a register has been given a value, does not mean it will retain that value until the `geninterrupt()` is encountered. Consider the following example.

```
#include <string.h>
#include <dos.h>

char stringToWrite[] = "some silly string";

void fn() {

    _AH = 0x13;             //write string function
    _AL = 0x00;             //cursor flags
    _BH = 0;                //page 0
    _CX = strlen(stringToWrite);
    _DH = row;
    _DL = col;
    _ES = FP_SEG(stringToWrite);
    _BP = FP_OFF(stringToWrite);
```

```
        geninterrupt(0x10);
}
```

This program segment has several problems. First, the call to `strlen()` will overwrite the value in `AH` so that when the `geninterrupt()` is encountered the value of `AX` will be unknown. Even were this not the case, the `FP_SEG()` macro would wipe out `AX` as well. Finally, the `BP` register must be saved and restored if it is to be modified.

By reordering the registers and saving the `BP`, the following code segment functions properly.

```
#include <string.h>
#include <dos.h>

char stringToWrite[] = "some silly string";
unsigned saveBP;

void fn() {
    saveBP = _BP;
    _CX = strlen(stringToWrite);   //call fns. first
    _ES = FP_SEG(stringToWrite);   //this destroys AX
    _BH = 0;
    _DH = 0;
    _DL = 0;
    _AH = 0x13; //write string function
    _AL = 0;
    _BP = FP_OFF(stringToWrite);   //destroy BP last
    geninterrupt(0x10);
    _BP = saveBP;                  //saveBP cannot be auto
}
```

The `SS` and `BP` registers should be the last to be modified, as automatic variables will no longer be accessible after `BP` is changed. Global and static variables will not be accessible once the `DS` register has been modified. Under no circumstances should the programmer change the `CS` register.

The AX register should be next to last to be loaded, as Turbo C++ uses this register most often. Function calls should be performed before any registers are loaded because they can change all registers except SI and DI.

If the interrupt changes the SI or DI registers, the program must save and restore them before returning. Turbo C++ caches values into these registers and assumes that their values remain intact across function calls. (This caching can be disabled from the Options/Compiler/Code Generation menu.)

The following program shows the EMS module presented in Chapter 7 rewritten to use geninterrupt().

```cpp
//Make an EMS class for manipulating EMS memory
//written using geninterrupt()
#include "ems.hpp"

//---------Implementation of the EMS methods--------
EMS::EMS (unsigned pageCount) {
    //first set to "none values"
    handle = 0xffff;
    noPages = 0;

    //if EMS memory not present, give up now
    if (EMSPresent() = = 0)
        return;

    //otherwise allocate that many from EMS handler
    _BX = pageCount;
    _AH = 0x43;
    geninterrupt(EMSInt);

    if (_AH == 0) {           //if okay...
        handle = _DX;         //...save handle
        noPages = pageCount;
    }
}
```

```cpp
EMS::~EMS () {
    //give the EMS member back (if we have any)
    if (handle != 0xffff) {
        _DX = handle;
        _AH = 0x45;
        geninterrupt(EMSInt);
    }
}

//map the specified page into the specified frameslot;
//return a 0 if successful
unsigned EMS::map (unsigned page, unsigned frameSlot) {
    if (handle == 0xffff)
        return 0xffff;
    _BX = page;
    _DX = handle;
    _AL = (char)frameSlot;
    _AH = 0x44;
    geninterrupt(EMSInt);
    return _AH;
}

unsigned EMS::status() {
    if (handle = = 0xffff)
        return 0xffff;
    return EMSStatus();
}

//------Implementation of the general functions-----
//EMSPresent - return a 0 if EMS handler is present;
//             otherwise, return the page frame address
void far* EMSPresent(void) {
    const char EMSName[] = "EMMXXXX0";
    struct EMSHandler {
        char padding [0x0a];
        char name [9];
```

Turbo C++ Advanced Features

```
    } far* EMSPtr;

    //get the address of the EMS handler (with 0 offset)
    _AL = EMSInt;
    _AH = 0x35;                //get interrupt address
    geninterrupt(0x21);
    EMSPtr = (EMSHandler far*)MK_FP(_ES, 0);

    //now check for the name of the EMS handler
    for (int i = 0; i < 8; i++)
        if (EMSPtr->name[i] != EMSName[i])
            return (void*)0;

    //okay, it's there - return the page frame address
    _AH = 0x41;
    geninterrupt(EMSInt);
    if (_AH)
        return (void*)0;
    EMS::frameSegment = _BX;
    return EMSSlotAddr(0); //return address of pageframe
}

//EMSSlotAddr - given a frame slot number,
//              calculate its address.
void far* EMSSlotAddr (unsigned slotnum) {
    const unsigned frameOffsets[] = {0x0000,
                                     0x4000,
                                     0x8000,
                                     0xC000};
    if (slotnum > 3)
        return 0;
    return MK_FP(EMS::frameSegment,
                 frameOffsets[slotnum]);
}

//EMSStatus - return the status of the EMS handler
```

```
unsigned EMSStatus (void) {
    _AH = 0x40;
    geninterrupt(EMSInt);
    return _AH;
}

//EMS_pagecount - return the number of unallocated pages
unsigned EMSPageCount (void) {
    _AH = 0x42;
    geninterrupt(EMSInt);
    if (_AH)
        return 0;
    return _BX;
}
```

Keyword *asm*

Turbo C++ allows the programmer to include inline assembly language by using the **asm** keyword. Turbo C++ object modules may be linked with object modules created from Turbo Assembler or the Microsoft MASM Assembler. However, writing such modules is not an easy assignment.

Assembly language modules must include the proper names for the code and data segments and their segment groups. In addition, the assembly program must know whether C style "_" prefixes are to be added to the entry point names or whether type-safe linking names are in effect. Worse yet, all of these conventions can be changed from the options window.

Writing functions using the *asm* directive avoids these problems. Since the functions are processed by Turbo C++, the same names are created as with other C++ functions, even if the entire function is written in assembly.

To use the *asm* keyword the programmer must own a copy of Borland's TASM Assembler. Whereas Turbo C requires the programmer to use TCC—the command line version of the Turbo C compiler—programmers can compile *asm* with functions from the Turbo C++ IDE. To do so, the user must specify how the Turbo Assembler is accessed in the Transfer menu and then make sure that the program TASM2MSG is either in the current directory or in the path. This program forms the bridge between TASM and the on-screen compile and error windows.

When the asm directive is encountered, Turbo C++ restarts the compilation process, generating an assembly source program which is then passed to TASM for assembly using the Transfer function. The programmer may avoid the restart by specifying #pragma inline at the beginning of the module (or by including the -B command line option when using TCC).

Each asm line is considered a legal C++ statement. These statements may be terminated with a semi-colon. However, an end-of-line command terminates the statement as well.

To include numbers of inline assembly language statements, the programmer need not put an asm in front of every statement. Multiple assembly lines may be enclosed within braces following a single asm keyword. Individual assembler statements can be separated either by new lines or by semi-colons. Comments within an assembly section appear either within /* */ or after //.

The programmer should avoid using assembly language directives other than actual opcodes, as they might conflict with directives already output by the compiler. Assembler lines may reference C variable names—Turbo C++ will select the proper addressing mode. For example, consider the following "do nothing" function.

```
unsigned x;
void f() {
    unsigned y;

    asm {
        mov ax,x        //line #1
        mov bx,y        //line #2
    }
}
```

The line marked #1 generates the instruction MOV AX, DGROUP:_x whereas line #2 generates a MOV BX, [BP-2] reflecting the difference in the storage class between the global variable x and the automatic variable y.

Some error checking is performed on inline assembly code. If the user modifies the `SI` or `DI` register, Turbo C++ will avoid caching a value there. However, Turbo C++ does not include an assembler and so cannot detect illegal or improperly formatted opcodes. Such errors are detected during the assembly phase.

Let us now return to the sieve program at the beginning of this section to see where inline assembly language could enhance performance. We will limit our attention to the two `for` loops, labeled A and B. The programmer should examine the assembly code generated by Turbo C++ to decide how it might be improved. Due to the `if` statements, not much can be done with the second loop. However, we can improve upon the first loop.

The 8086 instruction set includes an instruction called String instructions. This instruction belongs to a set that operates on blocks of data. In each case the address of the source, if there is one, is put in the `DS:SI` register pair, and the destination, if there is one, is stored into the `ES:DI` register pair. The number of members is stored in `CX`. After each operation, the `SI` and `DI` registers are updated and the `CX` register is decremented. The operation is repeated until the `CX` register reaches zero. Each cycle through the loop requires only a few clock cycles. The Store String instruction does not use the `SI` register, but stores the contents of the `AX` register each time.

The Store String command can be used to set every element of `flags` to `TRUE`. The resulting program appears as follows:

```
//The Sieve of Eratosthenes Prime Number Program
//   Contains asm sections to enhance performance

#pragma inline

#include <stdio.h>
#include <stdlib.h>

#define TRUE  1
#define FALSE 0
#define ITER  100
#define SIZE  8190
```

```c
//define our Boolean sieve
char flags [SIZE+1];

//Main - the sieve program
void main () {
    int i,k;
    int iter, count;

    printf ("%d iterations. "
            "Hit enter and start stop watch\n", ITER);
    getchar ();
    printf ("Start...");

    asm cld              //set transfer direction to forward

    for (iter = 1; iter <= ITER; iter++) {
        count = 0;

        //set the array flags to all TRUE; same as:
        //for (i = 0; i <= SIZE; i++)
        //      flags[i] = TRUE;
        asm {
            mov  dx,di
            mov  ax,0x0101
            mov  cx,SIZE/2
            lea  di,flags
            push ds
            pop  es
            rep  stosw
            mov  di,dx
        }

        //now search for primes
        for (i = 2; i <= SIZE; i++)
            if (flags[i]) {
                //found a prime; cancel multiples
```

```
                    for ( k = i + i; k <= SIZE; k += i )
                         flags[k] = FALSE;
                    count++;
               }
          }

          printf ("stop!\n\n%d primes\n", count);
}
```

The first asm instruction sets the copy direction to forward for the remainder of the program. If the direction flag is set, the SI and DI registers are decremented instead of incremented. The flag need only be cleared once—it retains its value until set in a subsequent instruction. The second section performs the loop; the C++ loop has been retained as a comment for comparison.

Since TRUE has been defined as one, the AX register is set to 0x0101. By using word transfers, the program can set two members of flags at one time and cut the number of loops in half. This is why CX is loaded with SIZE/2 and not SIZE. The REP STOSW performs the String Store.

By using pseudo-registers, we can reduce the number of asm statements considerably. Although the number of machine instructions and the performance are not affected, readability is improved. The pseudo-register version of the loop appears as follows:

```
//set the array flags to all TRUE; same as:
//for (i = 0; i <= SIZE; i++)
//     flags[i] = TRUE;
_DX = _DI;
_ES = FP_SEG(flags);
_DI = FP_OFF(flags);
_CX = SIZE / 2;
_AX = 0x0101;
asm rep stosw
_DI = _DX;
```

It was not necessary to load the registers in any particular order in the `asm` case since we had direct control of all registers. Here, however, the AX register must be loaded last.

I find this more readable. However, the programmer must be careful that the assembly language generated is what was expected. Once a sequence such as the preceding has been coded, the programmer should use the Turbo Debugger to confirm that no register will be inadvertently lost before it is needed.

__emit__

The function `__emit__` allows Turbo C++ programmers to enter inline assembly in a Turbo Pascal-type hexadecimal style. This intrinsic command resembles, but is not, a function call with any number of constant values. The constant values supplied with `__emit__` are inserted into the code as they appear. No attempt is made to interpret the arguments as anything other than strings of numbers. Variable names are not expanded into addresses as they are with `asm`.

When using `__emit__`, the programmer must be certain that the size of the operand is correct. Constants of type character occupy one byte and those of type integer a word. No error checking is performed. Since no interpretation is performed by Turbo C++, the programmer cannot write functions that are insensitive to changes in memory model or argument passing convention.

Even with its dangers, `__emit__` is a powerful tool. First, `__emit__` is the only way to include assembly language in a Turbo C++ function if Turbo Assembler is not available (or if it is not known to be available, as would be the case with a commercial library). Second, because `__emit__` does not require the assembly step, functions containing `__emit__` compile faster than those containing `asm` sections.

While not sufficiently flexible for long segments of assembly language, `__emit__` is adept at generating the few lines of assembly sometimes needed. Consider the following function, which reads the flag register.

```
unsigned flags() {
    __emit__(0x9C,      //PUSHF
             0x58);     //POP AX
    return _AX;         //has to return something
}
```

The first two instructions place the value of the flag register in AX. Since AX would have been returned anyway, the `return _AX` statement does nothing more than confirm that we are returning something. The `return _AX` does not generate any code.

The hexadecimal values for the PUSHF and POP AX were determined by assembling with the A command of the DOS DEBUG debugger. DEBUG was supplied with versions of DOS prior to 3.2.

Register pseudo-variables are especially useful in reducing the size of the `__emit__` section or when accessing variable names. Consider the following two functions, each of which returns the product of its two arguments. Notice how much more readable `mult2()` is than `mult1()` even though they generate the same machine code.

```
unsigned mult1(unsigned a, unsigned b) {
    __emit__(0x8b,0x46,0x04);  //MOV AX,[BP-4]
    __emit__(0x8b,0x56,0x06);  //MOV DX,[BP-6]
    __emit__(0xf7,0xea);       //IMUL DX (AX = AX * DX)
    return _AX;
}
unsigned mult2(unsigned a, unsigned b) {
    _AX = a;
    _DX = b;
    __emit__(0xf7,0xea);       //IMUL DX (AX = AX * DX)
    return _AX;
}
```

The hexadecimal values of the instructions were found using the DOS DEBUG. The offsets of the arguments may be calculated by hand using the rule that the first argument is at BP-4 in Small or Compact memory models and BP-6 in the Medium, Large, or Huge memory models. However, it is easier to let Turbo C++ do the calculations. By examining the code generated from the following program, the programmer can determine where arguments a and b are on the stack.

```
unsigned trialMult(unsigned a, unsigned b) {
    a = 1;
    b = 2;
}
```

The trial function must be compiled in the same memory model that the final function will use.

Recoding the asm sections of the sieve program using __emit__ results in the following:

```
//set the array flags to all TRUE; same as:
//for (i = 0; i <= SIZE; i++)
//      flags[i] = TRUE;
_DX = _DI;
_ES = FP_SEG(flags);
_DI = FP_OFF(flags);
_CX = SIZE / 2;
_AX = 0x0101;
__emit__(0xfc);          //CLD
__emit__(0xf3, 0xab);    //REP STOSW
_DI = _DX;
```

Assembly Level Debugging

Even without indulging in the assembly language excesses described, the time comes when a programmer must get down to the assembly language level to see what the compiler has done with the C++ source code, especially when things appear to go wrong in the empty space between two C++ statements or when a function call never seems to arrive.

Turbo C++ is designed to work with Borland's Turbo Debugger. Although a separate product, specifying the proper path in the Transfer menu allows the programmer to move smoothly from the IDE to the Turbo

Debugger. The look and feel of the Turbo Debugger is the same as that of the built-in IDE debugger. The appearance of the screens is the same. Most of the commands are the same, except that the Turbo Debugger offers some options not available under the IDE debugger. Most important is the assembly language view and the assembly language single step that allows the programmer to execute individual machine instructions.

The Turbo Debugger comes in three forms, all of which feel the same but have different levels of resiliency. The basic Turbo Debugger occupies the same memory space as the program it is debugging. TD286, which uses the protected mode of the 80286, 80386, and 80486 processors, is most resistant to being overwritten, tending to trap offenders before they can do real harm. TD386 uses the virtual mode of the 80386 and 80486 to make itself virtually uncrashable. The virtual mode debugger takes almost no memory away from the application program, an important consideration for oversized programs. The TD386 can use the debugging registers of the CPU to set hardware breakpoints.

Even without the Turbo Debugger, a programmer can debug Turbo C++ programs at the assembly level. To use a non-symbolic debugger such as the DOS DEBUG, the programmer must generate a detailed load map containing the addresses of all global functions and variables. This is done by linking with the Detailed Map option in the Option/Link menu set. The programmer then generates assembly language listings of the programs to be debugged by compiling the program using TCC with the -S switch set. The assembly program generated includes the C++ source as comments showing which C++ statements generated what machine instructions.

The biggest difficulty with a non-symbolic debugger is getting started. Due to segment fix-ups, it is difficult to determine where a particular label will end up in memory. One solution for small programs is to select the Tiny compile model and generate a .COM executable file. This type of executable is simple and has no segment fix-ups. The offsets provided in the memory map can be applied directly off of the CS and DS in the debugger. Unfortunately, the .COM file format is not suitable for programs of significant size.

A second approach is to hard code breakpoints using the __emit__ keyword. A breakpoint is almost always set using the INT 3 command, which has the hexadecimal value 0xcc. INT 3 is built as a one-byte command to make it more attractive for use as a breakpoint. If the following program is executed under almost any debugger, execution will stop at the __emit__ as if the programmer had set a breakpoint there.

```
void main() {
    __emit__(0xcc);
```

These hard-coded breakpoints can be placed at key points throughout the program. Once the programmer knows where the program has stopped, the load map and assembly listings can be used to navigate further.

Hard-coded breakpoints can also be used as conditional breakpoints. For example, the following function will break whenever the first argument passed has a negative value.

```
void fn(int argA, int argB) {
    if (argA < 0)
        __emit__(0xcc);
```

Programmers can also use the INT 1 single-step breakpoint. This is coded as __emit__(0xcd, 0x01). INT 1 has the advantage that with some debuggers the programmer must manually increment the instruction pointer by one to get beyond the INT 3 breakpoint. This is never the case with the INT 1 breakpoint. With some debuggers, the programmer should single step the program once before starting to make sure that the interrupts are properly initialized.

The assembly source listing generated by Turbo C++ can often be combined with the CPU display window in the IDE debugger to make the application of an assembly language debugger unnecessary.

Interrupt Functions

A function may be declared to be an **interrupt function** as follows:

```
void interrupt function(unsigned bp, unsigned di,
                       unsigned si, unsigned ds,
                       unsigned es, unsigned dx,
                       unsigned cx, unsigned bx,
```

```
                         unsigned ax, unsigned ip,
                         unsigned cs, unsigned flags,
                         ...);
```

An interrupt function is called like a far function with the flag register pushed. Turbo C++ includes instructions at the beginning of the function to push all of the registers onto the stack before setting up the standard stack frame. The registers appear as arguments in the preceding declaration. The program may access and store values in the registers. Since the registers are popped back off of the stack when the function returns, changing one of the arguments changes the corresponding register upon return from the program.

An interrupt function may have arguments beyond the registers as well, as in the following:

```
void interrupt setFlags(unsigned bp, unsigned di,
                        unsigned si, unsigned ds,
                        unsigned es, unsigned dx,
                        unsigned cx, unsigned bx,
                        unsigned ax, unsigned ip,
                        unsigned cs, unsigned flags,
                        unsigned newFlagValue) {
    flags = newFlagValue;
}
```

Calling the function appears as follows:

```
setFlags(0x7123);
```

Only the argument beyond the registers is provided in the call to the function.

It is not necessary to list all of the arguments in the prototype of the interrupt function. The registers are saved and restored whether they have been listed or not. The registers must be included in the prototype only if the program needs access to them.

Interrupt functions are not normally called from other C++ functions. Interrupt functions are installed by placing the address of the function into one of the 256 interrupt vectors at the beginning of memory. For example, the function `clockTick()` in Chapter 11 is installed on interrupt 0x1C, the timer interrupt. Other programs can call this function by performing the appropriate soft interrupt. This is a convenient way to connect program sections written in different languages.

Interrupt functions can be used to write Terminate-and-Stay-Resident (TSR) programs. However, this is beyond the scope of this book. Interested readers are referred to *Turbo C: The Advanced Art of Program Design, Debugging, and Optimization* (Davis, M&T Books, Redwood City, CA, 1987) for a study of TSRs in Turbo C.

Special Forms of Flow Control

Versions of C prior to the ANSI standard provided a type of software interrupt known as a **signal function**. The programmer could declare a signal function to handle one of a set of events. If the event occured, the program could **raise** the event causing control to pass immediately to the signal function. Turbo C++ supports and expands upon signal functions.

Signals

A signal function is declared using the function `signal()` with the following prototype.

```
void (* signal(int event, void (* func)(int))) (int);
```

The `signal()` function accepts as its arguments an `int` representing the event being defined and the address of a function that takes a single `int` and returns a `void`. The function `signal()` returns the address of a function that takes a single `int` and returns a `void`. The pointer returned is the address of the previous handler for that event.

The list of events for which a signal may be defined appears in Table 10-2.

Table 10–2 Signal Events and Corresponding Signal Types

Signal Type	Value	Event
SIGABRT2	22	Abnormal termination
SIGFPE	8	Floating point trap
SIGILL	4	Illegal instruction
SIGINT	2	Control-Break interrupt
SIGSEGV	11	Memory access violation
SIGTERM	15	Program termination

The function `signal()` can be used to install a programmer-defined function or one of the three default event handlers listed in Table 10–3. When a signal function is first installed, `signal()` returns SIG_DFL as the previously installed function.

Table 10–3 Default Signal Functions

Signal Function	Value	Action
SIG_DFL	0	Terminate the program
SIG_IGN	1	Return to the caller
SIG_ERR	-1	Error return from signal()

When the signal function is called, the value of the signaled event is passed as the single argument. A single signal function may be installed for multiple events. By comparing the passed argument, the program can determine what event caused the signal function to gain control.

Signal functions may return to the caller, long jump to some saved location in the program, or terminate the program. Long jumping is discussed in Chapter 11.

The following program demonstrates the use of `signal()` and `raise()`.

```
#include <iostream.h>
#include <signal.h>

void terminateHandler(int sigType) {
```

```
        cout << "Program called terminate handler" << endl;
}

void main() {
    signal(SIGTERM, terminateHandler);

    cout << "In the function" << endl;

    raise(SIGTERM);
}
```

The function `terminateHandler()` is called from `raise()`. As written, `terminateHandler()` returns from the call and the program terminates normally. If `terminateHandler()` invoked `_exit()` or `abort()`, the function would not return and `atexit()` functions and destructors would not be invoked.

Three of the signals—SIGFPE, SIGSEGV and SIGILL—may be raised by Turbo C++. So that the signal handler can know whether the signal was raised by user-written software or by the system, Turbo C++ tacks an extra argument onto the call. The possible values for this argument, outlined in Table 10–4, are defined in FLOAT.H.

Table 10–4 Signal Types Defined in FLOAT.H and Their Values

Signal	Value	Meaning
SIGFPE Signal		
FPE_INTOVFLOW	126	80x86 interrupt on overflow
FPE_INTDIV0	127	80x86 integer divide by zero
FPE_INVALID	129	80x87 invalid operation
FPE_ZERODIVIDE	131	80x87 divide by zero
FPE_OVERFLOW	132	80x87 arithmetic overflow
FPE_UNDERFLOW	133	80x87 arithmetic underflow
FPE_INEXACT	134	80x87 precision loss
FPE_STACKFAULT	135	80x87 stack overflow
FPE_EXPLICITGEN	140	SIGFPE raise()'d by user

Table 10–4 Signal Types Defined in FLOAT.H and Their Values (Continued)

Signal	Value	Meaning
SIGSEGV Signal		
SEGV_BOUND	10	BOUND violation
SEGV_EXPLICITGEN	11	SIGSEGV raise()'d by user
SIGILL Signal		
ILL_EXECUTION	20	Illegal operation exception
ILL_EXPLICITGEN	21	SIGILL raise()'d by user

The first two `SIGFPE` signal types result from integer math error conditions detected by the CPU. The remaining conditions are generated by the Floating Point Unit or the FPU emulator and may be enabled or disabled via the `_control87()` standard library function. The call

`_control87(MCW_EM, MCW_EM);`

masks all error events from being signaled. The call

`_control87( 0, MCW_EM);`

reenables reporting for all events. Flags are defined in FLOAT.H to enable particular events and mask others.

The `SIGSEGV/SEGV_BOUND` event is signaled when a `BOUND` instruction detects a value out of range. This instruction is normally used to make sure an index is within the range of its array. The `BOUND` instruction does not exist on the 8086 and 8088 processors. Turbo C++ does not generate `BOUND` instructions. They would only occur in a Turbo C++ program if included in an `asm` or `__emit__` section.

The `SIGILL/ILL_EXECUTION` event is signaled when the processor detects an illegal instruction. The 8088, 8086, V20, and V30 processors cannot generate this exception. This signal usually indicates that the program has gotten lost and is in the process of crashing.

The signal handler function may ignore the second argument and treat all of the different types of events the same. In order to distinguish the events, a second integer argument must be declared. This makes installing the function more difficult since the prototype no longer matches that expected by `signal()`. This discrepancy can be resolved by recasting the address of the signal handler appropriately before passing it to `signal()`.

```
void mathHandler(int, int);
void (*tempFn)(int) = (void (*)(int))mathHandler;
signal(SIGFPE, tempFn);
```

The function `mathHandler()` is declared to accept both arguments passed for `SIGFPE` events. Its address must be recast into a pointer to a function taking a single argument before being passed to `signal()`.

A handler for one of the preceeding three events should not try to return to the caller without attempting to correct the problem. If the signal was raised by user-written software, data may be stored in global variables indicating the nature of the problem. If the problem was signaled by the system, the only evidence as to what caused the problem is in the registers.

When one of the floating point `SIGFPE` events occur, the registers are still in the FPU or the FP emulator and can be read out and analyzed. For the `FPE_INTOVFLOW`, `FPE_INTDIV0`, `SEGV_BOUND`, and `ILL_EXECUTION` events, the evidence is in the CPU registers. To enable the handler to analyze these conditions, Turbo C++ adds a third argument when raising one of these events. The third argument is a pointer to a structure containing the registers. The `CS:IP` stored in this structure points to the instruction that generated the event.

The following `SIGFPE` handler checks for a divide by zero. In the event that this is the reported error, the handler checks to make sure that the instruction is the expected `DIV` or `IDIV` (opcode = 0xF6 or 0xF7). If it is, the handler assumes a result of 0 and a remainder of 0 and skips over the instruction. Divide instructions may be two, three, and four bytes long, so the function must parse the instruction to determine how far forward to jump.

```
//Math signal handler

#include <iostream.h>
#include <stdlib.h>
```

```cpp
#include <signal.h>
#include <float.h>
#include <dos.h>

//structure containing registers passed for
//FPE_INTOVFLOW, FPE_INTDIV0, SEGV_BOUND and
//ILL_EXECUTION

struct REGLIST {
    unsigned bp;
    unsigned di;
    unsigned si;
    unsigned ds;
    unsigned es;
    unsigned dx;
    unsigned cx;
    unsigned bx;
    unsigned ax;
    unsigned ip;
    unsigned cs;
    unsigned flags;
};
void mathHandler(int signal, int type, REGLIST* reglist){
    cout << "Math error, signal = "
        << signal
        << ", type = "
        << type << endl;
    if (type = = FPE_INTDIV0 ) {
        reglist->ax  = 0;   //result of divide to 0

        //increment passed DIV or IDIV instruction
        char far * ipPtr =
            (char far *)MK_FP(reglist->cs,reglist->ip);
        if ((*ipPtr & 0xfe) != 0xf6) //make sure it's DIV
            cout << "Unknown instruction" << endl;
        else {
```

Turbo C++ Advanced Features

```cpp
            //check the R/M mode to determine instr size
            //(depends upon type of argument)
            char mode = (*(ipPtr + 1) >> 6) & 0x03;
            unsigned offset;
            switch (mode) {
                case 0:
                    if ((*(ipPtr + 1) & 0x7) = = 0x7)
                        offset = 4;   //16-bit address
                    else
                        offset = 2;   //register
                    break;
                case 1:
                    offset = 3;       //8-bit offset
                    break;
                case 2:
                    offset = 4;       //16-bit offset
                    break;
                case 3:
                    offset = 2;
            }
            reglist->ip += offset;
            return;
        }
    }
    cout << "Unrecoverable - aborting" << endl;
    _exit(1);
}

void main() {
    //declare a floating point event handler
    void (*fn)(int) = (void (*)(int))mathHandler;
    signal(SIGFPE, fn);

    //invoke a divide-by-zero error
    int x = 1, y = 0;
    x /= y;             //invokes abort with registers
```

```
        //raise an error manually
        raise(SIGFPE);    //invokes abort without registers
}
```

Control-break Handler

One of the most common events is the SIGINT or interrupt event. As a program is executing, DOS sets a flag if the user enters a Control-break from the keyboard. When the program next performs a DOS system call, DOS interrupts the operation by raising a SIGINT event. The default handler for SIGINT performs an INT 0x23 call.

The user program may define a new SIGINT event handler to intercept Control-breaks. Another approach is to intercept the interrupt 0x23 call with an interrupt function. Since the Control-break is such a common interrupt to intercept, the standard library routine cntrlbrk() allows the user to install a new break handler into interrupt 0x23. In practice, this appears as follows:

```
int breakHandler() {
    //output a message
    cout << "Control break entered";
    return 1;
}

void function() {
    ctrlbrk(breakHandler);
```

Execution continues from the point the signal is raised if the break handler returns a nonzero. If the handler returns a zero, execution terminates. In addition, the break handler may exit(), abort(), or long jump somewhere else in the program.

A break handler may declare another break handler. Control-break is normally used to terminate execution of a program. If Control-break is redefined to perform another operation, the programmer may enable the user to terminate the program by entering two or more Control-breaks in rapid

Turbo C++ Advanced Features

succession, so called "double breaks." This is demonstrated in the following program.

```cpp
#include <iostream.h>
#include <dos.h>
//Control Break count
unsigned count = 0;

int doubleBreakHandler() {
    cout << "\nTerminate" << endl;
    return 0;          //terminate program
}
int breakHandler() {
    //wait for double break
    ctrlbrk(doubleBreakHandler);
    delay(250);

    //output a message
    cout << "Control break entered";

    //return a non-zero to allow program
    //to continue
    ctrlbrk(breakHandler);
    count++;
    return 1;          //continue program
}

void main() {
    ctrlbrk(breakHandler);

    for (;;)
        cout << "Infinite loop __ break #"
             << count
             << endl;
}
```

When the user enters a single Control-break, the program outputs the message "Control break entered". When the user enters a double break, the program terminates.

This can also be useful if the break handler itself performs I/O. If a Control-break is detected during this operation, DOS invokes the break handler again resulting in an infinite loop. By deflecting the Control-break to a secondary handler, a break handler may perform system calls safely.

The standard library function `setcbrk()` sets a flag to inform DOS to check for a Control-break only when performing I/O system calls. Otherwise, DOS checks before every system call. The function `getcbrk()` returns the current setting of this flag.

Conclusion

Although it has many unique features, Turbo C++ remains as compatible with the ANSI C and AT&T C++ 2.0 standards as possible. The VROOMM system allows the programmer to write larger programs than would fit into 640K memory.

In Chapter 11, we will combine the C++ features into a sample `Task` class capable of introducing multitasking in user applications.

Chapter 11

Task Class Application

In this chapter we will develop a `Task` class to implement multitasking. Since it is handled from within the C++ program, this multitasking is independent of the operating system. Before we examine this application, however, we should consider what multitasking means and how it is achieved.

Theory

Think of a program as a forest. Within the woods are many paths and points at which the path splits in two, one path branching off in a new direction or doubling back to rejoin the main trail at an earlier point.

As it follows down the logical paths, the CPU plays the part of a hiker, deciding which path to take at each branch. Along the path, the CPU performs the requested operations.

Multitasking involves the creation of multiple hikers, known as multiple **execution threads** or **tasks**. Each program division is assigned its own thread.

When multiple CPUs exist, the program does have multiple hikers at its disposal. However, in all but the largest PCs, the execution threads must share a single processor. Each thread proceeds down the trail a way before control of the CPU is passed to the next thread. The state of the thread is saved so that when the CPU returns, the thread can be restored. The thread is not aware of having lost control of the CPU.

By creating more execution threads, multitasking makes modules less dependent upon each other. This is known as **decoupling**. For the most part, each decoupled module is written as a seperate program. Communication between modules is best handled through intertask messages, which can be easily documented.

The passing of messages is a major part of the object-oriented paradigm. In fully object-oriented languages, such as Smalltalk, function calls are implemented by passing messages to class objects. The member functions of C++ correspond to the types of messages that a Smalltalk class understands. The data is returned via a return message.

While C++ does not implement message passing internally for reasons of efficiency, class `Task` allows a programmer to build Smalltalk-like objects. The calling task sends a message to the task object. The object compares the request with its known methods to interpret the request. The difference is the caller continues executing while the task object processes the message.

Multitasking is a useful paradigm in other ways. The task that sends the message is unaware of how the receiving task performs its assignment. A well-written program might assign a task to handle printer output, for example, with different tasks for different printers. The remainder of the system need not know the details of accessing each printer. Other tasks simply send a message containing the information to be printed to the printer task.

In addition, each task need only control the printer type for which it is written. Tasks can be written to support virtual printers, saving the print requests to disk or sending them over a LAN. To the application tasks, the print messages all appear the same.

This technique can be used with devices other than hardware, such as a database. It is easier to write a database task that other tasks query with intertask messages than to write a database module to be called by different functions.

On projects involving several programmers, each programmer may be assigned a separate task. Given a description of the input and output messages, the programmer may implement the task in the optimum way. Debugging consists of sending test request messages and checking the response messages for accuracy. Since the message formats are documented, determining whether the task is working properly is simplified. Eventually the tasks from different programmers are placed in a single program. Developing the tasks separately reduces the amount of coupling via direct access to common assets.

The multitasking paradigm increases program performance. Giving the user a prompt while the program continues to execute in the background enables the programmer to compose the next command without waiting.

`setjmp/longjmp`

The key to multitasking is the **task switcher** or **rescheduler**. The task switcher saves the state of the current task so that it can be resumed later without a noticeable difference. This is called a **context save**. The rescheduler then finds the next execution thread to receive control and restores it to operation. This is called a **context switch**.

During the context switch, the instruction pointer and registers are saved into and read out of a structure which I will call the task object. Each task must have its own stack area so that return addresses are not overwritten. At task creation, a small area of memory is reserved and assigned for use as the task stack. The address of the task stack is retained in the task object. Automatic and register variables are not shared.

To save the complete context of a task would require saving all of the memory areas to which the task has access. In non-protected mode DOS, this would amount to all memory. Therefore, all threads share the same code and data space, thereby sharing the same functions and global variables.

A routine to perform the detailed register manipulation required for a context switch must be written in assembly language. The pseudoregisters in Turbo C++ do not provide sufficiently fine register control but the Turbo C++ run-time library contains a function that does.

The functions `setjmp()` and `longjmp()` were introduced in Unix C and have been retained in ANSI C and C++. Consider the following program.

```
#include <dos.h>

void main() {
    int option;
    int breakRoutine();

    ctrlbrk(breakRoutine);
    for(;;) {
        option = mainMenu();        //present main menu
        switch (option) {
            case option1:
                processOne();
                break;
            case option2:
                processTwo();
                break;
```

```
            }
        }
}
void processOne() {
    while(someCondition)
        keepProcessing();
}

int breakRoutine() {
    //how do we get back to the main menu?
}
```

After presenting the user with a menu of options, the program processes the user's input in a different function for each option. Before starting, a break routine is declared so that if the user enters the Control-break key, the program can stop, return to the main loop, restore the menu to the screen, and start over. How does the function `breakRoutine()` work?

Wherever it is called, the function `setjmp()` saves the state of the machine and returns a zero. In a single-tasked C application, all the registers are saved into a structure passed to the function. The structure for this purpose is of type `jmp_buf` and is defined in `setjmp.h`.

The program can return to the point of the `setjmp()` call by invoking `longjmp()` with the same structure and a return value. The program re-emerges from the `setjmp()` call with a new return value.

The return value from `setjmp()` tells the program whether the return is from the initial `setjmp()` call to store the context or from a subsequent `longjmp()`. The `longjmp()` function cannot return a zero. Calling `longjmp()` with a zero results in a return value of one reappearing from `setjmp()`.

We can now solve our problem as follows:

```
#include <dos.h>
#include <setjmp.h>

jmp_buf buffer;
```

```
void main() {
    int option;
    int breakRoutine();
    int retVal;

    ctrlbrk(breakRoutine);
    for(;;) {
        retVal = setjmp(buffer);//save the context
                //   retVal = 0 -> first call
                //          = 1 -> return from longjmp

        option = mainMenu();    //present main menu
        switch (option) {
            case option1:
                processOne();
                break;
            case option2:
                processTwo();
                break;
        }
    }
}

void processOne() {
    while(someCondition)
        keepProcessing();
}

int breakRoutine() {
    longjmp(buffer, 1);//return to the setjmp() call
}
```

The Control-break from the keyboard forces execution to the `breakRoutine()` function. The break function long jumps back to the main program loop to start over again.

C++ programmers must be careful when using `longjmp()`. Consider what would happen if `processOne()` were written as follows:

```
struct ClassWithDestructor() {
    ClassWithDestructor();
    ~ClassWithDestructor();
};

void processOne() {
    ClassWithDestructor anObject;

    while(someCondition)
        keepProcessing();
}
```

When the function `processOne()` is called, `anObject` of class `ClassWithDestructor` is created. Presumably the destructor is present to return whatever assets are allocated by the constructor for this class. However, if the program long jumps back to the `main()` function without executing a return from `processOne()`, the destructor is not invoked and the assets are not returned. The next time that `processOne()` is called, a new `anObject` will be created and the assets will be lost. No problem arises, however, if no objects for classes with destructors are created between the `setjmp()` and the `longjmp()` call.

In addition, a program can only long jump to a function calling the current function. Consider the `longjmp()` possibilities shown in Figure 11–1.

A program like the following is not legal.

```
jmp_buf buffer;

void fn1() {
    fn2();
    if (someCondition)
        longjmp(buffer, retVal);
}
```

Task Class Application

```
void fn2() {
    setjmp(buffer);
    //further processing
}
```

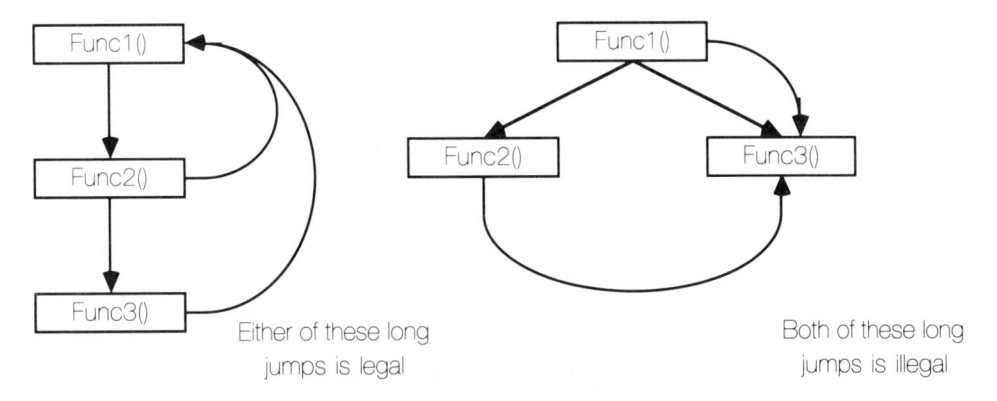

Figure 11-1 Legal longjmp() Possibilities

A function may long jump to a `setjmp()` call within the same function.

Rescheduler

A program may have more than one jump buffer at a time. The program can then decide to which context it will long jump. By storing the jump buffers in a linked list, a program can save and restore the `jmp_buf` contexts cyclically. We can use this technique to write a rescheduler using the following outline.

```
//declare a class to link setjmp() buffers together
struct Task : public LinkedList {
    jmp_buf buffer;
};
```

```
void reschedule() {
    static Task* taskPtr;   //currently active task

    //save the context of the current task (the caller)
    if (setjmp(taskPtr->buffer))
        return;          //upon return from longjmp() return

    //find next task to schedule
    taskPtr = findNextTask(taskPtr);

    //give the next task control
    longjmp(taskPtr->buffer);
}
```

With the program subdivided into multiple execution threads, (how this is accomplished is discussed later), one task can pass control to another by calling the reschedule function as shown in Figure 11–2. The reschedule function saves the context of the current task by calling `setjmp()`, then finds the next task to schedule. Control passes to the new task by long jumping to its saved context.

This is the basic approach we will use to implement the `Task` class.

Task Class

Each object of class `Task` is an independent execution thread capable of receiving control of the CPU. The task comes into existence when the object is created and ceases to exist when the object goes out of scope. The constructor and destructor initiate and terminate the task.

The constructor allocates the memory that the task will require. It then adds the object to the scheduling linked list and prepares the object to run when the rescheduler reaches it. The destructor removes the task from the scheduler list and returns any dynamically allocated memory to the heap.

Task Class Application

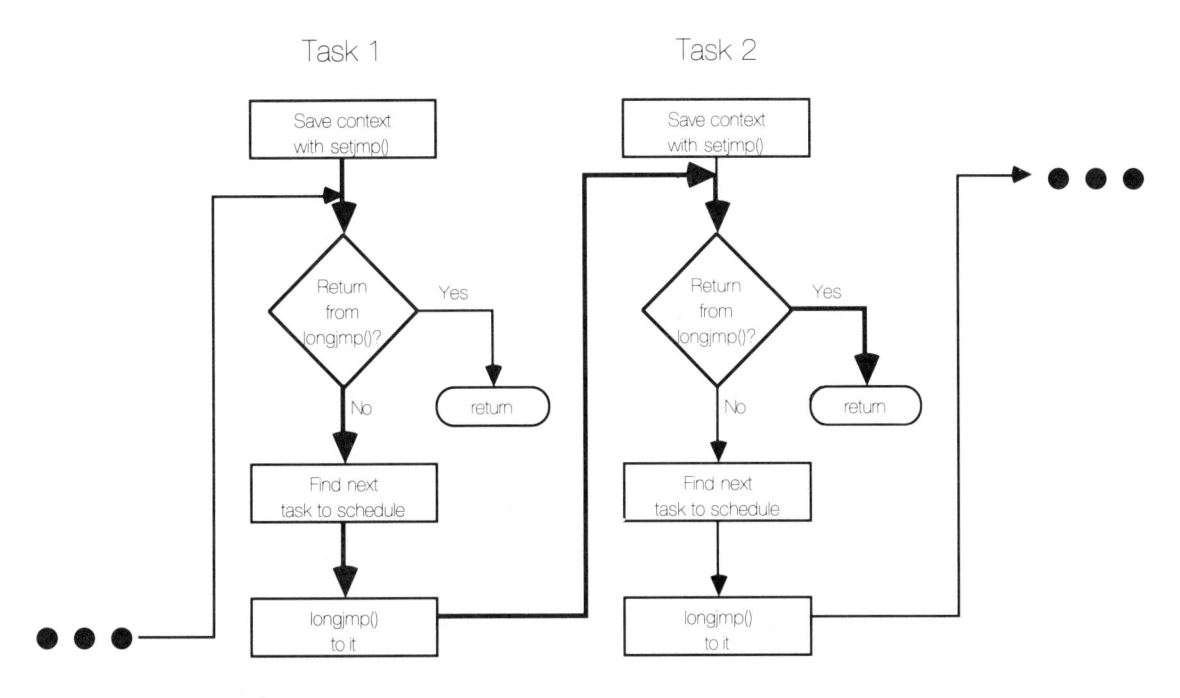

[Figure: Task Switching flowchart with two tasks showing Save context with setjmp(), Return from longjmp() decision, Find next task to schedule, and longjmp() to it]

Figure 11–2 Task Switching with scheduler() (path through one switch darkened)

The `Task` class needs other members to support a full-function multi-tasker. For example, not all tasks are scheduled every time through the loop. A task may be temporarily suspended pending some event. To support this, the class task contains a task status and several counters.

A task may be assigned a priority so that some tasks may be allocated more execution time than others. This type of information must also be stored in the class.

Often a parent task spawns a child task to perform a particular operation. To resynch with the child task later on, the task object needs a completion status. The child task sets the completion status to indicate whether the request was carried out successfully. The parent task can query and wait for completion status.

To support message passing, each task object requires a queue to store messages waiting to be processed. When the task requests the next message to process, the first message is taken from the queue and returned to the task. If the queue is empty, the task is suspended until a message appears.

Application software must not be given direct access to the internal members of the task class nor should it know intimate details of the task class's inner workings. Public member functions are provided to control access to the private flags and pointers.

Finally, an interrupt function is called by the hardware clock, which ticks 18.2 times per second. This function can time out tasks waiting for events to occur. The interrupt function can allow tasks to delay or wait for messages up to a certain length of time.

Comparison of Features

The biggest limitation of the multitasking proposal is that it implements **voluntary** or **non-preemptive scheduling**. That is, once a task gains control of the CPU it retains that control until the rescheduler function is called.

In operating systems such as DESQview, Unix, and OS/2, the scheduling of tasks is not controlled from the application software. In such preemptive multitaskers, a task that is executing has control taken away and passed to other tasks without any special call being made.

The scheduling of tasks in preemptive systems is based upon the hardware clock. In a process known as **time slicing** each task is assigned a period of time. A task can shorten its time slice by suspending itself or explicitly calling the rescheduler, but a task cannot extend its time slice beyond that allocated.

Preemptive scheduling is a better model for controlling multitasking in many respects. The sharing of assets should be under control of the scheduler. However, preemptive multitasking is more difficult to implement because the application has no idea when control is likely to be expropriated. In a non-preemptive system, the scheduler must rely on the application tasks to return control after a fair amount of time. A single task that gets lost in an infinite loop without calling the rescheduler halts the entire system.

Time slicing gives a more objective measure of asset division. It may be difficult for an application to determine that it should give up control after

1,000 iterations through a particular loop; however, allowing an application two 18-millisecond clock ticks is easily quantified and brutally fair.

DOS was written as a single-tasking operating system and is inherently non-reentrant. When an application task is in the middle of a DOS system call, another task cannot start a DOS call without crashing the first task. A preemptive task scheduler based on DOS must take precautions to prevent one task from making a DOS call when another DOS call is being executed.

In addition, applications must avoid data collisions that can arise in preemptive schedulers. The following scenario involves two application tasks, `TaskA` and `TaskB`, both of which have access to global variable `accountTotal`. To add $100 to `accountTotal`, `TaskA` reads the contents of `accountTotal` and then adds 100.00. Before `TaskA` can write the result into `accountTotal`, its time slice expires and it loses control of the CPU.

As the next in line, `TaskB` begins to execute. `TaskB` subtracts $200 from `accountTotal`. When `TaskA` regains control, it picks up where it left off by writing its result to `accountTotal`, thus overwriting the $200 debit made by `TaskB`. This is graphically depicted in Figure 11-3.

This scenario results in a **data collision**. The window of opportunity for the preceding data collision consists of only a few CPU instructions. However, similar data collision windows can be quite large, covering many functions. Data collisions can cause garbled output or system crashes as well as loss of data.

Preemptive systems also do a certain amount of thrashing, which levies needless overhead on the system. Consider the following scenario. Suppose that `TaskA` requires 20 milliseconds to process a message but its time slice is only 18 milliseconds. A time line of `TaskA`'s progress is shown in Figure 11-4.

Two extra context switches are performed that would not be necessary if `TaskA` were given a few more milliseconds to complete the message it started. Depending upon how long tasks execute between reschedulings, the time to perform a context switch may be significant.

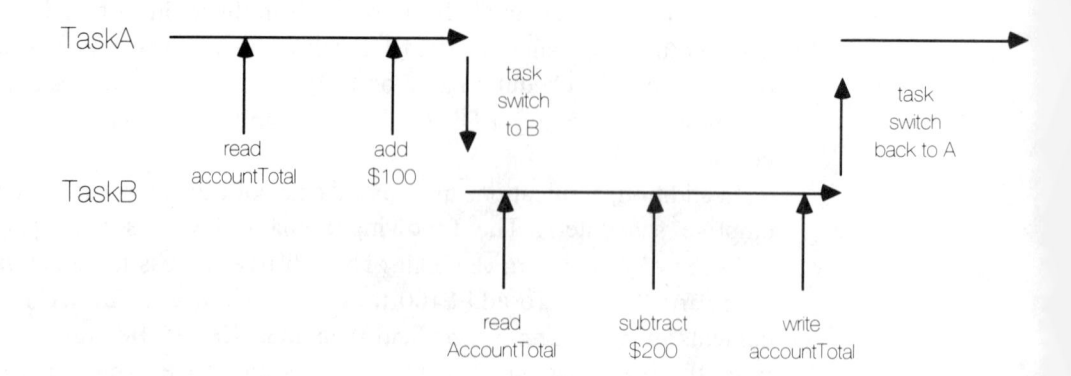

Figure 11-3 Time Line for Data Collision

In a non-preemptive system, `TaskA` would retain control of the CPU until the message was processed, only two milliseconds longer than the time slice version in the example. The overhead of the extra context switches would be avoided.

The `Task` class presented here includes task initialization and termination, suspension, delaying, intertask message passing, and task synchronization. The only major limitation is that no more than one task may call a VROOMM overlay. If two tasks access overlayed functions, one task could cause another's overlay to be paged out. When the first task resumes, the code it was executing would no longer be there.

Implementing Class Task

The complete source code for class `Task` is contained in Appendix A. This section contains a breakdown and description of the main points.

The structure of the `Task` class is contained in the include file MTASK.HPP. The member variables of class `Task` appear as follows:

```
#include <iostream.h>
#include <setjmp.h>
```

Task Class Application

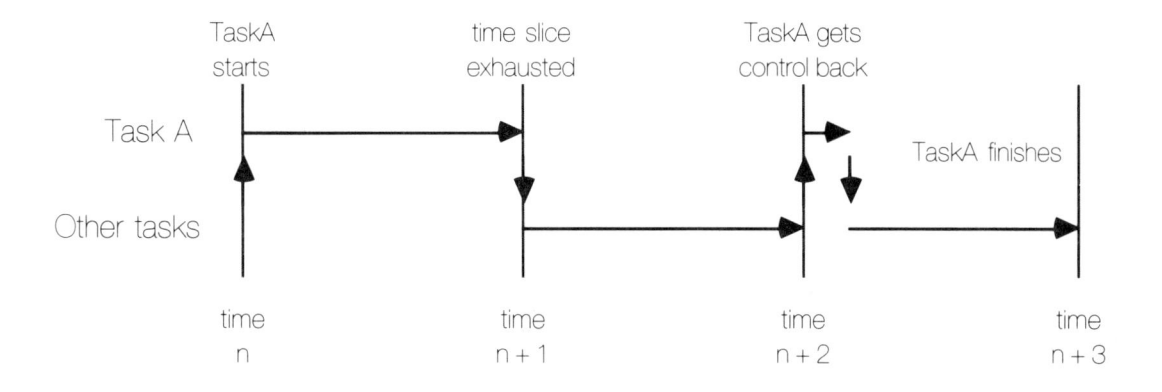

```
                TaskA              time slice         TaskA gets
                starts             exhausted          control back
                  │                    │                   │
    Task A        ├────────────────────►                   ├──►
                  │                    │                   │ │     TaskA finishes
                  │                    │                   ▼ ▼
    Other tasks   │                    ├───────────────────►───────────────────►
                  │                    │                   │                   │
                time                 time                time                time
                 n                   n+1                 n+2                 n+3
```

Figure 11–4 Time Line for TaskA

```
#include "slist.hpp"

//The Task class
class Task : public LinkedList {
  private:

    static Task* currentTaskPtr; //the RUNNING task
    static unsigned taskCount;

    char     taskName[40]; //identification
    unsigned taskId;       //simple ordinal count

    unsigned status;       //current task status
    unsigned loopCount;
    unsigned delayCount;   //no. clock ticks to wait
    Task*    retTask;      //task waiting for retVal
```

```
        jmp_buf  regs;             //saved registers
        unsigned *stackPtr;        //pointer to bottom of stack
        unsigned ssize;            //stack size
        unsigned releaseStack;     //1->release stack on exit

        unsigned noMsgs;           //no. of queued messages
        Message  queue;            //message queue

    public:
        unsigned retVal;           //task return value
        unsigned cpuTime;          //time spent within task

        enum TaskStatus {          //flags for 'status'
          READY         = 0x00,
          SUSPENDED     = 0x01,
          DYING         = 0x02,
          DEAD          = 0x04,
          AWAITING_MSG  = 0x08,
          DELAYED       = 0x10,
            RUNNING     = 0x80
        };
        enum TaskErrors {          //values for fn.s and 'retVal'
              OK          =  0,  //worked correctly
              GENERROR    = -1,  //unspecified task error
              NOSTACK     = -2,  //no stack or overflow
              QUEFULL     = -3,  //queue is full
              OUTOFRANGE  = -4   //not a legal value
        };
};
```

The `Task` class is a subclass of `LinkedList`, which is defined in the include file `SLIST.HPP`. The `Task` objects reside in a circular linked list. The currently active task is the object pointed at by `currentTaskPtr`. Rescheduling always begins with the next object in the list after `*currentTaskPtr`.

A `Task` object is always in one of several states defined in the enumerated type `Task::TaskStatus`. The state of the object is stored in the member `Task::status`.

A task marked `READY` is ready to be scheduled, but is not currently running. The task marked `RUNNING` is the task currently in control of the CPU. No more than one task may be marked `RUNNING` at any given time. No task is marked `RUNNING` when the rescheduler is searching for another task to execute. A `RUNNING` task is implicitly `READY`.

Tasks marked `SUSPENDED`, `AWAITING_MSG`, or `DELAYED` are waiting for an external event to occur and are not ready to run. For example, a task attempting to retrieve the next input message to process will be assigned state `AWAITING_MSG` if the input queue is empty. The `AWAITING_MSG` state is cleared when a message is sent to the queue from some other task.

A task may be assigned more than one waiting state. For example, a task might be suspended while waiting for an input message. This task will not be marked `READY` until both an input message has arrived and another task has unsuspended it.

When a `Task` object is destructed, it is removed from the scheduler list and its state is set to `DEAD`. Tasks are marked `DYING` while they are in the process of being killed. The state transition diagram is shown in Figure 11-5.

An error indication is returned from member functions. These errors are defined in the enumerated type `Task::TaskErrors`. Tasks may also return one of these values as a completion status when terminating. Negative values were chosen for errors in order to allow functions to return positive numbers as no-error data values.

Errors are not propagated. The class does not have an error state that must be cleared before subsequent task requests are acknowledged.

Task Creation

The class `Task` has two constructors which are defined as follows:

```
Task::Task(void (*fn)(),
           void* stack, unsigned stackSize,
           char* tNamePtr) {
```

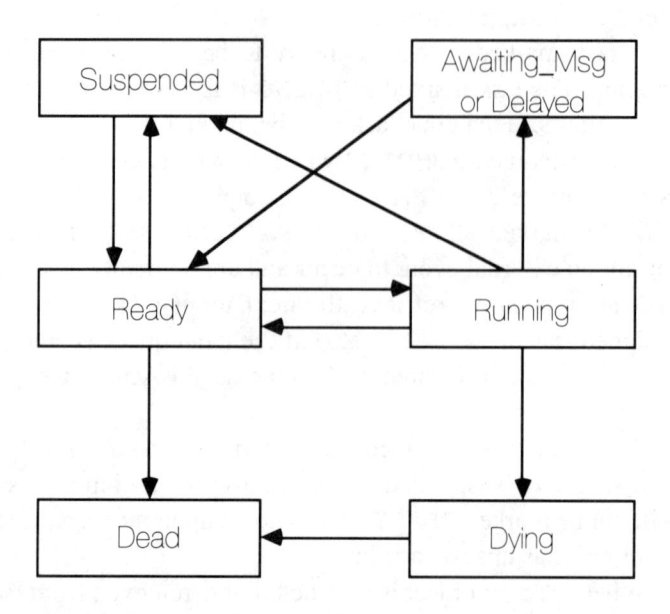

Figure 11–5 State Transition Diagram for `Task`

```
        releaseStack = 0;
        initTask(fn, stack, stackSize, tNamePtr);
}

Task::Task(void (* fn)(),
           unsigned stackSize,
           char* tNamePtr) {
    void* stack = new unsigned[stackSize];
    releaseStack = 1;
    initTask(fn, stack, stackSize, tNamePtr);
}
```

The first argument provides the address of the function where execution of the task will start the first time the task is given control.

Task Class Application

The constructors differ in the second argument. In the first constructor, the caller provides a pointer to a buffer area that the task will use for its stack. With the second constructor, the caller provides only the stack size. The second constructor allocates the stack memory from the heap. The `releaseStack` flag indicates whether the stack area should be returned to the heap when the task is terminated.

The final argument gives the task a name. This is optional and defaults to a null string.

Both functions call `initTask()` to perform the task initialization. Its definition follows with special notes added as reference points for discussion.

```
void Task::initTask(void (*fn)(), void* stack,
                unsigned stackSize,
                char* tNamePtr) {
    //save the name and id of the new task       Note A
    taskId = ++Task::taskCount;
    taskName[0] = '\0';
    if (tNamePtr)
        memcpy(taskName, tNamePtr, sizeof taskName - 1);
    taskName[sizeof taskName - 1] = '\0';

    //set up the new task's stack;               Note B
    //if no stack abort start
    ssize = stackSize;
    stackPtr = (unsigned*)stack;
    if (stackPtr == 0) {
        cout << "Could not start task" << *this << endl;
        retVal = Task::NOSTACK;
        status = Task::DEAD;
        return;
    }

    //set stack to call killSelf() on return     Note C
    unsigned* endStackPtr = &stackPtr[stackSize-1];
    *--endStackPtr = FP_SEG(killSelf);
```

```
    *--endStackPtr = FP_OFF(killSelf);

    regs[0].j_sp   = FP_OFF(endStackPtr);      //Note D
    regs[0].j_ss   = FP_SEG(endStackPtr);

    regs[0].j_ip   = FP_OFF(fn); //and the fn address
    regs[0].j_cs   = FP_SEG(fn);

    regs[0].j_ds   = _DS;   //seg regs are important
    regs[0].j_es   = _ES;
    regs[0].j_flag = 0x7246; //a "good" value for flags

    regs[0].j_si   = 0;     //these regs not important
    regs[0].j_di   = 0;
    regs[0].j_bp   = 0;

    //now add the task descriptor to the list    Note E
    status = Task::READY;   //mark task ready
    loopCount = 0;          //set count and...
    noMsgs = 0;             //...message queue size to 0
    retVal = 0;             //no return value and...
    retTask = (Task*)0;     //...no task waiting
    if (currentTask() == 0)//when initing first task...
        currentTask(this); //...save it as the root;...
    else
        addAfter(currentTask()); //...add to root
}
```

At Note A the function assigns a `taskId` and increments the static counter `taskCount`. Up to 39 characters of the task name are copied into `taskName` and a NULL is attatched to the end. Both of these fields are used for identification, primarily during debugging.

The Note B fragment checks the stack space. If the address is NULL, as would be the case if `new` returned a NULL in the constructor, `initTask()` marks the task DEAD and does not add it to the list. Setting the `retVal` to `NOSTACK` informs the parent task of the child task's fate in the event it later queries for return value.

The stack grows downward on an 80x86 machine. Thus, the line

```
unsigned* endStackPtr = &stack[lastLoc];
*--endStackPtr = 1;
```

has the effect of pushing a 1 onto the top of the stack in the same way as a PUSH instruction might.

The code fragment beginning with Note C points the local variable `endStackPtr` to the last location of the task's stack. The address of the function `killSelf()` is pushed first. If the task attempts to return from its top level function, it will "return" to the function `killSelf()` which will remove the task from the scheduling list. This resembles the way in which a normal program terminates itself by returning from the function `main()`.

The Note D section initializes the `jmp_buf` structure, which includes the values that will be loaded into the registers when the task is first scheduled. Setting `CS:IP` to `fn` causes execution to begin with the function pointed at by `fn`. The `DS`, `ES`, and `flags` registers must be initialized with proper values. I hard coded a reasonable value for the flags. The values of the overflow, parity, and half-parity bits are not important. No initial value is assigned to the `AX`, `BX`, `CX` and `DX` registers.

In the section beginning with Note E, the constructor initializes the other members of the `Task` class. If the current object is the first to be constructed, it is made the `currentTask` and left in the circular linked list of one. If other `Task` objects exist, the current object is linked onto the existing list to be scheduled in its turn.

In use, the constructors appear as follows:

```
#include "mtask.hpp"
void f1(), f2(), f3();

Task globalTask1(f1, 0x100, "Global Task #1");

int taskBuffer[0x100];
Task globalTask2(f1, taskBuffer, 0x100,
```

```
                    "Global Task #2");

void f1() {
    //perform work and then call...
    f2();
}

void f2() {
    Task localTask1(f3, 0x100, "Local Task #1");

    int localBuffer[0x100];
    Task localTask2(f3, localBuffer, 0x100,
                    "Local Task #2");
    //continue processing
```

The task `globalTask` is constructed when the program starts and begins executing at function `f1()` when the rescheduler is enabled. When `globalTask` calls the function `f2()`, the object `localTask` is instantiated and added to the scheduling list.

In the preceding example, both `globalTask` and `localTask` are instantiated twice, once with each constructor. The first constructor call allocates the 256 words of stack from the heap. The second objects use array buffers for stack space. A locally declared automatic buffer may be used as a stack area as long as the buffer does not go out of scope before the object.

Task Rescheduling

Task rescheduling is based upon the function `reschedule()` shown in the following listing.

```
void reschedule(unsigned count) {
    Task* currTPtr = currentTask();

    //first mark the task as no longer running
    currTPtr->status &= ~Task::RUNNING;
```

Task Class Application

```
//then store the registers                    Note A
currTPtr->loopCount = count;
if (setjmp(currTPtr->regs))    //once we get control...
    return;                    //...return to calling task
currTPtr->regs[0].j_di = _DI;//fix bug in setjmp()

//search active task descriptor list for a candidate
//start with the current Task
Task* tdPtr = currTPtr;                       //Note B
Task* prevTdPtr;
for (;;) {
    prevTdPtr = tdPtr;
    tdPtr     = tdPtr->next();


//search active task descriptor list for a candidate
//start with the current Task
Task* tdPtr = currTPtr;
Task* prevTdPtr;
for (;;) {
    prevTdPtr = tdPtr;
    tdPtr     = tdPtr->next();

    //if we find a task that is not the current
    //task to terminate, do it
    if (tdPtr->taskStatus() & Task::DYING)
        if (tdPtr != currTPtr) {
            tdPtr->killTask();
            tdPtr = prevTdPtr;//restart with prev td
        }

    //for tasks with a loop count > 0, decrement it
    if (tdPtr->loopCount) {
        tdPtr->loopCount--;
        continue;
    }
```

```
            //as soon as we find a ready task,
            //make it the current task and give it control
            if (tdPtr->taskStatus() == Task::READY) {
                currentTask(tdPtr);
                tdPtr->status |= Task::RUNNING;
                longjmp(currentTask()->regs, 2);
            }
        }
    }
}
```

Although not a member function, `reschedule()` is a friend of `Task` so that `reschedule()` can have access to private members.

The rescheduler starts by clearing the RUNNING flag in the status of the current task. The address of the currently active task object is returned by the function `currentTask()` which is defined in MTASK.HPP: as follows:

```
inline Task* currentTask() {
    return Task::currentTaskPtr;
}
```

At Note A the rescheduler sets the `loopCount`. Finally `reschedule()` calls `setjmp()` to save the registers into the `regs` member structure. When `setjmp()` returns the value zero, the program skips over the return.

The next line fixes a bug in early versions of Turbo C++ which caused the DI register to be saved improperly. Since `setjmp()` restores DI upon return, `reschedule()` can store the register into the structure where it belongs.

At Note B `reschedule()` begins searching with `tdPtr->next()` for the next task to schedule. The `next()` method returns `LinkedList::next()` recast to `Task*`.

```
Task* next() {
    return (Task*)LinkedList::next();
}
```

Task Class Application

If the next task is marked `DYING`, then `reschedule()` calls `killTask()` and restarts with the previous entry. The function `killTask()` cannot kill the current task.

If the `loopCount` is not zero, `reschedule()` decrements it and continues with the next object in the list. This implements a crude but effective priority scheme. The `loopCount` field was initialized when the task called `reschedule()`. Setting `loopCount` to a value other than zero allows a task to be executed less often. For example, setting the count to one causes a task to be scheduled half as often as a task with a `loopCount` of zero.

The final check is for `status`. If the status is `READY`, then `reschedule()` marks it as the current task with the private friend function `currentTask(Task*)` defined in MTASK.HPP as follows:

```
inline void  currentTask(Task* tdPtr) {
    Task::currentTaskPtr = tdPtr;
}
```

The task status is marked `RUNNING` and `reschedule()` long jumps to it. The `longjmp()` call "reappears" from the `setjmp()` call at Note A with the value two. With a nonzero value, `reschedule()` returns to allow the new task to proceed.

Task Termination

Terminating involves removing a task from the rescheduling list and calling the rescheduler. A task that is not a member of the list will never be scheduled again. Task termination is handled by the member function `killTask()`, which is defined as follows:

```
void Task::killTask() {
    //ignore requests to kill dead tasks
    if (taskStatus() & Task::DEAD)
        return;

    //if another task is waiting on a return value
```

```
        //unsuspend that task
        if (retTask) {                                  // Note A
            retTask->unsuspendTask();
            retTask = (Task*)0;
        }

        //if task trying to kill itself,
        //mark it for later removal
        if (currentTask() = = this) {                   // Note B
            status |= Task::DYING;
            if (numTasks() = = 0) {//quit if no tasks left
                cout << "Killed last task #"
                    << *this << endl;
                status |= Task::DEAD;
                stopScheduler();
                return;
            }
            reschedule();       //just have to wait
        }

        //okay, to kill the task                        // Note C
        cout << "Killing #" << *this << endl;
        if (noMsgs)
            cout << "    " << noMsgs
                << " messages lost" << endl;
        status |= Task::DEAD;   //mark the task as dead
        if (releaseStack)       //if stack came from heap...
            delete stackPtr;    //...put the stack back
        this->remove();         //and remove it from list
    }
```

If the task is already DEAD— i.e., killTask() has been accidentally invoked twice on the same object—the function returns without taking any action.

The check at Note A is for a task waiting for a return value. The address of a parent task waiting for the current task to terminate is stored in the member `retTask`. The parent task is unsuspended and `retTask` is cleared.

The check at Note B determines whether the program is trying to kill the current task. It is not safe to kill the task we are executing. If `this` is the current task, it should be marked as `DYING` and rescheduled. When the rescheduler reaches this task object again, `killTask()` will be called from a different task to terminate it completely.

A program must have at least one ready or potentially ready task. Killing the last task terminates the program. When asked to kill the final task, `killTask()` inserts a message to standard output and exits the program via the `stopScheduler()` function.

Normally `stopScheduler()` disables the scheduler and returns to `main()` without returning to the caller. If the scheduler has already been stopped, however, `stopScheduler()` returns to the caller without taking any action. This normally only occurs when `Task` objects are being destructed as part of program termination. In such cases, `killTask()` returns to the destructor.

At Note C the task object should be terminated. Messages left in the input queue generate a lost data warning. The function then marks the task as `DEAD` and removes the `Task` object from the list. If `releaseStack` is set, indicating that the stack area was allocated from the heap, the stack is deleted as well. If dynamically allocated, the stack for the last task is returned to DOS with the remainder of the program's memory.

The function `killSelf()` should be used by a task to terminate itself. This function appears as follows:

```
void killSelf() {
    currentTask()->killTask();
    abort();
}
```

Since `killTask()` results in the specified task being terminated, this function does not return.

The destructor `~Task()` terminates a task when its object goes out of scope. The destructor checks to see if the task has been terminated. If the `DEAD` flag is set, the destructor inserts a message and returns. The destructor is invoked for each global `Task` object when `main()` exits, even if killTask() has already terminated the tasks. If the task is not already terminated, the destructor invokes killTask() and returns.

```
Task::~Task() {
    //if task is still alive, kill it quick
    if (taskStatus() & Task::DEAD)
        cout << "Dead task #" << this <<
                " went out of scope" << endl;
    else
        killTask();
}
```

In use, task termination appears as follows:

```
#include "mtask.hpp"
void f1(), f2(), f3();
Task globalTask(f1, 0x100, "Global Task");

//globalTask starts here
void f1() {
    //perform work and then call...
    f2();
}

void f2() {
    int localBuffer[0x100];
    Task localTask(f3, localBuffer, 0x100, "Local Task");
    for(;;) {
        reschedule(); //give other tasks a chance
        //processing loop of some type

        //under certain conditions, kill localTask
        if (someCondition)
            localTask.killTask();
    }
} //localTask terminated here if not already
```

```
//localTask starts here
void f3() {
    //a task may decide to terminate itself as well
    if (someCondition)
        killSelf();

    //returning from main function also kills task
    if (someOtherCondition)
        return;

    for(;;) {
        //enter processing loop
    }
}
```

As `globalTask` enters `f2()`, the subtask `localTask` starts. During the execution of `f2()`, `globalTask` can terminate the subtask by applying `killTask()` to the `localTask` object. The subtask can call `killSelf()` to terminate itself. The destructor for `localTask` is executed when `globalTask` exits the function `f2()`. If `localTask` is not already terminated, the destructor terminates it.

Starting and Stopping the Scheduler

The original execution thread that executes `main()` cannot be multitasked since it has no task object. After performing any setup functions, must pass control to the rescheduler using the function `startScheduler()`, which is defined as follows:

```
jmp_buf returnToMain;           //path back to main()
void startScheduler() {
    Timer OneOfThese;           //install the timer now
    returnToMain[0].j_di = _DI;//this fixes a bug in
                                //early TC++ setjmp()

    if (setjmp(returnToMain))
```

```
        return;
    schedulerEnabled = 1;
    longjmp(currentTask()->regs, 1);
}
```

This function starts by instantiating the `Timer` object to enable the timer. It then saves the current position into the structure `returnToMain`. After setting the `schedulerEnabled` flag to true, `startScheduler()` long jumps to the current task.

The first task object declared is the first current task. Before `startScheduler()` is called, at least one task must be declared.

The scheduler is disabled by calling the function `stopScheduler()`. This function clears the `schedulerEnabled` flag and long jumps back to `startScheduler()` to return to `main()` from the point at which the scheduler was enabled. The `main()` function may perform whatever cleanup work is necessary before terminating.

```
void stopScheduler() {
    if (schedulerEnabled) {
        schedulerEnabled = 0;
        longjmp(returnToMain, 1);
    }
}
```

Calling `stopScheduler()` after the scheduler has been disabled has no effect. Thus, if `killTask()` calls `stopScheduler()` when the objects are being destructed at the end of the program, no harm will be done because the `schedulerEnabled` flag will have already been cleared.

Task Return Value

The simplest form of intertask communication is the task return. A parent task may spawn a subtask to execute one logical path, while the parent executes another with the intent of eventually recombining the two branches as shown in Figure 11-6.

Task Class Application

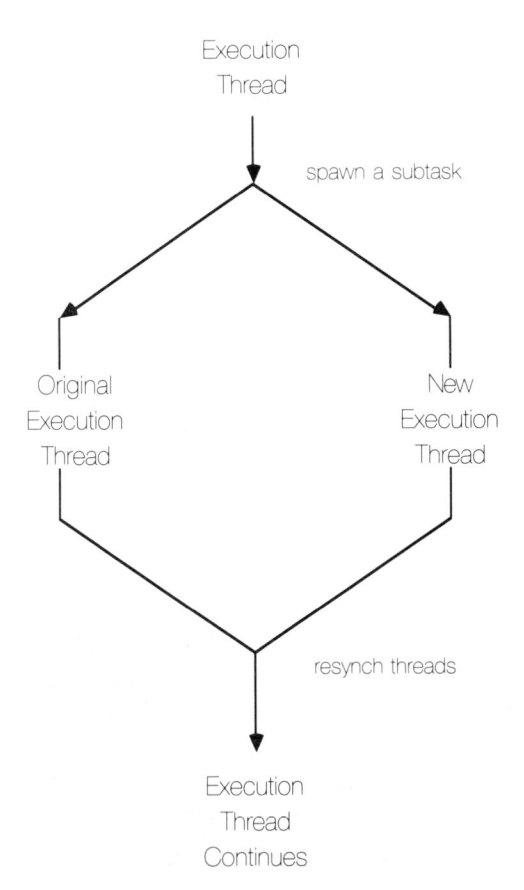

Figure 11-6 Spawning and Resynching Subtasks

Resynching two tasks is accomplished through the `setReturnValue()` and `getReturnValue()` methods shown.

```
int Task::setReturnValue(int value) {
    if (value < 0) {
        cout <<
          "Negative return values reserved for system\n";
        return Task::OUTOFRANGE;
    }
    retVal = value;
    return Task::OK;
```

}

```
int Task::getReturnValue(Task& td){
    while ((td.taskStatus() &
            (Task::DEAD|Task::DYING)) = = 0){
        if (td.retTask)
            return Task::QUEFULL;
        else {
            td.retTask = this;
            suspendTask();
            reschedule();
        }
    }
    return td.retVal;
}
```

The `setReturnValue()` method allows a task to store a return value. The return value cannot be negative, since class `Task` reserves negative values for system error indications. If this is a problem, the size of `retVal` can be expanded to a `long int`.

A task may set its return value more than once. For example, a task may set its return value to a "Successfully Completed" indication at the outset of the task and change it in the event of an error. The `Task` constructor initializes the `retVal` to zero.

The `getReturnValue()` is the method a task A uses to read the return value of another task B. If task B is not dead or dying when the call is made, task A is suspended. The address of the waiting task is stored in the member `retTask` which is of type `Task*`. Only one task may wait on another. If a task is already waiting for task B, then `getReturn-Value()` returns an immediate error condition.

When task B terminates itself, the function `killTask()` restarts the waiting task A. When restarted, `getReturnValue()` returns task B's return value.

Task Class Application

If Task B was never started completely, the `Task` constructor sets the status and return value so that Task A will receive an indication of that failure when it calls `getReturnValue()`.

The following are non-member equivalents to the functions previously defined in `MTASK.HPP`. Each invokes the corresponding member function on the current task.

```
inline int returnTaskValue(int value) {
    return currentTask()->setReturnValue(value);
}
inline int getTaskValue(Task& td) {
    return currentTask()->getReturnValue(td);
}
```

In practice, these functions appear as follows:

```
#include "mtask.cpp"

void parentFunc() {
    //begin execution

    //parent task may fork off subtask at any time
    void childFunc();
    Task childTask(childFunc, 0x100);

    //now parent may continue executing

    //eventually parent wants to link back up
    int childValue = getTaskValue(childTask);

    //continue on
}

void childFunc() {
```

```
    int result;
    //child task performs some work

    //now return the result and quit
    returnTaskValue(result);
}
```

The body of `parentFunc()` and `childFunc()` are omitted for brevity.

Intertask Message Passing

Message passing is a more sophisticated communications path than task return values. The member `Task::queue` points to a FIFO queue of messages. The number of messages in the queue is maintained in the member `Task::noMsgs`.

A message should be defined as publicly derived from class `Message`, which is defined in MTASK.HPP as follows:

```
class Message : public LinkedList {};
```

The following message might be used to submit disk read requests to a disk control task.

```
struct DiskRequest : public Message {
    int    function;    //0 -> read, 1 -> write
    int    diskSector;
    int    numOfSectors;
    void*  bufferAddress;
}
```

A task can send messages to another task's queue up to a maximum of `maxQueSize`, using the method `sendMsg()`, which is defined as follows:

Task Class Application

```
const int maxQueSize = 20;
int Task::sendMsg (Message* msgPtr) {
    Message* lastMsgPtr;

    if (noMsgs > maxQueSize)
        return Task::QUEFULL;

    lastMsgPtr = (Message*)queue.previous();
    msgPtr->addAfter(lastMsgPtr);
    noMsgs++;
    unwaitTask();
    return Task::OK;
}
```

Attempts to queue up more than `maxQueSize` messages return an immediate indication that the queue is full.

Once `sendMsg()` determines that room is available in the queue, the address of the last message is located using the function `LinkedList::previous()`. The message is added to the queue using the method `LinkedList::addAfter()`. Finally it "unwaits" the task in case the task is waiting for a message to appear.

A task reads its queue using the method `getTMsg()` defined as follows:

```
Message* Task::getTMsg(unsigned N) {
    Message* nextMsgPtr;

    if (noMsgs = = 0) {                               //Note A
        waitTask(N);
        reschedule();
    }
    if (noMsgs) {                                     //Note B
        noMsgs--;
        nextMsgPtr = (Message*)queue.next();
        nextMsgPtr->remove();
```

```
            return nextMsgPtr;
    } else
        return (Message*)0;
}
```

The argument to `getTMsg()` specifies the number of clock ticks the task will wait for a message to appear. If N equals zero, the task will wait forever. To avoid being delayed, a task must check to see if any messages are available before calling `getTMsg()`. The member function `msgCount()` returns the number of messages in the queue.

At Note A, the function determines if any messages are in the queue. If not, it holds the task for up to N clock ticks. The task will be released when a message is sent to the queue or the prescribed time expires.

At Note B, `getTMsg()` dequeues the first message and returns its address. If no messages are present, a NULL is returned.

One task should not read another's queue. The normal procedure for a task to use when reading its own queue is `getMsg()`, which is defined as follows:

```
Message* getMsg(unsigned N) {
    return currentTask()->getTMsg(N);
}
```

The preceding functions are applied in the following example.

```
#include "mtask.hpp"

//format of disk request and response messages
struct DiskRequest : public Message {
    int    function;          //0 -> read, 1 -> write
    int    diskSector;
    int    numOfSectors;
    void*  bufferAddress;
    Task*  requestingTask;
};
```

Task Class Application

```
struct DiskResponse : public Message {
    int diskStatus;
};

//DiskTask - read, process and respond to disk requests
void diskFunc();
Task diskTask(diskFunc, 0x100, "Disk Task");

void diskFunc() {
    DiskRequest* rqstPtr;
    int    status;
    Task* sendAnswerTo;
    DiskResponse* sendBackPtr;

    //sit in infinite loop, performing disk operations
    for (;;) {
        //read a request
        rqstPtr = (DiskRequest*)getMsg(0);
        sendAnswerTo = rqstPtr->requestingTask;

        //perform disk operation

        //respond when finished
        sendBackPtr = new DiskResponse;
        sendBackPtr->diskStatus = status;
        sendAnswerTo->sendMsg(sendBackPtr);
    }
}

//readDisk - send a read request to the disk task and
//           return the completion status
int readDisk(int sector, int noSectors, void* bufferPtr){
    //build a read request message
    DiskRequest& read = *new DiskRequest;
    read.function      = 0;     //read request
```

```
    read.diskSector      = sector;
    read.numOfSectors    = noSectors;
    read.bufferAddress   = bufferPtr;
    read.requestingTask  = currentTask();
    diskTask.sendMsg(&read);    //send the message

    //the wait for a response
    DiskResponse* responsePtr;
    responsePtr = (DiskResponse*)getMsg(0);

    //return messages to heap
    delete(&read);
    int returnStatus = responsePtr->diskStatus;
    delete(responsePtr);

    //return response to caller
    return returnStatus;
}
```

The task `diskTask` is in an infinite loop, reading disk access request messages, performing them, and responding with the completion status. (The code to perform the disk operation has been omitted.) The response message is sent to the task object address contained in the request message.

The function `readDisk()` provides an interface between other tasks and `diskTask`. When calling `readDisk()`, a task builds a read request message containing its arguments. The read request message must also include the address of the caller's task object in order for the caller to receive a response. Any task can call `readDisk()` so that several requests may be pending at the same time.

If the caller does not know the target task's object address, the function `directory()` allows the caller to look up a task by name. The definition is as follows:

```
Task* directory(char* targetName) {
    Task* tdPtr = currentTask();
    int strLength = strlen(targetName);
```

```
    do {
        if (strLength == strlen(tdPtr->taskName))
            if (strncmp(targetName,
                        tdPtr->taskName,
                        strLength) == 0)
                return tdPtr;
        tdPtr = tdPtr->next();
    } while (tdPtr != currentTask());
    return (Task*)0;
}
```

Starting with the current task, `directory()` searches for the first `taskName` that matches the `targetName`. If no match is found, `directory()` returns a NULL.

If `readDisk()` did not know the address of the `diskTask` object, it could find the address using the known task name "Disk Task" as follows:

```
//send to task "Disk Task"
Task* diskTaskPtr;
if (diskTaskPtr = directory("Disk Task"))
    diskTaskPtr->sendMsg(&read);        //send the message
```

The directory function is convenient when communicating between tasks that reside in separate programs. In addition, accessing by name rather than address reduces the bonding between tasks.

Finally, `sendMsg()` does not copy the message into a buffer before sending it. Thus, the programmer must confirm that the message is still valid when it is received. For example, the following is not valid.

```
struct MyMessage : public Message {
    int data;
}

void sendAMessage(Task* taskPtr, int inputData) {
    MyMessage msgBuf;
```

```
        msgBuf.data = inputData;
        taskPtr->sendMsg(&msgBuf);
}
```

In this example `sendAMessage()` allocates `msgBuf` from its local stack and then sends the address of the block to the task `*taskPtr`. However, the function then returns to the caller, thereby freeing the stack memory containing `msgBuf`. By the time that `*taskPtr` reads the message its contents will have been destroyed.

This problem can be avoided in two ways. One is to allocate the buffer statically, thereby insuring its integrity. The other solution is to allocate the message from the heap as follows:

```
void sendAMessage(Task* taskPtr, int inputData) {
    MyMessage* msgBufPtr = new MyMessage;

    msgBufPtr->data = inputData;
    taskPtr->sendMsg(msgBufPtr);
}
```

The program allocates from the heap a block large enough to hold a `MyMessage`. The message is then sent to the receiving task. The receiving task must `free` the message when finished. This was the approach used in the `DiskTask` example earlier.

Time

Functions must be able to slow down to match slow external devices, such as humans, by delaying execution for specified lengths of time. For example, the following three lines beep the speaker at 400 Hz for one half second.

```
sound(400);
delay(500);
nosound();
```

Without the `delay()` call, the time between the `sound()` and `nosound()` calls would be so short that no sound could be heard.

The delay functions provided by single tasking libraries work by executing in a tight loop either counting cycles through a carefully measured instruction sequence or watching a global time increment until the specified length of time has transpired.

In a multitasking environment, while one task is waiting, other tasks should be performing useful work. If a task calls the `delay()` function provided in the Turbo C++ library, all tasks are suspended since `delay()` contains no calls to `reschedule()`. The class `Timer`, also defined in `MTASK.CPP`, forms the basis for implementing a multitasked version called `tDelay()`.

The definition for class `Timer` follows:

```
const unsigned clockInt = 0x1c;
class Timer {
    friend unsigned getTime();
  private:
    static void interrupt (far * oldfn)(...);
    static unsigned           globalTime;

  public:
    Timer();
    static void interrupt clockTick(...);
    ~Timer();
};
```

The constructor for `Timer` is defined as follows:

```
Timer::Timer() {
    oldfn = getvect(clockInt);
    setvect(clockInt, Timer::clockTick);
}
```

The constructor saves the address of the interrupt service routine for interrupt 0x1C. That interrupt is called from the hardware clock interrupt once every 55 milliseconds. The constructor then installs the interrupt routine `Timer::clockTick()`.

Executing the constructor for the single `Timer` object `OneOfThese` from the function `startScheduler()` installs the function `clockTick()` immediately before control is passed to the rescheduler.

The destructor for class `Timer` is set up similarly.

```
Timer::~Timer() {
    if (oldfn) {
       setvect(clodkInt, Oldfn);
       oldfn = 0:
    }
}
```

When `OneOfThese` is destructed as `startScheduler()` returns, the destructor reinstalls the previous interrupt service routine. Zeroing `oldfn` guarantees that the interrupt service routine is not reinstalled more than once.

The interrupt function `clockTick()` is defined as follows:

```
void interrupt Timer::clockTick() {
Task *tdPtr;
//don't do anything if scheduler not enabled
if (schedulerEnabled) {
    //increment the current time
    globalTime++;                                         //Note A

    //tick each task descriptor in the list;
    //if current task is RUNNING, increment its
    //CPU counter
    tdPtr = currentTask();
    if (tdPtr->taskStatus() & Task::RUNNING)
    tdPtr->cpuTime++;                                     //Note e B
    //loop through the tasks, tick each one
    do {                                                  //Note C
       tdPtr->oneClockTick();
       tdPtr = tdPtr->next();
    } while (tdPtr != currentTask());
```

```
}

//chain to the "old" timer function now
(*oldfn)();                                             //Note D
```

Once `clockTick()` is installed, it is given control every clock tick. If the scheduler is enabled, `clockTick()` increments a static member `Timer::globalTime` at Note A. This variable may be read with the function `getTime()`.

```
unsigned getTime() {
    return Timer::globalTime;
```

The preceding provides tasks with the number of clock ticks since the multitasker began. Although less sophisticated, this function is quicker than the standard C++ functions for measuring time.

At Note B, `clockTick()` increments the `cpuTime` member of the current task if it is in state RUNNING. This provides a crude measure of the tasks that consume the most time.

Schedulers in systems that maintain an accurate measure of CPU usage read the clock when starting a task and again when taking control. The difference between the two readings is the time used by the task. By adding up the time between the context switches of every task, the system can accurately measure how much time each task requires.

However, the PC timer is too coarse to measure short periods of time. Although the timer chip can be accelerated, doing so requires difficult programming and may conflict with application software that attempts to do the same thing.

The timer approach is statistical. Tasks that use most of the CPU time are more likely to be running when the clock interrupt occurs; thus, their `cpuTime` field tends to increment faster. While no more than a rough indication of CPU usage, the overhead in `cpuTime` is very low. Since the `cpuTime` member is not used by the scheduler, it is publicly available to applications functions.

The main job of `clockTick()` is to count down tasks that are delayed. This is handled in the loop starting at Note C. For each task in the list, `clockTick()` calls the method `Task::oneClockTick()`.

At Note D, `clockTick()` calls the interrupt service routine previously installed at interrupt 0x1C. This allows a program to chain to other timer routines, perhaps installed by earlier TSRs.

The function `Task::oneClockTick()` is defined as follows:

```
void Task::oneClockTick() {
    if (delayCount)
        if (--delayCount == 0) {
            if (taskStatus() & Task::AWAITING_MSG)
                unwaitTask();
            if (taskStatus() & Task::DELAYED)
                undelayTask();
        }
}
```

The variable `delayCount`, a member of the class `Task`, is nonzero whenever the task is waiting for a length of time, in other words, a certain number of clock ticks, to pass.

The function `oneClockTick()` checks the value. If the value is not zero, `oneClockTick()` decrements it. If the result is zero, then the delay time has expired and the task is resumed.

The several methods that allow one task to suspend another are defined as follows:

```
void Task::suspendTask() {
    status |= Task::SUSPENDED;    //set suspended bit
}
void Task::unsuspendTask() {
    status &= ~Task::SUSPENDED;   //clear suspended bit
}
void Task::waitTask(unsigned N) {
    status |= Task::AWAITING_MSG;//set message waiting
    delayCount = N;
}
void Task::unwaitTask() {
    if (taskStatus() & AWAITING_MSG){
```

Task Class Application

```
            status &= ~Task::AWAITING_MSG;
            delayCount = 0;
        }
    }
    void Task::delayTask(unsigned N) {
        status |= Task::DELAYED;      //set the delay flag
        delayCount = N;
    }
    void Task::undelayTask() {
        if (taskStatus() & Task::DELAYED) {
            status &= ~Task::DELAYED; //clear msg waiting bit
            delayCount = 0;
        }
    }
```

The first two functions, suspend() and unsuspend(), set and clear the SUSPENDED flag. With this flag set in the task object's status, the rescheduler will no longer schedule the task. No timer is associated with the suspended flag.

The waitTask() and delayTask() methods set the AWAITING_MSG and DELAYED flags, respectively. However, these tasks also set the delayCount to the value of the argument N. If the count is non-zero, then oneClockTick restarts the tasks when it decrements the delayCount to zero. If the count is zero, the task waits until another task specifically frees it, as with the suspend() function.

The functions waitTask() and unwaitTask() work with the message send and receive functions. User tasks should use the delayTask() and undelayTask() functions to delay each other.

The following code fragment shows how these functions are used.

```
typedef Task* TaskPtr;
TaskPtr task1Ptr, task2Ptr, task3Ptr;
void fn() {
    task1Ptr->suspend();            //suspend Task1
    task2Ptr->delayTask(3 * 18);//wait Task2 3 seconds
    task3Ptr->unsuspend();          //unsuspend Task3
}
```

The first call suspends the task `*task1Ptr`, the second call suspends `*task2Ptr` for three seconds, and the last call unsuspends `*task3Ptr`.

To suspend or delay itself a task should use the `tSuspend()` and `tDelay()` functions included in `MTASK.CPP`. These are defined as follows:

```
void tDelay(unsigned N) {
    currentTask()->delayTask(N);
    reschedule();
}

void tSuspend() {
    currentTask()->suspendTask();
    reschedule();
}
```

These functions set the `status` and `delayCount` of the calling task so the scheduler will not schedule them and then surrender control via the call to `reschedule()`. A task that calls `tSuspend()` is suspended until another task unsuspends it. A task calling `tDelay()` is delayed for N clock ticks or until another task undelays it.

The following code fragment waits for a key from the keyboard for up to 10 seconds. If no key arrives, the program times out and continues with a default key.

```
#include "mtask.hpp"
#include "conio.h"

//Define message to hold keystroke
struct KeyMessage : public Message {
    char key;
};

//keyFunc - read a keystroke from keyboard
//          and send it to mainTask
```

Task Class Application

```
KeyMessage response;
void keyFunc() {
    //wait until a character hit
    while (!kbhit())
        reschedule();

    //put the keystroke into response message
    response.key = getch();

    //now send it
    mainTask.sendMsg(&response);
}

//readKey - wait for up to 10 seconds for a key from the
//          keyboard, if no key arrives return default
char readKey(char defaultChar) {
    Task keyTask(keyFunc, 0x200);
    KeyMessage* responsePtr;

    //wait for message with keystroke in it
    responsePtr = (KeyMessage*)getMsg(10 * 18);
    if (responsePtr)
        return responsePtr->key;
    else
        return defaultChar;
}
```

When called, the function `readKey()` starts the subtask `keyTask` which cycles in a loop checking the keyboard for the appearance of a keystroke. As long as no key is present, the task surrenders control by calling `reschedule()`. If a keystroke arrives, `keyTask` reads the key, stores it into a message, and returns it to `readKey()`.

Note that `keyTask` does not read the keyboard directly. Since the multitasker is not built into the operating system, any task that becomes suspended without calling `reschedule()` stops all tasks.

After starting the subtask, `readKey()` waits for up to 180 clock ticks (10 seconds) for a message. If a message arrives, `readKey()` returns the key contained in the message to the caller; otherwise, `readKey()` returns a default character. The `keyTask` object is destructed and the task is terminated when `readKey()` returns.

Task Output

The `Task` member functions include several output statements. Although these statements can (and should) be removed once the applications program is working properly, they are necessary during development to provide the programmer with insight as to what the multitasker is doing. Class `Task` also includes several functions designed to give the programmer visibility into the status of the task objects.

A `Task` inserter can be defined to display the task Id and name.

```
inline ostream& operator<<(ostream& s, Task& td) {
    return s << td.taskId << " - " << (char*)td.taskName;
}
```

The following small code fragment uses the `Task` inserter

```
Task globalTask(globalFunc, 0x100, "Global Task 1");

void fn() {
    Task localTask(localFunc, 0x100, "Local Task 1");

    cout << "The current tasks are\n"
         << globalTask << "\n"
         << localTask  << endl;
```

to generate the following output.

```
The current tasks are
1 - Global Task 1
2 - Local Task 1
```

The member function `showTask()` allows the programmer to periodically display the state of specific task objects. This function is defined as follows:

```
void Task::showTask() {
   unsigned stackDepth =
              regs[0].j_sp - FP_OFF(stackPtr);

   cout << dec <<
     "Task #"            << *this   <<
     "\n  nomsgs = "     <<  noMsgs <<
     "  return value = " <<  retVal <<
     "  status = ";

   //output status information as an ASCII string
   static char* statuses[] = { "Suspended ",
                               "Dying ",
                               "Dead ",
                               "Awaiting Msg ",
                               "Delaying ",
                               "Running "};
   static enum TaskStatus statusBits[] =
                                    {Task::SUSPENDED,
                                     Task::DYING,
                                     Task::DEAD,
                                     Task::AWAITING_MSG,
                                     Task::DELAYED,
                                     Task::RUNNING};
   for (int i = 0; i < 6; i++)
      if (status & statusBits[i])
         cout << statuses[i];

   cout << hex <<
       "\n  stackdepth = " <<   stackDepth <<
       "  stacksize = "    <<  ssize * 2;
```

```
    cout << dec <<
            "\n  CPU time = "    <<   cpuTime;

    cout << endl;
}
```

This function calculates the stack depth by comparing the current value of the stack pointer saved in the task descriptor with the known location of the beginning of the task's stack. This information is displayed along with the most important class information.

The task status is interpreted by matching an ASCII string with each status bit. The task status is ANDed with the array of status bits. When the result is not zero, the corresponding ASCII string is output.

The function `showAllTasks()` provides an overview of all tasks by executing `showTask()` on all of the tasks in the scheduling list.

```
void showAllTasks() {
    Task *tdPtr = currentTask();

    do {
        tdPtr->showTask();
        tdPtr = tdPtr->next();
    } while (tdPtr != currentTask());
}
```

A task can be built that will wait for a predefined condition such as a message or a time interval before calling `showAllTasks()`. The following task waits five seconds and dumps the state of all tasks.

```
void showIt() {
    tDelay(5 * 18);    //5 second delay
    showAllTasks();
    killSelf();
}
Task showTask(showIt, 0x100, "Display Task");
```

When added to the `readKey()` program in the previous example, the output appears as follows:

```
Task #2 - Display Task
  nomsgs = 0   return value = 0   status = Running
  stackdepth = 1da  stacksize = 200
  CPU time = 0
Task #1 - Task which calls ReadKey()
  nomsgs = 0   return value = 0   status = Awaiting Msg
  stackdepth = 35c  stacksize = 400
  CPU time = 0
Task #3 - Task to Poll Keyboard
  nomsgs = 0   return value = 0   status =
  stackdepth = 3e2  stacksize = 400
  CPU time = 68
```

Three tasks are defined. The task that calls `showAllTasks()` always appears first in the list and is always the currently running task. This task was created with 0x200 bytes of stack space, of which 0x1da bytes are available. In addition, there are no messages in this task's input queue, the task has a return value of zero, and no CPU time has been accumulated. A task does not accumulate CPU time while it is waiting, delayed, or suspended.

The second task in the list is called `readKey()`. This task is awaiting a message from `keyTask` and was allocated 0x400 bytes of stack. No CPU time has been accumulated.

The third task is associated with `keyTask`. This task has no status, which means it is ready to run. Almost four seconds of processing time accumulated during the five seconds before `showTask` displayed this status. The remaining time was spent in the rescheduler.

Sample Application

Some of the most common applications for multitasking are simulation programs. These programs simulate different types of objects interacting asynchronously.

Time independence is difficult to simulate with conventional, control loop-based solutions. In this type of a solution, the order of function calls is predefined and fixed.

With one CPU, the order of events in a multitasking solution can be predicted. Unlike the control loop solution, however, the tasks that simulate the objects do not know what the order is. Variability can be added by including delays of random lengths of time.

Example 1: Orbiting Planets

To demonstrate the `Task` class multitasker, let us model a system of planets moving through space. The full source code listing for this program appears in Appendix B.

As planets move they interact with each other through the gravitational pull that each exerts. The force one body exerts on another is represented by the following equation:

$$\vec{F}_{ij} = \frac{G m_i m_j}{r_{ij}^2} \hat{r}_{ij}$$

The resulting acceleration is proportional to the mass of the object. Thus, the acceleration that a body experiences due to the gravitational pull of another is represented by the following formula:

$$F = ma$$

$$\vec{a}_{ij} = \frac{G m_j}{r_{ij}^2} \hat{r}_{ij}$$

If more than one other body exists, then the acceleration is the vector sum of all of the acceleration vectors.

$$\vec{a}_i = \sum_{j <> i} \frac{G m_j}{r_{ij}^2} \hat{r}_{ij}$$

Task Class Application

Barring collision, a planet travels along a path determined by adding the constantly changing acceleration vector to the planet's velocity vector, independent of other events. The interaction of independent bodies is ideally suited to a multitasking solution.

The following class `Planet` is a subclass of `Task`.

```
class Planet : public Task {
  private:
    Location loc;
    Velocity vel;
    double mass;

  public:
    char  identifier;
    virtual unsigned isA() { return 1;}

    Planet(void* stack, unsigned stackSize,
          Location& iLoc, Velocity& iVel,
          double iMass, char* pName, char id) :
        loc(iLoc), vel(iVel),
        Task(planetFunc, stack, stackSize, pName){
        mass = iMass;
        identifier = id;
    }
    Planet* nextPlanet();
    Planet& operator<<(char c);

    Vector calcAcceleration();
    void update(Vector& acc) {
        vel.update(acc);
        loc.update(vel);
    }
};
```

The first three members of `Planet` contain the planet's mass, current location, and current velocity. The member identifier is the character that the program uses to display the planet on the screen.

The constructor for `Planet` specifies the task information, the initial location, initial velocity, and the identification character.

The virtual method `isA()` is used to determine the subclass of `Task`. `Task::isA()` returns a zero. I arbitrarily designated `Planet::isA()` to return a one. For example, the member function `nextPlanet()` uses the `Task next()` method to return the next task in the scheduling list.

```
Planet* Planet::nextPlanet() {
    Task* tPtr;
    do {
        tPtr = next();
    } while (tPtr->isA() != 1);
    return (Planet*)tPtr;
}
```

If `tPtr->isA()` is not equal to one, then `tPtr` points to a `Task` object other than a `Planet` and the function continues searching. One could generalize such a function into a member function that returns the next `Task` object of the same subclass as the caller as well.

```
Task* nextThing() {
    Task* tPtr;
    do {
        tPtr = next();
    } while (tPtr->isA() != this->isA());
    return tPtr;
}
```

The `Planet& operator<<(char)` function displays the character argument on the screen at the location of the planet. To keep the simulation simple, this function displays in 80x25 character mode.

Task Class Application

```
static unsigned far& screen(unsigned xloc,unsigned yloc){
    static unsigned (far* screenMatrix)[25][80] =
        (unsigned (far*)[25][80])0xB8000000L;
    return   (*screenMatrix)[yloc][xloc];
}
void putText(unsigned xloc, unsigned yloc,
            unsigned color, unsigned symbol){
    unsigned fullChar = ((unsigned)color << 8) + symbol;
    screen(xloc, yloc) = fullChar;
}
Planet& Planet::operator<<(char c) {
    int cTemp = c;
    int xloc = 40.5 + loc.loc.x / 100.;
    int yloc = 12.5 - loc.loc.y / 140.;
    if (xloc >= 0)
        if (yloc >= 0)
            if (xloc < 80)
                if (yloc < 25) {
                    putText(xloc, yloc, 0x03, cTemp);
                    return *this;
                }
    cout << "\nGone off screen" << endl;
    killSelf();
    return *this;//
}
```

The x and y locations of the planet are arbitrarily scaled and then centered about the middle of the screen. Different scaling factors are used for x and y to make circles appear round on the character screen. If the character location is off the screen, a message is displayed and the task is terminated.

The last two member functions calculate the acceleration due to other planets and update the planet's `Velocity` and `Location`.

The classes `Velocity` and `Location` are defined as follows:

```
struct Velocity {
    Vector vel;
    unsigned lastTime;

    Velocity(double xVel,double yVel) : vel(xVel, yVel) {
        lastTime = getTime();
    }
    void update(Vector&);
};

struct Location {
    Vector loc;
    unsigned lastTime;

    Location(double xLoc,double yLoc) : loc(xLoc, yLoc) {
        lastTime = getTime();
    }
    void update(Velocity& vel);
};
```

The `Velocity` and `Location` classes contain the velocity and location vectors plus the time of the last update. Updating the `Velocity` consists of multiplying the acceleration by the time since the last update and adding it to the previous velocity. Updating `Location` is similar.

```
void Location::update(Velocity& vel) {
    double tDiff = (getTime() - lastTime) / 18.2;
    lastTime = getTime();
    loc = loc + tDiff * vel.vel;
}
void Velocity::update(Vector& acc) {
    double tDiff = (getTime() - lastTime) / 18.2;
    lastTime = getTime();
    vel = vel + tDiff * acc;
}
```

Task Class Application

No consideration is given to the fact that the acceleration and velocity change continuously. The update functions assume that these values are constant over the time interval. This approximation is acceptable as long as the intervals are short enough that the acceleration and velocity do not change significantly in one interval.

Since all constants in this simulation have been arbitrarily scaled to match the display dimensions, the programmer can remove the 18.2 factor to make the simulation move faster. Doing so makes the simulation more coarse.

The `Vector` class is similar to the `Complex` class, consisting of a two-dimensional number pair. The program also defines the common operators for class `Vector`.

```
struct Vector {
    double x;
    double y;

  public:
    Vector(double iX, double iY) : x(iX), y(iY) {}
    Vector(Vector& v) {
        x = v.x;
        y = v.y;
    }
    Vector() : x(0), y(0) {}

    double mag2() {
        return x * x + y * y;
    }
    Vector unitVector();
};
```

The `unitVector()` method calculates the unit vector parallel to the vector provided.

```
Vector Vector::unitVector() {
    double mag = sqrt(mag2());
```

```
    return Vector(x / mag, y / mag);
}
```

Also defined for `Vector` are the common arithmetic operations.

```
Vector operator+(Vector& a, Vector& b) {
    return Vector(a.x + b.x, a.y + b.y);
}
Vector operator-(Vector& a, Vector& b) {
    return Vector(a.x - b.x, a.y - b.y);
}
Vector operator*(double& a, Vector& b) {
    return Vector(a * b.x, a * b.y);
}
Vector operator/(Vector& a, double& b) {
    if (b == 0) {
        cerr << "Planet collision";
        killSelf();
    }
    return Vector(a.x / b, a.y / b);
}
```

The core of the program, `calcAcceleration()`, calculates the acceleration that a `Planet` experiences from other planets nearby.

```
Vector Planet::calcAcceleration() {
    Planet* planetPtr = this;
    Vector distance;
    double magnitude;
    Vector accVector;
    const double G = 1000.;
    Vector acc(0, 0);

    while ((planetPtr=planetPtr->nextPlanet()) != this) {
        distance = planetPtr->loc.loc - loc.loc;
        magnitude= (G * planetPtr->mass)/distance.mag2();
```

```
        accVector= magnitude * distance.unitVector();
        acc = acc + accVector;
    }
    return acc;
}
```

Starting with an acceleration of (0,0), `calcAcceleration()` loops through all of the `Planets` in the scheduling list. For each one it calculates the vector distance. From this the magnitude of acceleration is determined. The gravitational constant G used here is arbitrary to make the simulation run at a reasonable rate. The acceleration vector due to the other planet is equal to the acceleration magnitude times the unit vector toward that planet.

The process is repeated for each planet found and the results are accumulated in the `Vector acc`.

The base function for class `Planet`, `planetFunc()`, displays the planet, then calculates the planet's new velocity and location, and redisplays it.

```
void planetFunc() {
    Vector acc;
    Planet& currPlanet = *(Planet*)currentTask();

    for(;;) {
        currPlanet << currPlanet.identifier;
        tDelay(1);
                                                        //Note A
        if (kbhit()) {           //stop if char entered
            getch();             //flush the character
            killSelf();
        }
        currPlanet << ' ';                              //Note B
        acc = currPlanet.calcAcceleration();
        currPlanet.update(acc);
    }
}
```

The call to `tDelay()` leaves the planet's character on the screen long enough to remain visible. Even so, planets shimmer as their identifiers are removed and replaced.

The code fragment marked Note A checks for a keystroke. If one is detected, the planet terminates itself. The user can remove planets in this way until the program terminates. Removing the line marked Note B causes the planets to leave a trail of their past locations behind them.

To test the foregoing functions, I used a `main()` program that declares three planets of mass 1, 10, and 1,000 and named these planets Earth, Jupiter, and Sun. The relationship of the masses of the real planets are very different. I used the smaller ratios to allow the planets to have a noticeable effect on the sun.

The stack for these tasks was allocated in local globally defined arrays.

```
unsigned int stackBuf1[0x800];
unsigned int stackBuf2[0x800];
unsigned int stackBuf3[0x800];
void main() {
    //create a few planets
    int initX, initY;
    cout <<"Enter initial X and Y velocity for Sun:";
    cin >> initX >> initY;           //typical 0, 0
    Planet sun(stackBuf1, 0x800,
            Location(0, 0), Velocity(initX, initY),
            1000, "Sun", '*');

    cout <<"Enter initial X and Y velocity for Earth:";
    cin >> initX >> initY;           //typical -40, 0
    Planet earth(stackBuf2, 0x800,
            Location(0, 600), Velocity(initX,initY),
            1, "Earth", '.');

    cout <<"Enter initial X and Y velocity for Jupiter:";
    cin >> initX >> initY;           //typical 50, 0
    Planet jupiter(stackBuf3, 0x800,
            Location(0,-1000), Velocity(initX,initY),
```

```
                    10, "Jupiter", '@');

    //now start the tasks going
    clrscr();
    startScheduler();
}
```

The suggested initial velocities of (0,0), (-40, 0), and (50, 0) are good starting places for experimentation.

Without Jupiter, the Earth forms an elliptical orbit that follows the same track repeatedly. With Jupiter present, the orbit of the Earth precesses noticeably. However, if the Earth and Jupiter come close enough to each other, the Earth will be thrown completely off the screen.

Example 2: Worms

In the first example all communication between tasks was asynchronous. Each planet queried the other about its location, but there was no query-response, two-way communication. In addition, only one task type was involved.

The following game demonstrates communication between tasks of different types using intertask messages. In this simulation, the moving tasks are called worms. Worms scamper across the screen, leaving a trail behind them. Worms may not leave the screen nor may they cross a worm trail. When a worm can no longer move, it is terminated. The last worm left on the screen is the winner.

Worms are ignorant creatures. Before each move they must ask a worm driver task in which direction to move. The worm driver decides which path the worms will take and kills the worms when no legal possibility is left for them.

To allow the user to play, there are two types of worm drivers. Most worms query the automatic driver that scans the display looking for a likely place for the worm to go. One worm queries the manual driver, which then gets its instructions from the arrow keys of the numeric keypad. Thus, the user competes with the automatic driver to keep its worms alive the longest. The game is terminated when the user enters the End key from the numeric keypad. The entire listing for the worm game appears in Appendix C. Here I will discuss only the main features.

Drivers are based upon the `Direction` class which is defined as follows:

```
class Direction : public Task {
  public:
    Direction(void (*myF)(), char* name) :
           Task(myF, 0x0200, name){}
};
```

Worms are based upon the `Worm` class which is defined as follows:

```
class Worm : public Task {
    friend ostream& operator<< (ostream& s, Worm& td);
  private:
    char      color;         //color+location of worm
    char      ourChar;       //its character
    unsigned xloc, yloc;     //its location

    unsigned direction;      //direction of travel

    Direction* driverPtr;    //address of driving task

  public:
    Worm(unsigned c, unsigned x, unsigned y, char symbol,
        Direction* dPtr) : Task(wormTask, 0x0100,"Worm"){
        color     = c;
        ourChar   = symbol;
        xloc      = x;
        yloc      = y;
        direction = c & 0x03; //start each worm in a
                              //different direction
        driverPtr = dPtr;
    }
    void    getNewDirection();
    void    updateLoc();
```

};

Each worm has a display color and character that distinguishes it from other worms. Each worm also has a direction of travel and a location. Finally, a worm knows the address of the task object it is to query for directions. These values are initialized in the `Worm` constructor. In the simulation, we use the three-argument `Task` constructor to allocate stack space from the heap.

Worms begin execution with the function `wormTask()`.

```
void wormTask() {
    Worm& ourWorm = *(Worm*)currentTask();
    for (;;) {
        tDelay(1);    //slow worms down to human speeds
        ourWorm.getNewDirection();
        ourWorm.updateLoc();
        cout << ourWorm;
    }
}
```

The call to `tDelay()` slows the worms to human speeds. Without this call, the game ends before the human player can react.

The outline of the remainder of the function is straightforward. A worm asks for the direction to travel with `getNewDirection()`, updates its screen location with `updateLoc()`, and outputs its symbol using the `operator<<(ostream&, Worm&)`.

The function `getNewDirection()` formulates and sends a message to the appropriate driver task. It then waits for and stores the response.

```
void Worm::getNewDirection() {
    //build a request message and send it
    RequestMsg request(this);
    driverPtr->sendMsg(&request);

    //await a response, store the answer and return msg
    AnswerMsg& answer = *(AnswerMsg*)getMsg();
    direction         = answer.direction;
```

}

The `RequestMsg` and `AnswerMsg` structures are defined as follows:

```
struct RequestMsg : public Message {
    Worm*     wormPtr;
    RequestMsg(Worm* wPtr) { wormPtr = wPtr;}
};
struct AnswerMsg : public Message {
    unsigned direction;
};
```

Notice that `getNewDirection()` must store the address of its own `Task` object in the message before sending it; otherwise, the `Direction` task would not know where to send the response.

The `Direction` task begins execution with one of the driver functions. The automatic driver code segment is as follows:

```
void autoWormDriver() {
    RequestMsg*    msgPtr;
    AnswerMsg*     ansPtr;
    Worm*          wormPtr;
    unsigned       d;
    unsigned       turn;
    static         tryNext[3] = {-1, 0, 1};
                                 //left, straight, right
    unsigned       foundOne;

    for (;;) {
        //first get the request
        msgPtr = (RequestMsg*)getMsg();           //Note A
        wormPtr = msgPtr->wormPtr;

        //now decide a direction
        for (turn = 0; turn < 3; turn++) {        //Note B
            d = (wormPtr->getDirection() +
                tryNext[turn]) & 0x03;
```

```
                if (foundOne =
                    !collisionCheck(wormPtr->nextXloc(d),
                                    wormPtr->nextYloc(d)))
                    break;
            }

            //inform the worm of the direction to turn
            if (!foundOne) {

                //no way out, delete the task (he's stuck)
                wormPtr->killTask();
            } else {

                //answer the question using the same message
                ansPtr = (AnswerMsg*)msgPtr;          //Note C
                ansPtr->direction = d;
                wormPtr->sendMsg(ansPtr);
            }
        }
    }
```

The task starts by waiting for a message. Since no time out time is provided, it defaults to zero. When the address of the request message arrives, `autoWormDriver()` saves the worm address and begins searching, first left, then straight, and finally right, for a free space. If none is found, the worm is terminated by the call to `killTask()`.

If a safe direction is found, it is sent to the worm by recasting the request into a response message and storing the information. This is a safe method as long as the response message is not longer than the request message. Declaring the response message on the `autoWormDriver()` stack is not an acceptable alternative since the next response might overwrite this response message before the worm can read it.

The requester can allocate the space for a larger response on its own stack and store the address in the request message. The alternative would be to allocate the response message from the heap and have the receiving task delete it.

The response is sent back to the requesting worm using the `send-Msg()` method.

Worms update and display their location using the following two functions.

```
void Worm::updateLoc() {
    unsigned newXloc=nextXloc(direction);//calculate...
    unsigned newYloc=nextYloc(direction);//...location...
    if (!collisionCheck(newXloc, newYloc)){//...is it ok?
        xloc = newXloc;         //yes - update it
        yloc = newYloc;
    }
}

ostream& operator<< (ostream& s, Worm& td) {
    putText(td.xloc, td.yloc, td.color, td.ourChar);
    return s;
}
```

The main program starts four worms.

```
#include <conio.h>
#include "mtask.hpp"
#include "worm.hpp"

//declare two direction tasks (one manual and one auto)
Direction keyboardTask(manualWormDriver,"manual driver");
Direction computerTask(autoWormDriver,"auto driver");

//declare two worms (assign them unique colors and symbols)
Worm w1(0x07, 40, 10, '*', &keyboardTask);
Worm w2(0x03, 39, 10, '@', &computerTask);
Worm w3(0x05, 40, 11, '$', &computerTask);
Worm w4(0x06,  0, 10, '#', &computerTask);
```

Task Class Application

```cpp
//main() - clear screen and pass control to scheduler
void main() {
    clrscr();
    startScheduler();
}

//For debug purposes, define a dump task function to
//run every 5 seconds to show state of all tasks
void dumpFn() {
    for(;;) {
        tDelay(int(5 * 18.2));
        cout << "\n-------------------------------\n";
        showAllTasks();
        cout << "\n-------------------------------\n";
    }
}

class DumpTasks : public Task {
    public:
        DumpTasks():Task(dumpFn, 0x0200, "Dump Task") {}
};
DumpTasks dT;
```

Each of the four worms is started with a different symbol at different locations. The first worm is attached to the keyboard driver, the other three are attached to the automatic driver.

Watching the output from the program develop, the user has little trouble keeping the brightly colored worms apart. Making sense of a static screen capture is quite different, however. Figure 11–10 represents the game three to four seconds after it has started but before the screen has become too confused. The screen has been edited to improve readability.

454   Hands-On Turbo C++

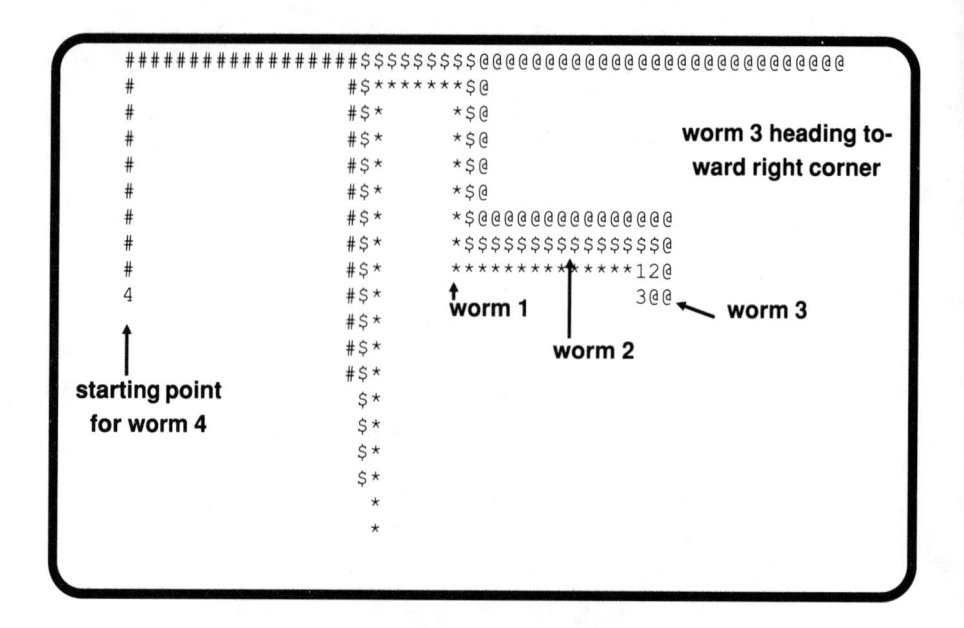

```
###################$$$$$$$$$@@@@@@@@@@@@@@@@@@@@@@@
#                  #$*******$@
#                  #$*      *$@
#                  #$*      *$@              worm 3 heading to-
#                  #$*      *$@              ward right corner
#                  #$*      *$@
#                  #$*      *$@
#                  #$*      *$@@@@@@@@@@@@@@
#                  #$*      *$$$$$$$$$$$$$$$@
#                  #$*      **********↑****12@
4                  #$*      ↑              3@@  ← worm 3
                   #$*    worm 1
↑                  #$*
                   #$*          worm 2
                   #$*
starting point     $*
for worm 4         $*
                   $*
                   $*
                    *
                    *
```

Figure 11-7 Three Worms Racing For Bottom of Screen

In Figure 11-7, the number of each worm was placed at its starting point. Notes were added as a further aid. Worm 3 was making its way toward the upper right-hand corner of the screen and the other three worms were racing for the bottom when the action was captured.

The `DumpTask` has been included in this example to give a dump of the state of the tasks every five seconds. To keep the dump from interfering with the worms, standard output should be directed to the printer using a command like the following to start the program.

```
WORMS >LPT1:
```

The following dump shows the status five seconds into a game.

```
-------------------------------
Task #7 - Dump Task
  nomsgs = 0   return value = 0   status = Running
  stackdepth = 1d6  stacksize = 200
  CPU time = 0
```

```
Task #6 - Worm
  nomsgs = 0   return value = 0   status =
  stackdepth = 3d2   stacksize = 400
  CPU time = 0
Task #5 - Worm
  nomsgs = 0   return value = 0   status =
  stackdepth = 3d2   stacksize = 400
  CPU time = 0
Task #4 - Worm
  nomsgs = 0   return value = 0   status =
  stackdepth = 3d2   stacksize = 400
  CPU time = 0
Task #3 - Worm
  nomsgs = 1   return value = 0   status =
  stackdepth = 3ac   stacksize = 400
  CPU time = 0
Task #2 - auto driver
  nomsgs = 0   return value = 0   status = Awaiting Msg
  stackdepth = 3b4   stacksize = 400
  CPU time = 0
Task #1 - manual driver
  nomsgs = 0   return value = 0   status = Awaiting Msg
  stackdepth = 3b8   stacksize = 400
  CPU time = 0

------------------------------
```

`DumpTasks` is the task currently running since it is producing the output. Notice that none of the worms is awaiting a response. One of the worms has a response message to process when it is next scheduled. The other three worms were waiting at their `tDelay()` call but are now ready. It is not unusual for all the worms to be ready—their time delay is so short that it expires while the status for the first task was being printed. Both driver tasks are awaiting query messages.

Depressing the End key terminates the program. Removing the task dump information for a typical game resulted in the following output upon terminating.

```
Killing #5 - Worm         <-- worms terminated during game
Killing #6 - Worm


Killing #7 - Dump Task    <-- tasks terminated at game end
Dead task #6 - Worm went out of scope
Dead task #5 - Worm went out of scope
Killing #4 - Worm
   1 messages lost
Killing #3 - Worm
Killing #2 - auto driver
Killed last task #1 - manual driver
```

Two worms ran into dead ends and were terminated by the `auto-WormDriver` task before the user stopped the game. When the destructors for the task objects were invoked upon exiting the program, tasks 5 and 6 were already terminated. When task 4 was killed, a response message was waiting to be processed.

Areas for Improvement

`Task` could be improved in several ways. When a task is terminated from `killTask()`, the destructors for locally declared objects are not invoked. This could have serious repercussions, especially if a parent task terminated itself without terminating its children.

Resolving this problem is difficult. One approach would be to define a new state, `killThySelf`. The functions of a task could periodically query the parent. If `killThySelf` appeared, the task would return to the base function for termination. This approach is clumsy. Turbo C++ has the same problem: calling `exit()` from a function does not invoke the destructors for objects created by the function(s) that called it.

The voluntary nature of rescheduling is also a problem. To make it preemptive, the call to `reschedule()` would have to be moved into the timer interrupt, but that would create new problems.

DOS is not reentrant and the Turbo C++ library may not be reentrant either. Checking devices would have to be added to all such calls to prevent two tasks from entering reschedule calls simultaneously.

In addition, tasks must be able to protect themselves from data collisions caused by rescheduling at unfortunate times. `Task` would have to include semaphores for controlling access to critical regions.

As it is written, `Task` is locked into the Large compilation model in order to reduce the number of variables to test. Allowing different memory models would require four times as many tests to allow for both near and far code and data pointers; however, there is no fundamental reason why this could not be done.

A final area of concern is stability. `Task` was written as a teaching tool. As such, the types of checks necessary to make `Task` foolproof are missing. For example, declaring a stack too small generally crashes the system. Fortunately, problems are usually easy to find. Single-stepping task switching with the IDE or Turbo Debuggers is straightforward and entertaining.

Comparisons with AT&T Task Class

AT&T offers a multitasker based upon a standard `task` class. While the basic concept of a non-preemptive multitasker is the same, many differences exist.

In the AT&T model, message queues are separate from tasks. A task sends a message to a queue. Another task may read that queue to receive the message. Both `task` and `queue` are built upon a base class called `object`.

This approach enables one task to read from different message queues. Thus, a task may read a response queue while temporarily ignoring a command input queue until the command has been completely processed.

In addition, task queues are built to be extensible by the user. A task can wait on other types of objects besides message queues. New object types may be defined by the user.

When a task attempts to add a message to a full queue, the task is suspended just as a task reading an empty queue. Not only is this more symmetric than returning an error message, but it is necessary to support queue **cutting** and **splicing**.

Individual tasks are frequently used as **filters**. Messages that appear at the input queue are processed and sent to an output queue to be picked up by the next task. This allows a problem to be decomposed into a series of independent tasks. Cutting allows the programmer to intercept input to a message queue and force it through another task, thereby inserting a filter into a path without the sending or receiving tasks being aware.

While these features make AT&T classes easier to use, they also increase its complexity. The class `Task` presented in this chapter is intended to give the reader insight into the basic workings of a multitasker.

Conclusion

Readers interested in learning more about Turbo C++ may refer to the suggested readings. However, no amount of reading will take the place of sitting at the terminal and grappling with real problems. Experiment with the power of C++. Turbo C++ will not disappoint.

Appendix A

Program Listing of Task Class

Program Listing of Task Class

This appendix contains the full listing of the `Task` class discussed in Chapter 11. `Task` is a publicly derived class of `LinkedList`, which is declared in the include file `SLIST.HPP` and defined in the source field `SLIST.CPP`. Task itself is defined in the source file `MTASK.CPP` and declared in the include file `MTASK.HPP` for use in programs that use multitasking.

The `SLIST.HPP` include file is defined as follows:

```
//SLIST.HPP
//Implement a singly linked list

#ifndef SLIST_HPP
#define SLIST_HPP

//The single linked list class with associated methods
class LinkedList {
   private:
     LinkedList* nextPtr;         //link to next element

   public:
                   LinkedList();
     LinkedList*   next();
     LinkedList*   previous();
     int           addAfter(LinkedList* prevMemberPtr);
     int           remove();
     int           removeNext();
};
#endif
```

The `SLIST.CPP` source file appears as follows:

```
//SLIST.CPP
//Implement a general singly linked list

#include "slist.hpp"
```

```cpp
//--------Implement the SLIST methods----------
LinkedList::LinkedList() {
    nextPtr = this;
}

LinkedList* LinkedList::next() {
    return nextPtr;
}

LinkedList* LinkedList::previous() {
    LinkedList* memberPtr;

    memberPtr = nextPtr;
    while (memberPtr->nextPtr != this)
        memberPtr = memberPtr->nextPtr;
    return memberPtr;
}

int LinkedList::addAfter(LinkedList* prevMemberPtr) {
    nextPtr               = prevMemberPtr->nextPtr;
    prevMemberPtr->nextPtr = this;
    return 0;
}

int LinkedList::remove() {
    LinkedList* prevMemberPtr;

    prevMemberPtr = previous();
    return prevMemberPtr->removeNext();
}

int LinkedList::removeNext() {
    LinkedList* nextMemberPtr = nextPtr;
    nextPtr = nextMemberPtr->nextPtr;
    nextMemberPtr->nextPtr = 0;
    return 0;
}
```

Program Listing of Task Class

The `MTASK.HPP` include file is defined as follows:

```
//MTASK.HPP
//Task class
//   Implements a nonpreemptive switcher based on setjmp()
//   and longjmp(). Declaring a new class Task
//   object adds the task to the scheduling list so that it
//   starts getting time. When the object goes out
//   of scope, the task is removed from the list and
//   killed. When no more
//   active tasks are left, the system quits. A task may
//   send a message to another task object. That task may
//   read the message—reading an empty queue suspends
//   the calling task up to the specified number of clock
//   ticks (0 -> wait forever).
//

#ifndef MTASK_HPP
#define MTASK_HPP
#ifndef __LARGE__
    #error Must be compiled under Large Memory Model
#endif

#include <iostream.h>
#include <setjmp.h>
#include "slist.hpp"   //use list structure to link td's


//The Message class - a message is a special case
//                    of a linked list
class Message : public LinkedList {};

//The Task class - a task object must exist for each task
class Task : public LinkedList {
  private:
    friend void    currentTask(Task* tdPtr);
```

```cpp
    public:
        friend Task*    currentTask();
        friend void     reschedule(unsigned count = 0);
        friend void     startScheduler();
        friend Task*    directory(char*);
        friend ostream& operator<< (ostream&, Task& td);

    private:
        static Task*    currentTaskPtr; //the currently
                                        //active task
        static unsigned taskCount;

        char     taskName[40]; //identification
        unsigned taskId;       //simple ordinal count

        unsigned status;       //current task status
        unsigned loopCount;
        unsigned delayCount;   //no. clock ticks to wait
        Task*    retTask;      //task waiting for retVal

        jmp_buf  regs;              //saved registers
        unsigned *stackPtr;         //pointer to bottom of stack
        unsigned ssize;             //stack size
        unsigned releaseStack;      //1->delete stack on exit
        unsigned noMsgs;            //no. of queued messages
        Message  queue;             //message queue

    public:
        unsigned retVal;       //task return value
        unsigned cpuTime;      //time spent within task
        enum TaskStatus {      //flags for 'status'
                READY        = 0x00,
                SUSPENDED    = 0x01,
                DYING        = 0x02,
                DEAD         = 0x04,
                AWAITING_MSG = 0x08,
```

Program Listing of Task Class

```
                    DELAYED     = 0x10,
                    RUNNING     = 0x80
};
enum TaskErrors {          //values for fn.s and 'retVal'
        OK          = 0,  //worked correctly
        GENERROR    = -1, //unspecified task error
        NOSTACK     = -2, //stack overflow
        QUEFULL     = -3, //queue is full
        OUTOFRANGE  = -4  //not a legal value
};
                           //constructor to start a task
Task (void (* fn)(),
      unsigned stackSize,
      char* tNamePtr = (char*)0);
Task (void (* fn)(),
      void* stack, unsigned stackSize,
      char* tNamePtr = (char*)0);
void initTask (void (* fn)(),
               void* stack, unsigned stackSize,
               char* tNamePtr);
                           //status access methods
unsigned taskStatus() {return status;}
unsigned msgCount()   {return noMsgs;}
virtual unsigned isA(){return 0;}

void    suspendTask();
void    unsuspendTask();
void    waitTask(unsigned N = 0);
void    unwaitTask();
void    delayTask(unsigned N = 0);
void    undelayTask();
void    oneClockTick();
                           //message methods
int     sendMsg(Message* msgPtr);
Message* getTMsg(unsigned N = 0);
                           //return value methods
```

```
    int      setReturnValue(int value);
    int      getReturnValue(Task& td);

    void     showTask();    //display task information
    void     killTask();

    Task*    next() {       //return next Task object
        return (Task*)LinkedList::next();
    }

    ~Task();
};

//Prototypes for non-method, non-friend functions
    Message* getMsg(unsigned wait = 0);
    void     tDelay(unsigned time);
    void     tSuspend();
    void     showAllTasks();
    unsigned numTasks();
    void     killSelf();

    unsigned getTime();     //get current time function

    void     stopScheduler();

//Implement commonly used friend functions inline
                            //store and set current task
inline Task* currentTask() {
    return Task::currentTaskPtr;
}
inline void currentTask(Task* tdPtr) {
    Task::currentTaskPtr = tdPtr;
}
                            //set or get task return value
inline int returnTaskValue(int value) {
    return currentTask()->setReturnValue(value);
```

```cpp
}
inline int getTaskValue(Task& td) {
    return currentTask()->getReturnValue(td);
}

                        //output task name
inline ostream& operator<<(ostream& s, Task& td) {
    return s << td.taskId << " - " << (char*)td.taskName;
}
#endif
```

The MTASK.CPP source code file appears as follows:

```cpp
//MTASK.CPP
//Cooperative task switcher based on setjmp()/longjmp()
//   Declaring a new class Task object adds the task to
//   the scheduling list. When the object goes out of scope,
//   the task is removed from the list and killed. When
//   the last active task is killed, the system quits.
//      A task may suspend itself, causing it to not receive
//   any more time until another task unsuspends it. It may
//   also delay a given no. of clock ticks. Another task may
//   undelay a task at any time. A task may send a message to
//   another task object. That task may read the
//   message-reading
//   an empty queue suspends the calling task up to
//   the specified number of clock ticks (0 -> wait forever).
//      Time is maintained by the Timer class. Only one object
//   of class Timer may exist. The constructor for this object
//   installs an interrupt function onto the hardware clock.
//   The only functions available to the user are getTime()
//   which returns the current time in clock ticks and
//   disableClock() which deinstalls the clock interrupt
//   function.
//
```

```cpp
#include <dos.h>
#include <process.h>
#include <string.h>
#include "mtask.hpp"

//--------------The timer class-----------------
//The Timer class—only one of these should ever be
//instantiated. Its purpose is to install the timer.
const unsigned clockInt = 0x1c;
int schedulerEnabled = 0;     //start with scheduler disabled
class Timer {
    friend unsigned getTime();
  private:
    static void interrupt (far * oldfn)(...);
    static unsigned              globalTime;

  public:
    Timer();
    static void interrupt clockTick(...);
    ~Timer();
};

//----------------------the methods---------------------
//The constructor for this class merely installs the timer
//interrupt routine, while the destructor puts the timer
//back.
Timer::Timer() {
    oldfn = getvect(clockInt);
    setvect(clockInt, Timer::clockTick);
}
Timer::~Timer() {
    if (oldfn) {
        setvect(clockInt, oldfn);
        oldfn = 0;
```

Program Listing of Task Class

```
        }
}

//the clockTick() method executes each tick of the hardware
//clock. It loops thru each of the waiting tasks
//decrementing their timers.
void interrupt Timer::clockTick(...) {
    Task *tdPtr;

    //don't do anything if scheduler not enabled
    if (schedulerEnabled) {

        //increment the current time
        globalTime++;

        //tick each task descriptor in the list;
        //if current task is RUNNING, increment its
        //CPU counter
        tdPtr = currentTask();
        if (tdPtr->taskStatus() & Task::RUNNING)
            tdPtr->cpuTime++;

        //loop through the tasks, tick each one
        do {
            tdPtr->oneClockTick();
            tdPtr = tdPtr->next();
        } while (tdPtr != currentTask());
    }

    //chain to the "old" timer function now
    (*oldfn)();
}

//----------------------the friend function-------------
//the single friend function allows users to get current time
unsigned getTime() {
```

```cpp
        return Timer::globalTime;
}


//---------------Implementation of Class Task------------
//-----------------------the methods-------------------

//Set up a task to start at *fn() the next time it is
//scheduled to execute; build a "kill self" function
//and put the return address of this function on the
//task's stack so that if the task returns, it will kill
//itself and avoid a crash
Task::Task(void (* fn)(),
           unsigned stackSize,
           char* tNamePtr) {
    void* stack = new unsigned[stackSize];
    releaseStack = 1;
    initTask(fn, stack, stackSize, tNamePtr);
}


Task::Task(void (*fn)(),
           void* stack, unsigned stackSize,
           char* tNamePtr) {
    releaseStack = 0;
    initTask(fn, stack, stackSize, tNamePtr);
}

void Task::initTask(void (*fn)(), void* stack,
                    unsigned stackSize, char* tNamePtr) {
    //save the name and id of the new task
    taskId = ++Task::taskCount;
    taskName[0] = '\0';
    if (tNamePtr)
        memcpy(taskName, tNamePtr, sizeof taskName - 1);
    taskName[sizeof taskName - 1] = '\0';

    //set up the new task's stack; if no stack abort start
```

Program Listing of Task Class

```
    ssize = stackSize;
    stackPtr = (unsigned*)stack;
    if (stackPtr == 0) {
        cout << "Could not start task" << *this << endl;
        retVal = Task::NOSTACK;
        status = Task::DEAD;
        return;
    }

    unsigned* endStackPtr = &stackPtr[stackSize-1];
    *--endStackPtr = FP_SEG(killSelf); //if Task returns,...
    *--endStackPtr = FP_OFF(killSelf); //...it kills itself

    regs[0].j_sp   = FP_OFF(endStackPtr);//set up stack ptr
    regs[0].j_ss   = FP_SEG(endStackPtr);

    regs[0].j_ip   = FP_OFF(fn); //and the function address
    regs[0].j_cs   = FP_SEG(fn);

    regs[0].j_ds   = _DS;    //seg regs are important
    regs[0].j_es   = _ES;
    regs[0].j_flag = 0x7246; //a "good" value for flags

    regs[0].j_si   = 0;      //these regs are not important
    regs[0].j_di   = 0;
    regs[0].j_bp   = 0;

    //now add the task descriptor to the list
    status = Task::READY;    //mark task ready
    loopCount = 0;           //set count and...
    delayCount = 0;          //...delay count...
    noMsgs = 0;              //...message queue size to 0
    retVal = 0;              //no return value and...
    retTask = (Task*)0;      //...no task waiting
    if (currentTask() == 0)  //when initing first task...
        currentTask(this);   //...save it as the root;...
```

```cpp
            else
                addAfter (currentTask()); //...add the rest to root
}

//Kill the specified task
void Task::killTask() {
    //ignore requests to kill dead tasks
    if (taskStatus() & Task::DEAD)
        return;

    //if another task is waiting on a return value
    //unsuspend that task
    if (retTask) {
        retTask->unsuspendTask();
        retTask = (Task*)0;
    }

    //if task trying to kill itself, mark it for later
      removal
    if (currentTask() = = this) {
        status |= Task::DYING;
        if (numTasks() = = 0) {//quit if no tasks left
            cout << "Killed last task #" << *this << endl;
            status |= Task::DEAD;
            stopScheduler();
            return;
        }
        reschedule();          //just have to wait
    }

    //okay, to kill the task
    cout << "Killing #" << *this << endl;
    if (noMsgs)
        cout << "    " << noMsgs << " messages lost" << endl;
    status |= Task::DEAD;            //mark the task as dead
    if (releaseStack)                //if stack came from heap...
```

Program Listing of Task Class

```
        delete stackPtr;          //...put the stack back
    this->remove();               //and remove it from list
}

//Methods to change task status
void Task::suspendTask() {
    status |= Task::SUSPENDED;    //set suspended bit
}
void Task::unsuspendTask() {
    status &= ~Task::SUSPENDED;   //clear suspended bit
}
void Task::waitTask(unsigned N) {
    status |= Task::AWAITING_MSG;//set message waiting bit
    delayCount = N;
}
void Task::unwaitTask() {
    if (taskStatus() & AWAITING_MSG){
        status &= ~Task::AWAITING_MSG;
        delayCount = 0;
    }
}
void Task::delayTask(unsigned N) {
    status |= Task::DELAYED;      //set the delay flag
    delayCount = N;
}
void Task::undelayTask() {
    if (taskStatus() & Task::DELAYED) {
        status &= ~Task::DELAYED; //clear msg waiting bit
        delayCount = 0;
    }
}
void Task::oneClockTick() {
    if (delayCount)
        if (--delayCount = = 0) {
            if (taskStatus() & Task::AWAITING_MSG)
                unwaitTask();
```

```cpp
            if (taskStatus() & Task::DELAYED)
                undelayTask();
        }
}

//Methods to send and receive a message
const int maxQueSize = 20;
int Task::sendMsg (Message* msgPtr) {
    Message* lastMsgPtr;

    if (noMsgs > maxQueSize)
        return Task::QUEFULL;

    lastMsgPtr = (Message*)queue.previous();
    msgPtr->addAfter(lastMsgPtr);
    noMsgs++;
    unwaitTask();
    return Task::OK;
}

//receive method = if N = 0 then wait forever for a message;
//                 if N > 0 then wait N clock ticks, return
//                          0 if timeout
Message* Task::getTMsg(unsigned N) {
    Message* nextMsgPtr;

    if (noMsgs = = 0) {
        waitTask(N);
        reschedule();
    }
    if (noMsgs) {
        noMsgs--;
        nextMsgPtr = (Message*)queue.next();
        nextMsgPtr->remove();
        return nextMsgPtr;
    } else
```

Program Listing of Task Class

```
            return (Message*)0;
}

//Display a task's diagnostic information
void Task::showTask() {
    unsigned stackDepth = regs[0].j_sp - FP_OFF(stackPtr);

    cout << dec <<
            "Task #"              << *this <<
            "\n   nomsgs = "      << noMsgs <<
            "   return value = "  << retVal <<
            "   status = ";

    //output status information as an ASCII string
    static char* statuses[] = { "Suspended ",
                                "Dying ",
                                "Dead ",
                                "Awaiting Msg ",
                                "Delaying ",
                                "Running "};
    static enum TaskStatus statusBits[] = {Task::SUSPENDED,
                                           Task::DYING,
                                           Task::DEAD,
                                           Task::AWAITING_MSG,
                                           Task::DELAYED,
                                           Task::RUNNING};
    for (int i = 0; i < 6; i++)
        if (status & statusBits[i])
            cout << statuses[i];

    cout << hex <<
            "\n   stackdepth = " << stackDepth <<
            "   stacksize = "    << ssize * 2;

    cout << dec <<
            "\n   CPU time = "   << cpuTime;
```

```cpp
        cout << endl;
}

//Save and return the return value of a task;
int Task::setReturnValue(int value) {
    if (value < 0) {
        cout <<
            "Negative return values reserved for system\n";
        return Task::OUTOFRANGE;
    }
    retVal = value;
    return Task::OK;
}

int Task::getReturnValue(Task& td){
    while ((td.taskStatus() & (Task::DEAD|Task::DYING)) == 0){
        if (td.retTask)
            return Task::QUEFULL;
        else {
            td.retTask = this;
            suspendTask();
            reschedule();
        }
    }
    return td.retVal;
}

Task::~Task() {
    //if task is still alive, kill it quick
    if (taskStatus() & Task::DEAD)
        cout << "Dead task #" << *this <<
            " went out of scope" << endl;
    else
```

Program Listing of Task Class

```cpp
        killTask();
}


//--------------------the friends-----------------------
//Pass control to next ready task
void reschedule(unsigned count) {
    Task* currTPtr = currentTask();

    //first mark the task as no longer running
    currTPtr->status &= ~Task::RUNNING;

    //then store the registers
    currTPtr->loopCount = count;
    if (setjmp(currTPtr->regs))   //once we get control back...
        return;                   //...return to calling task
    currTPtr->regs[0].j_di = _DI;//this fixes bug in setjmp()

    //search active task descriptor list for a candidate
    //start with the current Task
    Task* tdPtr = currTPtr;
    Task* prevTdPtr;
    for (;;) {
        prevTdPtr = tdPtr;
        tdPtr     = tdPtr->next();

        //if we find a task that is not the current
        //task to terminate, do it
        if (tdPtr->taskStatus() & Task::DYING)
            if (tdPtr != currTPtr) {
                tdPtr->killTask();
                tdPtr = prevTdPtr;//restart with previous td
            }

        //for tasks with a loop count > 0, decrement it
        if (tdPtr->loopCount) {
```

```cpp
                tdPtr->loopCount--;
                continue;
            }

            //as soon as we find a ready task,
            //make it the current task and give it control
            if (tdPtr->taskStatus() == Task::READY) {
                currentTask(tdPtr);
                tdPtr->status |= Task::RUNNING;
                longjmp(currentTask()->regs, 2);
            }
        }
    }

    //look up a task by name; if not found, return a 0
    Task* directory(char* targetName) {
        Task* tdPtr = currentTask();
        int strLength = strlen(targetName);

        do {
            if (strLength == strlen(tdPtr->taskName))
                if (strncmp(targetName,
                        tdPtr->taskName,
                        strLength) == = 0)
                    return tdPtr;
            tdPtr = tdPtr->next();
        } while (tdPtr != currentTask());
        return (Task*)0;
    }

    //start the scheduler; this function never returns
    jmp_buf returnToMain;        //path back to main()
    void startScheduler() {
        Timer OneOfThese;        //install the timer now
```

```c
        if (setjmp(returnToMain))
            return;
        returnToMain[0].j_di = _DI;//this fixes bug in setjmp()
        schedulerEnabled = 1;
        longjmp(currentTask()->regs, 1);
}
void stopScheduler() {
    if (schedulerEnabled) {
        schedulerEnabled = 0;
        longjmp(returnToMain, 1);
    }
}


//----------------------the general functions---------
//Read msg from input queue; wait up to N clock
//ticks (0 -> wait forever)
Message* getMsg(unsigned N) {
    return currentTask()->getTMsg(N);
}

//Delay self for N clock ticks
void tDelay(unsigned N) {
    currentTask()->delayTask(N);
    reschedule();
}

//Suspend the calling task
void tSuspend() {
    currentTask()->suspendTask();
    reschedule();
}
//Dump the status of all tasks in the scheduling queue
void showAllTasks() {
    Task *tdPtr = currentTask();
```

```cpp
        do {
            tdPtr->showTask();
            tdPtr = tdPtr->next();
        } while (tdPtr != currentTask());
}

//Count the number of runnable tasks
unsigned numTasks() {
    Task* tdPtr = currentTask();
    unsigned count = 0;
    unsigned status;

    do {
        status = tdPtr->taskStatus() &
                    ~(Task::RUNNING|Task::DELAYED);
        count += (status == Task::READY);
        tdPtr = tdPtr->next();
    } while (tdPtr != currentTask());
    return count;
}

//Allow a task to kill itself at any time
void killSelf() {
    currentTask()->killTask();
    abort();                    //*** if it gets here, quit
}
```

Programs that use `Task` must include either the object files `SLIST.OBJ` and `MTASK.OBJ` in the link step or `SLIST.CPP` and `MTASK.CPP` in the project file.

Appendix B

*Source Code
for Example 1—Orbit*

Source Code for Example 1—Orbit

The simulation example presented in Chapter 11 is contained in the file ORBIT.CPP.

```cpp
//ORBIT.CPP

#include <dos.h>
#include <conio.h>
#include <math.h>
#include "mtask.hpp"

//----------------define a vector class------------------
struct Vector {
    double x;
    double y;

  public:
    Vector(double iX, double iY) : x(iX), y(iY) {}
    Vector(Vector& v) {
        x = v.x;
        y = v.y;
    }
    Vector() : x(0), y(0) {}

    double mag2() {
        return x * x + y * y;
    }
    Vector unitVector();
};

Vector Vector::unitVector() {
    double mag = sqrt(mag2());
    return Vector(x / mag, y / mag);
}

Vector operator+(Vector& a, Vector& b) {
    return Vector(a.x + b.x, a.y + b.y);
```

```
    }
    Vector operator-(Vector& a, Vector& b) {
        return Vector(a.x - b.x, a.y - b.y);
    }
    Vector operator*(double& a, Vector& b) {
        return Vector(a * b.x, a * b.y);
    }
    Vector operator/(Vector& a, double& b) {
        if (b == 0) {
            cerr << "Planet collision";
            killSelf();
        }
        return Vector(a.x / b, a.y / b);
    }


    //-----------------define the location classes-------------
    struct Velocity {
        Vector vel;
        unsigned lastTime;

        Velocity(double xVel, double yVel) : vel(xVel, yVel) {
            lastTime = getTime();
        }
        void update(Vector&);
    };

    struct Location {
        Vector loc;
        unsigned lastTime;

        Location(double xLoc, double yLoc) : loc(xLoc, yLoc) {
            lastTime = getTime();
        }
        void update(Velocity& vel);
    };
```

Source Code for Example 1—Orbit

```cpp
//-----------------implement the methods------------------
//Update - update the location based on the velocity and
//         the time since last update
void Location::update(Velocity& vel) {
    double tDiff = (getTime() - lastTime) / 18.2;
    lastTime = getTime();
    loc = loc + tDiff * vel.vel;
}
//Update - update the velocity based on the acceleration and
//         the time since last update
void Velocity::update(Vector& acc) {
    double tDiff = (getTime() - lastTime) / 18.2;
    lastTime = getTime();
    vel = vel + tDiff * acc;
}

//-----------------now the Planet class-------------------
void planetFunc();
class Planet : public Task {
  private:
    Location loc;
    Velocity vel;
    double mass;

  public:
    char  identifier;
    virtual unsigned isA() { return 1;}

    Planet(void* stack, unsigned stackSize,
          Location& iLoc, Velocity& iVel,
          double iMass, char* pName, char id) :
       loc(iLoc), vel(iVel),
       Task(planetFunc, stack, stackSize, pName){
       mass = iMass;
       identifier = id;
    }
```

```
    Planet* nextPlanet();
    Planet& operator<<(char c);

    Vector calcAcceleration();
    void update(Vector& acc) {
        vel.update(acc);
        loc.update(vel);
    }
};

//-----------------Planet methods-----------------
//NextPlanet() - return the address of the next planet
Planet* Planet::nextPlanet() {
    Task* tPtr;
    do {
        tPtr = next();
    } while (tPtr->isA() != 1);
    return (Planet*)tPtr;
}

//PutText() - put a character to a screen at specific
//            row and column; for mono change address to
//            0xB0000000L; for 80x43 mode simply change
//            dimensions
static unsigned far& screen(unsigned xloc, unsigned yloc) {
    static unsigned (far* screenMatrix)[25][80] =
        (unsigned (far*)[25][80])0xB8000000L;
    return  (*screenMatrix)[yloc][xloc];
}
void putText(unsigned xloc, unsigned yloc,
             unsigned color, unsigned symbol){
    unsigned fullChar = ((unsigned)color << 8) + symbol;
    screen(xloc, yloc) = fullChar;
}
//operator<<() - display a planet on the screen; if goes off
//               screen boundaries, terminate the task
```

Source Code for Example 1—Orbit

```cpp
Planet& Planet::operator<<(char c) {
    int cTemp = c;
    int xloc = 40.5 + loc.loc.x / 100.;
    int yloc = 12.5 - loc.loc.y / 140.;
    if (xloc >= 0)
        if (yloc >= 0)
            if (xloc < 80)
                if (yloc < 25) {
                    putText(xloc, yloc, 0x03, cTemp);
                    return *this;
                }
    cout << "\nGone off screen" << endl;
    killSelf();
    return *this;
}

//CalcAcceleration - calculate the acceleration of a planet
//                   due to gravity of other planets
Vector Planet::calcAcceleration() {
    Planet* planetPtr = this;
    Vector distance;
    double magnitude;
    Vector accVector;
    const double G = 1000.;
    Vector acc(0, 0);

    while ((planetPtr = planetPtr->nextPlanet()) != this) {
        distance = planetPtr->loc.loc - loc.loc;
        magnitude = (G * planetPtr->mass) / distance.mag2();
        accVector = magnitude * distance.unitVector();
        acc = acc + accVector;
    }
    return acc;
}

//PlanetFunc - track planet along its path across screen
```

```cpp
void planetFunc() {
    Vector acc;
    Planet& currPlanet = *(Planet*)currentTask();

    for(;;) {
        currPlanet << currPlanet.identifier;
        tDelay(1);
        if (kbhit()) {
            getch();            //flush the character
            killSelf();
        }
        currPlanet << ' ';
        acc = currPlanet.calcAcceleration();
        currPlanet.update(acc);
    }
}

//Main() - orbit planets around the sun
unsigned int stackBuf1[0x800];
unsigned int stackBuf2[0x800];
unsigned int stackBuf3[0x800];
void main() {
    //create a few planets
    int initX, initY;
    cout << "Enter initial X and Y velocity for Sun:";
    cin >> initX >> initY;          //typical 0, 0
    Planet sun(stackBuf1, 0x800,
            Location(0, 0), Velocity(initX, initY),
            1000, "Sun", '*');

    cout << "Enter initial X and Y velocity for Earth:";
    cin >> initX >> initY;          //typical -40, 0
    Planet earth(stackBuf2, 0x800,
            Location(0, 600), Velocity(initX, initY),
            1, "Earth", '.');
```

Source Code for Example 1—Orbit

```
    cout << "Enter initial X and Y velocity for Jupiter:";
    cin >> initX >> initY;              //typical 50, 0
    Planet jupiter(stackBuf3, 0x800,
            Location(0,-1000), Velocity(initX,initY),
            10, "Jupiter", '@');

    //now start the tasks going
    clrscr();
    startScheduler();
}
```

To build the Orbit example, the project file must include `ORBIT.CPP`, `MTASK.CPP`, and `SLIST.CPP` or their object files in the link step.

Appendix C

Source Code for Example 2—Worms

Source Code for Example 2—Worms

The second multitasking example is based on the WORM.HPP include file and the WORM.CPP source code file that define the Worm class. The driver class is defined in the source file DIRECT.CPP. The starter program is included in the source code file TESTMT.CPP.

The WORM.HPP include file is defined as follows:

```cpp
//WORM.HPP
//---------Define the direction deciding task class--------
class Direction : public Task {
  public:
    Direction(void (*myF)(), char* name) :
            Task(myF, 0x0200, name){}
};

//---------Define the worm task class---------------------
void wormTask();
class Worm : public Task {
    friend ostream& operator<< (ostream& s, Worm& td);
  private:
    char    color;           //color+location of worm
    char    ourChar;         //our character
    unsigned xloc, yloc;     //its location

    unsigned direction;      //direction of travel
    static unsigned deltaX[4]; //the meanings of...
    static unsigned deltaY[4]; //...of the directions

    Direction* driverPtr;    //address of driving task

  public:
    Worm(unsigned c, unsigned x, unsigned y, char symbol,
         Direction* dPtr) : Task(wormTask, 0x0200, "Worm"){
        color    = c;
        ourChar  = symbol;
        xloc     = x;
        yloc     = y;
```

```
            direction = c & 0x03;  //start each worm in a
                                   //different direction
            driverPtr = dPtr;
        }
        unsigned getDirection() { return direction;}
        unsigned nextXloc(unsigned d) {return xloc + deltaX[d];}
        unsigned nextYloc(unsigned d) {return yloc + deltaY[d];}
        void     getNewDirection();
        void     updateLoc();
};

//-------Define the direction request and answer messages--
struct RequestMsg : public Message {
    Worm*    wormPtr;
    RequestMsg(Worm* wPtr) { wormPtr = wPtr;}
};
struct AnswerMsg : public Message {
    unsigned direction;
};

//-------Now the prototypes for the helper functions-------
unsigned collisionCheck(unsigned xloc, unsigned yloc);
void     putText(unsigned xloc, unsigned yloc,
                 char color, char symbol);
char     getText(unsigned xloc, unsigned yloc);

//-------Prototypes for the task functions----------------
void wormTask();
void autoWormDriver();
void manualWormDriver();
```

The `TESTMT.CPP` driver program is defined as follows:

```
//TESTMT.CPP
//Worm game -
//  Exercise the class Task multitasker. Create several
```

Source Code for Example 2—Worms

```cpp
//  worm tasks. Each worm scampers across the screen trying
//  to stay within the screen and avoid the trails left by
//  other worms. Decisions of which way to turn are actually
//  made by one of two separate worm steering tasks. When a
//  worm can no longer move, the steering task kills it. The
//  user kills his own worm by depressing the END key.

#include <conio.h>
#include "mtask.hpp"
#include "worm.hpp"

//declare two direction tasks (one manual and one automatic)
Direction keyboardTask(manualWormDriver, "manual driver");
Direction computerTask(autoWormDriver, "auto driver");

//declare two worms (assign them unique colors and symbols)
Worm w1(0x07, 40, 10, '*', &keyboardTask);
Worm w2(0x03, 39, 10, '@', &computerTask);
Worm w3(0x05, 40, 11, '$', &computerTask);
Worm w4(0x06,  0, 10, '#', &computerTask);


//The "main" program cannot execute since he is not a
//"task" - he simply clears the screen and gives up
//control via start_scheduler()
void main() {
    clrscr();
    startScheduler();
}

//For debug purposes, define a dump task function to
//run every 5 seconds to show state of all tasks
void dumpFn() {
    for(;;) {
        tDelay(int(5 * 18.2));
        cout << "\n-------------------------------\n";
```

```
            showAllTasks();
            cout << "\n-------------------------------\n";
      }
}

class DumpTasks : public Task {
    public:
        DumpTasks():Task(dumpFn, 0x0200, "Dump Task") {}
};
DumpTasks dT;
```

The WORM.CPP source file is defined as follows:

```
//WORM.CPP

#include <dos.h>
#include "mtask.hpp"
#include "worm.hpp"

//-------------Implement the Worm Methods------------------
//Define the primary directions
unsigned Worm::deltaX[] = { 0,  1,  0, -1};
unsigned Worm::deltaY[] = {-1,  0,  1,  0};

//Request direction to travel from wormDriver
void Worm::getNewDirection() {
    //build a request message and send it
    RequestMsg request(this);
    driverPtr->sendMsg(&request);

    //now await a response, store the answer and return msg
    AnswerMsg& answer = *(AnswerMsg*)getMsg();
    direction         = answer.direction;
}

//update the worm's location
```

Source Code for Example 2—Worms

```cpp
void Worm::updateLoc() {
    unsigned newXloc = nextXloc(direction);//calculate...
    unsigned newYloc = nextYloc(direction);//...location...
    if (!collisionCheck(newXloc, newYloc)){//...is it legal?
        xloc = newXloc;      //yes - update it
        yloc = newYloc;
    }
}

//---------Implement Worm Friend Functions----------------
//Write the worm's current location to the screen
ostream& operator<< (ostream& s, Worm& td) {
    putText(td.xloc, td.yloc, td.color, td.ourChar);
    return s;
}

//---------Implement Worm Helper Functions----------------
//Simple getText() and putText() functions
static unsigned far& screen(unsigned xloc, unsigned yloc) {
    static unsigned (far* screenMatrix)[25][80] =
        (unsigned (far*)[25][80])MK_FP(0xB800,0x0000);
    return  (*screenMatrix)[yloc][xloc];
}
void putText(unsigned xloc, unsigned yloc,
             char color, char symbol){
    unsigned fullChar = ((unsigned)color << 8) + symbol;
    screen(xloc, yloc) = fullChar;
}
char getText(unsigned xloc, unsigned yloc){
    return (char)(screen(xloc, yloc) & 0xff);
}

//Check for a collision at a given location
unsigned collisionCheck(unsigned xloc, unsigned yloc) {
    //first check for collision with the walls
    if (xloc > 79)
```

```cpp
            return 1;
        if (yloc > 24)
            return 1;

        //now check for collisions with other worm trails
        return getText(xloc, yloc) != ' ';
}
//-------------Implement the Worm Task--------------------
//Request a direction of travel and then go that way
void wormTask() {
    Worm& ourWorm = *(Worm*)currentTask();
    for (;;) {
        tDelay(1);          //slow worms down to human speeds
        ourWorm.getNewDirection();
        ourWorm.updateLoc();
        cout << ourWorm;
    }
}
```

The `DIRECT.CPP` source code file is defined as follows:

```cpp
//DIRECT.CPP
//Worm direction tasks -
//   Worms send direction request message to tasks of this
//   class. The direction class returns a direction to the
//   worm.

#include <conio.h>
#include <stdlib.h>
#include "mtask.hpp"
#include "worm.hpp"

//-------------Direction Task(s)---------------------------
//When a worm asks a direction, decide one automatically
void autoWormDriver() {
    RequestMsg* msgPtr;
```

Source Code for Example 2—Worms

```cpp
    AnswerMsg*   ansPtr;
    Worm*        wormPtr;
    unsigned     d;
    unsigned     turn;
    static       tryNext[3] = {-1, 0, 1}; //search pattern:
                                  //left, straight, right
    unsigned     foundOne;

    for (;;) {
        //first get the request
        msgPtr = (RequestMsg*)getMsg();
        wormPtr = msgPtr->wormPtr;

        //now decide a direction
        for (turn = 0; turn < 3; turn++) {
            d = (wormPtr->getDirection() +
                tryNext[turn]) & 0x03;
            if (foundOne =
                !collisionCheck(wormPtr->nextXloc(d),
                            wormPtr->nextYloc(d)))
                break;
        }
        //inform the worm of the direction to turn
        if (!foundOne) {

            //no way out, delete the task (he's stuck)
            wormPtr->killTask();
        } else {

            //answer the question using the same message
            ansPtr = (AnswerMsg*)msgPtr;
            ansPtr->direction = d;
            wormPtr->sendMsg(ansPtr);

        }
    }
}
```

```cpp
//When a worm asks a direction to go let the user decide one
void manualWormDriver() {
    RequestMsg* msgPtr;
    AnswerMsg*  ansPtr;
    Worm*       wormPtr;
    unsigned d;

    for (;;) {
        //first get the request
        msgPtr = (RequestMsg*)getMsg();
        wormPtr = msgPtr->wormPtr;

        //now get a direction from the keyboard (if key
        //pressed, just continue present course)
        d = wormPtr->getDirection();
        if (kbhit())
            if (getch() == 0)
                switch (getch()) {
                    case 72: d = 0; break; //up    arrow
                    case 75: d = 3; break; //left  arrow
                    case 77: d = 1; break; //right arrow
                    case 79: stopScheduler(); //end key - quit
                    case 80: d = 2; break; //down  arrow
                }

        //answer the question using the same message
        ansPtr = (AnswerMsg*)msgPtr;
        ansPtr->direction = d;
        wormPtr->sendMsg(ansPtr);
    }
}
```

Either the project file for this example must include TESTMT.CPP, WORM.CPP, DIRECT.CPP, MTASK.CPP, and SLIST.CPP, or the object files from these modules must be specified in the link step.

Bibliography

Bibliography

The following is a list of books I can recommend to readers interested in continuing their education in C++ and object-oriented programming.

The original definition of C++ was included in the now dated:

Stroustrup, Bjarne, *The C++ Programming Language*, Addison-Wesley Series in Computer Science. Addison-Wesley, Reading, MA, 1986.

This book has been superseded by the more readable and more recent:

Ellis, Margaret A. and Bjarne Stroustrup, *The Annotated C++ Reference Manual*. Addison-Wesley, Reading, MA, 1990.

The reader should take note that both of these books are intended for the sophisticated programmer. Other worthwhile C++ books include:

Pohl, Ira, *C++ for C Programmers*. The Benjamin-Cummings Publishing Company, Redwood City, CA, 1989.

Wiener, Richard S. and Lewis J. Pinson, *An Introduction to Object Oriented Programming and Smalltalk*. Addison-Wesley, Reading, MA, 1988.

Wiener, Richard S. and Lewis J. Pinson, *The C++ Workbook*. Addison-Wesley, Reading, MA, 1990.

AT&T also produces a series concerning developing issues in C++. These are collectively known as the *Unix System V, AT&T C++ Language System*. The current release (Fall, 1990) is Release 2.1. These are available from AT&T at 1-800-432-6600.

There is a wide range of books to choose from to expand a C background. I would suggest the following:

Harbison, Samuel P. and Guy L. Steele, Jr, *C: A Reference Manual*. Tartan Laboratories, Prentice-Hall Software Series, Englewood Cliffs, New Jersey, 1987.

Kernighan, Brian W. and Dennis M. Ritchie, *The C Programming Language*. Prentice-Hall, Englewood Cliffs, New Jersey, 1978.

Many of the beginning principles of Turbo C programming are covered in:

Davis, Stephen R., *Turbo C: The Art of Advanced Program Design, Optimization and Debugging*. M&T Publishing, Redwood City, CA, 1987.

Those interested in learning Smalltalk, the progenitor of object-oriented languages, may refer to either of the following:

Goldberg, Adele and David Robson, *Smalltalk-80: The Language and its Implementation*. Addison-Wesley Series in Computer Science, Addison-Wesley, Reading, MA, 1983.

Pinson, Lewis J. and Richard S. Wiener, *An Introduction to Object Oriented Programming and Smalltalk*. Addison-Wesley, Reading, MA 1988.

Readers interested in learning more about the different memory types on the PC are referred to:

Duncan, Ray, Charles Petzold, M. Steven Baker, Andrew Schulman, Stephen R. Davis, Ross P. Nelson and Robert Moote, *Extending DOS*. Addison-Wesley, Reading, MA, 1990.

The articles referenced in *Hands-On Turbo C++* are:

Coplien, James O., Stephen C. Dewhurst, and Andrew R. Koenig, "C++: Evolving Toward a More Powerful Language", *AT&T Technical Journal*. July/August 1988.

Stroustrup, Bjarne, "What is Object Oriented Programming?", *USENIX Proceedings*, C++ Workshop. Santa Fe, NM, 1987.

Toutongh, Michael, "21st Century Assembler", *Computer Language Magazine*. June, 1990.

Wegner, Peter, "Learning the Language", *Byte Magazine*. March, 1989.

White, Eric, "Object Oriented Programming As a Programming Style", *C Users Journal*. February, 1990.

Index

abort() function, 188, 195, 379, 384
Abstract classes, 269-270
Abstraction, data, 7-10
Access
    controlling, 45-48, 63, 138-139
    to inherited members, 244-248
    to structures, 41-44
Ada language, 8, 199
addAfter() user-defined function, 421
Address user-defined class, 48-50
Addresses
    of base classes, 276-279
    with 80x86 processors, 87-93
    of functions, 95
    operator for (&), 28-31
    passing, to functions, 97
    this for, 143
    See also Reference operator and variables
adjustfield constant, 301
Aliases, 28-31, 101-103
always option, 11
Ambiguous objects with multiple inheritance, 273-276
Ampersands (&). *See* Reference operator and variables
Anonymous objects, 168
Anonymous unions, 37-38, 159
ANSI C, 11
Arguments
    const with, 30
    with constructors, 51, 54, 163-164, 166, 168
    custom manipulators with, 308-320
    default (*See* Default arguments)
    and function overloading, 38-39, 123-128
    for inline functions, 116
    for interrupt functions, 375-376
    with new, 233-234
    with operator overloading, 58-59
    and polymorphism, 262
    reference variables for, 30-31, 103, 105-107
    with signal(), 378, 381
    type checking for, 12, 27
    variable number of, 13, 28, 82-83, 127-128
    and void, 14
Arrays
    for class objects, 144-147
    huge, 100-101
    initializing, 167-168
    and pointers, 95
    of strings, reading, 341
    virtual, 212-229
asm directive, 366-371
Assembly language
    with constructors, analysis of, 177-180
    debugging, 373-375
    extern "C" directive for, 134
    inline, 24, 355-357, 366-373
    and structured languages, 4
    support for, 23-24
Assignment operator, default, 203
Associativity, 201-202, 295
atexit() function, 192-193, 379

auto storage class and variables, 79, 150
    construction of, 52, 163
    destruction of, 163, 187-188
    on stack, 90, 110
autoWormDriver() user-defined function, 450-451
AWAITING_MSG task state, 403, 431
AX register, modifying, 363

bad() function, 338
badbit error flag, 336-337
Bakward user-defined class, 282-284
Base classes, 62
    addresses of, 276-279
    and inheritance, 243, 251
basefield constant, 301
BASIC language, 5
Binary operators, overloading, 200
Binding, 68-69, 128-129, 201-202, 261
bios() function, 359
Blocks, declarations within, 31-33, 109-111
Books, 503-504
BOUND instruction, 380
BP register, modifying, 362
Braces ({ })
    for blocks, 109
    for inline assembly language, 367
break statement and destructors, 111
Breakpoints
    for debugging, 374-375
    and this, 144
breakRoutine() user-defined function, 392-393
Buffers
    for error messages, 331
    jump, 395-396
    and stream I/O, 292-293, 305-306, 321-323
BusinessAddress user-defined class, 65-66
BYTEREGS structure, 359

C and C++, 11-21
.C files, 11
C-I (copy-initializer) constructors, 169-171, 181, 185-186
calcAcceleration() user-defined function, 444-445, 486-487
CALL instruction, 23
calloc() function, 34-35
Casting, 12, 87
cerr object, 330-331
Chaining
    of extractors, 322
    of inserters, 294
changeDivider() user-defined function, 317, 319
Chaos paradigm, 5, 9
char data type and variables, 80
    constants, 86
    extractors for, 321
    inserters for, 297
    range and size of, 80
Child tasks, 397
cin object, 70-71, 306, 330-331

Classes, 45-48
    abstract, 269-270
    ambiguous, with multiple inheritance, 275-276
    arrays for, 144-147
    base, 62, 243, 251, 276-279
    constants for, 168-169
    definitions of, 45-46
    derived (*See* Derived classes)
    enumeration members of, 153-155
    friends of, 155-157
    inheritance with (*See* Inheritance)
    organization of, 137-141
    pointers with, 47, 147-150, 253
    static members of, 150-153
    and structures, 41-45, 139
    with this, 142-144
    and unions, 157-159
clear() function, 338
clockTick() user-defined function, 377, 427-430, 469
clog object, 330-331
cntrlbrk() function, 384
COBOL language, 5
Code, reusing, 9
Code segment, 89
Coercion operators, 209-212, 253
Collisions, data, 399-400, 457
Colons (:) with scope resolution operator (::), 35-36
.COM files
    debugging, 374
    generating, 91
Comma operator (,), overloading, 203
Commas (,) in argument lists, 28
Comments
    C vs. C++, 36
    with inline assembly language, 367
Compact compile model, 90
Compilation
    conditional, 97-98
    models for, 90, 97
    options for, 22
    and overlays, 346
Complex user-defined class
    coercion operator with, 210-211
    constants for, 168-169
    I/O operators for, 72-74
    overloading operators for, 57-61, 205-209
Composite data types, 6
Compound new operator, 233-239
Conditional compilation, 97-98
Conditional operator (?:), overloading, 202-203
Conflicts with overlays, 346-347
const storage type and variables, 15-16, 81-82
    with arguments, 30
    for #define, 35
Constants
    class, 168-169
    passing, as referential arguments, 108-109
    type for, 85-86
Constructors, 50, 163

arguments with, 51, 54, 163-164, 166, 168
for array objects, 144
assembly language code generated by, 177-180
calling, from `new`, 186-187
calling `new` from, 182-186
and class constants, 168-169
copy-initializer, 169-171, 181, 185-186
creating objects with, 52-56, 180-181
default, 164-165
for derived classes, 64-65, 248-249
for file stream classes, 331-333
format of, 51-52
global, 192
initializing objects with, 167, 170-171
inline, 163
with multiple inheritance, 271
overloading of, 54, 164
passing objects by value with, 171-173
for `Planet` class, 439-440
returning objects by value with, 173-177
for `Task` class, 396, 403-408
for `Timer` class, 427
and variable declarations, 32-33
`cont` statement and destructors, 111
Containing classes
vs. derived classes, 249-251
and doubly linked lists, 280-282
Context saves, 390
Context switches, 391, 399
Control-break handler, 384-386
Control structures, variable declarations within, 32
`control87()` function, 380
Coprocessor, 80-81
Copy-initializer constructors, 169-171, 181, 185-186
Costs, 9
`cout` object, 70-71, 294, 306, 330-331
.CPP files, 11
CS register, modifying, 362
`currentTask()` user-defined function, 410-411, 477-478
Custom extractors, 323-330
Custom inserters, 306-308
Custom manipulators
with general argument types, 315-320
with restrictive argument types, 308-315
`CustomManip` user-defined class, 328
Cutting of queues, 458

Data
abstraction of, 7-10
collisions between, 399-400, 457
defining types for, 7-8 (*See also* Typing and type checking)
encapsulation of, 6-7, 44-48
in programming concepts, 5-6
Data segment, 89
DEAD task state, 403, 406, 412
DEBUG command (DOS), 374
Debugging, 22
assembly @LEVEL =, 373-375
 functions, 115
 modules, 390
 406
 144
 ants, 85-86

Declaration
within blocks, 31-33, 109-111
of enumerated types, 154
of friends, 156, 205
of functions, 27-28
of member functions, 46
of pointers, 93-98
prototype, 11-14
tentative, 99-100
of variables, 31-33, 79-85, 109-111
Decoupling modules, 389
Default accessibility, 245
Default arguments, 27-28, 83-84
with constructors, 54, 168
and overloaded functions, 126-127
and pointers, 98-99
Default assignment operator, 203
Default constructors, 164-165
Default pragma priority, 194
Default scope for classes, 138-139
Default storage classes, 79
`#define` directives, 33-34
vs. `const` variables, 35
and overloading, 40
Definitions, class, 45-46
`delay()` function, 427
DELAYED task state, 403, 431
`delayTask()` user-defined function, 431, 473
`delete` keyword, 34-35
for array objects, 145-146
balancing, with `new`, 185
bypassing, 111
for object deletion, 52, 118-120, 188-189
overloading, 229-239
Derived classes, 62, 243
access from, 244-248
constructors for, 64-65, 248-249
vs. containing classes, 249-251
destructors for, 64-65
and inheritance, 251-259
initializing, 64-65
and inline functions, 115
multiple inheritance with, 66-67
pointers to, 67-68, 190-191
and private members, 138
and virtual functions, 67-70
`Derived` user-defined class, 284-287
Destructors, 51-52
for array objects, 144
balancing, with constructors, 185
bypassing, 111, 394
for derived classes, 64-65
invoking, 187-189
and `longjmp()`, 394
for objects deletion, 52, 56, 189-190
for `Task` class, 396, 413-415
virtual, 190-191
Development costs, 9
DI register, modifying, 363
DIRECT.CPP file, 498-500
`Direction` user-defined task, 448
`directory()` user-defined function, 424-425
`diskTask()` user-defined function, 424
Display, standard object for, 331
`DLinkedList` user-defined class, 280-284
DOS, non-reentrancy of, 399, 457
Double breaks, handler for, 385-386

`double` data type and variables
constants, 86
inserter for, 298
range and size of, 80
Double precision calculations, 20-21
`doubleBreakHandler()` user-defined program, 385-386
Doubly linked lists, 279-284
DS register, modifying, 362
DYING task state, 403, 411-412

Early binding, 68, 261
Efficiency, programming, 9-10
Ellipses (...)
and function overloading, 127-128
for variable arguments, 13, 28, 82-83
`_emit_` function, 371-373
EMS memory
class for, 363-366
for virtual arrays, 216-229
`EMSArray` user-defined class, 216-229
`EMSPageCount()` user-defined function, 218, 221-222, 366
`EMSPresent()` user-defined function, 218, 220-221, 364-365
`EMSSlotAddr()` user-defined function, 218, 221, 365
`EMSStatus()` user-defined function, 218, 221, 365-366
Encapsulation of data, 6-7, 44-48
`endl` inserter manipulator, 305
`enum` statements, 6
Enumeration members, 153-155
`eof()` function, 338
Error handling
with assembly language, 368
and function overloading, 39
standard object for, 331
for streams, 336-338
with `Task` class, 403
Escape sequences, C vs. C++, 21
EXE2BIN utility, 91
Execution order and pragmas, 195
Execution threads, 389
`exit()` function, 188, 191, 195, 384
`_exit()` function, 188, 195, 379
`exit` pragma, 20, 193-195
Expanded memory
class for, 363-366
for overlays, 353
for virtual arrays, 216-229
Expressions, typed, 85-87
Extended memory for overlays, 353
`extern "C" {}` directive, 132-134
`extern` storage class, 79, 81
Extra segment, 89
Extractors, 292-293, 320-322
chaining, 322
custom, 323-330
overloading, 292

`factorial()` user-defined function, 116-117
`fail()` function, 338
`failbit` error flag, 321, 325, 336-338
Far addresses, 90-91
Far pointers, 94, 96, 127
`FileArray` user-defined class, 213-214
`filebuf` class, 331

Index

Files
  .C and .CPP, 11
  include, 13, 132
  pointers to, 335-336
  seeking within, 334-335
  standard objects for, 330-331
  tying, 335
  user, 331-334
  for virtual arrays, 213-216
`fill()` function, 304
Filters, tasks for, 458
`flags()` function, 300
`float` data type and variables
  constants, 86
  extractors for, 321
  inserter for, 298
  range and size of, 80
`floatfield` constant, 301
FLOAT.H file, 379
Floating-point routines
  C vs. C++, 20-21
  signals for, 379-380
Flow control, signals for, 377-384
`flush()` function, 215
`flush` inserter manipulator, 305
`for` loops, variable declarations within, 32
Formatting with stream I/O, 71-72, 299-305, 308-320
Fortran language, 5
`Forward` user-defined class, 282-284
`FPE_x` signals, 379
`fprintf()` function, 291
`free()` function vs. `delete`, 34-35, 118
Friends, 155-157, 204-209
`fstream` class, 215, 331
`fstream.h` file, 215
Functions
  addresses of, 95
  and data passing, 6
  declaring, 27-28
  as friends, 155-157
  inline, 33-34, 40, 112-118
  interrupt, 375-377
  member (*See* Member functions)
  operators as, 57
  outline, 112-113, 116-118
  overloading, 38-40, 123-134
  passing addresses to, 97
  prototyping for, 11-14
  referential, 107-108
  with referential arguments, 105-107
  virtual, 67-70, 261-262

`geninterrupt()` function, 359-366
`get()` function, 339
`getcbrk()` function, 386
`getMsg()` user-defined function, 422-423
`getNewDirection()` user-defined function, 449-450, 496
`getReturnValue()` user-defined function, 417-419, 476
`getTime()` user-defined function, 429, 469-470
`getTMsg()` user-defined function, 421-422, 474-475
Global constructors, 192
Global storage class and variables
  construction of, 52, 54, 163
  destruction of, 163, 188

far, 90
initializing, 50-51
secondary effects from, 6
`good()` function, 338
`goto` statement and variable declarations, 111
Graphic User Interface, 4
Greater than symbol ()
  for redirection, 331
  with stream I/O (>), 70-71

.H files, 13
`hardfail` error flag, 336-337
Heap objects
  construction and destruction of, 163
  memory allocation for, 34-35
  See also Memory and memory allocation
Hexadecimal numbers
  for assembly language entry, 371-372
  constants, 85
  escape sequences for, C vs. C++, 21
Hiding data, 6-7, 44-48
Hierarchies, abstract classes for, 270
.HPP files, 13
Huge compile model and objects, 90-91, 100-101

`Id` user-defined class, constructor for, 182-186
IDE debugger, 374
IEEE floating point standard, 81
`if` statement and variable declarations, 111
`ifstream` class, 331
Include files, 13, 132
Increment operators, overloading, 203
Inheritance, 8, 62-66
  and abstract classes, 269-270
  and derived classes, 251-259
  multiple, 66-67, 270-284
  with `new` and `delete`, 230
  and polymorphism, 260-268
  simple, 243-251
  virtual, 284-287
  and virtual functions, 68-70
`initAddress` user-defined function, 44
Initializing, 50-51, 191
  arrays, 167-168
  with constructors, 167, 170-171
  derived classes, 64-65
  and `main()`, 192-195
  protected and public members, 249
  reference variables, 29
  static member variables, 151-152
  unions, 157-158
`initTask()` user-defined function, 405, 470-471
Inline assembly language, 24, 355-357
  `asm` for, 366-371
  debugging, 373-375
  `__emit__` for, 371-373
  pseudo-registers and `geninterrupt()` for, 358-366
Inline constructors, 163
Inline functions, 33-34
  efficiency of, 112-115
  with outline, 116-118
  overloading, 40
  problems with, 115-116
`inline` pragma, 18, 367

Input/output. *See* Extractors; Inserters; Stream I/O
Inserters, 291-292, 295-296
  associativity of, 295
  chaining, 294
  custom, 306-308
  format control for, 299-305
  manipulators with, 308-320
  overloading, 292
  for `Task` class, 434
  types for, 297-299
Inspect command, 22
Inspect Window, 144
Instantiating
  arrays, 144
  classes, 46, 137, 269
`int` data type and objects
  constants, 86
  inserter for, 298
  range and size of, 80
INT instruction, 23
`int86()` function, 359
`int86x()` function, 359
Integers
  extractors for, 321-322
  variables for, 80
Interactive debugger, 22
Interactive Development Environment (IDE), 21-23
Interrupt functions, 375-377
Intrinsic operators, 7-8, 199
I/O functions, libraries for, 56-57
  See also Extractors; Inserters; Stream I/O
`iomanip.h` file, 71, 304, 310, 330
`iOnly` user-defined manipulator, 312-313, 318, 327, 330
`ios` class, 299, 302, 336
`iostream.h` file, 71, 292, 301, 304, 320, 331
`isA()` function, 263-264, 440
`istream` class, 71, 331
`istrstream` class, 340-341

`jAlso` user-defined manipulator, 312, 314, 318, 328, 330
`jmp_buf` type, 392, 395

Keyboard, standard object for, 331
`killSelf()` user-defined function, 407, 480
`killTask()` user-defined function, 411-414, 416, 418, 451, 456, 472-473

Languages, object-oriented, 4-5
Large compile model, 90-91
Late binding, 68-69, 261
Less than symbol ()
  for redirection, 331
  with stream I/O (<), 70-71, 294-295
Libraries for I/O functions, 56-57
Linked lists, 254-259
  doubly linked, 279-284
  for jump buffers, 395-396
  with polymorphism, 264-268
`LinkedList` user-defined class, 254-259, 280-284, 402
Linking, 22, 128-129
  C modules, 132-134
  and overlays, 346

type safe, 128-134
Lists. *See* Linked lists
Loading overlays, 346-349
`Location` user-defined class, 441-442, 484
Lockout problems with overlays, 346, 348
Logical addresses, 87, 89
`long double` data type and variables
    constants, 86
    inserter for, 298
    range and size of, 80
`long int` data type and variables
    constants, 86
    range and size of, 80
`longjmp()` function, 390-394
Loops
    assembly language for, 355-357
    and overlays, 345
Lvalues
    with conditional operator, 203
    operators as, 202
    referential functions as, 108
    `this` as, 144

Macros
    vs. inline functions, 33-34
    overloading, 40
    transfer, 22-23
`main()` function and initialization, 192-195
`malloc()` function
    vs. `new`, 34-35, 118-119
    and object construction, 52
Manipulators, stream I/O, 71-72, 299-305, 308-320
`map()` user-defined function, 218-220, 227-228, 364
Mapping EMS pages, 217
Masking functions with overloading, 40
Math coprocessor, 80-81
`mathHandler()` user-defined function, 381-384
Medium compile model, 90
Member functions, 45-48, 137
    accessing, 46, 138-139
    constructors for, 50-56
    defining, 47-48
    as inline functions, 112
    pure virtual, 269
    `static`, 153
    `volatile` and `const` with, 81-82
Member objects
    constructors for, 180-181
    destructors for, 189-190
Member operators (.)
    vs. friend operators, 204-209
    overloading, 202
Member pointer operator (-), overloading, 202
Memory and memory allocation
    c-i constructors for, 185-186
    with `delete`, 34-35, 118-120, 185
    with `new`, 34-35, 118-120, 185, 229
    protection of, 88-89
    stream I/O with, 340-341
    See also Expanded memory; Overlay systems
    ..., 389-390
    97-398, 420-426, 457
    mulation, 447-456
    ber functions

Modular programming, 6-7
Modules
    C, linking, 132-134
    decoupling, 389
    and function overloading, 128
`msgCount()` user-defined function, 422
`MTASK.CPP` file, 432, 467-480
`MTASK.HPP` file, 400, 419-420, 461, 463-467
Multiple inheritance, 66-67, 270-272
    and ambiguous classes, 275-276
    and ambiguous objects, 273-275
    and base class addresses, 276-279
    and doubly linked lists, 279-284
Multiprogramming, memory protection with, 88
Multitasking, 389-390
    rescheduler for, 395-396
    `setjmp()` and `longjump()` for, 390-394
    See also `Task` class application
`MyClass` user-defined class
    for extractors, 323-330
    for inserters, 307-308, 312-315, 317-320

Names
    of constructors, 51
    conventions for, 46
    type safe, 129-130
Near addresses, 90-92
Near pointers, 127
Nested `for` loops, variable declarations within, 32
`new` keyword, 34-35
    arguments with, 233-234
    calling, from constructors, 182-186
    calling constructors from, 186-187
    for object construction, 52, 118-120
    overloading, 229-239
`next()` user-defined function, 255, 281-284, 410
Non-preemptive scheduling, 398
Non-reentrancy of DOS, 399, 457
Numeric extractors, 321-322
Numerical Coprocessor, 80-81

`object` class, 457
Object-oriented programming, 3-10
Objective C, 3
Octal constants, 85
`ofstream` class, 331
`oneClockTick()` user-defined function, 429-431, 473-474
OOP (object-oriented programming), 3-10
`open()` function, 333
Operators
    associativity of, 201-202, 295
    coercion, 209-212, 253
    defining, 7-8
    as friends, 157, 204-209
    intrinsic, 7-8, 199
    overloading (*See* Overloading, operators)
    precedence of, 61, 201-202, 295-296
Optimization and register variables, 17
`option` pragma, 18-20
`ORBIT.CPP` file, 483-489
Orbiting planets
    source code for, 483-489
    as `Task` class application, 438-447

`ostream` class, 71, 294, 331
`ostrstream` class, 340-341
Outline functions, 112-113, 116-118
Overlay flag, 351
Overlay Support flag, 351
Overlay systems
    conventional, 345-348
    with multitasking, 400
    thrashing with, 351-354
    VROOMM, 23, 348-354
Overloading
    constructors, 54, 164
    functions, 38-40
    and C module linking, 132-134
    default arguments with, 126-127
    differentiating, 123-128
    stream I/O, 74
    and type safe linking, 128-132
    operators, 56-61, 199-200
    and coercion operators, 209-212
    friend vs. member, 204-209
    insertion and extraction, 292
    limitation on, 201-204
    `new` and `delete`, 229-239
    precedence and associativity of, 201-202
    and virtual arrays, 212-229
`_Ovrbuffer` global variable, 354
`_OvrInitEms()` function, 353
`_OvrInitExt()` function, 353-354
`_OvrSize` global variable, 354
`_OvrTrapCount` global variable, 354

Paged memory
    conventional, 88-89
    EMS, 217
Paradigms, programming, 4-5
Parent tasks, 397
Parentheses ()
    with functions, 95
    with insertion operator, 296
    as operator, 202
Pascal language, 4-5
Performance
    with assembly language, 368
    with inline functions, 112-115
    with multitasking, 390
    with overlays, 345, 353
`permWidth()` user-defined function, 312, 314, 318-319, 328, 330
Physical addresses, 87
PL/1 language, 12
`Planet` user-defined class, 439-440, 485-486
`planetFunc()` user-defined function, 445, 485-488
Planets, orbiting
    source code for, 483-489
    as `Task` class application, 438-447
Pointers
    and arrays, 95
    assignment of, 96
    to base classes, 253
    to class objects, 47, 147-150
    coercion paths with, 211
    to constants, 16
    declaring, 93-100
    and defaults, 98-99
    with derived classes, 67-68, 190-191

Index

and destructors, 188
far, 94, 96, 127
to functions, methods as, 140
huge, 100-101
inserter for, 298
near, 127
and overloaded functions, 125, 127
and reference operator, 29-31, 102
to streams, 335-336
tentative declarations of, 99-100
to `void`, 14, 100
Polymorphism, 8, 67-70, 260-262
`isA()` with, 263-264
linked list example with, 264-268
Positioning files, 334-335
Postincrement operators, overloading, 203
`#pragma`s, 18-20, 193-195
Precedence, 201-202
of insertion operator, 295-296
of overloaded operators, 61
of types, 86
`precision()` function, 303
Preemptive scheduling, 398
Preincrement operators, overloading, 203
Preprocessor directives vs. inline functions, 33-34
`prev()` user-defined function, 281-284
`previous()` user-defined function, 255, 421
Prime numbers program, 91-92
with inline assembly language, 368-370
timing analysis of, 355-357
`printf()` function, 70-71, 291, 340
Priorities of pragmas, 193-195
Private data, 7
Private members, 46, 137-138
access to, 244-246
and friends, 155-157
Program listings
for orbiting planets simulation, 483-489
for `Task` class, 461-480
for Worms game, 493-500
Programming paradigms, 4-5
`protected` keyword, 138, 244
Prototyping, function, 11-14
Pseudo-registers, 23, 358-366, 370-372
Public data, 7
Public members, 46, 137-138
access to, 244-245
for unions, 157
Publicly derived classes, 62
Pure specifiers, 269
Pure virtual member functions, 269
`put()` function, 339

Queues for message passing, 397-398, 420-426, 457
Quiet changes, 20-21

Radix for extractors, 322
`raise()` function, 377-379
RAM disks for overlays, 354
Range of data types, 80
`rdstate()` function, 338
`read()` function, 215, 339
`readDisk()` user-defined function, 424-425
`readKey()` user-defined function, 433-434, 437

`READY` task state, 403, 411
Recursion and inline functions, 116-117
Redirection of I/O, 331
Reference operator (&) and variables, 28-31, 101-103
for arguments, 30-31, 103, 105-109
declaration of, 32-33
for functions, 107-108
for inline functions, 116
and overloaded functions, 126
types for, 104-105
Referencing arrays, 213
Registers and `register` storage class and variables, 17, 79, 90
destructors for, 187-188
for interrupt functions, 375-376
pseudo, 23, 358-366, 370-372
and `volatile` storage type, 15
`REGS` union, 359-360
`reschedule()` user-defined function, 408-411, 432-433, 457
Rescheduler, 390-391, 395-396
Return types
with functions, 12, 82
and overloaded functions, 125
with `Task` class, 416-420
Reuse, software, 9
`RUNNING` task state, 403, 410-411

`saveregs` pragma, 18
Scaling with orbiting planets simulation, 441, 443
`scanf()` function, 70-71, 291
Scheduler for `Task` class, 415-416
Scope
and blocks, 110-111
default, 138-139
and default arguments, 84
of members, 137-138
of static variables, 151
Scope resolution operator (::), 35-36, 48, 62, 202
Secondary effects from global variables, 6
`seekg()` function, 215, 334
Seeking within files, 334-335
`seekp()` function, 215, 334
Segment register, 89
Segmented memory model, 87-93
Semi-colons (;) with inline assembly language, 367
`sendAMessage()` user-defined function, 426
`sendMsg()` user-defined function, 420-421, 425, 452, 474
`setcbrk()` function, 386
`setDivider()` user-defined function, 315-317, 319, 329-330
`setf()` function, 300-301, 305
`setFlag()` user-defined function, 310-311
`setiosflags()` function, 305
`setjmp()` function, 390-394, 396, 410-411
`setjmp.h` file, 392
`setprecision()` function, 309-310
`setReturnValue()` user-defined function, 417-418, 476
`setw()` function, 304, 322
`showAllTasks()` user-defined function, 436-437, 479-480

`showTask()` user-defined function, 435-436, 475-476
SI register, modifying, 363
Side effects from global variables, 6
Sieve of Eratosthenes program, 91-92
with inline assembly language, 368-370
timing analysis of, 355-357
`SIGFPE` signal, 378-380
`SIGILL` signal, 378-380
`SIGINT` signal, 378, 384
`signal()` function, 377-384
signed variables
for overloaded function arguments, 124
range and size of, 80
`SIGSEGV` signal, 378-381
Simulation, `Task` class applications for, 438-439
Single precision calculations, 21
Single-stepping
with `__emit__`, 375
and inline functions, 115
and `this`, 144
Singly linked lists, 254-259, 264-268
`sizeof` keyword with `malloc()`, 34
Slashes (/) for comments (//), 36, 367
`SLIST.CPP` user-defined file, 255, 461
`SLIST.HPP` user-defined file, 254-255, 402, 461
Slots, EMS, 217
Small compile model, 90
Smalltalk, 3-4, 389
`smanip_int` class, 310, 315
`smanip_long` class, 315
Software reuse, 9
Source code
for orbiting planets simulation, 483-489
for Worms game, 493-500
Spawning tasks, 397, 416-417
Splicing queues, 458
SS register, modifying, 362
Stability of `Task` class, 457
Stack
for `auto` variables, 90, 110
and constructors, 178-179
for multitasking, 391
for orbiting planets simulation, 446-447
for `Task` class, 406-407
Stack segment, 89
`startScheduler()` user-defined function, 415-416, 428, 478-479
`startup` pragma, 20, 193-195
`static` storage class and variables, 79
for class members, 150-153
for `const` variables, 81
construction of, 52, 163
destruction of, 163, 188
Status of tasks, 403
`status()` user-defined function, 218-220
`stderr` stream, 330-331
`stdin` stream, 330-331
`stdio.h` file, 291, 340
`stdout` stream, 330-331
`stopScheduler()` user-defined function, 413, 416, 479
Storage classes, 15-17, 79-82, 150-153
`Store String` instruction, 368
Stream I/O, 70-75, 291-294, 339
buffers for, 292-293, 305-306, 321-323
error handling for, 336-338

for files, 330-336
incore, 340-341
manipulators for, 71-72, 299-305, 308-320
mixing, with `stdio`, 340
See also Inserters; Extractors
`streampos` type, 215, 334
String instructions, assembly language, 368
Strings
inserter for, 298
reading arrays of, 341
Stroustrup, Bjarne, 4
`strstream.h` file, 340-341
`struct` keyword and structures, 6
anonymous unions for, 37
as arguments, 105
and classes, 41-45, 139
`malloc()` with, 35
variable sized, 237-239
Structured programming, 5-6, 9
Student records, linked list for, 256-259, 264-268
`studentGPA()` user-defined function, 258-259, 266
`studentList()` user-defined function, 258-259, 266-268
`studentNewGPA()` user-defined function, 258-259, 266
`studentPassing()` user-defined function, 258-259, 266-268
`studentStart()` user-defined function, 258-259, 265-268
`SubClass` user-defined class, 251-254
Subclasses. *See* Derived classes
Superclasses *See* Base classes
SUSPENDED task state, 403, 431
`suspendTask()` user-defined function, 430-431, 473

Take the address of operator (&), 28-31
`Task` class application, 396-397
vs. AT&T task class, 457-458
constructors for, 403-408
destructors for, 396, 413-415
features of, 398-400
implementing, 400-408
improvement areas for, 456-457
listing of, 461-480
message passing with, 420-426
for orbiting planets, 438-447
output of, 434-437
return value for, 416-420
schedule control with, 408-411, 415-416
terminating tasks with, 411-415
timing for, 426-434
for worms simulation, 447-456
See also Multitasking
Task switcher, 390-391, 395-396
TASM Assembler, 366
TASM2MSG program, 366-367
TCC.EXE and VROOMM, 354
TC.EXE and VROOMM, 354
TD286, 374
?86, 374
? user-defined function, 427, 432, ?479
?tant user-defined class,
?tion, 334

`tellp()` function, 334
Tentative declarations, 99-100
Terminate-and-Stay Resident programs, 23, 377
`terminateHandler()` user-defined function, 378-379
Termination of tasks, 411-415
`Test` user-defined class, 234-237
TESTMT.CPP driver program, 494-496
`this`, 142-144, 152-153
Thrashing
with multitasking, 399
with overlays, 351-354
`tie()` function, 306, 335
Tildes () for destructors, 52, 187-188
Time independence, applications for, 438-439
Time slicing, 398
`Timer` user-defined class, 427, 468
Timing comparisons, C vs. C++, 10
Timing for `Task` class, 426-434
Tiny compile model, 90-91
TLINK and type safe linking, 131
Transfer menu, 22-23
TSR (Terminate-and-Stay-Resident) programs, 23, 377
`tSuspend()` user-defined function, 432, 479
Turbo Assembler, 24
Turbo C vs. Turbo C++, 21-24
Turbo Debugger, 373-374
Turbo Linker, 130-132
Tying streams, 306, 335
Type conversions, anonymous unions for, 37-38
Type safe linking, 128-134
Typed expressions, 85-87
`typedef` statements, 6
Typing and type checking, 11-12, 27-28
of arguments, 12, 27
and declaring objects, 79-85
of enumerated members, 154
for inserters, 297-299
for reference variables, 104-105

Unary operators, overloading, 199-200
`undelayTask()` user-defined function, 431, 473
Unions, 157-158
anonymous, 37-38, 159
`unitVector()` user-defined function, 443-444, 483
Universal donor pointers, 14
`unsigned` modifier and variables
for arguments with overloaded functions, 124
constants, 86
range and size of, 80
`unsuspendTask()` user-defined function, 430-431, 473
`unwaitTask()` user-defined function, 430-431, 473
`updateLoc()` user-defined function, 449
User-defined types, overloading operators for, 57
User files, 331-334

Values
passing objects by, 171-173
returning objects by, 173-177

Variable arguments, 13, 28, 82-83
and function overloading, 127-128
Variable sized structures, 237-239
Variables
with assembly language, 367
construction of, 52, 54, 163
declaring, 31-33, 79-85, 109-111
destruction of, 163, 187-188
initializing, 50-51
range and sizes of, 80
and registers, 15, 17, 358-366
scope resolution operator for accessing, 35
stack for, 90, 110
`Vector` user-defined class, 443-444, 483-484
`Velocity` user-defined class, 441-443
Vertical bar (|) for redirection, 331
Video, BIOS routines for, 360
Virtual arrays, 212
EMS, 216-229
file, 213-216
Virtual destructors, 190-191
Virtual functions, 67-70, 261-262, 269
Virtual inheritance, 284-287
Virtual memory, 89
Virtual mode debugger, 374
Virtual Run-time Object-Oriented Memory Manager, 23, 348-354
`void` keyword, 14-15
Void pointers, 14, 100
`volatile` storage class and variables, 15-16, 81-82
Voluntary scheduling, 398
VROOMM overlay manager, 23, 348-354

`waitTask()` user-defined function, 430-431, 473
`warning` pragma, 18
Watch windows, 144
White space with extractors, 321-322
`width()` function, 302-303
WORDREGS structure, 359
`Worm` user-defined class, 448
WORM.CPP file, 496-498
WORM.HPP file, 493-494
Worms game
source code for, 493-500
as `Task` class application, 447-456
`wormTask()` user-defined function, 449, 493-494
`write()` function, 215, 339

`x_fill` field, 302-304
`x_flags` member, 299-300
`x_precision` field, 302
`x_width` field, 302, 322

Zoom boxes, 22

Hands-On Turbo C++ Source Code Order Form

Save yourself the trouble of typing in the listings from *Hands-On Turbo C++*. For only $10 (plus shipping and handling) you can receive all the example programs including the Task class from Chapter 11. Also available with this offer...

Would you like your application to look like Turbo C++, FoxPro, or Microsoft Windows? Don't worry, with C++ Windows Toolkit you can create any of them, or mix and match! C++ Windows Toolkit is a full C++ implementation of C Windows Toolkit from Magna Carta Software. It features:

Windows
- Create up to 255 windows simultaneously
- TRUE windowing. Windows may be written to even when out of view or when overlapped!
- Windows may be opened, closed, moved resized, and stored to disk.
- Send data from any window or virtual screen to a printer.
- Supports many printer formatting codes (bold, compressed, underline, etc.)
- Create Virtual Screens up to size of available memory

Menus
- High-level functions to create pop-up, pull-down, spreadsheet, and hypertext menus.
- Create an SAA-complaint interface with radio buttons and check boxes.
- Full transparent mouse support including scroll bars, elevator boxes, etc.

Data-entry
- Turn any window into an editor for memo fields, application notepad, etc.
- Full featured data-entry for strings, numbers, monetary amounts, floating point

Hardware Support
- Autodetect MDA, Hercules, CGA, EGA, MCGA, VGA adapters
- 43 lines on the EGA, 12/14/21/28/43/50 lines on the VGA
- Create custom fonts with our font editor FONTEDIT™

Save 30%

YES, I want to get my "Hands-On"....

☐ source code for programs appearing in "Hands-On Turbo C++" $10.00   _____

☐ C++ Windows Toolkit   regularly ~~$195.95~~ with this coupon $139.95   _____

Name: _____   Shipping and handling:*   _____

Address: _____   Texas residents add 8.25%:   _____

City: _____

State/Zip: _____   Total: _____

Check, money order or credit card   Specify 3.5" ☐   5.25" ☐
☐ Visa   ☐ Mastercard   Mail to:
_____ Exp Date _____   Magna Carta Software, Inc
                                                  P.O. Box 475594
Name on card: _____   Garland, TX 75047-5594
        Sig: _____

* Shipping and handling: US 48 states (ground) $5; US Domestic, Alaska, Hawaii (2-day air) $10; Canada (ground) $10; Canada and Mexico (air) $15; Europe/South America $20; elsewhere $25
  All orders prepaid in US funds; please allow 3 to 6 weeks